Professional Plone Development

Build robust, content-centric web applications with Plone 4

Martin Aspeli

PUBLISHING

community experience distilled

BIRMINGHAM - MUMBAI

Professional Plone 4 Development

First published: August 2011

Production Reference: 1180811

Published by Packt Publishing Ltd.
Livery Place
35 Livery Street
Birmingham B3 2PB, UK

ISBN 978-1-849514-42-2

www.packtpub.com

Cover Image by Charwak A (charwak86@gmail.com)

Credits

Author
Martin Aspeli

Reviewers
Andrew Burkhalter
David Glick
Hanno Schlichting
Jon Stahl
Eric Steele
Israel Saeta Pérez
Matthew Wilkes

Acquisition Editor
Steven Wilding

Development Editor
Maitreya Bhakal

Technical Editors
Shreerang Deshpande
Arun Nadar
Manasi Poonthottam
Aditi Suvarna

Project Coordinator
Michelle Quadros

Proofreader
Mario Cecere

Indexer
Tejal Daruwale

Graphics
Nilesh R Mohite

Production Coordinator
Adline Swetha Jesuthas

Cover Work
Adline Swetha Jesuthas

Foreword

Hi Eric: A long, long time ago, you made a foolish promise to write a foreword for PPD4.

I suspect Martin plied me to write this foreword while out one evening during the 2010 Plone Conference in Bristol. Full from an excellent dinner and even better conversation, beer in hand, who could say no?

I've long envied Martin's ability to write. Text and code flow from his fingers at a rate that I can't even begin to emulate. I, on the other hand, have been staring at a blank text editor for two weeks now, hoping for inspiration.

One of my first interactions with Martin was in early 2008. I'd been toying with developing a tool that would dramatically simplify editing Plone's layout, a daunting task for most beginners. In response to an early preview, Martin said, *I am also half convinced that this is a cruel joke...But if it isn't, then this could be the best thing for Plone since the invention of Firebug.* That comment, more than any other, motivated me to see the project through.

After all, it was Martin who inspired me to create it.

Earlier that year, Martin wrote a blog post titled *Pete and Andy Try Plone 4*, describing the steps two fictional characters might take to set up and deploy a functioning Plone site in 10 days using an array of new tools that greatly simplify the process. A bold declaration of the roadmap Martin envisioned for Plone, the post prompted a flurry of discussion within the community. Rereading it today, it's easy to see how significant an influence it has been on Plone's evolution. For me, in particular, it sparked an idea and touched off a series of events that ultimately led me to where I am today: Leading Plone's core development team and making sure that each new version puts its predecessors to shame.

And now to the book you hold in your hands.

The original edition of Martin's Professional Plone Development has held a prominent place on my desk since it was first published in 2007. Four years and hundreds of man-hours of Plone work later, I still find myself occasionally turning to it to find a snippet of code or to look up an unfamiliar function. I've been lucky enough to serve as an editor for this updated version. It's been a great read, and it's a reminder to me of just how far Plone has come in the last four years. What's more, I continue to find new and useful information within its pages – *Chapter 12, Relational Databases'* discussion of relational databases arrived in my inbox just as I was starting work on a project requiring the use of SQLAlchemy.

Martin has long been key to Plone's success. He's served as a member of the Framework Team, deciding which features belong in Plone, and he has led the Documentation Team. It's easy to recognize his handiwork in large sections of the Plone 3 and 4 releases. His ability to contribute so heavily to the codebase and then to turn around and describe it so well is a rare combination of skills indeed.

This book won't just tell you how to do things – it will tell you how to do things well. In *Chapter 2, Introduction to the Case Study*, he walks you through the basics of requirements gathering, use cases, mockups, and client interaction. From there, he shares his knowledge of proper development practices, and more specifically, proper Plone development practices. While the client is fictional, by the end of this book, you will have planned, built, and deployed a real Plone application.

Plone is by no means simple. What it provides in power and flexibility comes at the cost of a long learning curve. This book is your ladder.

Welcome to Plone.

– Eric Steele
Plone Release Manager
Pennsylvania State University's WebLion Group

About the Author

Martin Aspeli is an experienced Plone consultant and a prolific Plone contributor. He served on the Framework Team for Plone 3.0, and has contributed significantly for many of Plone's features, such as the portlets infrastructure, the content rules engine, the Dexterity content type framework, and the integration of Diazo theming engine into Plone.

He is a former leader of the Plone Documentation Team, has written a number of well-received tutorials available on `plone.org`, and is a regular speaker at Plone events and conferences. Martin was recognized in 2008 by Packt Publishing as one of the *Most Valuable People* in Open Source Content Management Systems for his work on the first edition of Professional Plone Development.

By day, Martin works for a 'Big Four' management consultancy, managing web development teams. He is passionate about Open Source, Agile, and high quality software.

About the Reviewers

A once-active contributor to several third-party Plone add-on products, integrator of Plone for environmental nonprofits, and occasional Plone core contributor, **Andrew Burkhalter** has more recently taken on the role of active lurker within the Plone community. Though he now spends his days writing iOS productivity apps using Objective-C and Cocoa, he still thinks fondly of Python code and web programming, and has loved the opportunity to review Professional Plone from the perspective of a semi-outsider looking in.

David Glick is a web developer at Groundwire in Seattle. He is a contributor to a number of Plone add-on products, a member of the Plone Foundation, and has participated in development of Plone in various capacities as a core developer, framework team member, and security team member since 2008.

Hanno Schlichting is one of the most prolific long-term Plone Core developers. He serves as the Zope 2 release manager, is a Zope Toolk release team member and has led the Plone internationalization team for many years in addition to many more informal roles and involvement in Plone Foundation committees. Hanno currently works for Jarn AS locate in Southern Norway. Jarn AS is an agile export consultancy company specializing in high-quality development and consulting in for Plone and employs some of the most recognized Plone community members worldwide.

Jon Stahl is a graduate student at the University of Washington Evans School of Public Affairs. Prior to that, he spent 15 years at Groundwire providing technology consulting services to environmental nonprofits. He has been working with Plone since 2005 and has served multiple terms on the Plone Foundation Board of Directors. He has contributed several chapters to *Practical Plone 3* and served as a reviewer for the first version of *Professional Plone Development*.

Eric Steele has been using Zope since 2002 and Plone since 2005. He is currently working as a developer for Penn State University's WebLion group. He is the author of several widely used Plone products, including GloWorm and FacultyStaffDirectory. Eric serves as the Plone release manager and is a member of the Plone Foundation.

Israel Saeta Pérez is a Physics student and computer enthusiast from Spain. He has contributed to several free-software projects and specially to Plone, helping with documentation and working on Deco/Tiles development during the Google Summer of Code 2010. Nowadays he's preparing to start a masters in Artificial Intelligence and does some freelance consulting in his free time.

I want to thank my parents for helping me become who I am today.

Matthew Wilkes has been working with Plone since 2005 at Team Rubber, as a freelance consultant and for Jarn AS in Berlin. During that time he was involved in developing many different Plone sites, from intranets to government consultation sites. He is an active Plone community foundation member, serving on the Plone 4 Framework Team and foundation membership committee as well as an active member of the Zope and Plone security teams.

www.PacktPub.com

Support files, eBooks, discount offers, and more

You might want to visit www.PacktPub.com for support files and downloads related to your book.

Did you know that Packt offers eBook versions of every book published, with PDF and ePub files available? You can upgrade to the eBook version at www.PacktPub.com and as a print book customer, you are entitled to a discount on the eBook copy. Get in touch with us at service@packtpub.com for more details.

At www.PacktPub.com, you can also read a collection of free technical articles, sign up for a range of free newsletters and receive exclusive discounts and offers on Packt books and eBooks.

http://PacktLib.PacktPub.com

Do you need instant solutions to your IT questions? PacktLib is Packt's online digital book library. Here, you can access, read and search across Packt's entire library of books.

Why Subscribe?

- Fully searchable across every book published by Packt
- Copy and paste, print and bookmark content
- On demand and accessible via web browser

Free Access for Packt account holders

If you have an account with Packt at www.PacktPub.com, you can use this to access PacktLib today and view nine entirely free books. Simply use your login credentials for immediate access.

Table of Contents

Part 2 – Customizing Plone

Part 3 – Developing New Functionality

Preface

Plone is a web content management system that features among the top two percent of open source projects and is used by more than 300 solution providers in 57 countries. Its powerful workflow system, outstanding security track record, friendly user interface, elegant development model, and vibrant community makes Plone a popular choice for building content-centric applications. By customizing and extending the base platform, integrators can build unique solutions tailored to specific projects quickly and easily.

If you want to create your own web applications and advanced websites using Plone 4, Professional Plone 4 Development is the book you need.

The first edition of this book remains one of the most widely read and recommended Plone books. This second edition is completely revised and up-to-date for Plone 4.1, covering new topics such as Dexterity, Diazo, jQuery, and z3c.form, as well as improved ways of working with existing technologies such as Buildout, SQLAlchemy, and the Pluggable Authentication Service. It retains the writing style and comprehensive approach that made the first edition so popular.

Built around a realistic case study, Professional Plone 4 Development will take you from an understanding of Plone's central concepts, through basic customization, theming, and custom development, to deployment and optimization.

What this book covers

This book is divided into four sections:

1. First, we will introduce Plone and the case study, and learn how to set up a development environment.
2. The second section covers basic customization, including theming a Plone site using Diazo.

3. The third section focuses on custom development – building new content types and user interfaces, customizing security, and integrating with the external databases.

4. The final chapters cover deployment and performance optimization.

Let us take a look at each chapter in a bit more detail:

Chapter 1, Plone in Context, discusses what Plone is and when it may be an appropriate choice, and introduces the Plone community.

Chapter 2, Introduction to the Case Study, introduces the case study that will be used as the basis for the examples throughout the book.

Chapter 3, The Development Environment, discusses how to set up a productive development environment with tools for source code management, debugging, and more.

Chapter 4, Basics of Customization, discusses the ways in which the Zope application server infrastructure allows us to customize various aspects of Plone.

Chapter 5, Developing a Site Strategy, will start the customization of Plone to meet the requirements of our case study by creating a "policy package" to contain configuration and new code.

Chapter 6, Security and Workflow, discusses Zope's security model and shows how to create a custom workflow and permission scheme for our application.

Chapter 7, Using Add-ons, shows how to safely install Plone add-ons.

Chapter 8, Creating a Custom Theme, uses the Diazo theming engine to turn an HTML mock-up of the final site into a fully functional Plone theme.

Chapter 9, Nine Core Concepts of Zope Programming, takes a break from the case study to allow us to go into detail of the core concepts that underpin all Zope programming.

Chapter 10, Custom Content Types, uses the Dexterity framework to model the case study's specific data requirements as new content types.

Chapter 11, Standalone Views and Forms, shows how to render pages that are not the views of content types, and use the z3c.form framework to generate forms automatically from declarative schemata.

Chapter 12, Relational Databases, shows how to query and manipulate an external relational database from within Plone.

Chapter 13, Users and their Permissions, shows how to manage personal information and create more advanced security schemes. We will also create a simple plugin to allow users to log into a Plone site using their Facebook account.

Chapter 14, Dynamic User Interfaces with jQuery, shows how to use jQuery, the popular JavaScript framework, to create dynamic user interfaces and manage client-side interactions.

Chapter 15, Summary and Potential Enhancements, summarizes the work that has gone into the case study and points to some potential future enhancements.

Chapter 16, Zope on the Server, discusses the differences between a Zope instance configured for development and ones configured for use on a server.

Chapter 17, Setting up a Production Server, discusses the services that are typically deployed alongside Zope, including web servers, caching proxies, and load balancers.

Chapter 18, Authenticating with LDAP and Active Directory, shows how to configure authentication against an organization's existing LDAP or Active Directory repository.

Chapter 19, Looking to the Future, briefly considers migrations, before bringing the book to a close.

What you need for this book

To follow the examples in the book, you will need a computer suitable for use as a Plone development environment. This may use either Windows, Linux, or Mac OS X, though you should ensure you have rights to install new software and that the operating system is recent enough for you to be able to install Python 2.6.

We will cover the details of setting up a development environment, including prerequisites that must be installed, in much more detail in *Chapter 3, The Development Environment*.

Who this book is for

This book assumes that the reader is familiar with Plone from the point of view of an administrator or power user, has a basic understanding of web application development, and is comfortable with the Python programming language.

Conventions

In this book, you will find a number of styles of text that distinguish between different kinds of information. Here are some examples of these styles, and an explanation of their meaning.

Code words in text are shown as follows: "The `bootstrap.py` script installs `zc.buildout` itself, and gives us the `bin/buildout` command."

A block of code is set as follows:

```
[instance]

eggs =
    Plone
    Products.PloneFormGen
```

When we wish to draw your attention to a particular part of a code block, the relevant lines or items are set in bold:

```
<browser:page
    name="list-contents"
    for=".interfaces.IMyType"
    layer=".interfaces.IMyLayer"
    permission="zope2.View"
    class=".browser.listcontents.ListContentsView"
    template="browser/listcontents.pt"
    />
```

Any command-line input or output is written as follows:

```
$ bin/buildout -c somefile.cfg
```

New terms and **important words** are shown in bold. Words that you see on the screen, in menus or dialog boxes for example, appear in the text like this: "It can be found on the **Properties** tab in the ZMI."

 Warnings or important notes appear in a box like this.

 Tips and tricks appear like this.

Reader feedback

Feedback from our readers is always welcome. Let us know what you think about this book—what you liked or may have disliked. Reader feedback is important for us to develop titles that you really get the most out of.

To send us general feedback, simply send an e-mail to feedback@packtpub.com, and mention the book title via the subject of your message.

If there is a book that you need and would like to see us publish, please send us a note in the **SUGGEST A TITLE** form on www.packtpub.com or e-mail suggest@packtpub.com.

If there is a topic that you have expertise in and you are interested in either writing or contributing to a book, see our author guide on www.packtpub.com/authors.

Customer support

Now that you are the proud owner of a Packt book, we have a number of things to help you to get the most from your purchase.

Downloading the example code

You can download the example code files for all Packt books you have purchased from your account at http://www.PacktPub.com. If you purchased this book elsewhere, you can visit http://www.PacktPub.com/support and register to have the files e-mailed directly to you.

Errata

Although we have taken every care to ensure the accuracy of our content, mistakes do happen. If you find a mistake in one of our books—maybe a mistake in the text or the code—we would be grateful if you would report this to us. By doing so, you can save other readers from frustration and help us improve subsequent versions of this book. If you find any errata, please report them by visiting http://www.packtpub.com/support, selecting your book, clicking on the **errata submission form** link, and entering the details of your errata. Once your errata are verified, your submission will be accepted and the errata will be uploaded on our website, or added to any list of existing errata, under the Errata section of that title. Any existing errata can be viewed by selecting your title from http://www.packtpub.com/support.

Piracy

Piracy of copyright material on the Internet is an ongoing problem across all media. At Packt, we take the protection of our copyright and licenses very seriously. If you come across any illegal copies of our works, in any form, on the Internet, please provide us with the location address or website name immediately so that we can pursue a remedy.

Please contact us at copyright@packtpub.com with a link to the suspected pirated material.

We appreciate your help in protecting our authors, and our ability to bring you valuable content.

Questions

You can contact us at questions@packtpub.com if you are having a problem with any aspect of the book, and we will do our best to address it.

Part 1

Getting Ready

Plone in Context

Introduction to the Case Study

The Development Environment

1
Plone in Context

Since its humble beginnings, Plone has grown from "just another open source Content Management System" into a platform from which many people make their living, with hundreds of service providers worldwide. Big and small businesses, NGOs and charities, governments and individuals are building websites, intranets, and specialized applications on top of Plone with great success.

Spurred by advances in Python and Zope, along with increased media attention and recognition, Plone has steadily improved over the past several years. Plone 2.1 (released in 2005) and Plone 2.5 (released in 2006) were largely focused on incremental improvements and laying the foundations for future leaps in functionality. Plone 3.0 (2007) brought not only important new features to put Plone on par with most "enterprise" web content management systems, but instigated a more mature development process that led to incremental improvements through versions 3.1 (2008), 3.2 (2009), and 3.3 (2009). Plone 4 sets a new benchmark for stability and scalability, improves end user experience with a new theme and new visual editor, and brings Plone up-to-date with the latest Python and Zope releases.

In this chapter, we will:

- Consider how Plone fits in with the ongoing evolution of Zope, and how the Zope Toolkit and newer Python technologies are changing web development practices
- Consider when Plone may be a good choice for solving your web development problems
- Discuss why and how you may want to become a part of the Plone community

A brief history of Plone

Plone is an application that runs on the Zope 2 application server. By now over a decade old, Zope was probably the first open source application server. It started life as an environment in which power users could build web applications through-the-web, and was at one point the "killer application" for the Python programming language. It has inspired various other applications and frameworks, as well as improvements in Python itself.

Zope 2 turned out to be a good platform for building content management systems, and the Content Management Framework (CMF) was created to make this easier. The CMF changed the emphasis of Zope programming towards filesystem-based development and applications that could be more easily packaged up and redeployed. It also brought us "tools", "skins", and many other concepts fundamental to Plone.

Plone was born as a user-friendly CMS using the CMF. It was initially a night-time collaboration between Norwegian Alexander Limi and Texan Alan Runyan, but other Zope and Python developers soon began to contribute as well.

As the Plone project built ever more functionality on top of Zope 2, the Zope developers were working on a successor, to be named Zope 3. This project aimed to start with a clean slate, drawing on the experiences (and mistakes) of Zope 2 and CMF to create a next-generation web development framework.

The main premise of Zope 3 was that small, reusable, easily testable, and well-documented components should be orchestrated into complete systems. The individual building blocks should also be usable from other Python applications. Eventually, the community realized that Zope 2 could become just such an application. By way of a piece of integration code called Five (hint: what is Zope 2 + Zope 3?), it became possible to use Zope 3 components and concepts directly in Zope 2 applications, including Plone.

Zope 3 and Five revitalized Zope 2 development. Zope 2.8 shipped with the components from Zope 3.0 as an add-on library. Subsequent versions continued to update parts of the Zope 2 internals with more modern components, in tandem with the evolution of Zope 3 itself.

Unfortunately, this co-mingling of Zope 2 and Zope 3 quickly became confusing, and Zope 3 never really took off as a standalone framework in the same way that Zope 2 had, not at least because by this time there were so many other Python frameworks to choose from.

In 2010, the Zope community decided to rebrand the "core" part of Zope 3 as the Zope Toolkit, or ZTK for short. The ZTK is used by a variety of applications, including Zope 2, and is advanced jointly by the developers of those projects. The application server and framework aspects of Zope 3 were moved out to a separate project called Blue Bream, which thus became another consumer of the ZTK. The name Zope 3 was retired, although you will still see it used in older documentation and code.

What is new in Plone 4?

The first edition of this book covered Plone 3. This edition has been updated to take into account new and changed components that come with Plone 4, as well as evolution in Plone 'best practice' over the past few years.

Some of the more exciting new features in Plone 4 include:

- Plone 4 uses Zope 2.12 (up from 2.10) and Python 2.6 (up from 2.4). Plone 4.1 updates Zope to 2.13.

- Binary files and images are now stored in so-called BLOBs by default, making Plone much better at serving large files.

- There is a new default visual theme, known as Sunburst.

- The default visual content editor has been changed from Kupu to the widely used TinyMCE editor. This is both better maintained and easier to extend, and should provide an improved user experience for content authors.

- Plone's core JavaScript functionality is now based on jQuery and jQuery Tools. The most obvious change is that many features are now presented in modal "overlay" dialog boxes.

- Portlet management has been improved with a better user interface for "blocking" portlets and per-group dashboard portlets, in addition to per-user ones.

It is now possible to let users log in with their e-mail address instead of a Plone-specific username.

By the time you read this book, Plone 4.1 should be out. This includes many incremental improvements, such as:

- A new *Site Administrator* role, for users who should be able to administer the site without having access to the lower-level developer- and system administrator-oriented tools in the Zope Management Interface.

- Better support for commenting on content, including moderation and Catpcha support, based on the new `plone.app.discussion` package.

- Inclusion of a new HTTP caching tool, `plone.app.caching`.

- A new standard approach to assign and look up universally unique identifiers (UUIDs) for content and other objects, based on the `plone.uuid` package.

- Integration into the core distribution of the form building tool `z3c.form`, which we will cover in *Chapter 11, Standalone Views and Forms*, the testing framework `plone.testing`, which we will use throughout the book, and `plone.app.registry`, which is used to manage site-wide settings and preferences. In addition, the `lxml` XML parsing library will be bundled with Plone's installers to simplify installation.

- Factoring out of some dependencies, so that it is possible to deploy a minimalist Plone installation without such things as the KSS Javascript framework, the Kupu visual editor, and OpenID support. The installers and standard distribution will continue to include these, of course, but by depending on the `Products.CMFPlone` distribution instead of the fully fledged `Plone` distribution, we can choose to only include those add-ons we need.

For more details, please see `http://plone.org/products/plone/releases/4.0` and `http://plone.org/products/plone/releases/4.1`.

 We will use Plone 4.1 as the basis for the examples in the book, but we will highlight where there are differences between Plone 4.0 and 4.1 and how you can stay compatible with both releases.

Plone-the-application and Plone-the-framework

New users sometimes appear on the Plone mailing lists asking for a comparison of Plone and PHP, the popular web programming language. On the face of it, this is a strange question, if you consider that PHP is a language and Plone is first and foremost a content management application. You can download Plone, put it on your server, configure a few options, perhaps install a third party add-on product or two, and use it to solve your everyday content management needs.

Thus, "Plone-the-application" is used to power intranets, public websites, document repositories, and a host of other web-based systems. Plone successfully competes in the "upper mid-tier" CMS market, and is often chosen over commercial systems such as OpenText RedDot and Microsoft SharePoint in head-to-head evaluations.

Plone is developed almost exclusively by volunteers. It is open source, which means that you can obtain and use it for free, and that you are free to modify the underlying source code. There is no official, commercial "high end" version. There is no single company behind Plone selling support or certifications (although professional support is available from a multitude of smaller vendors). There is no specific hardware tie-in. So why have thousands of man-hours gone into making Plone an ever more sophisticated CMS?

The answer is two-fold. We will consider the community drivers later in this chapter, but there are strong commercial reasons as well. The majority of Plone's core contributors make their living from what is often referred to as "Plone-the-framework". They are professional web developers who sell consulting services and support, and have found that by working off an advanced, common base platform, they can offer better value to their customers. A few Plone contributors work for companies with large Plone installations that have found paying someone to spend part of their time contributing to Plone and getting changes into the core to be cheaper than buying ad-hoc support and development resources.

This model is of course nothing new in open source, but it happens to fit content management systems quite well. Customers rarely need a CMS as it comes out of the box. Most will want to customize its look-and-feel, workflow, security, and site structure. Frequently, customers also need some integration with existing systems, or may wish to build a portal that includes not only web page content, but various interactive tools and mini-applications.

If a customer is going to pay for consultants or developers to create the system they need, buying an expensive software license as well seems unnecessary. Developing a complete system from scratch is normally prohibitively expensive and risky. Better then, to take a system which comes close to meeting their needs, turn off the parts that are not relevant, and add the pieces that are missing. That is where Plone comes in. Customers can also take comfort from the fact that there is a large community of companies and individuals who can work with Plone. They need not be locked into a single vendor.

Because the people who build Plone spend the rest of their time building these more specialized systems on top of it, Plone's architecture has evolved in such a way that it is easy to extend. Indeed, this kind of extensible application is how Zope 2 (the application server on which Plone runs) was originally marketed. Almost any part of Plone can be amended, changed, or modified in such a way that Plone itself can be upgraded later without needing to reapply changes to the actual code base. That is, you should never have to fork Plone for your own needs.

Additional considerations when deciding on Plone

Whether Plone is a good base for your application or not will depend on how much Plone offers you out of the box, and how difficult it will be to provide the rest. Usually, this means that your requirements can be modeled in a "content-centric" way, making use of Plone's infrastructure for managing hierarchical, semi-structured content. Being able to reuse Plone's workflow-based security model, tried-and-tested user interface and its infrastructure for things like user management, page layout, and administration tasks also tends to be a strong selling points. Furthermore, Plone's strong support for internationalization and localization is an important consideration for many users.

At the same time, it is important to realize that to get the most out of Plone, you will need to make an investment of time, money, or both. Zope and Plone are RAM-hungry and run best on a modern server. Proper infrastructure is never free, and requires some planning. Similarly, if this is your first Plone project and you are intending to customize Plone extensively, you should bear in mind that there will be a learning curve. Besides online documentation and books such as this one, various companies also offer training courses and specialized consultancy, should you need it.

Licensing

Most parts of Plone are licensed under the GNU General Public License (GPL) Version 2, with various components alternatively licensed under the Lesser General Public License (LGPL), MIT, and BSD licenses. You should seek qualified legal advice if you are concerned about the license.

In practical terms, the license means that you are free to modify and reuse parts of Plone for your own needs. However, if you build a custom application on top of Plone and you intend to distribute (for example, sell a license for, or a boxed version of) that application, you will need to distribute its source code as well. You do not need to make the source code available if you are simply deploying a solution on an internal server.

Plone's source code is legally owned by the Plone Foundation, and is protected by a contributor agreement drawn up with the aid of the Software Freedom Law Center. This "software conservancy" model is very similar to the framework used to protect the integrity of other major open-source projects, such as Apache and Mozilla. The Plone Foundation is able to negotiate alternative license arrangements in special circumstances. Please see http://plone.org/foundation.

The Plone Community, and why you belong there

The word "community" permeates any discussion of what Plone is and where it came from. In practical terms, Plone may be a piece of software, but in the truest sense, Plone is first and foremost a community. In the words of former Zope Corporation CEO Paul Everitt:

> *"Plone, the software is an artifact of Plone, the community."*

Almost all of Plone's core contributors are (or become) friends in real life. They arrange "sprints"—short, intense development sessions—sometimes in exotic locations like an Austrian castle, a former military base on a Norwegian island, and a cabin high up in the Alps. There is an annual conference and usually a symposium or two throughout the year. And every day, the developers meet in online chat rooms and on mailing lists.

This friendship and the mutual respect that developers have for each other, are important factors contributing to Plone's success. Many of us care quite passionately about making Plone the best it can be, and happily expend both personal and professional time on Plone-related activities without direct financial reward.

The Plone community itself is larger than just the two or three dozen core developers, though. First, Plone's sister communities—those of Zope, CMF, and Python—overlap with the Plone community and with each other in socially complex ways. Second, a large number of developers contribute third-party add-on products, answer questions from end users and other developers, and participate in discussions around the future of Plone. A larger number still are end users and Plone administrators, reporting bugs, offering praise and criticism, and joining in the discourse. This is where we hope you will connect with the community initially, if you have not done so already!

Most open source communities have a core of dedicated developers with some governance structure around it. In Plone's case, governance is provided by:

- The Plone Foundation, which is responsible for legal affairs and has a mission "to protect and promote Plone."
- The current Release Manager, who has the final say over what goes into a particular release. A release manager typically serves for one or two releases, before handing over the reins (and serving as a mentor) to the next release manager.

- The current Framework Team, who reviews contributions and make recommendations to the release manager during the early stages of the release cycle.

In practical terms, however, Plone's governance is extremely democratic, and there is very little conflict and very few emotional disputes.

Because of this, people generally find the Plone community open and approachable. Most developers are very happy to give help to those who ask for it, and questions on the mailing lists and in the chat room (see `http://plone.org/support`) are normally answered quickly. Many developers will also actively seek to involve more peripheral members of the community in improving Plone, for example through mentoring or invitations to sprints and other events.

One of the best qualities of the Plone community is its openness to new contributors and the deliberate way in which it develops new leadership from within. The users and developers which encircle the core will sometimes move closer to it through their own learning and participation. As they gain the trust and respect of other developers, they are given more decision-making powers and less supervision, and will be able to influence the future direction of Plone more directly.

Such influence is one strong benefit of actively engaging with the community, and it is not as difficult to attain as one might think. The main factor is attitude, not knowledge. For example, there are many people close to the core of the project who are less technical, but who want to help where they can. Ultimately, Plone would not survive without an influx of fresh blood and new perspectives from time to time.

Even if you are not enticed by rewards of responsibility and influence, being a member of the Plone community, however peripheral, will almost always be beneficial. By reading the mailing lists, for example, you will pick up much up-to-the-minute knowledge that may not be readily available elsewhere. When you are stuck, asking a question in the chat room or on a mailing list can often get you an answer in minutes or hours. By meeting Plone users and developers in real life, at user group meetings, sprints, conferences, and symposia, you will find yourself with a growing network of experts to draw upon when you need it the most. Save for Alan and Alexander, who started it all, every one of us was once a Plone newbie—many of us more recently than you might think!

Contribution to the community should be fun, fit your skills and interest, and give you something back. The easiest way to make a contribution is simply to start answering questions on the mailing lists. If you have some code you want to write, ask about how it may fit with existing projects, and how you may best contribute it to the community. If you feel there is a gap in the documentation and you would like to write a how-to or tutorial, you can do so at `http://plone.org/documentation` and submit it for review. If you would like to host a user group meeting or a sprint, get in touch! You will find that if you show a willingness to give a little, you will get a lot.

Summary

In this chapter, we have discussed:

- A brief history of Zope and Plone
- New features in Plone 4
- How Plone-the-application and Plone-the-framework are related
- Some considerations you should bear in mind when deciding to use Plone
- What the Plone community is and why you may consider knocking on its door

In the next chapter, we will introduce the example application, which will be used to illustrate key concepts over the course of the book.

2
Introduction to the Case Study

Throughout this book, we will build a semi-realistic application that will demonstrate various Plone technologies and concepts. The source code for this application can be found on the book's accompanying website. We will explain the various packages and modules over the next several chapters, but if you are the type of reader, who likes to start at the end, feel free to browse through the code now.

In this chapter, we will:

- Put the example application in the context of a case study
- Show our fictitious client's requirements
- Perform some high level modeling of what the application may look like in Plone.

Background and high-level requirements

Optilux Cinema Group is a mid-sized chain of cinemas. They currently have a limited web presence, but wish to expand it to offer moviegoers a better way to find out about the latest films and reserve tickets for screenings.

The following high-level requirements have been presented to potential vendors of the cinema's web content management system:

	Requirement	Importance	Chapter
1	The site should have a look and feel consistent with Optilux's corporate branding.	High	5 and 8
2	The site should show information about all of Optilux's cinemas.	High	10
3	Non-technical cinema staff should be able to update information about each cinema.	High	6 and 10
4	The site should allow staff to highlight promotions and special events. These may apply to one or more cinemas.	High	10
5	Cinema staff should be able to publish information about new films. It should be possible to update this information after publication.	High	6 and 10
6	Customers should be able to find out in which cinemas a particular film is showing, and which films are showing at a particular cinema. Note that the scheduling of films at cinemas is managed in an existing relational database.	High	12
7	Only films that are currently showing or will be shown in the near future should be viewable.	High	10
8	Customers should be able to search and browse films by cinema, location, and date/time or film name.	High	10 and 12
9	Customers should be able to reserve tickets online. Tickets will be picked up and payment taken at the cinema. Reservations must use Optilux's existing relational database-based ticketing system.	Medium	12
10	Any digital assets, such as images or other files, used on the website must be traceable using a special Digital Asset Management Code, which will be used to link the assets to a third party system.	Medium	10 and 11
11	Customers should not have to log in to use the site, but a username and password should be required when they wish to reserve tickets.	Medium	12 and 13
12	Logged-in customers should have easy access to their preferred cinema or cinemas, such as those in their area.	Medium	13 and 14
13	Customers should be able to log in using their Facebook account.	Medium	13
14	Customers should be able to email enquiries to the site manager if they have questions or feedback.	Low	11
15	Customers should be able to discuss and rate movies.	Low	14

As we become more experienced with Plone development, these requirements will start to ring a few bells. For example, we may identify content types by finding the nouns in the requirement descriptions (for example: #2, #3, #4, and #5), such as Cinema and Film. We may be able to satisfy a few requirements by using Plone's standard content types or simple extensions thereof – a Promotion (#4) could be an extension of an Event or News Item.

It is also likely that the various content types will require custom workflows and security (#5, and #7). We can identify user roles like Customer, Staff, and Management from the subjects in the various requirement descriptions and start to understand what permissions these roles may have.

For reservations and reporting, we will need some relational database connectivity (#9). This in turn will probably mean developing custom forms and templates which access the information in the database.

As the system requires management of member (user), data, and preferences (#11, and #12) we may need to add additional user properties. To support an external authentication mechanism such as the Facebook Graph API (#13) we need to write a custom plugin for the Zope **Pluggable Authentication Service (PAS)**.

Lastly, we must provide client-specific branding (#1). Plone provides user-friendly administrative pages and content management operations. We may also want to use the jQuery JavaScript framework to add dynamic user interface elements.

Modeling and mockups

We may, perhaps in conjunction with the client, decide to do some initial modeling of how the system should look. Some developers advocate very detailed modeling and strict adherence to relevant standards such as UML, the Unified Modeling Language. This depends on personal preference. In the author's opinion, the models themselves are not as important as the act of modeling—thinking through the client's requirements in terms of high-level components and interfaces.

Models can help structure a conversation with the client. Walking through a model and showing screen mockups or wireframes brings an abstract idea of an application to life.

For the purpose of this application, we will start by drawing a UML Use Case Diagram, which highlights the main types of users of the system and the types of things they may want to do with it:

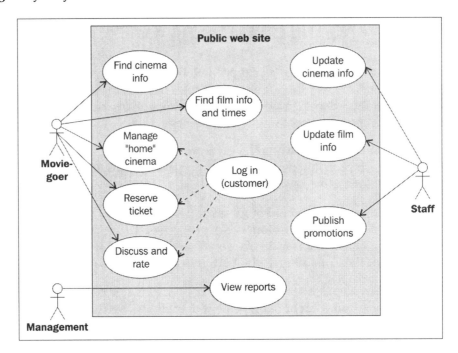

This diagram is by no means exhaustive, but it does give a quick visual representation of the kind of interaction the application will need to support.

From this, we can identify major system components, represented in a high-level class diagram. This also shows where external interfaces will be needed, in this case to the relational database holding film reservations.

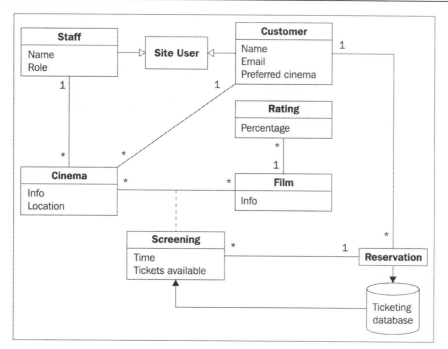

Again, this diagram is far from exhaustive, but it shows that we need to manage **Cinema** and **Film**, which is related by **Screening**. **Customer** and **Staff** are different types of site users, and **Customer** can make **Reservation** for particular **Screening**. **Customer** can also create **Rating** for a particular **Film**. In the content collaboration system, **Staff** can be members of various Projects, which contain documents that staff are working on.

We will also typically work with visual design mockups, drawn in a graphics program and/or provided as 'flat' HTML pages, to indicate how the site will look and feel:

In *Chapter 8, Creating a Custom Theme*, we will see how this mockup forms the basis of a custom site theme.

Information architecture

The design and requirements have implications for the site's information architecture. In Plone, content authors add folders, pages, and other content items to build site structure. This structure is automatically reflected in Plone's navigational aids—the top level tabs, breadcrumbs, navigation tree, and site map, that is, in the website's URLs.

 A logical site structure is an important step towards making a website user-friendly and easy to navigate, and can help improve search engine rankings.

Looking at the design mockup, the links across the top and in the left hand side navigation will most likely expose the main functionality of the site. Different options may appear for logged-in customers, cinema staff or managers, as appropriate. Note that the labels in the mockup are suggestions from the graphic designer. The actual information architecture may be different and may change over time, depending on how the site administrator wishes to set it all up.

The following table outlines initial information architecture for the site:

Section	Purpose	Content types	Visibility
Home	Front page, contains general information	*Folder, Page*	All
About Optilux	General information about Optilux Cinemas	*Folder, Page*	All
About membership	Information about membership benefits	*Folder, Page*	All
Films	Container for films, including film listing	*Film Folder*	All
First film	Information about a film currently showing	*Film*	All
Unpublished film	A film not yet visible to the public	*Film*	Staff
Cinemas	Container for cinemas, including listings	*Cinema Folder*	All
Region one	Container for cinemas in one region	*Cinema Folder*	All
Promotion	A promotion specific to Region one	*Promotion*	All
Cinema one	A cinema in Region one	*Cinema*	All
Screening times	Listing of screening times for films	*Screening*	All
Reserve	Form to reserve tickets for a screening	*Reservation*	Member
Cinema two	Another cinema in Region one	*Cinema*	All
Promotion	*A promotion specific to Cinema two*	*Promotion*	All
Future promotion	A promotion not yet visible	*Promotion*	Staff
Region two	Container for cinemas in another region	*Cinema Folder*	All
Corporate information	General corporate information	*Folder, Page*	All

Section	Purpose	Content types	Visibility
Project one	A project, visible to all staff	*Folder*	Staff
Project two	Another project, private to one group	*Folder*	Some staff

This structure should translate reasonably to a site map of the content hierarchy. Typically, a folder may represent a section or subsection, and contain pages or other content items as necessary. Most folders will have a 'front page' set as its default view, using Plone's **Display** menu, rather than use the standard folder listing view.

This pattern is also used for custom content types. For example, we will create a Cinema Folder type to contain Cinemas. The default view of the cinema folder will allow users to browse for cinemas. Custom types will be built in *Chapter 10, Custom Content Types*.

It is often helpful to prototype the site's information architecture using standard content types (mainly Folders and Pages) with placeholder text, even if some items will eventually be built using custom types. This makes it easier to test the navigation and any customizations.

Running the project

Project management is outside the scope of this book, and every developer and organization will have different ways of managing their development projects. It is probably fair to say, however, that most Plone consultants prefer to work according to "agile" principles (See http://agilemanifesto.org), which typically include rapid prototyping, short development iterations and a high degree of customer interaction throughout the design and development process.

Indeed, Python is often branded an 'agile' programming language, because it is quick to write, easy to read and lends itself well to code refactoring. Furthermore, since Plone gives you a fully featured system out-of-the-box, you will be able to have something tangible and usable up and running almost instantly, which you can incrementally refine with input from the client.

Many developers keep a live test server for the client to test, periodically deploying code updates to showcase new functionality. If you go down this route, you will probably want to set up an issue tracker for the client to report any problems they find. There are many options here. Trac (http://trac.edgewall.org) is a popular Python-based test server.

Getting a draft of the customer's desired branding up for testing quickly can be very valuable, as users often have trouble making the conceptual leap from vanilla Plone to their own requirements. Even just putting a logo and color scheme into a site otherwise using the standard Plone theme can give the client a greater sense of ownership and generate some excitement. It is normally advisable to turn off unneeded core Plone functionality sooner rather than later, to avoid initial confusion. Also remember that in general, you cannot assume that delivering something Plone does out of the box will involve zero effort. At the very least, you will have to test the functionality within the overall context of your application.

As you work with your client, you will get a better idea about what is important to them. Giving them what they want most first, getting them involved in testing early, and being receptive to changes in the specification is usually a very good idea.

Because of this, many Plone consultants prefer to work on a time-and-expenses basis and promise frequent code releases, allowing the project to grow with the client's understanding of their needs. This is not so different from how Plone itself grows as people discover new things they would like it to do. By following good development and project management practices and effectively leveraging Plone's base functionality, you can ensure that at any given point the client has a fully functional (but partially complete) application at their disposal for testing and experimentation.

Summary

In this chapter, we have been introduced to:

- A semi-realistic case study that will be used throughout this book
- High level requirements for the example application following this case study
- Some initial models that point the way to how the application will look and work
- Initial thoughts on the site's information architecture
- A few tips for running Plone development projects

In the next chapter, we will learn how to set up our development environment, before we start building the application for real.

3
The Development Environment

Before we can start building our application, we must set up a suitable development environment. This should mirror the final 'live' server configuration as closely as possible, so that we can test our software locally before deploying it. The environment should also provide appropriate tools to support us during development.

In this chapter we will learn about:

- The elements of Zope's software stack
- How these can be configured for development on various platforms
- Supporting technologies, such as distributions, Setup tools/Distribute, and Buildout
- Some useful development tools

Installers

Understanding your development environment is an important prerequisite to becoming a productive developer. If you need to get up and running quickly, however, you can start with one of the prepackaged Plone installers.

The Plone community generally discourages the use of third-party operating system packages such as RPMs or DEBs for installing Zope and Plone. These are often out of date, and sometimes make non-standard assumptions that make them difficult to support. Furthermore, as a developer you will need write access to the build configuration and source code of your own packages. As such, you should run Zope from within your home directory. We will cover production server deployment in the final part of this book.

Since Plone 3.2, the various platform-specific installers have been based on Buildout, Plone's preferred build tool. You can download the latest Plone 4 installer for your platform from `http://plone.org/downloads`.

The rest of this chapter will describe the building blocks of a development environment and illustrate how to set up such an environment from scratch. If you use an installer, the result may be slightly different, but once you understand how Buildout works, you will be able to customize the installer-configured environment as necessary.

Note that on Mac OS X, the **Unified Installer** is the best choice for developers, as it is more Buildout-friendly.

Glossary of terms

The table below summarizes the various terms and technologies which we will encounter in this chapter. It pays to be familiar with these, as you will find them again not only throughout this book, but also in other Plone documentation.

Term	Definition
Module	A single `.py` file of Python code.
Package	A bundle of Python modules and supporting files. At the most basic level, a package is a directory with an `__init__.py` file and zero or more other Python modules. Packages may be nested. See the Python documentation for details about how to create and import packages.
Setuptools / Distribute	Setuptools is a Python library that extends Python's built-in `distutils` library to support extended distribution metadata, including dependency management (see below). Distribute is a fork of Setuptools that provides some additional features and bug fixes. At the time of writing, it is the more actively maintained of the two, and the default choice for Plone 4.

Term	Definition
Namespace package	Nested packages can be used to build namespaces. For example, most Plone software lives in a top-level package called `plone`, for example `plone.browserlayer` and `plone.memoize`. This is useful to avoid clashes with other projects and to signal ownership over a particular package.
	Namespace packages, a feature of Setuptools/Distribute, allow such namespaces to be declared explicitly. This in turn makes it possible to release packages independently: `plone.browserlayer` and `plone.memoize` are independent distributions on PyPI (see below), which can be installed independently and/or concurrently.
Distribution	A means of packaging and distributing Python code. A distribution consists of a directory with a `setup.py` file, Python code, and potentially other resources. The metadata in `setup.py` may include a version, installation dependencies and license information.
	Tools based on Setuptools/Distribute, including Buildout, can use the metadata to manage concurrent installations of different versions of a given distribution, automatically fetch dependencies, and more.
	It is common to create a distribution containing, and named after, a single package. For example, the distribution `plone.memoize` contains the package `plone.memoize` (which may of course contain sub-packages). However, distribution names do not have to follow this pattern.
Egg	A binary distribution format used by Setuptools/Distribute. Each distribution archive is specific to a particular platform and Python version. Therefore, it is normally safer to use a source format when distributing packages, which is effectively just a compressed archive of the code and metadata. (Setuptools/Distribute will turn a source distribution into an egg specific to the local development environment upon installation.)
	The downside of using source distributions is that if a package has binary dependencies (for example Python extensions written in C), the necessary compiler and libraries need to be available wherever the distribution is installed. It is common to assume Linux and Mac OS X users have these tools available, but make binary eggs available for Windows.

Term	Definition
Develop egg	Normally, we let Setuptools/Distribute (via Buildout) manage the downloading and installation of distributions. For packages we are developing, however, we normally want to control the source code ourselves, and have the abilityto have changes reflected immediately without having to rebuild and reinstall a distribution. This can be achieved with develop eggs, which use a placeholder file to inform Setuptools/Distribute about the location of the in-development source code.
Product	Filesystem-based Python extensions for Zope 2 were originally called Products. Placed in a special directory (`Products/`), they would automatically be discovered by Zope at startup, and implicitly appear under the `Products.*` namespace. Although this method of deployment is still supported for legacy software, virtually all products have now been converted to regular packages.
	Products may contain an `initialize()` function, called when Zope starts up. For legacy reasons, this function is called automatically for packages in the `Products.*` namespace. Packages in other namespaces can opt into this behavior using the `<five:registerPackage />` directive in their `configure.zcml` file. This is mainly useful for registering new content types. We will see an example of this in *Chapter 10, Custom Content Types*.
	The term "product" is also sometimes used more generally to refer to add-ons that extend Plone, even if they are not actually packaged as old-style Zope 2 Products.
Python path	The Python path lists directories and distributions containing Python packages that are available for import by a running Python program. The current path is stored in the variable `sys.path`. We will use Buildout to ensure that this path contains the packages we need to run Plone and our custom software, and – ideally – no more.
The Python Package Index (PyPI)	Previously known as the "Cheese Shop", this is an online repository of Python distributions. Anyone can upload a distribution here. Setuptools/Distribute-based tools such as Buildout and `easy_install` can use PyPI to locate and install distributions and their dependencies.
easy_install	A command-line tool installed with Setuptools/Distribute, which searches PyPI for a given distribution and downloads and installs it.
	By default, `easy_install` puts packages in the global `site-packages` folder for the Python interpreter which was used to install `easy_install` itself. This, coupled with limited dependency version management features, makes `easy_install` unsuitable for installing Plone and Zope.

Term	Definition
Pip	A more advanced alternative to `easy_install`, which can better manage dependency versions and supports distribution uninstallation. This is rarely used in Plone development (and unsuitable for installing Plone itself), but useful for installing tools written in Python.
Buildout	A tool for managing a self-contained environment through a single configuration file (`buildout.cfg`). Buildout itself is installed by the `zc.buildout` distribution. We also use the noun 'buildout' (lowercase 'b') to describe a particular environment managed by Buildout (capital 'B'). Most Plone projects use Buildout to download, install, and configure Zope, Plone, and other dependencies. Buildouts are 'repeatable', meaning that they can be used to replicate a particular setup across multiple servers or developers' machines.
Known Good Set (KGS)	Zope and Plone consist of hundreds of distributions, all available on PyPI. These evolve semi-independently — new versions may be released at any time. By default, Buildout, `easy_install`, and Pip will download the most recent distributions of a package and its dependencies. This may be fine for simple projects, but for complex systems such as Zope or Plone, there is no guarantee that the latest versions of all dependencies will work together. Furthermore, a new release of a dependency could make a 'stable' build difficult to replicate in the future. To avoid such problems, the Zope and Plone developers publish 'known good sets' that 'pin' every distribution to a tested version. Custom projects usually start from a standard KGS, and then override or amend the version pins as necessary to accommodate additional software.
Virtualenv	Just as stray versions can destabilize an installation, so can conflicting packages installed globally into the Python interpreter's `site-packages` directory, e.g. using a tool like `easy_install` or `Pip`. Many operating systems also ship with Python installations that contain operating-system specific packages, some of which have been known to conflict with Zope and Plone. Virtualenv is a script that can be used to create a clean, isolated Python installation. It also allows distributions to be installed in a way that is local to this environment, so that they do not affect other installations.

Term	Definition
ZopeSkel	A collection of *Paste Script* templates for Zope and Plone development, accessible through the `zopeskel` command. We will use this to create new package distributions.

Prerequisites

Before we can get into the business of setting up a Plone development environment, we must install a few prerequisites:

- **Python interpreter**: This is suitable for running Plone. As of Plone 4.0, that means Python 2.6. If your operating system does not have Python 2.6 installed, you can get the latest version in the 2.6 series from `http://python.org/`. On Mac OS X, you can also use MacPorts (`http://www.macports.org/`) to install it. Some members of the Plone community have also created a cross-platform Buildout that can be used to build Python itself. This is particularly popular for installing Python 2.4 (used in Plone 3) on Mac OS X Snow Leopard. See `http://svn.plone.org/svn/collective/buildout/python`.

- **Python Windows Extensions** (On Windows only): It is an installer suitable for your Python version and architecture can be downloaded from `http://sourceforge.net/projects/pywin32/files/`. Presuming you installed Python to `C:\Python26`, you should add `C:\Python2.6;C:\Python2.6\Scripts` to your system `PATH`.

- **Python Imaging Library** (`PIL`): This should be installed for this Python interpreter. Download it from `http://www.pythonware.com/products/pil`. This may have other dependencies, such as the JPEG, PNG, and GIF libraries. On Mac OS X, you can use MacPorts to install `PIL`, if you also used MacPorts to install Python 2.6. On Windows, there is a PIL binary installer. On other operating systems, you may want to install the development versions of `libjpeg`, `libpng`, and `libgif` using operating system packages, and then install PIL manually from source. Simply unpack it and run python `setup.py` install from inside the newly unpacked directory, where python is the binary you intend to use to run Plone.

- **C compiler** (On Unix-like operating systems): You will need this to compile Zope and its dependencies. The default choice is GCC. On Mac OS X, this means installing XCode with command line tools from the Mac OS X DVD. On Linux, use your operating system's package manager to install the base GCC package. On Windows, there should be binary distributions available for all dependencies, making a compiler unnecessary.

- **An internet connection**: Buildout needs to download and install Plone. If your connection requires a proxy server, Python should respect the operating system proxy settings. If it does not, you may need to set the HTTP_PROXY environment variable to the proxy server's URL.

- **A programmer's text editor**: The editor should be preferably one with Python, XML, HTML, and CSS syntax highlighting. You should set up your editor, so that a tab or indent is output as four (4) spaces. This makes Python development a lot more predictable. Popular choices include TextMate on Mac OS X, vi or Emacs on Linux, and SciTE on Windows.

- **A shell**: Most examples in this book will show a Bash interpreter shell, though we will cover Windows syntax when it differs significantly. Remember, that path separators on Windows are backslashes (\), while other environments use forward slashes (/). Also, environment variables on Windows are referred to as %NAME%, whilst in most Unix shells, including Bash, variables are dereferenced with $NAME.

This book assumes that you are comfortable using the shell to move around the filesystem, run commands, and manipulate files; and that you know how the PATH environment variable works and how to change it.

Creating an isolated Python environment

If you installed or compiled a version of Python specifically for the purposes of Plone development, and you did not install anything else globally, you can skip this step.

This is likely to be the case if you are on Windows (see the next section), which is just as well, as it is tricky to install PIL into a Virtualenv on Windows.

If, however, you want to use an operating system-provided Python installation, or you intend to install anything into the global Python environment, you should create an isolated Python environment for Plone development using Virtualenv by executing the following steps:

1. First, make sure easy_install is available. You can try this on a command line with:

   ```
   $ easy_install -h
   ```

2. If this prints a help message, all is good. Otherwise, download `distribute_setup.py` from `http://python-distribute.org/` and run it with:

```
$ python distribute_setup.py
```

 If you get a permission denied error, you may need to run this command as root or under `sudo`.

3. You should then be able to install that latest version of Virtualenv using `easy_install`:

```
$ easy_install -U virtualenv
```

 Again, you may need to do this as root or under `sudo`. If the command is not found, look at the output of the `distribute_setup.py` command to find out where `easy_install` was configured, and add this to your `PATH` environment variable.

4. At this point, you should have a `virtualenv` command available. Use this to create a new environment, such as in your home directory. For example:

```
$ virtualenv --no-site-packages plone-python
```

 This will use the same Python interpreter as the one used by `easy_install`. If you want to use a different Python binary (for example: if `easy_install` does not run under Python 2.6), you can specify the full path to the `python` binary with the `-p` command line option.

This will install a 'clean' Python binary in `plone-python/bin/python`. The `--no-site-packages` ensures no global site packages 'bleed' into the environment.

1. This unfortunately also hides `PIL`, so you will need to install the Python components of this again. Download the latest version from `http://pythonware.com/products/pil/`. Unpack it to reveal the directory `Imaging-1.1.7` (assuming 1.1.7 is the version you downloaded). Then do:

```
$ cd /path/to/Imaging-1.1.7
$ /path/to/plone-python/bin/python setup.py install
```

 Please note that at the time of writing this book, `PIL` is not compatible with `setuptools` and thus cannot be installed with `easy_install` or Buildout.

A minimal buildout

With the prerequisites out of the way, we can now install Zope and Plone using Buildout. Later in this chapter, we will create a flexible development buildout, which we will use and extend throughout the book. First, however, we will illustrate a minimal Plone buildout and show how to stop and start Zope in debug mode.

1. First, we create a new directory to contain the buildout somewhere we have write access as a non-administrative (root) user, such as our home directory. It is preferable to use a short directory path, without spaces, as some older tools do not deal well with spaces in file paths.

2. Next, we download `bootstrap.py`, which is used to install Buildout itself. It is best to download the version used by the Plone developers: `http://svn.plone.org/svn/plone/buildouts/plone-coredev/branches/4.1/bootstrap.py` (adjust the version as necessary for Plone 4.2 and onward).

3. We place this file in our newly created directory. In the same directory, we use a text editor to create a `buildout.cfg` file with the following contents:

```
[buildout]
extends =
    http://dist.plone.org/release/4.1/versions.cfg
parts = instance

[instance]
recipe = plone.recipe.zope2instance
user = admin:admin
eggs = Plone
```

> The `extends` line is used to include a 'known good set' of distributions corresponding to a particular Plone release. You should adjust the version number (4.1 in this case, which is the latest release at the time of writing) as necessary.

4. To initialize the buildout, open a shell and move to the directory containing the two files. Then we run the following command line which will download Buildout and create a few directories and files.

```
$ python bootstrap.py --distribute
```

> If you want to use a different Python binary to run Plone, you can invoke one by absolute path. For example, using the Virtualenv example (shown earlier), you could run `/path/to/plone-python/bin/python bootstrap.py --distribute`.

5. We can then run:

```
$ bin/buildout
```

This will download, compile, and install Zope and Plone. The first time we do this, it can take a long time.

 You may also see some warnings about 'syntax errors' fly past when Setuptools/Distribute tries to pre-compile certain Python scripts. You can safely ignore these. They are issued because, these scripts are not normal Python modules, but rather scripts intended to be executed in Zope's untrusted scripting environment.

6. Once the buildout has finished, we can start Zope in debug mode with:

```
$ bin/instance fg
```

When we see the line Zope is ready to handle requests, we can open a web browser and go to http://localhost:8080. We should see a welcome page, inviting you to create a new Plone site. Using the administrative username and password (admin/admin) specified in the buildout.cfg file, we can do so. For now, we will leave all options at their default settings.

Presuming we kept Plone as the Plone site id, we should now be able to access our Plone site at http://localhost:8080/Plone.

When we are done, we can shut down Zope by pressing *Ctrl+C* in the terminal window.

Buildout basics

The simple buildout (mentioned in the previous section) illustrates most of Buildout's core features. Let us look at these in a bit more detail.

The bootstrap.py script installs zc.buildout itself, and gives us the bin/buildout command. This looks for build instructions in a file called buildout.cfg in the current directory. An alternative file may be specified with the -c command line option:

```
$ bin/buildout -c somefile.cfg
```

 The bin/buildout command must be re-run for any changes to the buildout configuration file to take effect.

To run a buildout in offline mode, we can use:

```
$ bin/buildout -o
```

This is useful if we are not connected to the internet, or simply to speed up buildout execution.

 An offline build will fail unless all required distributions and files are available on the local machine. This usually means that you need to run the buildout at least once already.

See the output of `bin/buildout --help` for other options.

The buildout configuration file consists of sections, in square brackets, containing options, given as name = value pairs. Options that accept multiple values use whitespace as a delimiter. Such values may also be given on multiple, indented lines:

```
[instance]
eggs =
    Plone
    Products.PloneFormGen
```

A value can be referenced from another value as `${section:option}`. For example:

```
[hosts]
devserver = localhost
[ports]
devserver = 8080
[instance]
recipe = plone.recipe.zope2instance
user = admin:admin
eggs = Plone
http-address = ${hosts:devserver}:${ports:devserver}
```

This kind of variable substitution becomes important once we start to define sections that are shared by multiple buildouts.

It is also possible to add to or remove from a multi-line option using `+=` and `-=`:

```
[instance]
eggs =
    Plone
    Products.PloneFormGen
# later, possibly in another file:
[instance]
eggs +=
    collective.googleanalytics
```

Lines beginning with a # are taken as comments and ignored.

In a buildout configuration file, the [buildout] section, which controls global options, usually comes first:

```
[buildout]
extends =
    http://dist.plone.org/release/4.1/versions.cfg
parts = instance
```

The extends line is used to include other configuration files, which can be specified by relative path or remote URL. All included files are merged into a single logical buildout. If, for a particular named section, an option in an extended file is also specified in the extending file, the latter's value is used.

The extends line references a known good versions set for Plone. If you open it in a web browser, you will see something like this (truncated for brevity):

```
[buildout]
extends =
        http://download.zope.org/zopetoolkit/index/1.0.3/zopeapp-
versions.cfg
        http://download.zope.org/Zope2/index/2.13.8/versions.cfg

[versions]
Plone                           = 4.1
Products.ATContentTypes   = 2.1.3
```

This file extends two other files, which in turn contain statements like (again truncated):

```
[buildout]
versions = versions

[versions]
Zope2 = 2.13.8
...
```

When these files are merged, Buildout will look for version pins in the [versions] section (as indicated by the ${buildout:versions} option). The Zope 2 has known good set pins numerous distributions in its [versions] block, to which the Plone known good set adds its own. We could also add or override some version pins using a [versions] section in our own top level buildout.cfg.

The parts option in the [buildout] section is used to list, in order, the steps that Buildout should follow when executing the build. Each part is defined by a section containing a **recipe** option.

A recipe is a named distribution which exposes the logic to perform a particular build task. It will be downloaded from PyPI as required. Most recipes accept and/ or require various options, read from the relevant part section. It is possible to use a given recipe multiple times (in different parts) in a single buildout.

 Writing a new recipe is beyond the scope of this book, but it is not particularly difficult. See http://buildout.org for details. With numerous recipes available on PyPI, however, custom recipes are rarely required. You can look for buildout recipes on PyPI: http://pypi.python.org/pypi?:action=browse&c=512

In the example above, we specified a single part, instance, which was defined in the following section:

```
[instance]
recipe = plone.recipe.zope2instance
user = admin:admin
eggs = Plone
```

This particular recipe is used to configure a Zope 2 instance, into which we install the Plone distribution, and configure an initial user called admin, with the password admin. See http://pypi.python.org/pypi/plone.recipe.zope2instance for details about other options supported by this recipe.

Several recipes, including plone.recipe.zope2instance, use the eggs option to define a **working set** of eggs that should be provided for any console scripts generated. When Buildout generates a script, it will embed the working set in the sys.path variable. For example, bin/instance will look something like this (truncated for brevity):

```
#!/usr/local/bin/python2.6
import sys
sys.path[0:0] = [
  '/path/to/buildout/eggs/Plone-4.1-py2.6.egg',
  '/path/to/buildout/eggs/bpython-0.9.7.1-py2.6.egg',
  '/path/to/buildout/eggs/plone.reload-1.5-py2.6.egg',
  ...
  ]

import plone.recipe.zope2instance.ctl

if __name__ == '__main__':
    plone.recipe.zope2instance.ctl.main(
        ["-C", '/path/to/buildout/parts/instance/etc/zope.conf']
        + sys.argv[1:])
```

This 'path mangling' ensures that the relevant packages, at the required versions, are available at runtime, and provides for isolation between scripts and buildouts.

The working set is calculated from all distributions listed in the `eggs` option, in addition to their dependencies. When the relevant part is executed, Buildout will download and install distributions from PyPI as necessary. Downloaded source distributions are kept in the `dist` directory in the downloads cache, if one is configured. Platform-specific egg installations are kept in the `eggs/` directory, either locally in buildout root or in a shared eggs cache.

Alternatively, we can specify one or more develop eggs. If no version pin says otherwise, a develop egg normally takes precedence over downloaded distributions. During development, we will usually manage all our custom code as develop eggs in the `src/` directory inside the buildout. Develop eggs must be explicitly listed in the `develop` option in the `'buildout'` section. For example:

```
[buildout]
develop =
    src/my.package
    src/my.otherpackage
```

It is also possible to use a wildcard match:

```
[buildout]
develop =
    src/*
```

We will demonstrate a more comprehensive buildout. For more details about Buildout, see `http://www.buildout.org/` and `http://pypi.python.org/pypi/zc.buildout`.

The buildout directory

Besides the buildout configuration and bootstrap files, a buildout consists of a number of directories and files, many of which are created and managed by Buildout and various recipes.

We always should put our build under source control, using a version control system such as Subversion or Git. As a rule of thumb, however, we should not version control any files generated by buildout. This usually means adding the relevant files or directories to the 'ignore' list for our source code management system.

Inside a Plone development buildout, we may find the following files and directories:

File or directory	Version control	Purpose
bootstrap.py	Yes	Installs zc.buildout in a freshly created buildout.
*.cfg	Yes	Buildout configuration files, including the default buildout.cfg.
.installed.cfg	No	Describes the currently installed buildout configuration. This allows buildout to run already-installed recipes in 'update', rather than 'install' mode.
.mr.developer.cfg	No	Describes currently installed develop eggs when using the mr.developer extension.
src/	Yes	The default location for custom distributions. You should version control the src/ directory itself, but if you use the mr.developer extension to manage your develop eggs, you should ignore src/* (all files inside the src/ directory) to avoid accidentally checking them into the build itself. See further for more details.
bin/	No	Contains installed scripts, such as bin/buildout and bin/instance.
eggs/	No	Contains all eggs ever installed from binary or source distributions. (The currently *active* set of eggs for a given runtime is embedded in the scripts in the bin/ directory.) It is possible to share an eggs directory among multiple buildouts.
develop-eggs/	No	Contains the placeholder files for currently active develop eggs.
parts/	No	Used by recipes to store internal files. Buildout is liable to delete or overwrite anything inside this directory at any time.
var/	No	Contains runtime configuration such as logs (var/logs/) and the Zope database files (var/filestorage/ and var/blobstorage/).
coverage/	No	Default output location for HTML test coverage reports created with z3c.coverage. We will describe this tool in more detail shortly.

File or directory	Version control	Purpose
*.pyc, *.pyo	No	These are byte-compiled Python files, which should never be under version control. They may appear in distributions inside the src/ directory, for example.

 If all goes wrong and you want to perform a hard reset on your buildout, delete the parts/ directory and the .installed.cfg file, and rerun buildout. If you think some installed eggs may have been corrupted, you can delete the eggs/ and develop-eggs/ directories as well, which will cause distributions to be reinstalled.

Buildout defaults

To save bandwidth, disk space, and build time, it is a good idea to share third party files between buildouts. Buildout allows us to specify shared directories for eggs, downloads, and remotely extended buildout files (such as known good version sets).

Buildout defaults are set in a file found in ~/.buildout/default.cfg, where ~ is our home directory.

 On Windows, you can find your home directory by opening the Python interpreter and running import os.path; print os.path.expanduser("~") at the interactive prompt.

We must first create the .buildout directory inside our home directory if it does not already exist. Inside .buildout, we then create the directories eggs, downloads, and extends to store the various types of downloads, and a file called default.cfg, containing:

```
[buildout]
eggs-directory = /path/to/.buildout/eggs
download-cache = /path/to/.buildout/downloads
extends-cache  = /path/to/.buildout/extends
```

 Be sure to update the paths to reflect the actual location of the .buildout directory on your system.

The default.cfg file can be used for other defaults if necessary. It behaves as if it is implicitly extended by any buildout you run.

Packages and distributions

Distributions using Setuptools/Distribute – include those we will write starting from *Chapter 5, Developing a Site Strategy* and use as develop eggs—consisting of a directory with a top-level `setup.py` file, and relevant source code, documentation, and other files.

`setup.py` contains metadata about the distribution itself, and declares its current version as well as any dependencies. Dependencies can be specified down to particular versions (such as ">=0.2,<1.0" means "later than version 0.2 but earlier than version 1.0"). Here is a sample `setup.py` file:

```
from setuptools import setup, find_packages
import os

version = '1.0'

setup(name='my.package',
      version=version,
      description="Description of my package",
      long_description=open("README.txt").read() + "\n" +
                  open(os.path.join("docs", "HISTORY.txt")).read(),
      author='Martin Aspeli',
      author_email='optilude@gmail.com',
      license='GPL',
      packages=find_packages(exclude=['ez_setup']),
      namespace_packages=['my'],
      include_package_data=True,
      zip_safe=False,
      install_requires=[
          'setuptools',
          'some.package >= 1.0',
      ],
      )
```

Here:

- The distribution name is `my.package`, and the version is 1.0.

- We have specified a short and long description, author information, and other metadata for PyPI. The long description is read from the files README. txt and docs/HISTORY.txt.

- We ask `Setuptools/Distribute` to find source code in the current directory, excluding the module `ez_setup` if found. By default, this is done by looking for any files under version control.

- We declare that `my.*` is a namespace package.

- We declare that the distribution cannot be run from a zipped archive, as this is unsupported by Zope and discouraged in general.
- We declare that this distribution depends on setuptools (to support namespace packages) and `some.package`. The latter has to be version 1.0 or later.

When a distribution is installed, `Setuptools/Distribute` will attempt to fulfill dependencies listed under `install_requires` by downloading and installing them if necessary. It will look for distributions on PyPI by default, but an alternative index can be specified if necessary, and secondary 'find-links' may be listed in the distribution itself.

It is possible to use `setup.py` to install a distribution into the global site packages of a given Python interpreter:

```
$ python setup.py install
```

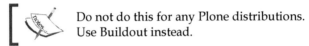

Do not do this for any Plone distributions.
Use Buildout instead.

To install a develop egg instead, we can run:

```
$ python setup.py develop
```

This creates a placeholder file that links to the distribution's source code, allowing it to be added to the Python path at runtime.

New packages can be released as source distributions, which are just zip files of the package with some additional metadata. We can build a source distribution of a package with:

```
$ python setup.py sdist
```

The new distribution will be placed in the `dist` subdirectory, which will be created if necessary.

Distributions can be uploaded to PyPI through a `setup.py` command:

```
$ python setup.py egg_info -RDb "" sdist register upload
```

On Mac OS X, you should make sure resource forks are not included in the archive, as they can confuse other operating systems. To do that, you can run two commands before the line above: export COPY_ EXTENDED_ATTRIBUTES_DISABLE=true and export COPYFILE_ DISABLE=true.

You will be asked to specify or create a PyPI account if this is the first time you run this command. The login details are stored in the `.pypirc` file in your home directory.

The `easy_install` script searches PyPI or a similar index for distribution to download and install into the global Python environment. The latest valid versions of any dependencies will be included automatically. For example, we installed Virtualenv with:

```
$ easy_install -U virtualenv
```

Some distributions have optional dependencies known as **extras**. These can be installed using square bracket notation, for example:

```
$ easy_install -U my.package [someextra]
```

The same notation is supported in the `install_requires` line for dependencies. For example, a distribution that wanted to declare an extra called `test` that added a dependency on `plone.testing` with the `z2` extra could add the following in its `setup.py` file:

```
extras_require={
    'test': ['plone.testing[z2]',]
},
```

Distributions can contain metadata about included plugins using a mechanism called **entry points**. This allows code to discover these plugins at runtime. Entry points are listed in `setup.py`, under the `entry_points` argument. For example, some Plone add-ons use an entry point like this to automatically register their configuration with Plone:

```
entry_points="""
[z3c.autoinclude.plugin]
target = plone
""",
```

> For more information about `Setuptools/Distribute` and `setup.py`, see `http://guide.python-distribute.org/`.

The development buildout

We will now create the development buildout that will be used throughout this book. You can find this in the book's accompanying source code.

We currently have three buildout configuration files, all found at the root of the buildout:

File	Purpose
versions.cfg	Contains our own known good set of distributions, allowing us to pin down custom dependencies and override any version pins from other known good sets we extend.
packages.cfg	Extends versions.cfg and other known good version sets, including the known good set for Plone, sets some global options, and defines various working sets. This file allows us to manage the distributions that make up our project in a way that can be reused by multiple top-level buildout configuration files.
buildout.cfg	This is the top-level buildout file for our development build, containing the parts and options we need to set up a development environment. Later in the book, we will add additional top-level buildout files for production deployment.

The first of these files, versions.cfg, is straightforward:

```
# Project-specific version pins
# =============================

[versions]
# Buildout
mr.developer = 1.17
collective.recipe.omelette = 0.10

# Development tools
bpython = 0.9.7.1
pygments = 1.4
Products.DocFinderTab = 1.0.4
Products.PDBDebugMode = 1.3.1
Products.PrintingMailHost = 0.7
z3c.coverage = 1.2.0
jarn.mkrelease = 3.0.9
setuptools-git = 0.4.2
setuptools-hg = 0.2

# ZopeSkel
ZopeSkel = 2.19
Cheetah = 2.2.1
Paste = 1.7.5.1
PasteScript = 1.7.3
PasteDeploy = 1.3.4
```

The version pins shown here were the most appropriate versions at the time of writing. You may want to update some of these versions. See the description of z3c.checkversions mentioned in the following sections for details.

Next up, packages.cfg is a little more interesting:

```
# Information about packages and known good version sets
# ========================================================
[buildout]
extensions = mr.developer buildout.dumppickedversions
extends =
# Known good sets of eggs we may be using
    http://dist.plone.org/release/4.1/versions.cfg
    versions.cfg

versions = versions
unzip = true

# Egg sets
[eggs]
main =
    Plone
test =
devtools =
    bpython
    plone.reload
    Products.PDBDebugMode
    Products.PrintingMailHost
    Products.DocFinderTab

# Checkout locations
[sources]
```

This first installs two **buildout extensions**: mr.developer, which is used to manage develop eggs, and buildout.dumppickedversions, which will print the picked versions for any unpinned distributions at the end of the buildout run. We will describe these in more detail in the next section.

Next, we extend two known good sets—the one for our chosen Plone version, and our own local versions.cfg, which should come last so that it can override any versions from the external sets.

We also set the `unzip` option to `true`, which means that buildout will always unzip eggs in `eggs/` directory. This makes debugging easier, avoids potential problems with Zope code that does not properly set the `zip_safe` flag to `False`, and is a prerequisite for using `collective.recipe.omelette`. Two recipe-less sections are then defined: `[sources]` is used by `mr.developer`, and will be described in a moment. `[eggs]` is used to define working sets that are referenced in other buildout sections:

Working set	Purpose
main	The minimal set of distributions required to run our application. Until we create some distributions of our own, we use the `Plone` egg here. In *Chapter 5, Developing a Site Strategy* we will replace this with our own 'policy package', which in turn will depend on all the software we need, including Plone.
test	This option lists all distributions for which we want to run automated tests. Usually, that means every custom distribution we create. If distributions have a [test] extra for test-only dependencies, this should be used here. Until we create our own distributions, this is empty.
devtools	Additional distributions that we want to install in the development environment, but not on a production server.

Finally, `buildout.cfg` contains the actual build instructions for our development environment:

```
# Development environment buildout
# ================================

[buildout]
parts =
    instance
    test
    coverage-report
    omelette
    zopepy
    zopeskel
    checkversions
    mkrelease

extends =
    packages.cfg

# Packages to check out/update when buildout is run
auto-checkout =

# Make sure buildout always attempts to update packages
always-checkout = force
```

```
# Development Zope instance. Installs the ``bin/instance`` script
[instance]
recipe = plone.recipe.zope2instance
http-address = 8080
user = admin:admin
verbose-security = on
eggs =
    ${eggs:main}
    ${eggs:devtools}

# Test runner. Run: ``bin/test`` to execute all tests
[test]
recipe = zc.recipe.testrunner
eggs = ${eggs:test}
defaults = ['--auto-color', '--auto-progress']

# Coverage report generator.
# Run: ``bin/test --coverage=coverage``
# and then: ``bin/coveragereport``
[coverage-report]
recipe = zc.recipe.egg
eggs = z3c.coverage
scripts = coveragereport
arguments = ('parts/test/coverage', 'coverage')

# Installs links to all installed packages to ``parts/omelette``.
# On Windows, you need to install junction.exe first
[omelette]
recipe = collective.recipe.omelette
eggs =
    ${eggs:main}
    ${eggs:devtools}

# Installs the ``bin/zopepy`` interpreter.
[zopepy]
recipe = zc.recipe.egg
eggs =
    ${eggs:main}
    ${eggs:devtools}
interpreter = zopepy

# Installs ZopeSkel, which can be used to create new packages
# Run: ``bin/zopeskel``
[zopeskel]
recipe = zc.recipe.egg
eggs = ZopeSkel

# Tool to help check for new versions.
```

```
# Run: ``bin/checkversions versions.cfg``
[checkversions]
recipe = zc.recipe.egg
eggs = z3c.checkversions [buildout]

# Tool to make releases
# Run: ``bin/mkrelease --help``
[mkrelease]
recipe = zc.recipe.egg
eggs = jarn.mkrelease
```

First, we list the parts to execute, and extend packages.cfg to gain access to our working- and known good version sets. The last two options in the [buildout] section, auto-checkout and always-checkout, are used by mr.developer and described below.

Next, we define our development Zope instance. This runs on port 8080, has an administrative Zope user called admin with password admin, provides additional debug information for security violations, and is installed with a working set combining ${eggs:main} and ${eggs:devtools}.

The subsequent parts install various development tools, which are described in more detail in the subsequent sections.

 You may have noticed that several parts use zc.recipe.egg. This recipe is used to install one or more distributions. If a distribution declares one or more **console scripts** (through an entry point), these are installed to the bin/ directory refer http://pypi.python.org/pypi/zc.recipe.egg for details.

Development tools

Let us now examine the various development tools that we will use throughout the book.

Buildout extensions

The first two development tools are extensions to buildout itself, which operate at build time.

mr.developer

We previously saw how to list develop eggs using the ${buildout:develop} option. As our projects grow, it is usually beneficial to version control the buildout separately from the distributions used as we develop eggs. This allows us to release, tag, and branch individual distributions independently of other distributions, and of the build itself. We can do this manually by checking out distributions to the src/ directory and keeping the develop option up to date, but this is cumbersome and error prone. The mr.developer extension was built to alleviate this. It can look for packages that may be used as develop eggs in the [sources] section, which we have placed in our packages.cfg file. For example:

```
[sources]
my.package = svn https://svn.example.org/repos/my.package/trunk
my.otherpackage = git https://github.com/myorg/my.otherpackage
```

Here, two distributions are configured for mr.developer, one found in a Subversion repository, and one found in a Git repository. (Other version control systems, including Mercurial, Bzr, and CVS are supported as well.) If a package is not (yet) checked in to any version control system, we can manually place it in the src/ directory and list it with the fs option (short for filesystem):

```
[sources]
optilux.policy = fs optilux.policy
```

> Most Plone distributions are found in one of the standard Plone repositories: http://svn.plone.org/svn/plone for core distributions, or http://svn.plone.org/svn/collective for community add-ons. If you need to use an unreleased distribution (for example to get access to a recent bug fix), you can add it to mr.developer's sources list with the appropriate Subversion URL as well.

With [sources] defined, we can tell mr.developer to automatically check out distributions and register them as develop eggs using the ${buildout:auto-checkout} option. For development purposes, we have placed this in our top-level buildout.cfg file. To use the two fictitious distributions in our previous example as develop eggs, we could do:

```
[buildout]
...
auto-checkout =
    my.package
    my.otherpackage
```

We do this in `buildout.cfg`, and not `packages.cfg`, because we only want to track the source code repository during development. In the final part of this book, we will describe how to make internal distribution releases suitable for production deployment.

If we also want to ensure that distributions are updated from the source code repository each time buildout is run, we can add `always-checkout = true` to the `[buildout]` section. By default, packages are checked out once, but must be manually updated.

There is always a chance that an update could result in a merge conflict if uncommitted local changes interfere with changes pulled from a remote repository. In this case, `mr.developer` will abort the buildout, allowing you to resolve the merge conflict before running the build again.

`mr.developer` also installs a script called `bin/develop`. This can be used to update one or all distributions tracked by `mr.developer`, activate or deactivate develop eggs, track the status of all distributions (even across multiple version control systems and repositories), and rerun buildout (which is required for distributions activations/deactivations to take effect). See the output of `bin/develop help` for details.

This covers the most basic use of `mr.developer`. See `http://pypi.python.org/pypi/mr.developer` for further options and usage patterns.

buildout.dumppickedversions

As previously discussed, it is important to pin down distribution versions as a project matures, to ensure a build can be safely repeated in the future without the risk of a new distribution uploaded to PyPI causing a build or runtime error. At the very least, Buildout should not be given free rein to pick any distribution versions when a project is released and deployed to a production server.

The `buildout.dumppickedversions` extension will print a summary of any versions that were picked by Buildout at the end of each buildout run. The output looks like this:

```
*************** PICKED VERSIONS ****************
[versions]
Products.PDBDebugMode = 1.1
Products.PrintingMailHost = 0.7
*************** /PICKED VERSIONS ***************
```

Here, we have neglected to pin `Products.PdbDebugMode` and `Products.PrintingMailHost`. Helpfully, `buildout.dumppickedversions` has listed them in a format suitable for copying into our `versions.cfg` file. Once we do that and rerun buildout, they should disappear from this list.

The picked versions block is output even if buildout encountered an error. This can sometimes make it harder to spot error messages. Be sure to look above the **PICKED VERSIONS** line to check that buildout completed successfully.

Development Zope instance

For development, we usually use a single Zope instance, controlled by the script `bin/instance` (the script name is taken from the part name in the buildout configuration), with a local `Data.fs` file and `blobstorage` directory containing the Zope database. This instance is optimized for use in a development environment, and has the **verbose-security** flag turned on, to give more details about security-related errors.

'Permission denied' errors are normally not reported in the error logs. To see them, go to the **Errors** control panel under Plone's **Site Setup** and remove **Unauthorized** from the list of ignored exception types.

During development, we normally run Zope in foreground mode, with:

```
$ bin/instance fg
```

Not only does this make it easier to see log messages and use the debugger, it also ensures that Zope runs in debug mode, which, among other things, ensures that page templates on the filesystem can be modified and their changes take effect without restarting Zope, and disables caching and merging of Plone's CSS and JavaScript resources.

Note that this renders the `debug-mode` option of `plone.recipe.zope2instance` obsolete.

We also install various development tools into the Zope instance. These are outlined in the subsequent sections.

plone.reload

Ordinarily, any change to Python or ZCML files requires a restart of Zope to take effect. This can be time consuming, especially if we are making frequent changes. `plone.reload` attempts to alleviate this by detecting changed code and reloading it.

 `plone.reload` only works when Zope is running in debug mode.

The reloader is invoked from the `@@reload` view at the root of the Zope instance. If Zope is running on port `8080`, that means going to `http://localhost:8080/@@reload`. Click **Reload Code** to reload any code changed since startup or the previous reload. Click **Reload Code and ZCML** to also reload ZCML component configuration.

 The reload mechanism works most of the time, but it is not perfect, and may fail to detect certain changes. In rare circumstances, a reload may also cause difficult-to-debug crashes. If you see any problems after a reload, or the reload did not appear to work, you should restart Zope before attempting any other debugging.

Products.PdbDebugMode

This package installs an exception hook that will drop us to a debugging prompt if any exceptions are raised, which is useful for diagnosing exceptions. See the following sections for more details about PDB, the Python debugger.

 Zope will not return a response while at a breakpoint, which may make the site appear to hang. Be sure to check the terminal where Zope is running for a break point if your browser does not complete a request as expected. Press *c* and then *Enter* to exit the debugger. You may need to do this multiple times if multiple threads have reached the same break point simultaneously.

`Products.PdbDebugMode` also provides a view called `@@pdb`, which can be used to drop into a PDB prompt at will. This is useful for ad-hoc introspection, or just to test a Python expression against a live site. Simply append `/@@pdb` to the URL of any content item (or the Plone site root), such as, `http://localhost:8080/Plone/@@pdb`. Use `self.context` at this prompt to inspect the relevant content object.

Products.PrintingMailHost

This package hooks into the Plone `MailHost` object to make it print the output of
mail messages to the console instead of sending them to a mail relay. This is useful
for testing and debugging code that sends e-mails.

Products.DocFinderTab

This package adds a **Doc** tab to most objects in the Zope Management Interface.
We can use this to look at the methods, variables, and base classes of a given
content object.

Test runner

Throughout this book, we will be writing automated tests for our code. To run
those tests, we need a test runner, which is installed with `zc.recipe.testrunner`.

 In Plone 3, we would normally use the command `bin/instance test`
to run tests. This is no longer supported in Zope 2.12, and thus Plone 4.

This recipe takes an `eggs` option, under which we list every distribution we want to
test. In our buildout, this is initialized from `${eggs:test}` from `packages.cfg`.

 Note that each distribution containing packages to test must be listed
explicitly, even if it is a dependency of another included distribution.

The test runner recipe generates a script called `bin/test` (the name is taken from
the test runner part's section). To run all tests, simply do:

```
$ bin/test
```

To run only the tests in a particular package, use the `-s` option:

```
$ bin/test -s my.package
```

To run only a test with a name matching a particular regular expression, use the `-t`
option:

```
$ bin/test -s my.package -t test_something
```

See the output of `bin/test --help` for other options.

Coverage reporting

Ideally, we should have automated tests covering every code path in our application. To help measure how good our code coverage is, we can use the test runner's coverage reporting tool. This is enabled with the `--coverage` option, which should indicate a directory for the coverage report. For example:

```
$ bin/test --coverage=coverage
```

 Coverage analysis significantly slows down the test runner, which is why this option is not enabled by default.

This will output summary statistics to the console, and place the raw coverage reports in the directory `parts/test/coverage`. To turn these into a user-friendly HTML report, we can use the `bin/coveragereport` script installed by the `z3c.coverage` package:

```
$ bin/coverage
```

This looks in the aforementioned directory and outputs a coverage report to the `coverage/` directory inside the buildout root. Open `coverage/all.html` in a web browser to see the full report, including line-by-line test coverage analysis.

Continuous integration

When working in a team, it is important to run the build tests regularly, with instant notification when either the build itself or a test breaks: early detection makes regressions easy to diagnose and resolve, and is an important element of code quality management. This style of working is known as **continuous integration**.

Instructions for setting up a continuous integration server are beyond the scope of this book, but you are encouraged to look at Hudson, an open source continuous integration tool that is easy to install and use. Hudson can be configured to execute a series of shell commands, including `bin/buildout` and `bin/test`. Recent versions of the test runner also support Subunit output, which can be converted to JUnit-style XML reports suitable for Hudson. See `http://hudson-ci.org/` and `http://pypi.python.org/pypi/python-subunit` for more information.

Omelette

It is useful to be able to search the 'active' source code for debugging and analysis purposes. With numerous distributions making up the Plone working set, however, it can be difficult to keep track of which packages are currently in use.

To make this easier, we can use `collective.recipe.omelette`. This presents a single 'virtual' source tree of the current working set by creating symbolic links to all packages in all (unzipped) eggs in the directory `parts/omelette`.

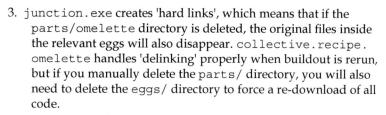

`collective.recipe.omelette` works on Windows, but there are three important caveats:

1. You must download `junction.exe` (see `http://technet.microsoft.com/en-us/sysinternals/bb896768.aspx`), copy it to a directory on the system `PATH`, and run it manually at least once to accept its license terms.

2. `junction.exe` is fairly slow and can affect buildout performance, especially on slower systems.

3. `junction.exe` creates 'hard links', which means that if the `parts/omelette` directory is deleted, the original files inside the relevant eggs will also disappear. `collective.recipe.omelette` handles 'delinking' properly when buildout is rerun, but if you manually delete the `parts/` directory, you will also need to delete the `eggs/` directory to force a re-download of all code.

If you prefer not to use `collective.recipe.omelette` on Windows, simply remove it from the `parts` list.

The zopepy interpreter

Python lets us quickly prototype code on the interactive interpreter prompt. This is very powerful and can save much guessing. To be able to import Zope and Plone code, however, we need the relevant set of packages available. This is achieved with the `bin/zopepy` script, which is simply a Python interpreter with the correct `sys.path` mangling applied.

Bear in mind that `zopepy` does not actually start Zope or load any of its configuration, so Zope runtime state like configured components or database connections will not be available. If you need that, you can run `bin/instance debug` instead, which will start up Zope and present an interactive prompt. Note that if you make changes to the ZODB, you will need to explicitly commit them with: `import transaction; transaction.commit()`.

ZopeSkel

ZopeSkel is a collection of skeleton templates that can be used to create new distributions quickly. It is installed as bin/zopeskel. We will see how to use this in *Chapter 5, Developing a Site Strategy,* but in the meantime, you can run bin/zopeskel --help to learn how to use it.

z3c.checkversions

We have extolled the virtues of pinning distributions a few times already, but one downside of maintaining version pins is that discovering new releases requires manually checking PyPI or other sources. For major components with their own known good version sets such as Plone, this is not so much of an issue, but for our various development tools and third-party dependencies, it can become a hassle.

To help with this, we can use the bin/checkversions script installed by z3c.checkversions. To run it against our versions.cfg file, we would do:

```
$ bin/checkversions versions.cfg
```

This will report the latest available version on PyPI. If we are only interested in bug fixes, we can restrict the check to minor versions, with:

```
$ bin/checkversions versions.cfg --level=2
```

See the output of bin/checkversions --help for more options.

jarn.mkrelease

Eventually, we will need to make releases of our distributions. For distributions we intend to release to the public that can mean uploading source distributions to PyPI. For internal distributions, we usually want to release to an internal distribution location, so that we have immutable, versioned distributions for deployment.

As we will show in the final part of this book, we can use bin/mkrelease, installed by jarn.mkrelease, to easily make releases. For more information, see http://pypi.python.org/pypi/jarn.mkrelease.

Tools in the browser

The humble web browser is an important part of our development environment. Not only does it allow us to manually test our site; modern browsers also come with development tools that allow us to debug JavaScript, understand what CSS is affecting what elements on the page, prototype JavaScript code, and CSS changes, inspect request and response headers, and inspect and modify the HTML structure on the fly.

Chrome and Safari both have built-in development tools. For Firefox, there is the ever popular Firebug. Get it from `http://getfirebug.com`, and wonder how you ever lived without it.

Learning to help yourself

During development, there will probably be times when you are stumped. Plone is fairly well-documented, but the documentation is certainly not perfect. The mailing lists and chat room are great resources if you need help, but it is also very important to learn how to help yourself.

Find the documentation

Documentation for Plone code can usually be found in one of the following places:

* High level and tutorial-style documentation is normally found at `http://plone.org/documentation`.

* Many distributions include documentation in their PyPI listings. For example, plone.testing's documentation can be found at `http://pypi.python.org/pypi/plone.testing`.

* Distributions often include documentation in their README file. This is often also the source of the documentation published to PyPI.

* Internal documentation in the form of comments or tests is often very valuable. Most packages use Zope interfaces (more on those in *Chapter 9, Nine Core Concepts of Zope Programming*) to describe their key APIs. Look for a file called `interfaces.py`.

Use the Source, Luke!

Python's readability is both a blessing and a curse. A blessing because it is normally possible to read the source code to find out what is going on. A curse because this sometimes makes developers a little lax about documentation.

One of the first hurdles new developers should overcome is any undue respect for the Python files that make up Zope and Plone. There is (almost) nothing magical about them. Earlier, we showed how to install an 'omelette' (in the `parts/omelette` directory inside the buildout root) that provides a single view of the source code that makes up the Plone runtime environment for a project. This is the best place to look for source code.

Get used to searching for code using `grep` or equivalent graphical tools, opening them and looking for specific classes and methods. Seeing what a piece of code does can often be faster than looking up documentation or examples. As time goes by, you will find that a few packages come up repeatedly, and finding code will be easier.

You can of course change these files as well. A backup is advisable, but if you think that temporarily raising an exception, adding a PDB break point, or printing a message from somewhere deep inside Zope helps you to solve a problem, go right ahead.

It is a bad idea to make permanent changes this way, however, not least because those changes will be overwritten if you upgrade or reinstall the particular component. In the next chapter, we will learn more about other ways of customizing code Zope and Plone. However, if you find a bug, please report it (at `http://dev.plone.org/plone`), and attach a patch if you can!

Become familiar with the debugger

PDB, the Python debugger, is your best friend. To insert a breakpoint in your code or in some other code that you are trying to debug add the following line and (re-)start Zope in the foreground in a terminal:

```
import pdb; pdb.set_trace()
```

To avoid a restart, you can usually use the `@@reload` view from `plone.reload`. Refer the previous sections.

When this line is encountered, execution will stop, and the terminal will display:

(pdb)

This is the interactive PDB prompt. Type `help` and press *Enter* to see available commands. The most important ones are `pp`, to print a variable or the result of an expression; `n` to step to the next line; `s` to step into a function call; `l` to show a listing of the source code around the current execution point; `tbreak` to add a temporary breakpoint at a particular line, and `c`, to stop debugging and continue execution until another breakpoint is encountered.

If you want to quickly test syntax or libraries, you can run Python's interactive interpreter, through the `bin/zopepy` script as described earlier.

Look at the logs

During development, you should typically run Plone in a terminal window, using `bin/instance fg`. This enables debug mode and prints log messages to the console. If anything goes wrong, you should inspect the log first.

If an exception is encountered, you will likely see a traceback. For example:

```
Traceback (innermost last):
Module ZPublisher.Publish, line 115, in publish
Module ZPublisher.mapply, line 88, in mapply
Module ZPublisher.Publish, line 41, in call_object
Module Products.CMFPlone.FactoryTool, line 361, in __call__
Module Products.CMFPlone.FactoryTool, line 147, in __getitem__
Module Products.CMFPlone.PloneFolder, line 406, in invokeFactory
Module Products.CMFCore.TypesTool, line 934, in constructContent
Module Products.CMFCore.TypesTool, line 345, in constructInstance
Module Products.CMFCore.TypesTool, line 357, in _finishConstruction
Module Products.CMFCore.CMFCatalogAware, line 145, in
notifyWorkflowCreated
Module Products.CMFCore.WorkflowTool, line 355, in notifyCreated
Module Products.DCWorkflow.DCWorkflow, line 392, in notifyCreated
Module Products.DCWorkflow.DCWorkflow, line 476, in _changeStateOf
Module Products.DCWorkflow.DCWorkflow, line 571, in _executeTransition
Module Products.DCWorkflow.DCWorkflow, line 435, in
updateRoleMappingsFor
Module Products.DCWorkflow.utils, line 60, in modifyRolesForPermission
Module AccessControl.Permission, line 93, in setRoles
AttributeError: appname
```

The actual error is usually on the last line of the traceback. If this is not in any code that you wrote, chances are something you did further up the stack caused the problem, if you passed an invalid argument to a function. Start from the end and work your way up the stack trace until you see some code that you wrote, and start debugging from there.

If you have `Products.PdbDebugMode` installed, you will usually end up at a `(pdb)` prompt when a traceback occurs. You can use this to investigate what is going on. The up and down PDB commands can be used to move up or down the stack. Use the c command to exit the debugger.

Summary

In this chapter, we have seen:

- How to prepare a development environment for Zope and Plone development
- How to set up a minimal Zope buildout and install a Plone site into it
- How Buildout and Setuptools/Distribute work
- How to set up a more sophisticated and flexible development buildout. This buildout will be used throughout the book
- Some important development debugging tools
- A few tips on how you can more effectively help yourself by learning to look at source code, using PDB effectively, prototyping things with zopepy, and looking at log files

This concludes Part 1 of the book. In Part 2, we will learn more about customizing Plone for our specific needs.

Part 2

Customizing Plone

Basics of Customization

Developing a Site Strategy

Security and Workflow

Using Add-on

Creating a Custom Theme

4
Basics of Customization

To a certain extent, all we ever do when we use Plone-the-platform is to customize Plone-the-product. Sometimes, that means building a system that barely resembles "out-of-the-box" Plone; other times, it simply means adding a few bells and removing a few unnecessary whistles.

In this chapter, we will cover the main types of customization that Plone supports, including:

- Persistent settings in the ZODB
- GenericSetup configuration
- CMF Skin layers
- The Zope Component Architecture

Starting with the next chapter, these techniques will be explained more fully and put into practice in the context of the Optilux Cinemas case study.

Persistent settings and the ZODB

The first type of customization most developers come across is in the form of settings exposed by various Zope Management Interface screens and Plone control panels. Sometimes, they may also build applications that depend on particular content items or site structure. In both cases, part of the application's configuration is stored in the **Zope Object Database (ZODB)**, rather than in source code or configuration files.

 The **Zope Object Database (ZODB)** is the primary data store for Plone content. It is a fast, hierarchical object store that natively persists Python objects. We will learn more about the ZODB in *Chapter 9, Nine Core Concepts of Zope Programming*.

Relying on persistent database state for configuration does not scale or repeat easily. Imagine a team of developers working on the same site. Ideally each developer would have their own sandbox, much like we saw in the previous chapter. This sandbox would need to be separate from the live environment. Manually replicating changes across such distributed environments is difficult and error-prone.

Further, because of the way the ZODB serializes Python objects (it uses the **pickle protocol**, a feature of the Python standard library — see http://docs.python.org/library/pickle.html), persistent objects can only be de-serialized with reference to the code that was used to create them. This means that extra care needs to be taken when renaming or relocating classes in the source code for objects that may be persisted.

These challenges led Tres Seaver, the creator of the Zope Content Management Framework (CMF), to formulate Seaver's Law:

> *"Persistence means always having to say you're sorry."*

This is so, because any setting that is persisted in a running application requires migration if the underlying code is modified (it's discussed in detail in the later sections of this chapter), and any setting that is made through-the-web is ephemeral if it has to be manually translated from a development environment to a production server (or vice-versa).

Where are persistent settings stored?

Persistent settings are stored in a few different places, including CMF tools, and the Plone site root itself.

A **tool** is a singleton persistent object, found in the root of the Plone site. Most tools have names starting with portal_, such as portal_membership or portal_types. They variously expose shared functionality and act as containers for configuration state. Most tools can be configured from the ZMI, and many of the Plone Site Setup control panels manage tool settings under the hood.

Some of the more common locations for customizations include:

- The portal_properties tool contains various property sheets, which in turn contain properties of various types. The two main property sheets are site_properties, containing general settings, and navigation_properties, containing settings related to site navigation.

- Some settings are stored as properties on the Plone site object. These can be found on the **Properties** tab in the ZMI, although it is better to manage them through Plone's Site Setup, not at least if you intend to use non-English characters.

- Settings related to content types, such as their title and default view, are stored in the various **Factory Type Information** (FTI) objects inside the `portal_types` tool.

- Workflow-related settings are stored in the `portal_workflow` tool and the workflow objects contained within it.

- Catalog (search) related settings, including search indexes, are stored in the `portal_catalog` tool.

- Information about actions – which are used to render links such those to log in, log out, access the dashboard or access Plone's Site Setup are stored in the `portal_actions` tool.

- The `portal_css` tool is used to control the inclusion and merging of CSS resources. Similarly, `portal_javascripts` is used to control JavaScript files.

- Information about themes, skin layers and through-the-web customizations of skin layer resources are stored in the `portal_skins` tool. Through-the-web customizations of browser views and viewlets are stored in the `portal_view_customizations` tool.

- Third party products (and likely in the future, Plone itself) may use the `portal_registry` tool to store configuration settings. This is installed by the `plone.app.registry` package. See `http://pypi.python.org/pypi/plone.app.registry` for more information.

Using GenericSetup for configuration

GenericSetup is one answer to Seaver's Law. In particular, it solves the translation-of-settings challenge and simplifies pre-configuration of persistent objects on site setup.

Each configurable component (such as a GenericSetup-aware tool) provides a pair of import and export handlers for importing and exporting its state to the filesystem. Each handler typically knows how to read and write an XML file with a particular name. For example, the file `skins.xml` will be read by the import handler for the `portal_skins` tool to set up skin layers (more on those in the next section).

See http://plone.org/documentation/manual/developer-manual/generic-setup for a listing of the standard GenericSetup handlers and their associated XML syntax.

For importing state, a collection of GenericSetup files can be placed in a directory, which is registered as a GenericSetup profile. There are two types of GenericSetup profiles:

A base profile aims to describe the complete configuration for a site, excluding its actual content. When a new Plone site is created, it is configured from a base profile found in `Products/CMFPlone/profiles/default/`. It is also possible to make changes through-the-web and then use the `portal_setup` tool to export a snapshot of those changes as an archive of XML files, which can be re-imported later.

When a base profile has been activated, we can install additional extension profiles on top of it. An extension profile is configured in the same way as a base profile and uses the same handlers, but it will normally only contain a subset of the settings which make up the site, either as overrides for those from the base profile, or as new entries. Whereas `portal_setup` will usually purge relevant settings before applying a base profile, extension profiles are applied on top of existing state. (Note that import steps may still overwrite values.)

 Extension profiles are useful for add-ons that need to be installable independently of the rest of the configuration of the site, as well as for site policies where the configuration will not deviate extensively from the base profile.

Both base and extension profiles are associated with profile metadata, stored in a `metadata.xml` file that provides a profile version and any profile dependencies. The version is usually a simple integer, starting from 1 (it is not related to the version of the distribution where the profile is found). After a package has been released and/or used in a production environment, the profile version should be incremented when the profile is updated. This enables support for profile upgrade steps, which we will cover in more detail in *Chapter 16, Zope on the Server*.

We will show how to create a new GenericSetup profile and set it up programmatically in the next chapter. For now, we will concentrate on how to take a snapshot of the current state of the site and manage profiles through the web. This can be useful for development, since the exported profiles can be adapted for use in an on-disk package. It can also help us roll back a site to a previous configuration, and inspect differences between a previous profile and the current state.

GenericSetup configuration is managed through the `portal_setup` tool, found in the ZMI at the root of a Plone site. On the **Profiles** tab, we see the active base profile:

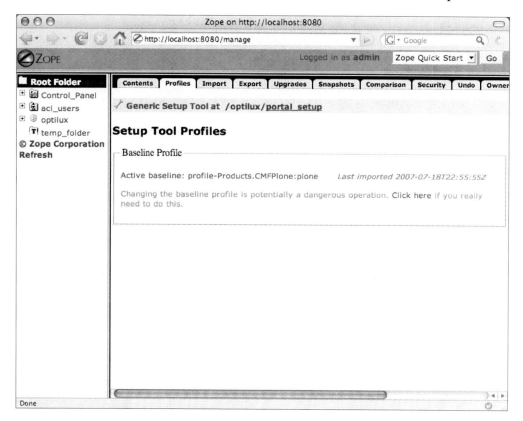

 As the text in the screenshot suggests, changing the base profile on a live site can lead to unexpected side effects unless the new base profile closely resembles the current base profile in structure.

The available import steps are listed under the **Import** tab. The default selection allows us to rerun the steps of the current base profile. We can instead select an appropriate extension profile or snapshot from the drop-down menu, and run some or all of its steps using the buttons at the bottom of the page.

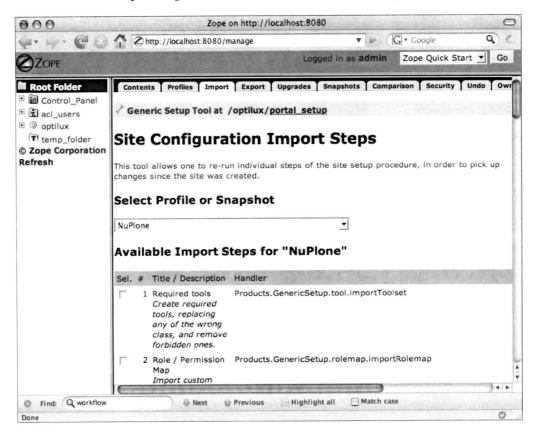

Note that when viewing the available import steps, there may be more handlers listed than the profile provides configuration for. (This is almost always the case for extension profiles.) Handlers with no corresponding import steps – that is, no corresponding XML files in the extension profile – will (usually) do nothing.

It can be useful to rerun individual steps after making changes to a profile during development. For example, say we have defined and imported a new workflow using an extension profile, as we will learn in *Chapter 6, Security and Workflow*. If we subsequently change the profile on disk, this will not be reflected in the site automatically. Rather than reimporting the entire profile and potentially resetting other configuration data, we can rerun the relevant workflow definition step in isolation. Lastly, import steps can be run from an uploaded .tar.gz archive. Such an archive can be created from the **Export** tab, where we can choose to export some or all of the currently available steps to the local machine.

It is also possible to create a snapshot of the site and store it in the ZODB (inside the portal_setup tool itself) rather than download it to the local machine. This is done from the **Snapshots** tab. Snapshots at different points in time can be compared using the **Comparison** tab. Here, we have taken a snapshot immediately before and after changing the site title:

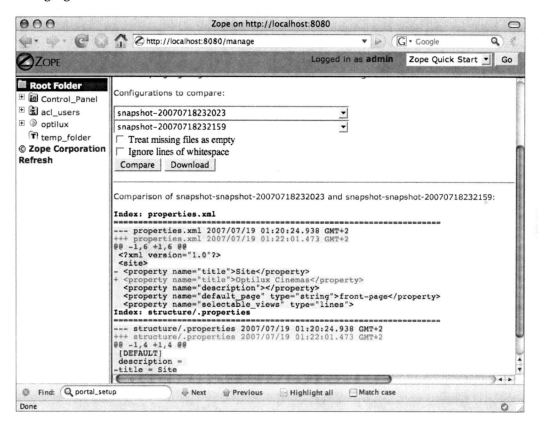

GenericSetup and Plone's Add-ons Control Panel

The user interface of the `portal_setup` tool can be a little cumbersome, especially for site administrators who do not understand the full depth of GenericSetup. `portal_quickinstaller`, the tool which powers Plone's **Add-ons** control panel, is GenericSetup-aware: if a package registers an extension profile, it will be available for an installation through the control panel. The tool also tracks the most common types of changes to the base configuration and is able to undo them upon uninstall.

In Plone 2, installation of third-party packages was achieved using an `Install.py` script. While this still works for legacy code, GenericSetup is easier to use and better supported. The main reason to use an `Install.py` script in Plone 3.0 was that GenericSetup at that time did not support automatically installing the package dependencies. As Plone 3.1, however, we have been able to use the `metadata.xml` file for this purpose, making `Install.py` scripts obsolete. We will see an example of package dependency installation in *Chapter 7, Using Add-ons*.

Acquisition and skin layers

Consider that Zope manages a hierarchy of objects, each of which has exactly one parent. In traditional object-oriented programming, a subclass can gain attributes and methods from its superclasses. Zope 2 acquisition wraps Python objects retrieved from the ZODB or being found during URL traversal in such a way that they can also 'acquire' attributes from their parents in the hierarchy.

URL traversal is the process Zope uses to resolve a URL requested by a web browser to a published object. It will be explained in more detail in *Chapter 9, Nine Core Concepts of Zope Programming*.

For example, some code may read:

```
context.getDefault()
```

In this statement, `context` may be the current content object, and `getDefault()` could be a method on this object, or its containing folder, or another folder higher up. `Closer` attributes always take precedence.

Other types of objects can also be acquired. For example, realize that each CMF tool is a persistent object in the root of the Plone site. Lazily written code sometimes looks like this:

```
return context.portal_membership.getAuthenticatedUser()
```

> The safer, more flexible version of this statement looks up the tool by
> name:
> ```
> from Products.CMFCore.utils import getToolByName
> mtool = getToolByName(context, 'portal_membership')
> return mtool.getAuthenticatedUser()
> ```

Here, we are acquiring the `portal_membership` tool from the `context` and calling
the `getAuthenticatedUser()` method on it. Again, `context` could be an object
anywhere in the Plone site. Acquisition also applies to templates. The following is
found at the top of most Plone page templates:

```
<html metal:use-macro="context/main_template/macros/main">
```

This means find the object `main_template`—be it an attribute on the context object,
an attribute on one of its parents, or a script or template or other object contained in
a parent folder and then get the `macros` dictionary (again, allowing for acquisition),
and from it the `main` key (ditto). Normally, of course, the first thing Zope finds in this
case will be Plone's main page template, which defines the overall layout of the site.

We also see acquisition take place during URL traversal. For example, the URL
`/Plone/front-page/document_view` will cause Zope to look for an attribute, object
or template called `document_view` relative to the front-page object. As it happens,
`document_view` is a page template, which is written in terms of an abstract `context`.
It is thus able to render a document-like object no matter where in the site it is.

In the early days of Zope 2 development, all objects, including page templates and
Python scripts used to implement logic, would be kept in the ZODB rather than
on the filesystem and edited through-the-web. Using acquisition, it is possible to
let specific templates and scripts in a subfolder take precedence over more general
ones higher up. Using more local objects to override general ones higher up in the
containment hierarchy is thus a way to customize an application.

Unfortunately, keeping application logic (scripts and templates) in the ZODB quickly
becomes a problem (recall Seaver's Law). CMF extends acquisition with a mechanism
known as **skin layers**, which lets us manage templates and scripts on the file system.

In the `portal_skins` tool in the ZMI, we can see a number of folders:

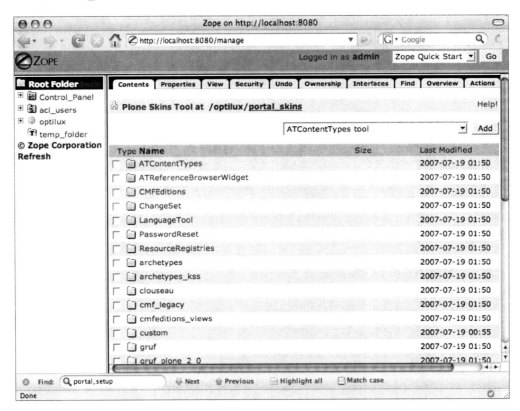

Save for the `custom` folder, which is managed in the ZODB, these are just views of directories on the filesystem, by convention found in a directory called `skins/` inside various packages.

On the **Properties** tab of `portal_skins`, we will see a list of skins (also called **themes**), of which one will be currently selected as the default (probably **Sunburst Theme** on a default Plone 4 installation).

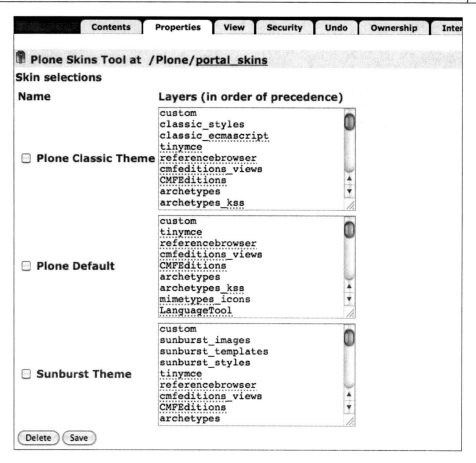

Each theme consists of an ordered list of **skin layers**, referring to the folders in the previous screenshot. Zope looks for an object to acquire 'up' the containment hierarchy, once it comes to the root of the Plone site, CMF will direct it 'down' the skin layers, in the order defined for the current skin. Similarly to location-based acquisition, items higher up in the skin layers (that is, those checked first) will take precedence. This means that a third party package can install a new skin layer near the top (conventionally, new skin layers are added just beneath custom) and override some of Plone's standard templates.

Furthermore, administrators can perform customizations through the web by placing items in the `custom` folder at the top of the layers. There is even a button to copy a script or template to the custom folder when we view an object inside one of the other skin layer folders in `portal_skins`. For serious development, however, through the web customization is not recommended, because it robs us of the ability to use source code management tools and has the same problems of deployment and repeatability as persistent settings. In the next chapter, we will see how a policy package can manage customizations more effectively.

Acquisition is very powerful (the same mechanism underpins Zope 2 security), but as you may have guessed, it can sometimes lead to unexpected results. Acquired objects, attributes, and templates essentially form one giant namespace. If an object `obj` has a method named `document_view()` it will be called when Zope traverses to `obj/document_view`. Of course, that may be what was intended (the method could for example explicitly call a different page template to deal with some special case), but it may not be. This also means Plone needs to reserve a number of content IDs to avoid strange errors caused by Zope not finding the right templates or tools.

Perhaps surprisingly, this is not as a big a problem in practice as it may seem. Most of the time, some testing and considerations of naming policy is all that is needed. However, as Plone grows, so does the strain of the single namespace. Luckily, the Zope Component Architecture, part of the Zope Toolkit, has a solution:

Overriding Component Architecture components

In the Zope Component Architecture, a **browser view** is a Python class and/or page template (depending on how it is configured) which acts as a page or form action. Unlike templates in skin layers, browser views are registered for a particular type of object, as described by a class or a Zope interface.

 An **interface** is a special Python object used to logically describe a component, such as a content object of a particular type. We will cover interfaces in full in *Chapter 9, Nine Core Concepts of Zope Programming*.

Views can also be distinguished from content objects and acquirable attributes explicitly. We will learn more about writing and configuring browser views in *Chapter 9, Nine Core Concepts of Zope Programming*, and *Chapter 11, Standalone Views and Forms*. But for now, consider the following registration in Zope's ZCML (Zope Configuration Markup Language) syntax:

```
<browser:page
    name="list-contents"
    for=".interfaces.IMyType"
    permission="zope2.View"
    class=".browser.listcontents.ListContentsView"
    template="browser/listcontents.pt"
    />
```

This statement, which could be found in a `configure.zcml` file in some package, configures a new browser view with the name `list-contents`, defined by a particular template and a class to house the view logic related to that template. It is protected by a standard View permission (`zope2.View`), and only available when its context provides the fictitious `IMyType` interface.

This view could be invoked with a URL like `/Plone/some-content/@@list-contents`. The `@@` part disambiguates it as a view. It is optional, but attributes and objects in folders will take precedence if there is a name conflict and the `@@` is omitted. If the `some-content` object did not declare support for the `IMyType` interface, `@@list-contents` would simply not be available and would result in a `NotFound` exception, with a *404 (HTTP Not Found)* error being shown to the user.

View registrations can be overridden for "more specific" interfaces. For example, say `some-context` above was of class `MyType`, which implemented the interface `IMyType` (the one the view is registered for). Let us say we had an object `other-context`, of type `MyOtherType` which was a subclass of `MyType` and happened to also provide an interface `IMyOtherType`. The `@@list-contents` view would be available on `other-context`, because of its superclass, but we could provide a more specific version just for objects providing `IMyOtherType` like so:

```
<browser:page
    name="list-contents"
    for=".interfaces.IMyOtherType"
    permission="zope2.View"
    class=".browser.listcontents.ListOtherContentsView"
    template="browser/listothercontents.pt"
    />
```

This allows specialization by object type, but it is also possible to specialize views by the request type (layer). Most of the time, of course, we use HTTP requests, but we can apply a **marker interface** to the request in various ways to create a more specific type of request:

- By associating an interface with a particular CMF theme, as selected in the `portal_skins` tool

- By installing an extension profile that registers a new browser layer using the `browserlayer.xml` GenericSetup syntax

- By using the `alsoProvides()` API in custom Python code

Once we have enabled our 'more specific' request type, we can use the `layer` attribute of the `<browser:page />` directive to register an alternative view that is used when the given request type is in effect:

```
<browser:page
    name="list-contents"
    for=".interfaces.IMyType"
    layer=".interfaces.IMyLayer"
    permission="zope2.View"
    class=".browser.listcontents.ListContentsView"
    template="browser/listcontents.pt"
    />
```

This approach of letting a more specific registration override another, more generic one as described by the interfaces provided by an object which permeates the Zope Component Architecture. As it happens, views are simply a special case of **adapters**, which are used to encapsulate particular aspects of an object's associated logic (in this case, the display logic). Very specific aspects of an application's behavior can thus be customized and general aspects can be reused with appropriate component registrations.

All of this will become clearer in *Chapter 9, Nine Core Concepts of Zope Programming* where we cover the syntax of views, adapters, and other components. For now, you should appreciate that the Zope Component Architecture's concept of customization by interface is an evolution of Zope 2's concept of customization by location and CMF's concept of customization by skin layer.

Customization best practices

We will see many examples throughout this book of customizations and extensions to Plone's out-of-the-box behavior, which will demonstrate sound working principles and practical patterns. There are a few general concepts that are worth understanding, though.

Using source control

In the previous chapter, we learned how to set up a development sandbox containing all the dependencies of our project. Development sandboxes are best treated as dispensable. Buildout makes it easy to re-create sandboxes, enabling us to start again if things go awry.

It is important to be able to revert to earlier versions of our code base, for example if we discover that we made a mistake at some point, perhaps weeks ago. Any serious project should use a source code management system, and all developers should learn how to use such systems effectively.

The most popular source control system among Plone developers is Subversion (`http://subversion.tigris.org`), because it is used by Plone itself, and works on all modern platforms. This fits the 'local sandbox' mode of development, because Subversion, like its predecessor CVS, assumes a distributed network of developers. Each developer checks out a local copy of the code to work on, and commits changes back regularly. If a file has been modified both locally and in the repository, Subversion will attempt to merge changes. If this fails, it will require the developer to resolve conflicts manually before being allowed to commit.

This works well, even for a large project like Plone. However, it requires some discipline, which is good practice even in small or one-person projects:

- Always update your local sandbox before you begin work. This ensures that you have the latest changes and are less likely to be subject to conflicts later.

- Commit one change at a time. Do not check in code only once a day (or week!). This makes it easier to 'undo' (revert) specific changes without affecting other ones.

- Write sensible commit log messages. If you need to find a particular revision again later, you will regret having committed it with a message saying only 'Committed latest changes'.

- If applicable, reference specific bug or issue numbers or items in the specification when writing commit log messages. This makes requirements and defects traceable.

- Run all the tests for a component (or better yet, the entire project) before checking in any changes. Otherwise, you may have broken something and not realized it. Leaving tests in a broken state for other developers to untangle is an unforgivable sin in large projects like Plone, and should be in your own work as well.

Writing tests

If source code management tools let us recover from our mistakes; then automated unit and integration tests help us make fewer mistakes in the first place. Test-driven development is hugely important, and is a habit that should be second nature to every developer. We will write tests for everything we do in this book, demonstrating several testing techniques.

The basic premise of unit testing is that after writing an interface or stub method for a particular piece of code, we write a test for it, ideally before we write the functionality itself. The test should assert the state of the application after the code under test has been called, to prove that the code works as expected.

 There are different opinions about the efficacy and practicality of the 'test-first' approach. What nobody disputes, however, is that it is vital to have good automated test coverage, whether the tests came first, last, or in tandem with the code. The author prefers a combination of writing tests before and during the development of a particular piece of functionality.

A unit test should be as small as possible, and test the most common cases and edge cases. Tests are run in isolation, and should not depend on one another in any way. The testing framework takes care of resetting the test fixture for each test. Tests are combined into a test suite and run automatically when the test suite is invoked. The test runner reports on which tests fail, and why.

Obviously, if a test is written before the code it tests, it should fail—if it does not, then either the test is invalid, or the code is not actually needed. The challenge is then to write code that makes the test pass, and ensure that it keeps on passing. Thus, if test coverage is good, developers can be more confident that they do not accidentally break code they thought was working. Automated testing is no substitute for testing by real users (often referred to as 'through-the-web testing' in the context of Plone), but neither is user testing a substitute for having decent automated test coverage.

 Code not covered by tests is by definition incomplete and almost certainly bad for your project.

When writing customizations, it is important to have tests that prove installation and setup code is working. As our local sandbox becomes more sophisticated, we may add something to the setup code to replicate a particular setting initially made manually through-the-web while exploring different approaches to solve a particular problem. Tests are the best way to know whether this would work on a new site, such as when the production environment is being set up.

There will be lots of examples of full tests in this book, but here is a short example of what a test may look like. In this case, we are checking that the `setTitle()` method of a standard Document (Page) works as expected:

```
import unittest2 as unittest
from plone.app.testing import PLONE_INTEGRATION_TESTING
from plone.app.testing import TEST_USER_NAME
from plone.app.testing import setRoles

class TestDocuments(unittest.TestCase):

    layer = PLONE_INTEGRATION_TESTING

    def testSetTitle(self):
        portal = self.layer['portal']
        setRoles(portal, TEST_USER_NAME, ('Manager',))

        portal.invokeFactory('Document', 'd1')
        portal['d1'].setTitle(u"New title")
        self.assertEqual(portal['d1'].Title(), "New title")
```

> For more information, the `plone.testing` and `plone.app.testing` documentation at `http://pypi.python.org/pypi/plone.testing` and `http://pypi.python.org/pypi/plone.app.testing` are essential reading, and will teach you a lot more about how to write tests in different styles and how to run them.

Considering migration requirements

Recall that the ZODB manages Python pickles—serializations of objects that can be stored on disk and resurrected. Pickles may reference specific classes and attributes. This is convenient because it absolves the developer from worrying about how persistent objects are managed.

> The only requirement is that the persistent class inherits from `persistent.Persistent`, either directly or indirectly.

However, if we change the code that was the original basis for the pickle, Zope may fail to read back the value that was stored. If a class was moved or removed, Zope may not be able to read the object at all. In this case, the ZMI may list a `BrokenObject`, a special kind of wrapper for broken pickles, instead of the object we were expecting.

A common solution to this problem is to create compatibility aliases to old code and emit deprecation warnings. This means that other code (including the ZODB) that tries to import the old object will still find it. The `zope.deferredimport` module can be used to write "lazy" imports that emit deprecation warnings. Search the Plone source code for calls to its `deprecated()` method to see some examples.

Where the persistent parts of classes have changed, we may need to perform ZODB migration. Migration code typically searches for objects that may be in the 'old' state and modifies them. This can sometimes be tricky, and requires careful testing.

If you have this need, a library called `Products.contentmigration`, which is used by Plone 4's new `plone.app.blob` package may be of help. See `http://pypi.python.org/pypi/Products.contentmigration`.

Plone itself uses GenericSetup upgrade steps to do its work. We can write our own upgrade steps for our own profiles, as we will demonstrate in *Chapter 16, Zope on the Server*.

Instead of writing one-off migrations, we may be able to write code that degrades gracefully, for example by checking for state that would have been produced by the 'old' code. Here is a reasonably common pattern to avoid the need for explicit migration:

```
def getValue(self):
    # We used to store the value in a variable called '_val'.
    # Now we store it as 'value', and we store the value as a number,
    # not a string

    value = getattr(self, 'value', None)
    if value is None:
        value = getattr(self, '_val', None)
        try:
            value = int(old_val)
        except ValueError:
            pass
    return value
```

As a rule of thumb, if users of your code would need a completely fresh site to ensure it is in a proper state after you made some change to the source code, you probably need migration when making new releases. Such persistence can feel a lot like saying sorry indeed.

Summary

In this chapter, we have covered:

- How persistent settings in the ZODB may need to be scripted or described using GenericSetup to make it possible to repeat a configuration across multiple environments
- The way in which Zope Acquisition and CMF skin layers are used to customize templates and scripts by context and arbitrary priority
- Briefly, the approach to customization exposed by the Zope Component Architecture. This will be covered in more detail as we introduce these concepts more fully in *Chapter 9, Nine Core Concepts of Zope Programming*
- A few things to remember when writing customizations, including the importance of using source control, writing unit and integration tests and managing migrations

Next, we will demonstrate how the configuration of our example application is encapsulated in its policy package, making use of these techniques.

Developing a Site Strategy

In the previous chapter, we learned about ways in which a developer can customize Plone changing the source code of Plone itself. We will now employ some of these techniques as we begin the process of turning an out of the box Plone installation into the site that will become the Optilux Cinemas website.

In this chapter, we will:

- Create the initial version of a policy package that will help us customize Plone to meet the requirements from *Chapter 2, Introduction to the Case Study*
- Add a GenericSetup extension profile to this package
- Write our first tests to prove that our customizations are working as expected

Creating a policy package

Our policy package is just a package that can be installed as a Plone add-on. We will use a GenericSetup **extension profile** in this package to turn a standard Plone installation into one that is configured to our client's needs.

 We could have used a full-site GenericSetup base profile instead, but by using a GenericSetup extension profile we can avoid replicating the majority of the configuration that is done by Plone.

We will use ZopeSkel, which we installed in *Chapter 3, The Development Environment*, to create an initial skeleton for the package, which we will call optilux.policy, adopting the optilux.* namespace for all Optilux-specific packages.

In your own code, you should of course use a different namespace. It is usually a good idea to base this on the owning organization's name, as we have done here. Note that package names should be all lowercase, without spaces, underscores, or other special characters. If you intend to release your code into the Plone Collective, you can use the collective.* namespace, although other namespaces are allowed too. The plone.* namespace is reserved for packages in the core Plone repository, where the copyright has been transferred to the Plone Foundation. You should normally not use this without first coordinating with the Plone Framework Team.

We go into the src/ directory of the buildout we created in *Chapter 3, The Development Environment*, and run the following command:

```
$ ../bin/zopeskel plone optilux.policy
```

This uses the *plone* ZopeSkel template to create a new package called optilux.policy. This will ask us a few questions.

We will stick with "easy" mode for now, and answer True when asked whether to register a GenericSetup profile.

Note that ZopeSkel will download some packages used by its local command support. This may mean the initial bin/zopeskel command takes a little while to complete, and assumes that we are currently connected to the internet.

A **local command** is a feature of PasteScript, upon which ZopeSkel is built. ZopeSkel registers an addcontent command, which can be used to insert additional snippets of code, such as view registrations or new content types, into the initial skeleton generated by ZopeSkel. We will not use this feature in this book, preferring instead to retain full control over the code we write and avoid the potential pitfalls of code generation. If you wish to use this feature, you will either need to install ZopeSkel and PasteScript into the global Python environment, or add PasteScript to the ${zopeskel:eggs} option in buildout.cfg, so that you get access to the bin/paster command.

Run bin/zopeskel --help from the buildout root directory for more information about ZopeSkel and its options.

Distribution details

Let us now take a closer look at what ZopeSkel has generated for us. We will also consider which files should be added to version control, and which files should be ignored.

Item	Version control	Purpose
`setup.py`	Yes	Contains instructions for how `Setuptools/Distribute` (and thus Buildout) should manage the package's distribution. We will make a few modifications to this file later.
`setup.cfg`	Yes	Contains additional distribution configuration. In this case, ZopeSkel keeps track of which template was used to generate the initial skeleton using this file.
`*.egg`	No	ZopeSkel downloads a few eggs that are used for its local command support (`Paste`, `PasteScript`, and `PasteDeploy`) into the distribution directory root. If you do not intend to use the local command support, you can delete these. You should not add these to version control.
`README.txt`	Yes	If you intend to release your package to the public, you should document it here. PyPI requires that this file be present in the root of a distribution. It is also read into the `long_description` variable in `setup.py`. PyPI will attempt to render this as `reStructuredText` markup (see `http://docutils.sourceforge.net/rst.html`).
`docs/`	Yes	Contains additional documentation, including the software license (which should be the GNU General Public License, version 2, for any packages that import directly from any of Plone's GPL-licensed packages) and a change log.

Item	Version control	Purpose
docs/HISTORY.txt	Yes	Used to manage the change log for any package releases, such as, README.txt, this is read into the long_description in setup.py. Again, if you delete this file, you must modify setup.py to not use it.
optilux.policy.egg-info/	No	Contains Setuptools/Distribute runtime information generated from setup.py and setup.cfg. This should not be under version control.
optilux/	Yes	The namespace package. Contains an __init__.py file with some Setuptools/Distribute boilerplate necessary for namespace packages to work.
optilux/policy	Yes	The root of the package itself. All our Python, ZCML, GenericSetup, and other files will end up in this directory and its subdirectories. If you installed an "omelette" (see *Chapter 3, The Development Environment*), this directory can also be found under parts/omelette/ optilux/policy.
optilux/policy/__init__.py	Yes	A usually empty file used to make this directory a package may also contain a Zope 2 product initialize() function. This is mainly needed for packages that install Archetypes content types, as we will see in *Chapter 10, Custom Content types*.
optilux/policy/configure.zcml	Yes	The main Zope configuration file for this package. This is automatically loaded by Plone at startup via an entry point in setup.py — see below.
optilux/policy/tests.py	Yes	Contains skeleton integration tests. We will replace these with our own tests later in this chapter.

Changes to setup.py

Before we can progress, we will make a few modifications to setup.py. Our revised file looks similar to the following code, with changes highlighted:

```python
from setuptools import setup, find_packages
import os

version = '2.0'

setup(name='optilux.policy',
      version=version,
      description="Policy package for the Optilux Cinemas project",
      long_description=open("README.txt").read() + "\n" +
          open(os.path.join("docs", "HISTORY.txt")).read(),
      # Get more strings from
      # http://pypi.python.org/pypi?%3Aaction=list_classifiers
      classifiers=[
        "Framework :: Plone",
        "Programming Language :: Python",
        ],
      keywords='',
      author='Martin Aspeli',
      author_email='optilude@gmail.com',
      url='http://optilux-cinemas.com',
      license='GPL',
      packages=find_packages(exclude=['ez_setup']),
      namespace_packages=['optilux'],
      include_package_data=True,
      zip_safe=False,
      install_requires=[
          'setuptools',
          'Plone',
      ],
      extras_require={
          'test': ['plone.app.testing',]
      },
      entry_points="""
      # -*- Entry points: -*-

      [z3c.autoinclude.plugin]
      target = plone
      """,
#     setup_requires=["PasteScript"],
#     paster_plugins=["ZopeSkel"],
      )
```

The changes are as follows:

1. We have added an author name, e-mail address, and updated project URL. These are used as metadata if the distribution is ever uploaded to PyPI. For internal projects, they are less important.

2. We have declared an explicit dependency on the `Plone` distribution, that is, on Plone itself. This ensures that when our package is installed, so is Plone. We will shortly update our `main` working set to contain only the `optilux.policy` distribution. This dependency ensures that Plone is installed as part of our application policy.

3. We have then added a `[tests]` extra, which adds a dependency on `plone.app.testing`. We will install this extra as part of the following `test` working set, making `plone.app.testing` available in the test runner (but not in the Zope runtime).

4. Finally, we have commented out the `setup_requires` and `paster_plugins` options. These are used to support ZopeSkel local commands, which we have decided not to use. The main reason to comment them out is to avoid having Buildout download these additional dependencies into the distribution root directory, saving time, and reducing the number of files in the build. Also note that, unlike distributions downloaded by Buildout in general, there is no "offline" support for these options.

Changes to configure.zcml

We will also make a minor change to the generated `configure.zcml` file, removing the line:

```
<five:registerPackage package="." initialize=".initialize" />
```

This directive is used to register the package as an old-style Zope 2 product. The main reason to do this is to ensure that the `initialize()` function is called on Zope startup. This may be a useful hook, but most of the time it is superfluous, and requires additional test setup that can make tests more brittle. See *Chapter 7, Using Add-ons*, for an example of tests that use the `installProduct()` function to deal with old-style Zope 2 products in test setup.

We can also remove the (empty) `initialize()` function itself from the `optilux/policy/__init__.py` file, effectively leaving the file blank. Do not delete `__init__.py`, however, as it is needed to make this directory into a Python package.

Updating the buildout

Before we can use our new distribution, we need to add it to our development buildout. We will consider two scenarios:

1. The distribution is under version control in a repository module separate to the development buildout itself. This is the recommended approach, as outlined in *Chapter 3, The Development Environment*.

2. The distribution is not under version control, or is kept inside the version control module of the buildout itself. The example source code that comes with this book is distributed as a simple archive, so it uses this approach.

Given the approach we have taken to separating out our buildout configuration into multiple files, we must first update `packages.cfg` to add the new package. Under the [sources] section, we could add:

```
[sources]
optilux.policy = svn https://some-svn-server/optilux.policy/trunk
```

Or, for distributions without a separate version control URL:

```
[sources]
optilux.policy = fs optilux.policy
```

We must also update the `main` and `test` working sets in the same file:

```
[eggs]
main =
    optilux.policy
test =
    optilux.policy [test]
```

Finally, we must tell Buildout to automatically add this distribution as a develop egg when running the development buildout. This is done near the top of `buildout.cfg`:

```
auto-checkout =
    optilux.policy
```

We must rerun buildout to let the changes take effect:

```
$ bin/buildout
```

We can test that the package is now available for import using the `zopepy` interpreter:

```
$ bin/zopepy
>>> from optilux import policy
>>>
```

The absence of an `ImportError` tells us that this package will now be known to the Zope instance in the buildout.

 To be absolutely sure, you can also open the `bin/instance` script in a text editor (`bin/instance-script.py` on Windows) and look for a line in the `sys.path` mangling referencing the package.

Working sets and component configuration

It is worth deliberating a little more on how Plone and our new policy package are loaded and configured.

At build time:

1. Buildout installs the `[instance]` part, which will generate the `bin/instance` script.
2. The `plone.recipe.zope2instance` recipe calculates a working set from its `eggs` option, which in our buildout references `${eggs:main}`.
3. This contains exactly one distribution: `optilux.policy`.
4. This in turn depends on the `Plone` distribution (we will add additional dependencies later in the book), which in turn causes Buildout to install all of Plone.

Here, we have made a policy decision to depend on a "big" Plone distribution that includes some optional add-ons. We could also have depended on the smaller `Products.CMFPlone` distribution (which works for Plone 4.0.2 onwards), which includes only the core of Plone, perhaps adding specific dependencies for add-ons we are interested in.

 When declaring actual dependencies used by distributions that contain reusable code instead of just policy, you should always depend on the packages you import from or otherwise depend on, and no more. That is, if you import from `Products.CMFPlone`, you should depend on this, and not on the `Plone` meta-egg (which itself contains no code, but only declares dependencies on other distributions, including `Products.CMFPlone`). To learn more about the rationale behind the `Products.CMFPlone` distribution, see `http://dev.plone.org/plone/ticket/10877`.

At runtime:

1. The `bin/instance` script starts Zope.

2. Zope loads the `site.zcml` file (`parts/instance/etc/site.zcml`) as part of its startup process.

3. This automatically includes the ZCML configuration for packages in the `Products.*` namespace, including `Products.CMFPlone`, Plone's main package.

4. Plone uses `z3c.autoinclude` to automatically load the ZCML configuration of packages that opt into this using the `z3c.autoinclude.plugin` entry point `target = plone`.

5. The `optilux.policy` distribution contains such an entry point, so it will be configured, along with any packages or files it explicitly includes from its own `configure.zcml` file. (We will see an example of the including additional dependencies in *Chapter 7, Using Add-ons*.)

Creating an extension profile

Let us now register an extension profile for the policy package. ZopeSkel has already done some of the work for us. In `configure.zcml`, we have:

```
<configure
    xmlns="http://namespaces.zope.org/zope"
    xmlns:five="http://namespaces.zope.org/five"
    xmlns:i18n="http://namespaces.zope.org/i18n"
    xmlns:genericsetup="http://namespaces.zope.org/genericsetup"
    i18n_domain="optilux.policy">

  <genericsetup:registerProfile
      name="default"
      title="Optilux Site Policy"
      directory="profiles/default"
      description="Turn a Plone site into the Optilux site."
      provides="Products.GenericSetup.interfaces.EXTENSION"
      />
  <!-- -*- extra stuff goes here -*- -->

</configure>
```

The XML standard requires that all namespaces be declared using the
`xmlns:` syntax seen on the first few lines of this file. A common mistake
is to use a directive such as `<genericsetup:registerProfile />`,
but forget to declare the `genericsetup` namespace. This will result in an
"unknown directive" error.

The `<genericsetup:registerProfile />` stanza registers a new profile. The title
and description (which we have edited from their generated defaults) will be shown
to the user when activating the policy package. The `name` is almost always `default`,
unless the package contains multiple profiles. The full profile name as known
to GenericSetup includes the package name, so in this case, it will be `profile-
optilux.policy:default`.

The `profile-` prefix indicates that this is an (extension) profile.
GenericSetup snapshots have names starting with `snapshot-`.

The `directory` argument tells GenericSetup where to look for the XML files which
the various import handles will read, relative to the package. By convention, this is
`profiles/default` for the primary profile.

We then create the profile directory (`src/optilux.policy/optilux/policy/
profiles/default`), and add a `metadata.xml` file inside it:

```
<metadata>
    <version>1</version>
    <dependencies>
    </dependencies>
</metadata>
```

This defines the profile version, which should always start at `1`. It will stay that
way until we need to worry about upgrades (see *Chapter 16, Zope on the Server*).
We have also added an empty dependencies list, as our package currently has no
dependencies. We will see how to install dependencies in *Chapter 7, Using Add-ons*.

Writing tests for customizations

We will begin by making a simple change: setting the browser window page title
and site description. These values are managed as properties called `title` and
`description` on the Plone site root. We can view these in the **Site** control panel
under **Site Setup** in Plone.

As good software developers, we will write automated tests before implementing the functionality. In this case, we will write integration tests that inspect the state of the Plone site after our package has been configured and activated.

By convention, tests go into a module or subpackage called `tests`. We already have such a module (`tests.py`) containing some example code, which we will replace with our own test code. Test fixture setup code conventionally lives in a module called `testing` (`testing.py`), which may be imported by other code that wishes to reuse a package's test setup.

> The boilerplate in the `tests.py` as generated by ZopeSkel at the time of writing uses the `Products.PloneTestCase` testing framework. Our code will use the newer `plone.app.testing` framework, which aims to replace `Products.PloneTestCase`. See the `plone.app.testing` documentation (`http://pypi.python.org/pypi/plone.app.testing`) for more details, including a comparison between the two.

Before we write the tests themselves, we will add a test layer that configures a shared test fixture for our integration tests.

> A **test layer** allows multiple tests to share the same fixture, alleviating the need for each test to set up and tear down a complex fixture. Test layers can also control the lifecycle of individual tests, for example to isolate each test in its own transaction.

In `testing.py`, we have:

```
from plone.app.testing import PloneSandboxLayer
from plone.app.testing import applyProfile
from plone.app.testing import PLONE_FIXTURE
from plone.app.testing import IntegrationTesting

from zope.configuration import xmlconfig

class OptiluxPolicy(PloneSandboxLayer):

    defaultBases = (PLONE_FIXTURE,)

    def setUpZope(self, app, configurationContext):
        # Load ZCML
        import optilux.policy
        xmlconfig.file('configure.zcml',
                optilux.policy,
                context=configurationContext
            )

    def setUpPloneSite(self, portal):
```

```
            applyProfile(portal, 'optilux.policy:default')
OPTILUX_POLICY_FIXTURE = OptiluxPolicy()
OPTILUX_POLICY_INTEGRATION_TESTING = IntegrationTesting(
        bases=(OPTILUX_POLICY_FIXTURE,),
        name="Optilux:Integration"
    )
```

This layer uses the `PloneSandboxLayer` helper from `plone.app.testing`. It first loads the package's configuration, and then installs its GenericSetup profile. All tests that use the `OPTILUX_POLICY_INTEGRATION_TESTING` layer will thus be able to assume the package has been configured and its profile applies to the Plone site that is set up by the `PLONE_FIXTURE` base layer.

The tests, in `tests.py`, look like this:

```
import unittest2 as unittest
from optilux.policy.testing import OPTILUX_POLICY_INTEGRATION_TESTING

class TestSetup(unittest.TestCase):

    layer = OPTILUX_POLICY_INTEGRATION_TESTING

    def test_portal_title(self):
        portal = self.layer['portal']
        self.assertEqual(
                "Optilux Cinemas",
                 portal.getProperty('title')
            )

    def test_portal_description(self):
        portal = self.layer['portal']
        self.assertEqual(
                "Welcome to Optilux Cinemas",
                 portal.getProperty('description')
            )
```

 If you have not done so already, you should read the documentation at `http://pypi.python.org/pypi/plone.testing` and `http://pypi.python.org/pypi/plone.app.testing` to familiarize yourself with testing concepts and APIs.

We should now be able to run the tests. Both of the preceding tests should fail, since we have not yet written the functionality to make them pass.

$ bin/test -s optilux.policy

Running optilux.policy.testing.Optilux:Integration tests:

```
...
Failure in test test_portal_description (optilux.policy.tests.TestSetup)
...
AssertionError: 'Welcome to Optilux Cinemas' != ''
...
Failure in test test_portal_title (optilux.policy.tests.TestSetup)
...
AssertionError: 'Optilux Cinemas' != u'Plone site'


  Ran 2 tests with 2 failures and 0 errors in 0.010 seconds.
```

The actual output is a little more verbose, but these lines tell us that both our tests failed, as expected.

Making a change with the extension profile

To implement the desired functionality, we create a file inside `profiles/default` called `properties.xml`, containing the following code:

```xml
<?xml version="1.0"?>
<site>
 <property name="title">Optilux Cinemas</property>
 <property name="description">Welcome to Optilux Cinemas</property>
</site>
```

> This was taken from the corresponding file in `Products/CMFPlone/profiles/default`, reduced to only the properties that we wanted to change. Plone's base profile is a good place to look for examples of GenericSetup syntax. See also `http://plone.org/documentation/manual/developer-manual/generic-setup`.

One of the import steps installed with Plone, *Site Properties*, knows how to read this file and set properties on the site root accordingly.

Our tests should now pass:

```
$ bin/test -s optilux.policy
Running optilux.policy.testing.Optilux:Integration tests:
...

  Ran 2 tests with 0 failures and 0 errors in 0.008 seconds.
```

Activating the package

Finally, we should verify that we can activate the package through the Plone interface. After starting Zope, we can go to our existing Plone site, log in as a user with Manager rights. Under **Site Setup**, in the **Add-ons** control panel, the new package should show up as shown in the following screenshot:

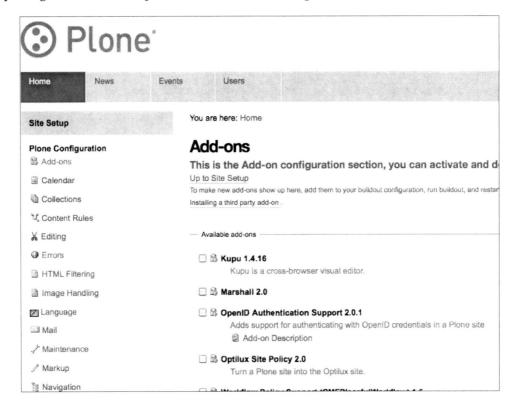

We can now activate it, and verify that this causes the title in the browser to change.

 If we are setting up a new site, we can activate the profile by selecting **Optilux Site Policy** on the **Create a Plone Site** screen.

Rebuildout, restart, reapply?

New Plone developers are often confused about when to rerun buildout, restart Zope, or reapply a profile in Plone. In this chapter, we have made three types of changes that required different types of reinitialization:

- Changes to the buildout configuration and distribution metadata (in `setup.py`). These types of changes only take effect once we rerun buildout.

- Changes to Python and ZCML code. These generally require a Zope restart, although we can often bypass this using `plone.reload`, as described in *Chapter 3, The Development Environment*.

- Changes to a GenericSetup extension profile. These require that the profile be reapplied through the `portal_setup` tool (or deactivated and re-activated through the **Add-ons** control panel). They do not require a Zope restart or reload. The exception is the `metadata.xml` file, which is read at Zope startup only.

Summary

In this chapter, we have seen:

- How to create a "policy package" to encapsulate a specific policy for a site

- How to use a GenericSetup extension profile to customize various aspects of Plone

- When to rerun buildout, restart Zope, and reinstall a package in Plone

As we build new functionality throughout the book, we will continue to add to the policy package. In the next chapter, we will extend it with custom workflow and security settings.

6
Security and Workflow

Security should never be an afterthought when building web applications. Zope and Plone provide a robust and flexible security model that lets us worry about our application logic instead of thinking too much about how to lock it down, so long as we understand a few basics.

In this chapter, we will:

- Explain the building blocks of Zope security: users, roles, and permissions
- Demonstrate the use of workflow, the primary mechanism for managing permissions in Plone
- Build a custom workflow for the Optilux website and add it to the policy package we created in the previous chapter.
- Discuss the differences between protected and trusted Python code in Zope

Security primitives

Zope's security is declarative: views, actions, and attributes on content objects are declared to be protected by permissions. Zope takes care of verifying that the current user has the appropriate access rights for a resource. If not, an `AccessControl. Unauthorized` exception will be raised. This is caught by an error handler which will either redirect the user to a login screen or show an **access denied** error page.

Permissions are not granted to users directly. Instead, they are assigned to roles. Users can be given any number of roles, either site-wide, or in the context of a particular folder, in which case they are referred to as **local roles**. Global and local roles can also be assigned to groups, in which case all users in that group will have the particular role. (In fact, Zope considers users and groups largely interchangeable, and refers to them more generally as **principals**.) This makes security settings much more flexible than if they were assigned to individual users.

Users and groups

Users and groups are kept in user folders, which are found in the ZMI with the name `acl_users`. There is one user folder at the root of the Zope instance, typically containing only the default Zope-wide administrator that is created by our development buildout the first time it is run. There is also an `acl_users` folder inside Plone, which manages Plone's users and groups.

Plone employs the **Pluggable Authentication Service (PAS)**, a particularly flexible kind of user folder. In PAS, users, groups, their roles, their properties, and other security-related policy are constructed using various interchangeable plugins. For example, an LDAP plugin could allow users to authenticate against an LDAP repository. We will revisit PAS in *Chapter 13, Users and their Permissions*, when we look at more advanced user management, and again in *Chapter 19, Looking to the Future*, when we configure LDAP authentication.

In day-to-day administration, users and groups are normally managed from Plone's **Users and Groups** control panel.

Permissions

Plone relies on a large number of permissions to control various aspects of its functionality. Permissions can be viewed from the **Security** tab in the ZMI, which lets us assign permissions to roles at a particular object. Note that most permissions are set to **Acquire**—the default—meaning that they cascade down from the parent folder. Role assignments are additive when permissions are set to acquire.

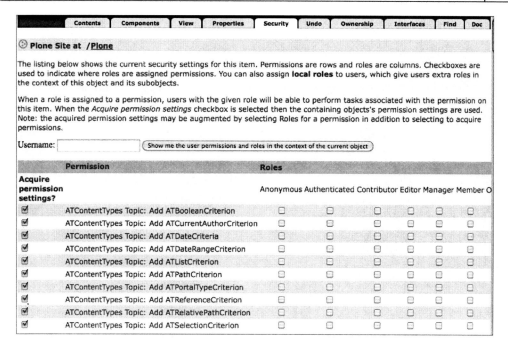

| Contents | Components | View | Properties | Security | Undo | Ownership | Interfaces | Find | Doc |

⊙ **Plone Site at /Plone**

The listing below shows the current security settings for this item. Permissions are rows and roles are columns. Checkboxes are used to indicate where roles are assigned permissions. You can also assign **local roles** to users, which give users extra roles in the context of this object and its subobjects.

When a role is assigned to a permission, users with the given role will be able to perform tasks associated with the permission on this item. When the *Acquire permission settings* checkbox is selected then the containing objects's permission settings are used. Note: the acquired permission settings may be augmented by selecting Roles for a permission in addition to selecting to acquire permissions.

Username: [   ] (Show me the user permissions and roles in the context of the current object)

Permission	Roles					
Acquire permission settings?	Anonymous	Authenticated	Contributor	Editor	Manager	Member
☑ ATContentTypes Topic: Add ATBooleanCriterion	☐	☐	☐	☐	☐	☐
☑ ATContentTypes Topic: Add ATCurrentAuthorCriterion	☐	☐	☐	☐	☐	☐
☑ ATContentTypes Topic: Add ATDateCriteria	☐	☐	☐	☐	☐	☐
☑ ATContentTypes Topic: Add ATDateRangeCriterion	☐	☐	☐	☐	☐	☐
☑ ATContentTypes Topic: Add ATListCriterion	☐	☐	☐	☐	☐	☐
☑ ATContentTypes Topic: Add ATPathCriterion	☐	☐	☐	☐	☐	☐
☑ ATContentTypes Topic: Add ATPortalTypeCriterion	☐	☐	☐	☐	☐	☐
☑ ATContentTypes Topic: Add ATReferenceCriterion	☐	☐	☐	☐	☐	☐
☑ ATContentTypes Topic: Add ATRelativePathCriterion	☐	☐	☐	☐	☐	☐
☑ ATContentTypes Topic: Add ATSelectionCriterion	☐	☐	☐	☐	☐	☐

> Sometimes, it is appropriate to change permission settings at the root of the Plone site (which can be done using the `rolemap.xml` GenericSetup import step — more on that follows), but managing permissions from the **Security** tab anywhere else is almost never a good idea. Keeping track of which security settings are made where in a complex site can be a nightmare.

Permissions are the most granular piece of the security puzzle, and can be seen as a consequence of a user's roles in a particular context. Security-aware code should almost always check permissions, rather than roles, because roles can change depending on the current folder and security policy of the site, or even based on an external source such as an LDAP or Active Directory repository.

Permissions can be logically divided into three main categories:

- Those that relate to basic content operations, such as **View** and **Modify portal content**. These are used by almost all content types, and defined as constants in the module `Products.CMFCore.permissions`. Core permissions are normally managed by workflow.

- Those that control the creation of particular types of content, such as **ATContentTypes: Add Image**. These are usually set at the Plone site root to apply to the whole site, but they may be managed by workflow on folders.

- Those that control site-wide policy. For example, the **Portlets: Manage portlets** permission is usually given to the *Manager* and *Site Administrator* roles, because this is typically an operation that only the site's administrator will need to perform. These permissions are usually set at the site root and acquired everywhere else. Occasionally, it may be appropriate to change them here. For example, the **Add portal member** permission controls whether anonymous users can add themselves (that is, "join" the site) or not. Note that there is a control panel setting for this, under **Security** in **Site Setup**.

Developers can create new permissions when necessary, although they are encouraged to reuse the ones in `Products.CMFCore.permissions` if possible. We will see examples of declaring new permissions (controlling the ability to add content of various types) when we create custom content types in *Chapter 10, Custom Content Types* and again in *Chapter 12, Relational Databases*.

The most commonly used permissions are:

Permission	Constant	Zope Toolkit name	Controls
Access contents information	`AccessContents Information`	`zope2.AccessContents Information`	Low-level Zope permission controlling access to objects
View	`View`	`zope2.View`	Access to the main view of a content object
List folder contents	`ListFolderContents`	`cmf.ListFolderContents`	Ability to view folder listings
Modify portal content	`ModifyPortalContent`	`cmf.ModifyPortalContent`	Edit operations on content
Change portal events	*N/A*	*N/A*	Modification of the Event content type (largely a historical accident)

Permission	Constant	Zope Toolkit name	Controls
Manage portal	`ManagePortal`	`cmf.ManagePortal`	Operations typically restricted to the Manager role.
Request review	`RequestReview`	`cmf.RequestReview`	Ability to submit content for review in many workflows.
Review portal content	`ReviewPortalContent`	`cmf.ReviewPortalContent`	Ability to approve or reject items submitted for review in many workflows.
Add portal content	`AddPortalContent`	`cmf.AddPortalContent`	Ability to add new content in a folder. Note that most content types have their own "add" permissions. In this case, both this permission and the type-specific permission are required.

The Constant column in the preceding table refers to constants defined in `Products.CMFCore.permissions`. The Zope Toolkit name column lists the equivalent names found in ZCML files in packages such as `Products.CMFCore`, `Products.Five` and (at least from Zope 2.13), `AccessControl`. They contain directives such as:

```
<permission
  id="zope2.View"
  title="View"
  />
```

This is how permissions are defined in the Zope Toolkit. Custom permissions can also be created in this way. Sometimes, we will use ZCML directives which expect a permission attribute, such as:

```
<browser:page
  name="some-view"
  class=".someview.SomeView"
  for="*"
  permission="zope2.View"
  />
```

The `permission` attribute here must be a Zope Toolkit permission ID. The title of the `<permission />` directive is used to map the Zope 2-style permissions (which are really just strings) to Zope Toolkit permission IDs.

To declare that a particular view or other resource defined in ZCML should not be subject to security checks, we can use the special permission `zope.Public`.

Roles

Roles can be assigned globally to users and/or groups from the **Users and Groups** control panel. It is usually easier to create logical groups that can be assigned a set of roles once, rather than manage those roles for each user. The default *Administrators* and *Reviewers* groups have the *Manager* and *Reviewer* roles, respectively. There is also a pseudo-group called **Logged-in users**, which can be used to manage global and local roles that should apply to everybody who logs into the site. Every user is automatically a member of this group.

The **Sharing** tab, which appears on most content items, can be used to search for users or groups and assign them local roles. Note that the set of roles on the sharing tab is limited to those explicitly white-listed.

The `sharing.xml` GenericSetup import step can be used to list additional local roles on the sharing tab. See `http://plone.org/ documentation/manual/developer-manual/generic-setup` for more details.

There are seven main roles in a default Plone installation.

Role	Purpose
Member	This is the default role for a Plone user. Quite a few permissions that normally apply to logged in users are given to this role. In CMF and Plone, the term **member** is also used more generally to describe users who are managed inside the site (as opposed to Zope-wide users).
Manager	This is the super-user role. Members of the *Administrators* group will have this role. Use it sparingly: a user with *Manager* rights has almost unlimited power over a Plone site.
Site Administrator	This role, which was introduced with Plone 4.1, allows us to define users with the ability to change the settings in Plone's control panels and view and edit almost all content, without giving them access to potentially destructive actions in the Zope Management Interface.
Reviewer	Users with this role, which is granted to the *Reviewers* group, can view and approve content that has been submitted for review.
Reader	This role is intended to be used as a local role only. It can be assigned from the **Sharing** tab, where it appears as **Can view**. When granted the *Reader* role, a user will usually be allowed to view a content object, even when normal *Members* cannot, for example, because the object is private.
Editor	This is the counterpart to *Reader*, is it used to assign modification rights locally. It is called **Can edit** on the **Sharing** tab. This allows content owners to delegate edit rights selectively to other users.
Contributor	This is used to delegate the right to add content items in folders. It appears on the **Sharing** tab under the title **Can add**.

If you create a new content type with a custom "add" permission, you should normally grant this to the *Contributor* role globally, using `rolemap.xml`. Similarly, if you have any custom permissions necessary to view an object, they should normally be granted to the *Reader* role, whilst any permissions necessary to modify an object should be granted to the *Editor* role.

In addition, Zope defines three automatically assigned roles:

Role	Purpose
Owner	This role is given to the owner of the current content item. Normally, this is the user who created it.
Authenticated	This is given to all logged-in users. This is more low-level than the Member role and cannot be revoked or granted explicitly. Therefore, it is usually better to rely on the Member role when designing a permission scheme for logged-in users.
Anonymous	This role refers to non-logged in users. There is a special user object, also called *Anonymous*, which is always granted this role.

Wherever a permission is granted to *Anonymous*, Zope will in effect stop checking the permission. This means that it is not possible to assign a permission to non-logged in users without also granting it to all authenticated users.

It is possible to create new roles through the `rolemap.xml` import handler in a GenericSetup profile (or through the **Security** tab in the ZMI).

Think carefully before adding too many new roles. A large number of custom roles is normally a sign that the security policy is not well thought-through. New roles usually require changes to the site's workflows.

Manipulating permissions and roles programmatically

To validate a permission in a particular context, such as the current content object, for the current user, we can do:

```
from AccessControl import getSecurityManager
from Products.CMFCore.permissions import ModifyPortalContent

sm = getSecurityManager()
if sm.checkPermission(ModifyPortalContent, context):
    # do something
```

Permissions are identified by strings, so we could use `"Modify portal content"` instead of importing and using `ModifyPortalContent`, but using the constant is less error-prone.

To grant a particular permission to a list of roles, we can do:

```
context.manage_permission("Portlets: Manage portlets",
        roles=['Manager', 'Site Administrator', 'Owner'], acquire=1)
```

Of course, it would be better to use a constant (provided there is one defined), but as the example shows, strings work too. Set `acquire=0` to turn off acquisition of role assignments.

To find out if the current user is logged in (that is, whether the user is "anonymous" or not), we can use the `portal_membership` tool:

```
from Products.CMFCore.utils import getToolByName

mtool = getToolByName(context, 'portal_membership')
if mtool.isAnonymousUser():
    # do something
```

Similarly, we can obtain the current member from this tool:

```
member = mtool.getAuthenticatedMember()
if member is not None:
    userId = member.getId()
```

 The user ID is a string that uniquely identifies the user. It should not be confused with the user's login name, which is the name used in combination with a password to log into the site. Sometimes, the user ID and login name are the same, but this is not always the case, particularly when authenticating against external user sources such as LDAP or Active Directory repositories.

Once we have a member object, we can look up member properties as in the following code:

```
fullName = member.getProperty('fullname')
email = member.getProperty('email')
```

 Member properties are enumerated on the **Properties** tab of the `portal_memberdata` tool.

We can also find members by ID, using the following line of code:

```
adminUser = mtool.getMemberById('admin')
```

 Take a look at the **Doc** tab of the `portal_membership` tool in the ZMI, or see `Products.CMFCore.MembershipTool` for more information about its API.

Keeping control with workflow

As we have alluded to before, managing permissions directly anywhere other than the site root is usually a bad idea. Every content object in a Plone site is subject to security, and will in most cases inherit permission settings from its parent. If we start making special settings in particular folders, we will quickly lose control.

However, if settings are always acquired, how can we restrict access to particular folders or prevent authors from editing published content whilst still giving them rights to work on items in a draft state? The answer to both of these problems is workflow.

Workflows are managed by the `portal_workflow` tool. This controls a mapping of content types to workflows definitions, and sets a default workflow for types not explicitly mapped.

 The workflow tool allows a workflow chain of multiple workflows to be assigned to a content type. Each workflow is given its own state variable. Multiple workflows can manage permissions concurrently. Plone's user interface does not explicitly support more than one workflow, but can be used in combination with custom user interface elements to address complex security and workflow requirements.

The workflow definitions themselves are objects found inside the `portal_workflow` tool, under the **Contents** tab. Each definition consists of states, such as *private* or *published*, and transitions between them.

Transitions can be protected by permissions or restricted to particular roles.

 Although it is fairly common to protect workflow transitions by role, this is not actually a very good use of the security system. It would be much more sensible to use an appropriate permission. The exception is when custom roles are used solely for the purpose of defining roles in a workflow.

Some transitions are automatic, which means that they will be invoked as soon as an object enters a state that has this transition as a possible exit (that is, provided the relevant guard conditions are met). More commonly, transitions are invoked following some user action, normally through the **State** drop-down menu in Plone's user interface. It is possible to execute code immediately before or after a transition is executed.

States may be used simply for information purposes. For example, it is useful to be able to mark a content object as "published" and be able to search for all published content.

More commonly, states are also used to control content item security. When an object enters a particular state, either its initial state, when it is first created, or a state that is the result of a workflow transition, the workflow tool can set a number of permissions according to a predefined permissions map associated with the target state.

The permissions that are managed by a particular workflow are listed under the **Permissions** tab on the workflow definition:

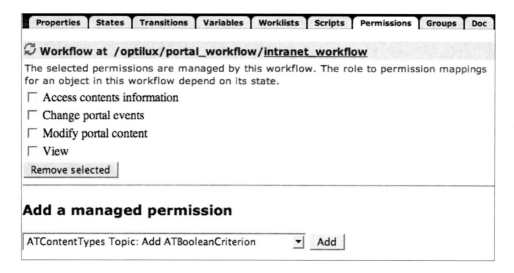

These permissions are used in a permission map for each state:

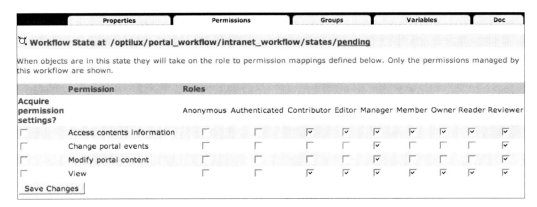

 If you change workflow security settings, your changes will not take effect immediately, since permissions are only modified upon workflow transitions. To synchronize permissions with the current workflow definitions, use the **Update security settings** button at the bottom of the **Workflows** tab of the `portal_workflow` tool. Note that this can take a long time on large sites, because it needs to find all content items using the old settings and update their permissions. If you use the **Types** control panel in Plone's **Site Setup** to change workflows, this reindexing happens automatically.

Workflows can also be used to manage role-to-group assignments in the same way they can be used to manage role-to-permission assignments. This feature is rarely used in Plone, however.

All workflows manage a number of workflow variables, whose values can change with transitions and be queried through the workflow tool. These are rarely changed, however, and Plone relies on a number of the default ones. These include the previous transition (`action`), the user ID of the person who performed that transition (`actor`), any associated comments (`comments`), the date/time of the last transition (`time`), and the full transition history (`review_history`).

Finally, workflows can define work lists, which are used by Plone's *Review list* portlet to show pending tasks for the current user. A work list in effect performs a catalog search using the workflow's state variable. In Plone, the state variable is always called `review_state`.

The workflow system is very powerful, and can be used to solve many kinds of problems where objects of the same type need to be in different states. Learning to use it effectively can pay off greatly in the long run.

Interacting with workflow in code

Interacting with workflow from our own code is usually straightforward. To get the workflow state of a particular object, we can do:

```
from Products.CMFCore.utils import getToolByName

wftool = getToolByName(context, 'portal_workflow')
review_state = wftool.getInfoFor(context, 'review_state')
```

However, if we are doing a search using the `portal_catalog` tool, the results it returns has the review state as metadata already:

```
from Products.CMFCore.utils import getToolByName

catalog = getToolByName(context, 'portal_catalog')
for result in catalog(dict(
    portal_type=('Document', 'News Item',),
    review_state=('published', 'public', 'visible',),
)):
    review_state = result.review_state
    # do something with the review_state
```

 The catalog tool will be covered in more detail in *Chapter 9, Nine Core Concepts of Zope Programming*.

To change the workflow state of an object, we can use the following line of code:

```
wftool.doActionFor(context, action='publish')
```

The `action` here is the name of a transition, which must be available to the current user, from current state of `context`. There is no (easy) way to directly specify the target state. This is by design: recall that transitions form the paths between states, and may involve additional security restrictions or the triggering of scripts.

 Again, the **Doc** tab for the `portal_workflow` tool and its sub-objects (the workflow definitions and their states and transitions) should be your first point of call if you need more detail. The workflow code can be found in `Products.CMFCore.WorkflowTool` and `Products.DCWorkflow`.

Installing a custom workflow

It is fairly common to create custom workflows when building a Plone website. Plone ships with several useful workflows, but security and approvals processes tend to differ from site to site, so we will often find ourselves creating our own workflows.

Workflows are a form of customization. Therefore, as we learned in *Chapter 4, Basics of Customization*, we should ensure they are installable using GenericSetup. However, the workflow XML syntax is quite verbose, so it is often easier to start from the ZMI and export the workflow definition to the filesystem.

Designing a workflow for Optilux Cinemas

It is important to get the design of a workflow policy right, considering the different roles that need to interact with the objects, and the permissions they should have in the various states. The requirements we saw in *Chapter 2, Introduction to the Case Study*, imply that only cinema staff should be allowed to create content. Draft content should be visible to cinema staff, but not customers, and should go through review before being published.

The following diagram illustrates this workflow:

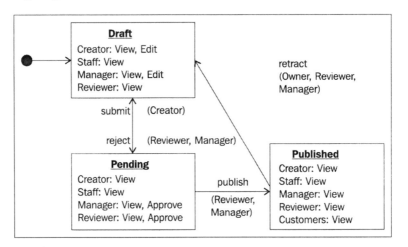

This workflow will be made the default, and should therefore apply to most content. However, we will keep the standard Plone policy of omitting workflow for the *File* and *Image* types. This means that permissions for content items of these types will be acquired from the *Folder* in which they are contained, making them simpler to manage. In particular, this means it is not necessary to separately publish linked files and embedded images when publishing a *Page*.

Because we need to distinguish between logged-in customers and staff members, we will introduce a new role called *StaffMember*. This role will be granted *View* permission by default for all items in the site, much like a *Manager* or *Site Administrator* user is by default (although workflow may override this). We will let the *Site Administrator* role represent site administrators, and the *Reviewer* role represent content reviewers, as they do in a default Plone installation. We will also create a new group, *Staff*, which is given the *StaffMember* role. Among other things, this will allow us to easily grant the *Reader*, *Editor* and *Contributor* role in particular folders to all staff from the **Sharing** screen.

> The preceding workflow is designed for content production and review. This is probably the most common use for workflow in Plone, but it is by no means the only use case. For example, the author once used workflows to control the payment status on an *Invoice* content type. As you become more proficient with the workflow engine, you will find that it is useful in a number of scenarios.

Building the workflow

We will build our workflow through the ZMI and then export it to the filesystem for incorporation into our policy package.

1. Before we can start, we must add the *StaffMember* role, so that we can use this in our workflow definitions. At the Plone site root, we go to the **Security** tab, and add the new role using the form at the bottom of the page.

2. Next, we ensure users with this role can view content by default, by finding the *View* permission in the listing (near the bottom), and ensuring the following roles are ticked: *Contributor, Editor, Manager, Site Administrator, Owner, Reader, StaffMember* before clicking **Save Changes**.

3. We then create a new skeleton workflow by copying one of the existing ones. This helps set up the standard Plone workflow and review state variables, for example.

4. In the ZMI, under the `portal_workflow` tool's **Contents** tab, we first copy and paste the `simple_publication_workflow`, which we immediately rename to `optilux_sitecontent_workflow`.

5. Clicking on the new workflow definition, we will be presented with its **Properties** tab. Here, we change the title and description as appropriate:

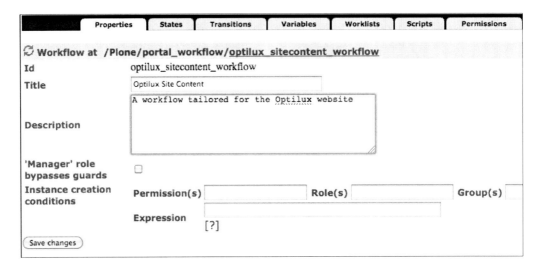

6. Next, we move to the **States** tab. Here, we can delete the `private` state, and add a new `draft` state. We must also set this as the initial state, by selecting it and clicking **Set Initial State**.

 It is important that every workflow has an initial state. Otherwise, you may get difficult-to-debug errors when creating content items using the workflow.

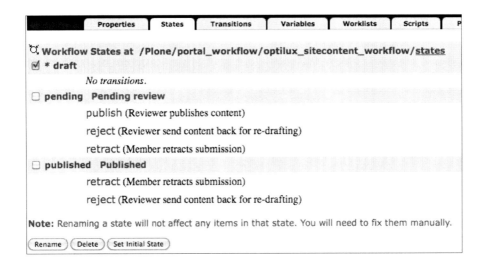

7. Clicking on the new state, we can set some properties—a title, description, and possible exit transitions:

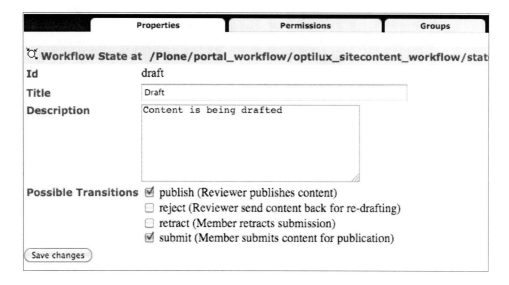

 It may be that the desired transitions have not been defined yet. In this case, you can always come back to the state definition later.

8. Next, we move to the **Permissions** tab, where we define the roles-to-permission map:

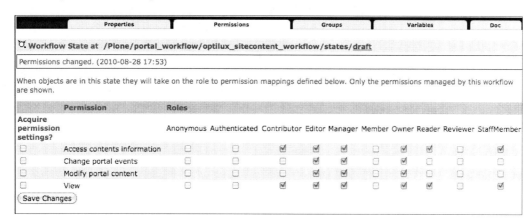

There are a few useful rules of thumb for setting up a workflow permission map for standard Plone content. These help ensure the **Sharing** tab works as expected:

The *View* and *Access contents information* permissions usually have the same role mappings.

If the *Owner* role has the *View* and *Access contents information permissions*, so should the *Reader* and *Editor* roles. Similarly, if the *Owner* role has the *Modify portal content* permission, so should the *Editor* role. If the *Add portal content* or any type-specific "add" permissions are managed, the *Owner* and *Contributor* roles should normally be in sync for such permissions.

We can now repeat this process for the other states, using our diagram above as a guide.

9. Next, we go back to the workflow definition and open the **Transitions** tab. Here, we notice that the `reject` and `retract` transitions still list the `private` state as their target.

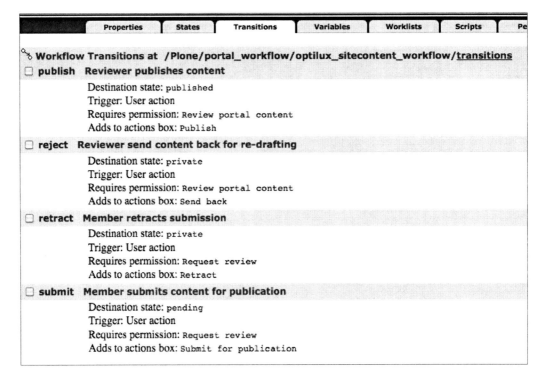

We can click on each to change it. For example:

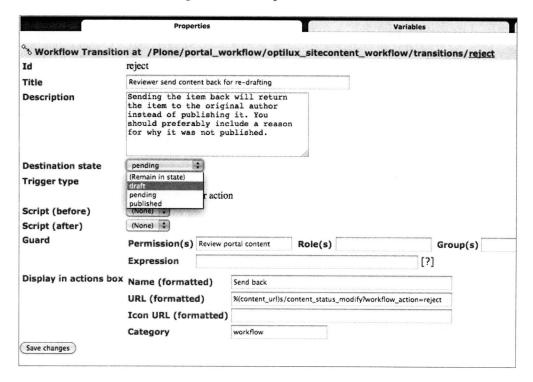

Notice the guard permission: **Review portal content** in this case. Also note that it is the **Display in actions box – Name (formatted)** value that is used for the **State** drop-down menu, while the **Title** is used as a tooltip.

The **URL (formatted)** is used to determine what the relevant item in the **State** menu links to. It is almost always a URL similar to the following one: `%(content_url)s/content_status_modify?workflow_action=<transition_id>`, where `<transition_id>` is the ID of the current transition. If this field is omitted, Plone will use this pattern as a default, so it is strictly speaking optional.

The **Category** must be `workflow` for the **State** menu to find the transition.

In this case, we do not need to remove or add any transitions, but had we needed to, we could have used the buttons at the bottom of the **Transitions** tab.

Once our states and transitions are defined, we can take a look at the work list we inherited from the `simple_publication_workflow`, under the **Worklists** tab on the workflow itself:

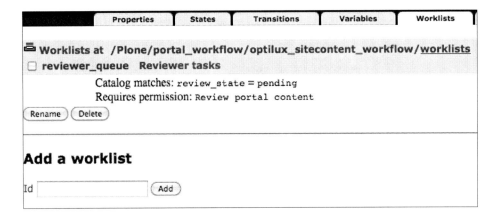

This work list is fine for our purposes, and will make content in the `pending` state show up in the *Review list* portlet.

It is common to assign the *Review list* portlet to the dashboard for the *Reviewers* group, so that all reviewers see it. This can be done from the **Users and Groups** control panel.

New work lists can be added using the form at the bottom. Be aware, though, that having too many work lists can have a performance impact on pages where the *Review list* portlet is shown. A work list definition looks similar to the following screenshot:

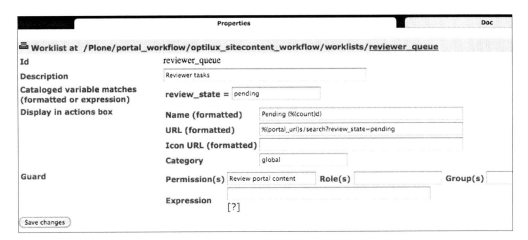

Notice how the state name is used in the **Cataloged variable matches** box, as well as in the **URL (formatted)** box. The former is what drives the work list. The latter is used to provide a link to a fuller work listing. The work list action category should be global, as shown. Guard permissions are used to control who can view the work list, which in this case is everyone who can approve content.

Exporting

With our workflow defined, we should test it through the web to ensure it is working as expected. When we are satisfied, we can create a GenericSetup export that contains our new settings. This will be used as the basis for our amendments to the policy package shortly.

In the portal_setup tool in the ZMI, we go to the **Export** tab, and select the export steps we are interested in: *Role / Permission Map* and *Workflow Tool*. At the bottom, we then click **Export selected steps**, which will present a .tar.gz archive for download. Expanding this, we should find the files rolemap.xml and workflows.xml, and the directory workflows/.

Amending the policy package

With our GenericSetup export in hand, we can now amend the optilux.policy package by selectively copying elements of the export into our custom GenericSetup profile.

To test these amendments through the web, we must reapply the policy package's GenericSetup profile through the portal_setup tool, or deactivate and reactivate it through the **Add-ons** control panel in Plone. Alternatively, we could create a new Plone site in the ZMI and apply our profile to it.

Role and permission settings

Roles and site-wide permission settings are managed using rolemap.xml, which should be placed in the profiles/default/ directory. Our export contains all roles and permissions in the site, which is much more than we want for our extension profile. The application-specific file we create from the export is much shorter:

```xml
<?xml version="1.0"?>
<rolemap>
  <roles>
    <role name="StaffMember" />
  </roles>
```

```
<permissions>
    <permission name="View" acquire="True">
      <role name="Owner" />
      <role name="Manager" />
      <role name="Site Administrator" />
      <role name="Contributor" />
      <role name="Reader" />
      <role name="Editor" />
      <role name="StaffMember" />
    </permission>
  </permissions>
</rolemap>
```

Here, we add the new *StaffMember* role, and then ensure members of this role can, by default, view any content, on par with users who have the *Manager* or *Site Administrator* role.

Workflow definition

Workflow definitions in a GenericSetup profile are stored in the `workflows/` directory, in which there should be one subdirectory named after each workflow. In this directory, a `definition.xml` file describes the workflow.

> The reason for this extra subdirectory is that some workflows may have associated Python scripts stored in the ZODB, which are exported here. These in-ZODB scripts are rarely used in Plone applications, however. In *Chapter 9, Nine Core Concepts of Zope Programming*, we will learn how to write event handlers that can be used to react to workflow changes.

Our workflow definition, in `profiles/default/workflows/optilux_sitecontent_workflow/definition.xml`, is shown below. For brevity, we have omitted some states, transitions and variable definitions. Please refer to the book's accompanying source code for the full listing.

> If you are looking for a more compact syntax for creating workflows directly on the filesystem, the `collective.wtf` package can be used to create workflows from a CSV file. It does not support every feature of the workflow tool, but has support for the bits Plone uses, and provides more Plone-like defaults. One major drawback, however, is that it does not support making workflows translatable. See `http://pypi.python.org/pypi/collective.wtf`.

The workflow definition begins with some basic information—its ID, title, description, state variable name, and initial state—followed by the list of permissions that the workflow will manage:

```
<?xml version="1.0"?>
<dc-workflow
    workflow_id="optilux_sitecontent_workflow"
    title="Simple Publication Workflow"
    description=""
    state_variable="review_state"
    initial_state="draft
    manager_bypass="False">

<permission>Access contents information</permission>
<permission>Change portal events</permission>
<permission>Modify portal content</permission>
<permission>View</permission>
```

Next, multiple states are defined, each with a list of available exit transitions and a role map for each managed permission.

```
<state state_id="draft" title="Draft">
 <description>Content is being drafted</description>
 <exit-transition transition_id="publish"/>
 <exit-transition transition_id="submit"/>
 <permission-map name="Access contents information"
    acquired="False">
  <permission-role>Contributor</permission-role>
  <permission-role>Editor</permission-role>
  <permission-role>Manager</permission-role>
  <permission-role>Site Administrator</permission-role>
  <permission-role>Owner</permission-role>
  <permission-role>Reader</permission-role>
  <permission-role>StaffMember</permission-role>
 </permission-map>
 <permission-map name="Change portal events" acquired="False">
  <permission-role>Editor</permission-role>
  <permission-role>Manager</permission-role>
  <permission-role>Site Administrator</permission-role>
  <permission-role>Owner</permission-role>
 </permission-map>
 <permission-map name="Modify portal content" acquired="False">
  <permission-role>Editor</permission-role>
  <permission-role>Manager</permission-role>
  <permission-role>Site Administrator</permission-role>
  <permission-role>Owner</permission-role>
```

```
    </permission-map>
    <permission-map name="View" acquired="False">
     <permission-role>Contributor</permission-role>
     <permission-role>Editor</permission-role>
     <permission-role>Manager</permission-role>
     <permission-role>Site Administrator</permission-role>
     <permission-role>Owner</permission-role>
     <permission-role>Reader</permission-role>
     <permission-role>StaffMember</permission-role>
    </permission-map>
   </state>

   . . .
```

The transitions are then defined, indicating the target state, guard conditions, trigger type (USER or AUTOMATIC), and an action URL which will be used for the corresponding link in the **State** menu in Plone.

```
   <transition transition_id="publish"
       title="Reviewer publishes content"
       new_state="published" trigger="USER"
       before_script="" after_script="">
    <description>Publishing the item makes it visible to other users.
    </description>
    <action
   url="%(content_url)s/content_status_modify?workflow_action=publish"
       category="workflow" icon="">Publish</action>
    <guard>
     <guard-permission>Review portal content</guard-permission>
    </guard>
   </transition>

   . . .
```

One or more work lists may also be defined. These are displayed in the *Review* portlet.

```
   <worklist worklist_id="reviewer_queue" title="">
    <description>Reviewer tasks</description>
    <action url="%(portal_url)s/search?review_state=pending"
      category="global" icon="">Pending (%(count)d)</action>
    <guard>
     <guard-permission>Review portal content</guard-permission>
    </guard>
    <match name="review_state" values="pending"/>
   </worklist>
```

Finally, a number of standard variables are defined, most of which are required for the proper operation of a workflow in Plone.

```
<variable variable_id="action"
  for_catalog="False" for_status="True" update_always="True">
 <description>Previous transition</description>
 <default>
  <expression>transition/getId|nothing</expression>
 </default>
 <guard>
 </guard>
</variable>

...

</dc-workflow>
```

Mapping workflows to types

Our new workflow definition must be explicitly registered with the workflow tool. It can then be associated with content types and/or set as the default workflow. Both are done using the `workflows.xml` file, which lives in the `profiles/default/` directory. As with `rolemap.xml`, the exported file should be pared down to only include the elements relevant to our extension profile:

```
<?xml version="1.0"?>
<object name="portal_workflow">
    <object name="optilux_sitecontent_workflow"
        meta_type="Workflow"/>
    <bindings>
        <default>
            <bound-workflow
                workflow_id="optilux_sitecontent_workflow"/>
        </default>
        <type type_id="File" />
        <type type_id="Image" />
    </bindings>
</object>
```

This syntax supports two further operations not shown in this example. To explicitly remove the workflow association (including a "no workflow" association) for a type and return it to use the default binding, use:

```
<type type_id="SomeType" remove="remove" />
```

To override the default workflow definition for one specific type, binding a different workflow:

```
<type type_id="SomeType">
    <bound-workflow workflow_id="some_workflow"/>
</type>
```

Adding the Staff group

Finally, to add the *Staff* group upon profile installation, we are faced with a conundrum: There is (currently) no GenericSetup syntax for creating groups. The solution here is to use **imperative configuration**, that is, configuration performed in Python code using the relevant APIs, as opposed to **declarative configuration**, which is performed using (XML) configuration files.

Imperative configuration in GenericSetup relies on a trick: we create a custom import handler which "reads" a placeholder file from the profile being imported. If the file is present, the import handler performs the necessary configuration.

> The placeholder file is very important. GenericSetup in effect always runs all registered import handlers for each profile it imports. It is up to each handler to decide how to act. Without some kind of marker to check, the imperative import handler will run indiscriminately for every profile imported into the Plone site.

To register our new import step, we can use the following syntax in `configure.zcml`:

```
<configure
    xmlns="http://namespaces.zope.org/zope"
    xmlns:five="http://namespaces.zope.org/five"
    xmlns:i18n="http://namespaces.zope.org/i18n"
    xmlns:genericsetup="http://namespaces.zope.org/genericsetup"
    i18n_domain="optilux.policy">

  <genericsetup:registerProfile
      name="default"
      title="Optilux Site Policy"
      directory="profiles/default"
      description="Turn a Plone site into the Optilux site."
      provides="Products.GenericSetup.interfaces.EXTENSION"
      />
```

```
<genericsetup:importStep
    name="optilux-various"
    title="Additional Optilux site policy setup"
    description="Optilux site policy configuration"
    handler="optilux.policy.setuphandlers.importVarious">
  <depends name="rolemap"/>
</genericsetup:importStep>

<!-- -*- extra stuff goes here -*- -->
</configure>
```

The name should be unique, so that it does not clash with other import steps. The title and description are used in the portal_setup user interface.

The nested <depends /> tag is used here to ensure that this handler executes after the rolemap import step, ensuring that the *StaffMember* role is available when we need it.

Most of the standard import steps are found in the exportimport/ configure.zcml file of Products.CMFCore.

The handler attribute gives the dotted name to a function implementing the import handler. The convention is to put this in a module called setuphandlers with a function called importVarious. In setuphandlers.py, we use the PAS and portal_ groups APIs to check for and add our new group. We explicitly check for a marker file, optilux.policy-various.txt, and abort if this is not found in the current profile.

```
from Products.CMFCore.utils import getToolByName

def setupGroups(portal):
    acl_users = getToolByName(portal, 'acl_users')
    if not acl_users.searchGroups(name='Staff'):
        gtool = getToolByName(portal, 'portal_groups')
        gtool.addGroup('Staff', roles=['StaffMember'])

def importVarious(context):
    """Miscellanous steps import handle
    """

    if context.readDataFile('optilux.policy-various.txt') is None:
        return

    portal = context.getSite()

    setupGroups(portal)
```

Take a look at the **Doc** tab for the `acl_users` and `portal_groups` objects inside the Plone site in the ZMI for details about their API.

Finally, we must add the `optilux.policy-various.txt` marker file to our `profiles/default/` directory. This file may be blank.

Writing the tests

Of course, we must not forget the tests for our new functionality. We amend `tests.py` as follows:

```python
def test_role_added(self):
    portal = self.layer['portal']
    self.assertTrue("StaffMember" in portal.validRoles())

def test_workflow_installed(self):
    portal = self.layer['portal']
    workflow = getToolByName(portal, 'portal_workflow')
    self.assertTrue('optilux_sitecontent_workflow' in workflow)

def test_workflows_mapped(self):
    portal = self.layer['portal']
    workflow = getToolByName(portal, 'portal_workflow')
    self.assertEqual(('optilux_sitecontent_workflow',),
        workflow.getDefaultChain())

def test_view_permisison_for_staffmember(self):
    portal = self.layer['portal']
    self.assertTrue('View' in [r['name']
        for r in portal.permissionsOfRole('Reader')
        if r['selected']])
    self.assertTrue('View' in [r['name']
        for r in portal.permissionsOfRole('StaffMember')
        if r['selected']])

def test_staffmember_group_added(self):
    portal = self.layer['portal']
    acl_users = portal['acl_users']
    self.assertEqual(1,
        len(acl_users.searchGroups(name='Staff')))
```

These tests make use of the `RoleManager`, `WorkflowTool`, and PAS user folder APIs to inspect the security settings in the site after creation.

Protected and trusted code

The preceding techniques—managing roles and permissions at the Plone site root and managing detailed permissions with workflows—are the staple of security configuration for integrators and customizers. As we continue to develop new functionality, we will ensure that it is properly protected by appropriate permissions, normally relying on the "core" permissions such as *View* and *Modify portal content* for which we have defined a policy in this chapter.

It is important, however, to understand when and how permissions are enforced. In particular, permissions are not generally enforced when we call methods in filesystem Python code.

 The exception are a few methods—notably `restrictedTraverse()`, which can be used to explicitly traverse to an object, `searchResults()` of `portal_catalog`, which only returns items the current user is allowed to view, `invokeFactory()`, which is available on container content types and used to create new subobjects, and `doActionFor()`, which we have seen previously, that explicitly checks the permissions of the current authenticated user, using the patterns shown earlier in this chapter.

Security is principally applied to things which are either created or accessed through-the-web. It is invoked on URL traversal when the browser requests a particular resource, or on "path traversal" in "untrusted" code—more on that in a moment. A "resource" here can mean a view of a content object, a particular method on a content object which returns something to the browser, a style sheet or indeed anything else which is published by Zope. We will look at the process of URL traversal and object publishing in more detail in *Chapter 9, Nine Core Concepts of Zope Programming*.

Security assertions are made in the following places:

- Zope Toolkit-style browser components, such as browser views and resources, which are declared in ZCML with an associated permission. We saw an example of declaring a view with `<browser:page />` above. These resources will not be available unless the current user has the given permission. We will see more examples of this in *Chapters 9, 10*, and *11*.

- Page templates and other resources in CMF skin layers, which may explicitly restrict access to particular roles. For example, the page template `prefs_install_products_form.pt` from the `plone_prefs` skin layer has an associated `prefs_install_products_form.pt.metadata` file containing the following lines:

  ```
  [security]
   View = 0:Manager
  ```

- Attributes and methods on content items, tools, and other persistent objects. These can be protected by permissions with ZCML, using the `<class />` and `<require />` directives, or in Python code using an `AccessControl.ClassSecurityInfo` object. We will see examples of both in *Chapter 10, Custom Content Types*.

In addition, the variable `__allow_access_to_unprotected_subjects__` can be added to a class to determine how (potentially acquired) attributes that do not themselves have security assertions should behave. It is set to `True` by one of the common base classes used for all Plone content types. This is necessary to enable the kind of generic user interface that Plone exposes, but it does mean that it is important to protect attributes of custom content types and other components.

Restricted Python

Zope allows sufficiently privileged users to create Page Templates, DTML methods, and Script's (Python) through-the-web. This was traditionally the way to build Zope applications, with scripts and templates coexisting with data objects in the ZODB.

In *Chapter 4, Basics of Customization*, we saw that the `portal_skins` tool allows us to manage acquirable resources such as page templates and scripts on the filesystem, and that this is generally preferable. To the underlying Zope architecture, however, resources in skin layers are no different to resources created in the ZMI. In both cases, expressions are subject to the controls imposed by **Restricted Python**.

 The Python classes and Page Templates used in Zope Toolkit browser views are "filesystem" code, and thus not subject to Restricted Python. Other filesystem code, such as methods of content types, tools, adapters, or utilities are also oblivious to Restricted Python.

Restricted Python ensures that users cannot create scripts or templates that access resources or perform operations they would not normally be allowed to invoke. Permissions are automatically checked when a script or template traverses the object graph or calls a method. Insufficient permissions result in an `Unauthorized` exception.

It is possible to define a **proxy role** for individual templates or scripts, either in the ZMI or using a `.metadata` file. For example, the `send_feedback.cpy` script needs to be able to access the site's email configuration, even if it is invoked by users not normally allowed to do so. The associated `send_feedback.cpy.metadata` contains:

```
[default]
proxy=Manager,Anonymous

[security]
View=0:Authenticated
```

> We describe `.metadata` files and proxy roles here mainly for completeness' sake. New code should use view components, as described in *Chapters 9, 10,* and *11*.

Restricted Python also ensures that scripts created through-the-web cannot access the server's filesystem, nor can they import unauthorized modules which may be used to compromise the server's security. Only those modules explicitly allowed, using the `allow_module()` and `allow_class()` methods from `AccessControl`, may be imported. In addition, methods and variables with names beginning with an underscore are considered private, and cannot be accessed. Lastly, any published class or method must have a docstring.

> These security restrictions are best thought of as ways to prevent administrators from making mistakes through the web. A malicious user with rights to create through-the-web scripts and templates could still cause a lot of harm, for example by sending all Zope threads into infinite loops or use up all of a server's memory.

Restricted Python is becoming less important as developers begin to prefer Zope Toolkit style browser views and resources. Here, the primary means of enforcing security is through the permission that applies to the entire view or resource, set in ZCML. Persistent objects such as content items also need to set appropriate permissions for their methods. We will see how in *Chapter 10, Custom Content Types*.

Summary

In this chapter, we have taken a look at Plone's approach to security, including:

- Key concepts such as users, groups, roles, and permissions
- A few examples of manipulating security settings in code
- The role played by workflows in managing security
- Creating custom workflow and apply it using GenericSetup
- How security is invoked during URL traversal and in Restricted Python

In the next chapter, we will learn about how to find and install third-party add-ons.

7
Using Add-ons

Throughout this book, we aim to develop reusable components. Of course, it is not very likely that someone else would want to reuse the Optilux site theme or policy, but developing for reusability encourages good practice. Besides, the client could come back next year wanting another site with the same basic look-and-feel.

Plone developers have created add-ons that do everything from making small improvements to core content types, to providing new functionality like forums, blogs, and database integration tools. Sometimes, developers will factor components built for customers into a reusable base package and another with customer-specific integration code. In the spirit of the Plone community, the vast majority of these packages are made available free under open source licenses.

In this chapter, we will:

- Discuss how to find, evaluate, and test Plone add-ons
- Demonstrate how to include PloneFormGen, a popular form building tool in the Optilux application
- Issue a few warnings: not all add-ons are created equal, and due diligence is usually required

Finding and evaluating add-ons

The main place to look for Plone add-ons is the **Products** area on the Plone website: http://plone.org/products. The Plone community encourages developers to list their packages here, and make use of the tools provided, such as issue trackers, roadmaps, and release management. Most modern packages also have distributions on PyPI (and sometimes only on PyPI), which can be found by searching http://pypi.python.org/pypi.

Many packages listed on the Plone website, and quite a few more, use the **Collective**, a community Subversion repository, to host their code. The Collective is located at `http://svn.plone.org/svn/collective`, and can be browsed at `http://dev.plone.org/collective/browser`.

If you have code you want to contribute to the Collective, you should ask on the mailing lists or chat room and then file a ticket with a request in the `plone.org` issue tracker (`http://dev.plone.org/plone`). The criteria for getting commit privileges to the Collective are not very onerous. See `http://dev.plone.org/collective`.

This also applies if you want to make fixes or improvements to other developers' code. If you are making changes to code you do not own, make sure you contact the maintainer of the package. For non-trivial changes, you should work on a branch. Members of the community in the chat room or on the mailing lists will be able to advise you if you are unsure about the etiquette of working with code in the Collective.

You can use `mr.developer` to track a package in the Collective (or any other repository) as a develop egg. See *Chapter 3, The Development Environment* for details.

There is no centralized review of add-ons. The Plone community thrives on contributions, and encourages developers to share their code. The downside to this is that sometimes add-ons overlap in scope or vary in quality.

In general, you cannot assume that an add-on has gone through the same quality control procedures as the Plone core. Though there are plenty of add-ons that are rock solid, there are also those that simply do not work or, worse, could damage your site when installed, for example by making unwise configuration changes.

You should always conduct some due diligence before choosing add-ons to rely on. Often, the best way to evaluate the quality of a particular add-on is to ask around for other community members' experiences or ask for recommendations on how to achieve a particular goal.

You may also wish to consider how well the add-on presents itself: is there a page in the products section of `plone.org`? Is there a release? Is it a final release, a release candidate, or a less mature pre-release? Has the author taken the time to explain the functionality of the add-on clearly, and is there a mention of outstanding issues or missing features? You could also take a look at the issue tracker and roadmap pages, if available, to get a flavor for how many outstanding issues there are and, perhaps more importantly, how quickly they are being resolved.

As you become a more experienced developer, however, the first thing you are likely to do is to browse through the source code. Over time, you will learn to spot whether an add-on is using good practices or not. A good initial benchmark is whether the package has any automated tests.

Playing it safe

When you have found one or more candidate add-ons to solve a particular problem, you will need to try them out. In doing so, there is one very important thing to remember:

> Never, ever install someone else's add-on package directly onto a live server without first testing it in your development environment. Even then, always, always take a backup of the Zope database before installing new software on a production server. An add-on could be perfectly stable on its own, but could still cause problems if it conflicts with other components that you have installed or developed.

To test an add-on, the usual procedure is to copy the Data.fs file from the live server to an environment with the same or a similar software configuration as the live server (that is, using the same buildout) and install the add-on here. Then, run the automated tests for your own code, as well as those for the add-on package itself, if applicable. These may tell you of conflicts that may not be obvious. You should, of course, also test it in the browser to ensure the new component behaves as expected.

Installing an add-on

To illustrate the installation of an add-on, we will show how to add the popular PloneFormGen package to our site. PloneFormGen installs content types that can be used by site administrators to build forms through the web. You can read more about it at http://plone.org/products/ploneformgen.

One way to install an add-on distribution is to list it directly in our Buildout configuration, by amending the working set that is installed for the Zope instance created by plone.recipe.zope2instance. For sites that do not have a policy package (like the one we created in *Chapter 5, Developing a Site Strategy*), this is the only way to install a new add-on. When using a policy package, however, it is better to consider all other packages (including Plone and any add-ons) as dependencies of the policy package. We will see an example of this shortly.

When installing an add-on directly using the buildout configuration, it is sometimes also necessary to load a ZCML slug. This is a file created by `plone.recipe.zope2instance` that tells Zope to load the package's configuration at startup.

 Slugs are not necessary for packages in the `Products.*` namespace, or packages that use the `z3c.autoinclude.plugin` entry point to register themselves with Plone, as described in *Chapter 5, Developing a Site Strategy*.

In a simplistic buildout, adding a new package with a ZCML slug could look similar to the following code:

```
[instance]
recipe = plone.recipe.zope2instance
eggs =
    Plone
    some.package
zcml =
    some.package
```

Slugs are installed for all packages listed in the `zcml` option.

Note that when using a policy package, it is preferable to explicitly load the package's configuration from `configure.zcml`, as we shall see in a moment.

Amending the buildout and policy package

Since we have a suitable policy package, we will install `PloneFormGen` by adding its distribution as a dependency of `optilux.policy`.

1. In the `setup.py` file of `optilux.policy`, we amend the `install_requires` argument as in the following code:

    ```
    install_requires=[
        'setuptools',
        'Plone',
        'Products.PloneFormGen',
    ],
    ```

2. Next, we should ensure the package's configuration will be loaded when our policy package is configured. This is strictly speaking not necessary in this case, since Zope will automatically load the configuration for any package in the `Products.*` namespace, but it is a good practice to explicitly load dependencies regardless. This also simplifies test setup. In `configure.zcml` in `optilux.policy`, we add:

```
<configure
    xmlns="http://namespaces.zope.org/zope"
    xmlns:five="http://namespaces.zope.org/five"
    xmlns:i18n="http://namespaces.zope.org/i18n"
    xmlns:genericsetup="http://namespaces.zope.org/genericsetup"
    i18n_domain="optilux.policy">

  <includeDependencies package="." />

    ...


</configure>
```

This will include the configuration for all packages listed in the `install_re-quires` list. If we wanted to be more explicit, we could do:

- `<include package="Products.PloneFormGen" />`

This would include the `configure.zcml` file of this package only.

3. Finally, we want to ensure the new dependency is automatically activated in the Plone site when `optilux.policy` is. To do that, we can use the `metadata.xml` file in the GenericSetup profile (`profiles/default`). We amend it as follows:

```
<metadata>
  <version>1</version>
    <dependencies>
     <dependency>profile-Products.PloneFormGen:default</dependency>
    </dependencies>
</metadata>
```

> Here, it is necessary to know the GenericSetup profile name for
> `Products.PloneFormGen`. Most well-behaved packages use the name
> `default`, but if in doubt, look for a GenericSetup registration in the
> package's ZCML files, or check its documentation.

4. Assuming we are happy to accept the latest available version of `Products.PloneFormGen` and its dependencies for the moment, we can now rerun buildout:

```
$ bin/buildout
```

The `buildout.dumppickedversions` extensions will report some new unpinned dependencies. At the time of writing, these are:

```
Products.PloneFormGen = 1.6.0
Products.PythonField = 1.1.3
Products.TALESField = 1.1.3
Products.TemplateFields = 1.2.5
```

We should ensure that we are happy with these versions by starting up Zope, reactivating the `optilux.policy` profile through the **Add-ons** control panel, and testing through the web. We can then copy the new versions to our `versions.cfg` file to lock them down.

Some more complex distributions are released with their own known good versions sets. These normally take the form of a URL that should be added to the `extends` line after the line that includes the Plone known good set. In our development buildout, that is done in `packages.cfg`. Check the relevant distribution's documentation for details. We will see an example of this style of installation in *Chapter 8, Creating a Custom Theme*.

Adding tests

We should also add a few tests for our new dependency. Here, we are mainly interested in testing that it was installed correctly. We assume the package itself has tests proving it works as advertised.

1. First, we need to ensure that `Products.PloneFormGen` is available in our tests. We thus amend our layer setup in `testing.py` as follows:

```
class OptiluxPolicy(PloneSandboxLayer):

    defaultBases = (PLONE_FIXTURE,)

    def setUpZope(self, app, configurationContext):
        # Load ZCML
        import optilux.policy
        xmlconfig.file(
                'configure.zcml',
                optilux.policy,
                context=configurationContext
        )

        # Install products that use an old-style initialize()
        # function
        z2.installProduct(app, 'Products.PythonField')
```

```
        z2.installProduct(app, 'Products.TALESField')
        z2.installProduct(app, 'Products.TemplateFields')
        z2.installProduct(app, 'Products.PloneFormGen')

    def tearDownZope(self, app):
        # Uninstall products installed above
        z2.uninstallProduct(app, 'Products.PloneFormGen')
        z2.uninstallProduct(app, 'Products.TemplateFields')
        z2.uninstallProduct(app, 'Products.TALESField')
        z2.uninstallProduct(app, 'Products.PythonField')

    def setUpPloneSite(self, portal):
        applyProfile(portal, 'optilux.policy:default')
```

This additional setup and tear-down is necessary because `Products.PloneFormGen` and three of its dependencies are registered as Zope 2 "products" and rely on the `initialize()` method for part of their startup configuration.

Virtually all packages in the `Products.*` namespace require this type of setup. For other namespaces, it may be necessary to look for an `initialize()` method in the package's `__init__.py` file, or a `<five:initializePackage />` line in its `configure.zcml` file.

Note that we do not need to load the packages ZCML here explicitly, since loading the `optilux.policy` configuration will include `Products.PloneFormGen` as a dependency.

2. Next, we add a test to `tests.py`, in the `TestSetup` class:

```
def test_PloneFormGen_installed(self):
    portal = self.layer['portal']
    portal_types = getToolByName(portal, 'portal_types')

    self.assertTrue("FormFolder" in portal_types)
```

3. We can now run our tests with:

```
$ bin/test
```

Summary

In this chapter, we have looked at:

- What add-ons are, and how they relate to the Plone core
- Where to find add-ons
- Tips for evaluating the viability of add-ons for your site
- Caveats around the use of add-ons
- Installing add-ons automatically, using our buildout and site policy package

In the next chapter, we will begin to build the visual look-and-feel of the Optilux site.

Creating a Custom Theme

8

Plone 4 ships with a default theme called **Sunburst**. This is designed to be clean, color neutral, and minimalist, and as such can be a good starting point for intranets and websites where branding is a secondary concern. Most projects, however, end up needing to customize the look and feel to meet organizational branding requirements.

In this chapter, we will demonstrate how to:

- Create a custom theme using the Diazo theming engine and `plone.app.theming`
- Customize templates and views
- Override a few of Plone's layout policies and visual elements

Background

In Plone 3, theming a Plone site involved selectively overriding page templates and resources such as stylesheets and images to modify the markup, styles, and images making up Plone's public face. This approach to theming is still possible in Plone 4, but it suffers from a fundamental problem—the more complex Plone's internals become, the harder it is to find all the templates and resources that need to be overridden, and to understand how they all fit together.

For more about the Plone 3 approach to theming, see the Plone Theme Reference at `http://plone.org/documentation/manual/theme-reference`.

Various solutions have been created to simplify Plone theming. The most promising of these is **Diazo** (formerly known as XDV), which offers something of a paradigm shift in theming. Diazo is not Plone-specific, but is integrated into Plone by a package called `plone.app.theming`. As the name suggests, `plone.app.theming` is intended to become a core part of Plone in the future, although at the time of writing, it remains an installable add-on.

Diazo enables an integrator to wrap a static HTML design around Plone, replacing placeholders with dynamic content and adding arbitrary markup where required. A simple yet powerful rule syntax makes it possible to build advanced themes without changing the original HTML theme or Plone's templates.

We will show how to customize Plone's various templates later in this chapter. In most cases, however, it will be easier to reach for the Diazo rules first, and only consider using Plone's customization mechanisms if Diazo falls short.

Diazo primer

A Diazo theme starts from a static HTML mockup of the website design, perhaps produced by a web designer with no knowledge of Plone. Diazo calls this the **theme**. Ideally, your base theme should consist of clean, well-structured HTML and CSS, making good use of IDs and CSS classes to identify the elements on the page. It should be possible to open the theme in a web browser without any server component running. Therefore, it should use relative paths when referencing images, stylesheets, and JavaScript files.

The theme is coupled with a set of **rules** that tell Diazo how to merge the content into the theme. They are held in an XML file, conventionally named `rules.xml`. The rules operate on the **content** being themed—in our case the HTML served up by 'plain' Plone. Any markup in the content not placed into the theme by a rule is discarded.

 Behind the scenes, Diazo compiles the theme and rules into a single XSLT transformation, which is run on the HTML output by Plone at the end of each request. When Zope debug mode is turned off, the overhead that this transformation adds is negligible.

Diazo rules operate on nodes in the markup of the theme and content. Nodes can be selected using either XPath expressions (which are more powerful) or CSS3 selectors (which are easier to write).

If you are unfamiliar with XPath or CSS 3, you should consult a good reference to learn the basics of the syntax. `http://w3schools.com` is a good place to start.

As an example, let us take a look at a rules file containing a few of the rules from the theme we will create in this chapter:

```xml
<?xml version="1.0" encoding="UTF-8"?>
<rules
    xmlns="http://namespaces.plone.org/diazo"
    xmlns:css="http://namespaces.plone.org/diazo/css"
    xmlns:xsl="http://www.w3.org/1999/XSL/Transform">

    <rules css:if-content="#visual-portal-wrapper">

        <theme href="index.html" />

        <replace css:content="#content"
                css:theme="#document-content" />

        <replace css:content-children="#portal-column-one"
                css:theme-children="#column-one" />
        <replace css:content-children="#portal-column-two"
                css:theme-children="#column-two" />

    </rules>

</rules>
```

The XML document is rooted in a `<rules />` tag which declares three namespaces:

- The main Diazo namespace that applies to most of the tags and attributes
- The `css` namespace, which is used for attributes containing CSS selectors
- The `xsl` namespace, which can be used to write advanced rules using inline XSLT syntax

We first reference a theme HTML file using the `<theme />` tag. The `href` attribute indicates the location to the theme, here using a path relative to the folder containing the `rules.xml` file.

We only apply this theme and its associated rules if the node indicated by the CSS selector `#visual-portal-wrapper` (that is, an element with that ID) exists in the content, using the `css:if-content` attribute on the nested `<rules />` block. This ID exists on all standard Plone pages, but not on things like dialog boxes shown in the visual editor, which we do not want to style.

It is also possible to use a path condition, which will match on the path of the page. For example, if-path="/news/" will match everything in the /news folder, including the folder itself. See the Diazo documentation for further details.

Using conditions, we can enable different themes for different content pages or sections of our website. Diazo will pick the first theme where the corresponding condition is true. If a <theme /> tag without a condition is found, it will be used as the default when no other theme matches. Themes may be declared inside the top-level <rules /> tag if they apply unconditionally.

Additionally, a <notheme /> element may be combined with an if-content or other condition to conditionally disable the theme for certain requests.

Conditions can be applied to any rule. To apply the same condition to multiple rules, we can use a nested <rules /> tag, as we have done previously. Rules without conditions are always executed.

Diazo supports the following rules:

Rule	Purpose
<replace />	Replaces a node in the theme, or the children of a node, with a node or the children of a node, from the content. If no node is matched in the content, the theme node will still be dropped. Conditional rules can be used to circumvent this behavior.
<before /> and <after />	Place the matched node(s) in the content before or after a matched node, or all the children of a node, in the theme.
<drop />	Removes a node in the theme or the content. Unlike the other rules, <drop /> allows only theme or content to be specified, not both. However, it is possible (and common) to drop a node in the theme using a conditional selector of the content, for example: with <drop css:theme="#something" css:if-content="#another-thing" />.
<merge />	Merges attributes of the node matched in the content into attributes on the node matched in the theme. The main use case is to merge space-separated CSS classes, for example: <merge css:theme="body" css:content="body" attributes="class" />.

Rule	Purpose
`<strip />`	Removes a node from the theme or content, leaving its children intact.
`<copy />`	Copies attributes of a node matched in the content into the node matched in the theme.

The rules are controlled by a number of attributes. These are:

Attribute	Used for	Purpose

`content`
 	
`css:content`
 	
`content-children`
 	
`css:content-children`
	All rules	Select a content node to operate on, either by XPath or CSS3 selector. The `content-children` variant selects on all children (including text and comment nodes) of the matched node, but not the node itself.

`theme`
 	
`css:theme`
 	
`theme-children`
 	
`css:theme-children`
	All rules	Select a theme node to operate on, either by XPath or CSS3 selector. The `theme-children` variant selects all children (including text and comment nodes) of the matched node, but not the node itself. Hence, `<replace />` with `theme-children` leaves the matched node in place, but replaces all its children, while `<after />` with `theme-children` appends the nodes from the content as the last nodes inside the matched theme node.

`if`	All rules	Make the rule or nested set of rules conditional upon a specific XPath expression. This can be used to test variables, which may be passed into the theme from the **Theming** control panel.
`if-path`	All rules	Make the rule or nested set of rules apply only when the user is viewing a page matching the specified path. A leading / (forward slash) indicates the path should match at the start of the URL. A trailing / (forward slash) indicates the paths should match at the end. For an exact match, use both a leading and a trailing /.

Attribute	Used for	Purpose

attributes	`<replace />`
	`<drop />`
	`<copy />`
	`<merge />`
		A space-separated list of attributes to operate on. If specified for `<replace />` or `<drop />`, this indicates these will operate on attributes instead of nodes.
		
		Use `attributes="*"` to operate on all attributes in the content.

separator	`<merge />`	Separator is used when merging attribute values. Defaults to a single space.

method	`<replace />`
	`<before />`
	`<after />`
		If you have any `<drop />` or other rules that manipulate the content, and you do not want those manipulations to be taken into account when performing a replacement, you can add `method="raw"` to the rule to ensure it runs before any manipulation of the content.

> The choice of XPath or CSS selectors is arbitrary, and we can mix and match as appropriate. Behind the scenes, Diazo compiles a CSS selector down to an XPath expression. Note that some valid CSS3 expressions may not be compilable to XPath, forcing you to use XPath directly. If this happens, you will see an error message pinpointing the invalid expression in the console output and an un-themed site.

Diazo also allows the theme to be modified directly by the rules, by omitting the content attribute and instead including the relevant content in the rules file itself. For example:

```
<after theme-children="/html/head">
    <style type="text/css">
        .highlight { color: red; }
    </style>
</after>
```

It is even possible to use XSLT directly in this way. Here is an example that turns a two-column table into a definition list. The `xsl:for-each` loop operates on the content.

```
<replace css:theme="#details">
  <dl id="details">
        <xsl:for-each css:select="table#details > tr">
            <dt><xsl:copy-of select="td[1]/text()"/></dt>
```

```
        <dd><xsl:copy-of select="td[2]/node()"/></dd>
    </xsl:for-each>
  </dl>
</replace>
```

 For more information and documentation about Diazo, see http://diazo.org.

Creating a Diazo theme

Diazo themes may be deployed in various ways when using `plone.app.theming` to integrate Diazo with Plone:

- In a ZIP archive uploaded through the Diazo Theme control panel in Plone
- In a special Zope-wide resources directory on the filesystem
- In a resource directory inside a filesystem Python distribution

We will use the last option here which, although it requires a little more setup, affords us the most flexibility. Of course, it is possible to switch between these deployments modes, so we could have started with filesystem resource directory and then moved to a distribution later. See `http://pypi.python.org/pypi/plone.app.theming` for further details.

For this example, we use a static HTML mockup of the Optilux website, which looks similar to the following screenshot:

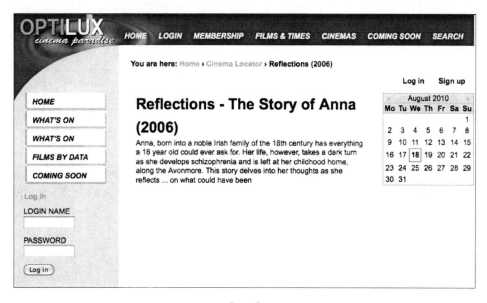

The Diazo version of the Optilux theme was kindly created by Rob Gietema of Four Digits (`http://fourdigits.nl/`).

Before we begin any Plone integration, we would procure or build this theme and test it in all relevant web browsers. This is also a good time to identify the key elements in the site, and consider how they may map to Plone's navigation, content, and other elements:

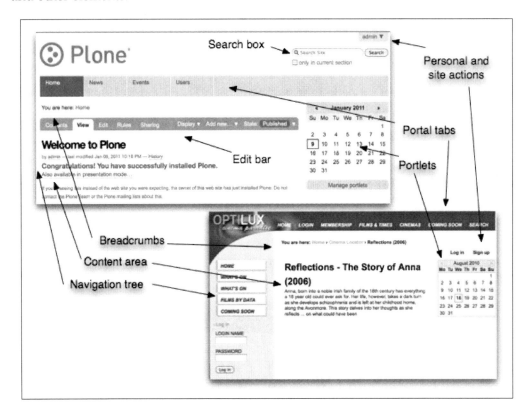

Creating a theme distribution

With the static theme ready, we can create a distribution for it to live in. As in *Chapter 5, Developing a Site Strategy*, we use `zopeskel` to create a basic distribution structure.

1. From within the `src/` directory, we run:

```
$ ../bin/zopeskel plone optilux.theme
```

- ◦ Again, stick with 'easy' mode and answer True when asked to create a GenericSetup profile.

2. As before, we will edit the generated setup.py file. We first update the install_requires line to add plone.app.theming as a dependency and add an extras_require line to enable the [test] extra:

```
install_requires=[
    'setuptools',
    'plone.app.theming',
],
extras_require={
    'test': ['plone.app.testing',]
},
```

We can also comment out or remove the setup_requires and paster_plugins line as we did in *Chapter 5, Developing a Site Strategy.*

3. Next, we will add some infrastructure to the optilux.theme package. We update the generated configure.zcml to look similar to the following code:

```
<configure>
    xmlns="http://namespaces.zope.org/zope"
    xmlns:i18n="http://namespaces.zope.org/i18n"
    xmlns:genericsetup="http://namespaces.zope.org/genericsetup"
    xmlns:plone="http://namespaces.plone.org/plone"
    i18n_domain="optilux.theme">
  <includeDependencies package="." />
  <plone:static
      directory="resources"
      type="theme"
      />
  <genericsetup:registerProfile
      name="default"
      title="Optilux Theme"
      directory="profiles/default"
      description='Extension profile for the "Optilux" Plone
theme.'
      provides="Products.GenericSetup.interfaces.EXTENSION"
      />
</configure>
```

Here, we include the plone.app.theming package as a dependency and register the installation profile. We also create a **static resource directory** of type theme for this package. This is where we will put the theme shortly. The <plone:static /> directive references a directory resources/ in the same directory as configure.zcml. We must create this directory manually.

Do not forget to declare the `plone` namespace on the root `<configure />` element and add the `<includeDependencies package="." />` line before using the `<plone:static />` directive.

4. Finally, we edit `profiles/default/metadata.xml` to make sure `plone.app.theming` is installed automatically when we install our theme add-on into Plone:

```
<?xml version="1.0"?>
<metadata>
  <version>1</version>
  <dependencies>
    <dependency>profile-plone.app.theming:default</dependency>
  </dependencies>
</metadata>
```

Adding the theme distribution to the buildout

With the outlines of our theme distribution in place, we can ensure it is installed with the buildout.

1. First, we edit `packages.cfg` to register the new distribution. We also add the Diazo known good version set to our `extends` list to ensure we have appropriate versions of all dependencies:

```
[buildout]
extensions = mr.developer buildout.dumppickedversions
extends =
# Known good sets of eggs we may be using
    http://dist.plone.org/release/4.1rc2/versions.cfg
    http://good-py.appspot.com/release/plone.app.
theming/1.0b8?plone=4.1rc2
    versions.cfg

versions = versions
unzip = true

# Egg sets
[eggs]
main =
    optilux.policy
test =
    optilux.policy [test]
    optilux.theme [test]
```

```
devtools =
    bpython
    plone.reload
    Products.PDBDebugMode
    Products.PrintingMailHost
    Products.DocFinderTab
[sources]
optilux.policy = fs optilux.policy
optilux.theme  = fs optilux.theme
```

Here, we have used version 1.0b8 of `plone.app.theming` as the base. This may not be the most appropriate release, so refer to the Diazo and `plone.app.theming` documentation as necessary.

2. Next, we will update the `optilux.policy` package to ensure `optilux.theme` is installed as a dependency. We edit `src/optilux.policy/setup.py` to make the `install_requires` parameter:

```
install_requires=[
        'setuptools',
        'Plone',
        'Products.PloneFormGen',
        'optilux.theme',
    ],
```

Since we used `<includeDependencies />` in `optilux.policy`, we do not need to explicitly include the `optilux.theme` configuration in `Optilux policy`'s `configure.zcml`.

3. We then edit `profiles/default/metadata.xml` to add:

```
<dependencies>
    <dependency>profile-Products.PloneFormGen:default</dependency>
    <dependency>profile-optilux.theme:default</dependency>
</dependencies>
```

4. With this in place, we should be able to run buildout again and see our new distribution and its dependencies, including `plone.app.theming` and `diazo`, to be downloaded and installed. So, we run:

```
$ bin/buildout
```

Installing lxml in Mac OS X

Diazo uses the lxml library to parse XML and execute XSLT. lxml in turn depends on the readily available libxml2 and libxslt C libraries. Unfortunately, Mac OS X at the time of writing ships with versions of these libraries that can cause problems for lxml, including seemingly random crashes.

To work around this, you can use a statically compiled version of lxml. Diazo depends on a version of lxml that should have static builds available for most platforms, but if you experience lxml problems, you can install your own static build by adding the following to your buildout.cfg:

```
[lxml]
recipe = z3c.recipe.staticlxml
egg = lxml
```

Add lxml as the first entry in the parts list and rerun buildout.

Adding the theme and rules

With our theme distribution created and installed, we can now build our rules file.

1. First, we add the static theme wholesale to the static directory we created inside the optilux.theme package. We also add a rules.xml file here, initially just a skeleton:

    ```
    <?xml version="1.0" encoding="UTF-8"?>
    <rules
        xmlns="http://namespaces.plone.org/diazo"
        xmlns:css="http://namespaces.plone.org/diazo/css"
        xmlns:xsl="http://www.w3.org/1999/XSL/Transform">

        <!-- Rules applying to standard Plone pages -->
        <rules css:if-content="#visual-portal-wrapper">

            <theme href="index.html" />

        </rules>

    </rules>
    ```

2. We can now start up Zope and go to the Plone **Add-ons** control panel to install Optilux Theme. This should install the **Diazo theme** control panel (as shown in the next screenshot).

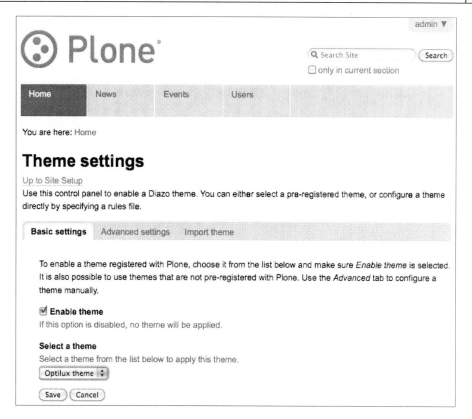

3. `optilux theme` should appear in the drop-down list. If we select it and choose **Enable theme**, we should see the static theme appear. Since we have not added any rules yet, this will in effect hide all of Plone's dynamic content.

If you are running Zope on `localhost`, make sure to access Plone using `localhost` as the hostname (for example: `http://localhost:8080/Plone`) instead of the IP address `127.0.0.1`. As a failsafe, `127.0.0.1` is added to the list of un-themed hostnames by default. Also note that the **Diazo theme** control panel itself explicitly disables theming by setting an `X-Theme-Disabled` response header.

4. We now need to add some rules. We will start with some boilerplate to copy over the page title for all Plone pages using Plone's default look-and-feel (which all have an element with the ID `visual-portal-wrapper`). We also add Plone's Meta tags and copy a few important attributes over from the `<body />` tag.

```
<?xml version="1.0" encoding="UTF-8"?>
```

```
<rules
    xmlns="http://namespaces.plone.org/diazo"
    xmlns:css="http://namespaces.plone.org/diazo/css"
    xmlns:xsl="http://www.w3.org/1999/XSL/Transform">

    <rules css:if-content="#visual-portal-wrapper">

        <theme href="index.html" />

        <drop theme="/html/head/meta" />
        <drop theme="/html/head/title" />

        <after content="/html/head/meta"
            theme-children="/html/head" />
        <after content="/html/head/title"
            theme-children="/html/head" />

        <copy attributes="class id dir"
            content="/html/body"
            theme="/html/body" />

    </rules>
</rules>
```

As long as Zope remains in debug mode (that is, it was started with `bin/instance fg`), changes should be reflected instantly, so we can reload the page. The only visual change so far will be the title of the web browser, but we can look at the page source to see Plone's `<meta />` and tags and `<body />` attributes.

Managing CSS and JavaScript resources

At this point, we have two important decisions to make:

- Do we want to include any of Plone's CSS and JavaScript resources?

- Do we want to make use of Plone's resource registries – the `portal_css` and `portal_javascripts` tools in the ZMI – to manage our resources?

We are about to pull in a lot of markup from Plone. It is unlikely that the theme's CSS will fully style this. There are three approaches we can take here:

- Pull in all of Plone's CSS. This styles everything, but can lead to CSS clashes and almost certainly means some CSS will be unused.

- Only use the theme's CSS. This usually means having to re-style some of Plone's markup from scratch.

- Strike a balance by pulling in only some of Plone's CSS resources.

For the Optilux theme, we will opt to include all of Plone's CSS.

The same argument goes for JavaScript, but here pulling in everything is usually the right choice, especially if we want to expose Plone's editing user interface through the theme.

On the second question, for high-performance sites it is usually advantageous to use Plone's resource registries to manage even the resources in the theme. Plone will merge resources and manage caching response headers, both of which are important for performance. However, we would still like the theme to render correctly without Plone running, so we cannot just move the resources out.

With this in mind, we take the following approach:

1. Register the CSS and JavaScript resources from the theme with `portal_css` and `portal_javascripts`, using GenericSetup.

2. Add conditions to these resources so that they are only rendered when the theme is in effect.

3. Optionally, also add conditions to the default resources so that they are not rendered when the theme is in effect.

4. Add a rule to the Diazo theme that drops all CSS and JavaScript resources from the theme; and another rule that copies all of Plone's CSS and JavaScript resources into the theme, in the order that Plone renders them

5. If necessary, add an additional stylesheet to the `portal_css` registry as the last entry, containing overrides and fixes for any conflicts between Plone's CSS and our theme's

To add the CSS files from the theme to the `portal_css` registry, we add a file in `profiles/default/cssregistry.xml` containing:

```
<?xml version="1.0"?>
<object name="portal_css">

  <stylesheet id="++theme++optilux.theme/stylesheets/main.css"
              expression="request/HTTP_X_THEME_ENABLED | nothing"
              applyPrefix="True" />

  <stylesheet id="++theme++optilux.theme/stylesheets/iefixes.css"
              expression="request/HTTP_X_THEME_ENABLED | nothing"
              conditionalcomment="IE"
              applyPrefix="True" />

</object>
```

The id is also the relative path to the resource. The `++theme++optilux.theme` prefix allows Plone to traverse to the `resources/` resource directory (the name is taken from name of the package containing the `configure.zcml` file where the `<plone:static />` directive appears). Inside this directory, we have `stylesheets/main.css` and `stylesheets/iefixes.css`.

The `expression` checks for a request header that is set by `plone.app.theming` when the theme is in effect. `applyPrefix` should be set to `True` for stylesheets registered in this way to ensure any background images and other resources specified with the `url()` syntax in the stylesheet work when Zope runs in non-debug mode and resource merging is in effect. The `conditionalcomment` can be used to set an Internet Explorer conditional comment, so that the relevant stylesheet is only used for Internet Explorer.

If we wanted to selectively turn off some Plone stylesheets when the theme is in effect, we could have added a tag such as:

```
<stylesheet id="public.css"
    expression="not:request/HTTP_X_THEME_ENABLED | nothing"
/>
```

The `id` should refer to an id already found in the `portal_css` tool in the ZMI.

The Optilux theme does not have any custom JavaScript, but the approach for themes that do is similar. The GenericSetup file is called `jsregistry.xml`, and could look something like this:

```
<?xml version="1.0"?>
<object name="portal_javascripts">

 <javascript
    id="++theme++my.theme/js/some-file.js"
    expression="request/HTTP_X_THEME_ENABLED | nothing" />

</object>
```

With these files added, we need to reinstall the `Optilux Theme` package in Plone's **Add-ons** control panel. We should now see the new resources in `portal_css`, but no changes to the themed pages until we add the following rules:

```
<?xml version="1.0" encoding="UTF-8"?>
<rules
    xmlns="http://namespaces.plone.org/diazo"
    xmlns:css="http://namespaces.plone.org/diazo/css"
    xmlns:xsl="http://www.w3.org/1999/XSL/Transform">

    <rules css:if-content="#visual-portal-wrapper">

        ...
```

```
<drop theme="/html/head/base" />
<drop theme="/html/head/style" />
<drop theme="/html/head/script" />
<drop theme="/html/head/link" />
<drop theme="/html/head/comment()" />

<after
    content="/html/head/base | /html/head/style | /html/head/
script | /html/head/link | /html/head/comment()"
    theme-children="/html/head"
    />

    ...

    </rules>
</rules>
```

Note that the XPath expression to append the resources to the theme's <head /> section uses an "or" to match a variety of tags. This ensures all <base />, <style />, <script />, and <link /> tags and comments (for IE conditional comments) are copied in the order they appear in the content relative to each other.

> *Why the* <base /> *tag?* Plone needs the <base /> tag to be included for relative links to work on folders with default pages set. There is some precarious use of conditional comments for the base tag to work reliably with Internet Explorer, which is why we include it in the combined <append /> rule.

Adding the rest of the rules

We are now ready to start replacing the placeholders in the theme with elements from the content. To make this easier, we can use two browser windows or tabs. In the first tab, we open a representative page in Plone with the theme enabled. In the second tab, we open the same URL, but append the query string parameter ?diazo.off=1. This will turn off the theme, assuming Zope is in debug mode.

> If you are running Zope locally, you can also bypass the theme by accessing Plone over http://127.0.0.1:8080 instead of http://localhost:8080.

We can now use a tool like Firebug in Firefox or the built-in inspector in Google Chrome to identify the HTML IDs, CSS classes, or XPath expressions of the elements we want to replace in the theme, and the corresponding elements in the content. We can then add rules one by one, reloading the themed page to check our work regularly.

Besides Firebug, which is a must-have for any web developer, the author regularly uses the Firefox XPath Checker add-on to test and debug XPath expressions.

After this process, we end up with the following rules file:

```
<?xml version="1.0" encoding="UTF-8"?>
<rules
    xmlns="http://namespaces.plone.org/diazo"
    xmlns:css="http://namespaces.plone.org/diazo/css"
    xmlns:xsl="http://www.w3.org/1999/XSL/Transform">

    <!-- Rules applying to standard Plone pages -->
    <rules css:if-content="#visual-portal-wrapper">

        <theme href="index.html" />

        <!-- Copy standard header tags, including base (very
             important for Plone default pages to work correctly),
             meta, title and style sheets/scripts, in the order they
             appear in the content.
          -->
        <drop theme="/html/head/meta" />
        <drop theme="/html/head/title" />
        <drop theme="/html/head/base" />
        <drop theme="/html/head/style" />
        <drop theme="/html/head/script" />
        <drop theme="/html/head/link" />
        <drop theme="/html/head/comment()" />

        <after content="/html/head/meta"
               theme-children="/html/head" />
        <after content="/html/head/title"
               theme-children="/html/head" />

        <after
            content="/html/head/base | /html/head/style | /html/head/
script | /html/head/link | /html/head/comment()"
               theme-children="/html/head"
            />

        <!-- Copy over the id/class attributes on the body tag.
             This is important for per-section styling -->
        <copy attributes="class id dir" content="/html/body"
               theme="/html/body" />

        <!-- Logo (link target) -->
        <copy attributes="href" css:content="#portal-logo"
```

```
                css:theme="#logo" />
        <!-- Site actions -->
        <replace css:content="#portal-siteactions li"
                css:theme-children="#actions" />

        <!-- User actions -->
        <!-- The logged-in actions are a list... -->
        <after css:content="#portal-personaltools li"
                css:theme-children="#actions" />
        <!-- ... but for anonymous users, it's a dl, so we build
            list elements using XSL directives
          -->
        <after css:theme-children="#actions">
            <xsl:for-each css:select="#anon-personalbar > a">
                <li><xsl:copy-of css:select="a"/></li>
            </xsl:for-each>
        </after>
        <!-- Global navigation -->
        <replace css:content='#portal-globalnav li'
                css:theme-children='#global-navigation' />

        <!-- Breadcrumbs -->
        <replace css:content-children='#portal-breadcrumbs'
                css:theme-children='#breadcrumbs' />

        <!-- Document Content -->
        <replace css:content="#content"
                css:theme="#document-content" />

        <!-- Edit bar -->
        <before css:content="#edit-bar"
                css:theme="#document-content" />

        <!-- Status messages not inside #content -->
        <drop css:content="#content .portalMessage"/>
        <before css:content=".portalMessage"
                css:theme="#document-content"
                method="raw" />

        <!-- Drop navtree images -->
        <drop css:content="dl#portletNavigationTree img" />

        <!-- Columns -->
        <replace css:content-children="#portal-column-one"
                css:theme-children="#column-one" />
        <replace css:content-children="#portal-column-two"
                css:theme-children="#column-two" />

        <!-- Footer -->
        <after css:content="#kss-spinner"
                theme-children="/html/body" />

    </rules>

</rules>
```

Notice how we have replaced the #document-content element in the theme with the entire #content div from Plone. This allows us to retain the ID #content as an indicator of the location of the main content area on the page. Much of Plone's CSS and JavaScript use this ID to target document content specifically, so it is usually a good idea to keep it in the themed site. Without it, you may find that things like JavaScript overlays do not work as expected.

As most of the rules mentioned earlier are straightforward, we will only discuss two of them in any detail:

First, note the two rules that both target the #actions area in the theme. The first one copies the elements from Plone's #portal-personaltools list, which is shown for logged-in users. The second builds a similar list for anonymous users. However, Plone outputs anonymous users' actions (such as **Log in**) as simple links not wrapped in a list. To avoid having to change the theme to accommodate this, we wrap the <a /> tags from Plone in <li /> tags using inline XSLT.

Second, we have had to use a pair of rules to manage status messages (with the CSS class portalMessage). These may appear both inside and outside the #content container, which we copy into the theme wholesale. To avoid duplicate messages, we drop from the content any .portalMessage inside #content, but we make sure the <before /> rule still sees such messages when copying them into the theme, by using method="raw".

At this point, our themed Plone site looks similar to the following screenshot:

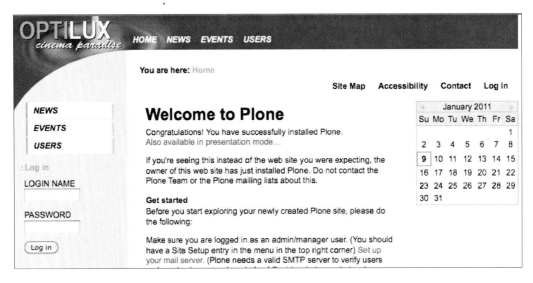

For this screenshot, we have also tweaked the portlet assignments at the root of the site, setting the `Navigation` portlet start level to `0`, adding a `Login` portlet in the left column, as well as a `Calendar` portlet in the right column.

Enabling the theme automatically

To support our goal of repeatable deployments, we would like the theme to be automatically configured when we install the `optilux.theme` package into Plone. We therefore add a `theme` file to `profiles/default/` containing:

```
<theme>
    <name>optilux.theme</name>
    <enabled>true</enabled>
</theme>
```

This will configure the theme in the configuration registry and enable it automatically.

Adding tests

As always, we will add tests to our theme. First, we add a `testing.py` module to the root of the `optilux.theme` package containing:

```python
from plone.app.testing import PloneSandboxLayer
from plone.app.testing import applyProfile
from plone.app.testing import PLONE_FIXTURE
from plone.app.testing import IntegrationTesting
from plone.app.testing import FunctionalTesting

from zope.configuration import xmlconfig

class OptiluxTheme(PloneSandboxLayer):

    defaultBases = (PLONE_FIXTURE,)

    def setUpZope(self, app, configurationContext):
        # Load ZCML
        import optilux.theme
        xmlconfig.file('configure.zcml', optilux.theme,
                            context=configurationContext)

    def setUpPloneSite(self, portal):
        applyProfile(portal, 'optilux.theme:default')

OPTILUX_THEME_FIXTURE = OptiluxTheme()
OPTILUX_THEME_INTEGRATION_TESTING = IntegrationTesting(
    bases=(OPTILUX_THEME_FIXTURE,), name="OptiluxTheme:Integration")
```

```
OPTILUX_THEME_FUNCTIONAL_TESTING = FunctionalTesting(
    bases=(OPTILUX_THEME_FIXTURE,), name="OptiluxTheme:Functional")
```

This is the same boilerplate we saw in *Chapter 5, Developing a Site Strategy* except that we also create a layer for functional testing.

Our tests all live in a single module called `tests.py`. We first define some integration tests that ensure the CSS registry is configured and that the theme is registered:

```python
import unittest2 as unittest
import transaction

from optilux.theme.testing import OPTILUX_THEME_INTEGRATION_TESTING
from optilux.theme.testing import OPTILUX_THEME_FUNCTIONAL_TESTING

from plone.testing.z2 import Browser
from plone.app.testing import SITE_OWNER_NAME
from plone.app.testing import SITE_OWNER_PASSWORD

from zope.component import getUtility
from Products.CMFCore.utils import getToolByName

from plone.registry.interfaces import IRegistry
from plone.app.theming.interfaces import IThemeSettings

class TestSetup(unittest.TestCase):

    layer = OPTILUX_THEME_INTEGRATION_TESTING

    def test_css_registry_configured(self):
        portal = self.layer['portal']
        cssRegistry = getToolByName(portal, 'portal_css')
        self.assertTrue(
                "++theme++optilux.theme/stylesheets/main.css"
                in cssRegistry.getResourceIds()
            )
        self.assertTrue(
                "++theme++optilux.theme/stylesheets/iefixes.css"
                in cssRegistry.getResourceIds()
            )

    def test_theme_configured(self):
        registry = getUtility(IRegistry)
        settings = registry.forInterface(IThemeSettings)
        self.assertEqual(settings.enabled, True)
        self.assertEqual(settings.rules,
                "/++theme++optilux.theme/rules.xml"
            )
        self.assertEqual(settings.absolutePrefix,
                "/++theme++optilux.theme"
            )
```

Next, we define a **functional test** using the **test browser** to simulate browser interaction. This needs to use the functional testing layer, and we need to commit any changes to the test fixture before opening the test browser. We then attempt to render two pages—a Plone page, and a ZMI page, checking that the theme markup appears in the former, but not the latter.

```
class TestRendering(unittest.TestCase):

    layer = OPTILUX_THEME_FUNCTIONAL_TESTING

    def test_render_plone_page(self):
        app = self.layer['app']
        portal = self.layer['portal']

        transaction.commit()

        browser = Browser(app)

        browser.open(portal.absolute_url())
        self.assertTrue('<div id="wrapper">' in browser.contents)

    def test_render_zmi_page(self):
        app = self.layer['app']
        portal = self.layer['portal']

        transaction.commit()

        browser = Browser(app)
        browser.addHeader('Authorization', 'Basic %s:%s' % (
                SITE_ OWNER_NAME, SITE_OWNER_PASSWORD,))

        browser.open(portal.absolute_url() + '/manage_main')
        self.assertFalse('<div id="wrapper">' in browser.contents)
```

 To learn more about the test browser and functional testing, refer to the plone.testing documentation at http://pypi.python.org/pypi/plone.testing.

Variations on the theming approach

The Optilux example demonstrates the most common approach to theming Plone using Diazo. There are however, a few other approaches that are worth being aware of, as we will discuss in the following sections.

Separate public and editing interfaces

For the Optilux side, we have chosen to integrate Plone's editing user interface into the theme. This retains Plone's traditional in-place editing capabilities and WYSIWYG (what you see is what you get) editing. For some designs, finding a place for Plone's various user interface elements can be tricky, and it may be preferable to avoid pulling in any of Plone's CSS or JavaScript at all and let content authors use an 'un-styled' view of Plone.

To set this up, you need to configure a dedicated domain name for content authors, typically a subdomain such as `admin.example.org`. You can then turn off the theme for this URL using a rule like:

```
<notheme if-host="admin.example.org" />
```

We will cover how to set up Plone on a public-facing domain in *Chapter 16, Next Steps* and *Chapter 17, Setting up a Production Server*.

Reading the theme from a separate server

It is possible to load the theme and/or rules from a separate web server. This allows you to deploy themes for multiple Plone installations centrally, or even use an existing website as the basis for a theme—great for demos or a quick proof-of-concept.

In the **Diazo theme** control panel, use the **Advanced settings** tab to enter an URL for a rules file. This can be a remote URL, a local `file://` URL on the server, or even a file uploaded to Plone. In the rules file, use a `<theme />` tag such as:

```
<theme href="http://example.org/index.html" />
```

If the theme HTML uses relative URL, set the absolute URL prefix in the **Diazo theme** control panel as required. Finally, make sure **Read network** is enabled.

Sharing a theme across multiple systems

As previously mentioned, Diazo is not Plone-specific. It is possible to deploy a compiled Diazo theme (an XSLT file) directly into web servers such as Apache or nginx. This makes it possible to theme any system, or even to share a single theme (perhaps with different rules files) across multiple applications to create seamless user experiences. Refer to the Diazo documentation for details.

Overriding visual elements

Diazo is a powerful theming engine, and as long as Plone outputs sufficient markup, we can achieve virtually any look and feel by combining Diazo with CSS. However, there are a few situations where we need to modify the markup that Plone produces.

As we saw in *Chapter 4*, *Basics of Customization*, Zope provides a multitude of hooks that can be used to customize skin layer resources, browser views, viewlets, and portlets, the core display technologies used in Plone. However, such customization can be cumbersome and requires an understanding of each of the aforementioned concepts. For theming purposes, we can normally get away with a lighter touch.

Registering a browser layer

Before we can make visual customizations, we need to register a **browser layer**. This is a Zope marker interface that is applied to the request during traversal when our theme distribution is installed in our Plone site, allowing Zope to determine when the customizations are to take effect. We put the interface in a module called `interfaces.py` in the `optilux.theme` package:

```
from zope.interface import Interface

class IOptiluxTheme(Interface):
    """Marker interface that defines a ZTK browser layer.
    """
```

To install this browser layer when the theme package is installed, we add the following in `profiles/default/browserlayer.xml`:

```
<layers>
    <layer
        name="optilux.theme"
        interface="optilux.theme.interfaces.IOptiluxTheme"
        />
</layers>
```

As with all GenericSetup configuration, we must reinstall the package in Plone for the changes to be applied.

The layout policy view

In the Optilux theme, we always want to show the left hand side column. Plone explicitly hides this for certain templates, such as the search results form, to provide more space for their main content. This policy is controlled by a helper view (that is, one that is not rendered, but contains logic that is consulted by other views) called plone_layout, which looks for the request parameters disable_plone.leftcolumn and disable_plone.rightcolumn to determine whether the columns should be hidden. The plone_layout view is defined in plone.app.layout.

For the purposes of the Optilux website, we will customize the plone_layout view with our own implementations of two of its methods:

- have_portlets(): This is used to tell Plone whether there are any portlets to render. Here we short-circuit the hook that is used to disable a column for the left column only.

- bodyClass(): This is used to calculate the CSS classes set on the <body /> tag. Here, we add a CSS class noRightColumn if the right column is disabled, so that we can use this in our stylesheet to ensure pages with no right column work correctly.

We will add our custom layout policy view to a module called layout.py in optilux.theme. This begins with:

```
from zope.component import getMultiAdapter
from zope.component import queryMultiAdapter
from zope.component import queryUtility

from plone.portlets.interfaces import IPortletManagerRenderer
from plone.portlets.interfaces import IPortletManager

from plone.app.layout.globals.layout import LayoutPolicy
from plone.memoize.view import memoize

class OptiluxLayoutPolicy(LayoutPolicy):
```

We first override the have_portlets() method, short-circuiting evaluating when asked to determine whether the right-hand column should be shown:

```
@memoize
def have_portlets(self, manager_name, view=None):

    if manager_name != 'plone.leftcolumn':
        force_disable = self.request.get(
            'disable_' + manager_name, None)
        if force_disable is not None:
            return not bool(force_disable)
```

The rest of this method is a copy of the Plone 4 default implementation:

```
context = self.context
if view is None:
    view = self

manager = queryUtility(IPortletManager, name=manager_name)
if manager is None:
    return False

renderer = queryMultiAdapter(
    (context, self.request, view, manager),
    IPortletManagerRenderer)
if renderer is None:
    renderer = getMultiAdapter(
        (context, self.request, self, manager),
        IPortletManagerRenderer)

return renderer.visible
```

Next, we override the `bodyClass()` method to add a custom CSS class when the right column is hidden.

```
def bodyClass(self, template, view):
    bodyClass = super(OptiluxLayoutPolicy, self).bodyClass(
                    template, view)
    if not self.have_portlets('plone.rightcolumn', view):
        bodyClass += ' noRightColumn'
    return bodyClass
```

 Do not worry if you do not recognize all the functions and patterns shown in the previous code just yet. If you compare this with the original from `plone.app.layout`, you will see that we have not made many changes.

We can now register this view as an override that is to be used when our browser layer has been enabled. In `configure.zcml` we have:

```
<configure
    xmlns="http://namespaces.zope.org/zope"
    xmlns:i18n="http://namespaces.zope.org/i18n"
    xmlns:genericsetup="http://namespaces.zope.org/genericsetup"
    xmlns:browser="http://namespaces.zope.org/browser"
    xmlns:plone="http://namespaces.plone.org/plone"
    i18n_domain="optilux.theme">
```

```
    . . .
    <!-- Override the layout policy view -->
    <browser:page
        name="plone_layout"
        for="*"
        layer=".interfaces.IOptiluxTheme"
        permission="zope.Public"
        class=".layout.OptiluxLayoutPolicy"
        allowed_interface="plone.app.layout.globals.interfaces.
ILayoutPolicy"
        />
</configure>
```

If we now restart Zope and reinstall the theme package through the **Add-ons** control panel, we should see the new policy take effect.

Overriding templates

To fully customize a Zope resource, we normally need to make a ZCML registration like the one we saw previously, or install a custom CMF skin layer, as illustrated in *Chapter 4, Basics of Customization*. For theming purposes, however, we are usually only interested in customizing the markup in a Zope Page Template (`*.pt` or `*.cpt`) file. Any Python logic or detailed resource registration can be left as it is.

For such simple template customizations, we can use the template customization support in `plone.app.themingplugins`. As its name suggests, `plone.app.themingplugins` contains a set of plugins for `plone.app.theming` that provide additional, advanced functionality for Diazo theme developers. To enable it, we must add it as a dependency in `setup.py` of the `optilux.theme` and rerun the buildout:

```
install_requires=[
    'setuptools',
    'plone.app.theming',
    'plone.app.themingplugins',
],
```

The template customization support in `plone.app.themingplugins` is based on `z3c.jbot` ("just a bunch of templates"). This allows us to swap out the page template file used in a view, viewlet, portlet or skin layer resource by employing a simple convention: We place page template files in an `overrides/` directory inside the theme resource directory with a name made up of the dotted name of the Python package where the original template is found and its filename.

At the time of writing, template overrides only work on the filesystem. They will be ignored for themes imported through the **Diazo theme** control panel as a ZIP archive.

For example, if we wanted to customize the template `dashboard.pt` found in the `plone.app.layout.dashboard` package, the override file would be called `plone.app.layout.dashboard.dashboard.pt`. This also works for resources in file system directory views, so `search_form.pt` in `Products.CMFPlone`'s `skins/plone_forms` directory becomes `Products.CMFPlone.skins.plone_forms.search_form.pt`.

 In *Chapter 3, The Development Environment* we used `collective.recipe.omelette` to create links to all installed distributions in `parts/omelette`. We can use this to find templates to customize. For example, we can perform a full-text search in this directory to locate templates containing markup or text we see in the browser. The dotted name then becomes the file's path relative to the `parts/omelette` directory with (back) slashes replaced by dots.

We first create the `overrides/` directory in `resources/` directory of the `optilux.theme`, alongside `rules.xml`. We can then put override templates into this directory. As an example, we will make a small tweak to the template for Plone's `path_bar` viewlet, which contains the **You are here** breadcrumbs. We want to change the separators between the breadcrumbs from right angle quotes (`&raquo;`) to right arrows (`&rarr;`).

A full text search of the `parts/omelette` directory reveals that this template is found in the package `plone.app.layout.viewlets` and is called `path_bar.pt`. We therefore create a copy of this file in our `overrides/` directory called `plone.app.layout.viewlets.path_bar.pt`. We can then modify this file as required.

After a Zope restart, we should see the changes take effect, provided our theme and browser layer have been installed.

 For more details refer to the `plone.app.theming` documentation at `http://pypi.python.org/pypi/plone.app.theming`.

Summary

In this chapter we have covered:

- The Diazo theming engine
- Creating a Python distribution for a Diazo theme
- Configuring and testing a Diazo theme for a Plone site
- Overriding Plone's layout policy
- Customizing templates using `z3c.jbot` conventions

We have not spent much time discussing fundamental web technologies such as HTML and CSS. Creating usable, accessible, maintainable, standards-compliant, and cross-browser compatible designs with HTML and CSS deserves a book in its own right. There are plenty of good resources online as well. If you are the type of web developer who uses a `<font />` tag every now and then, manages all layout with `<table />` and is not quite sure how to float a box to the right of a block of text, you owe it to yourself to spend some time with a good CSS reference.

This concludes Part 2 of the book. In Part 3, we will sink our teeth into Python, as we learn how to develop new content types, views, and other components.

Part 3

Developing New Functionality

Nine Core Concepts of Zope Programming

Custom Content Types

Standalone Views and Forms

Relational Databases

Users and their Permissions

Dynamic User Interfaces with jQuery

Summary and Potential Enhancement

Nine Core Concepts of Zope Programming

Now that we have learned how to set up and customize Plone, we are nearly ready to start developing brand new functionality for our application. This often means writing new content types, with custom views and forms to manage them. Sometimes, we will also need to create forms and pages that are not connected to any particular content type.

However, before we continue with Optilux Cinemas, we will take a look at the core principles that underpin Zope programming. Writing software for Zope is a little different from writing software for other web programming platforms such as PHP or ASP.NET. Having a solid understanding of Zope's core concepts will help you understand the examples which follow in this book, and help you apply what you learn to your own applications.

In this chapter, we will cover:

- **Object publishing** and **traversal**, which is how Zope relates URLs to content objects
- **Persistence**, Zope's transparent data storage mechanism
- **The catalog**, which is used for indexing and searching content
- **Interfaces**, which are used to describe components and their behavior
- **Component configuration** with ZCML or convention-over-configuration techniques
- **Utilities**, which are used to register global services or collections of related components
- **Adapters**, which are used to apply additional behavior to objects or classes of objects without modifying the objects themselves

- **Views** and **viewlets**, Zope's fundamental presentation components
- **Events**, which can be used to execute custom logic when content is added, modified, and so on

About the examples

The examples in this chapter are kept intentionally frivolous, and demonstrate concepts in isolation. They use Python **doctest** syntax, and most of them can be found in the `optilux.codeexamples` distribution that accompanies this book.

You can build and run these tests using:

```
$ cd optilux.codeexamples
$ python2.6 bootstrap.py --distribute
$ bin/buildout
$ bin/test
```

If you are brand new to Zope and Plone programming, you may find this chapter a little intense on first reading. If so, do not get discouraged! It may be easier to skim this chapter first, and come back to it as you encounter different concepts again in subsequent chapters. Alternatively, you may want to explore and play with the `optilux.codeexamples` package.

Object publishing and traversal

Consider a URL: `http://example.org/guitars/fender/strat.html`.

If this server was running Apache serving up HTML pages, then `guitars` and `fender` would probably be directories, and `strat.html` could be a static HTML page. If the server was using PHP, then perhaps `strat.html` would be called `strat.php` and consist of HTML with PHP code for branching, looping, and other logic. Languages such as ASP.NET and Cold Fusion are similar. Other frameworks, such as Ruby on Rails or Django rely on URL pattern matching to dispatch a request to a particular controller.

In Zope, the different parts of the URL are (in most cases) related to object publishing. For example, `guitars` and `fender` may be container objects, and `strat.html` could be the name of an object inside the `fender` container. `strat.html` could also be the name of an attribute or method on `fender`, a view (more on those in a little while) or a method alias. As we saw in *Chapter 4, Basics of Customization*, parts of the path could also be acquired from a skin layer or parent folder.

In the words of *Jon Stahl*, former Plone Foundation Board President: "Data in Zope is like a flowchart. Data in other web application frameworks is like a spreadsheet".

The process of determining which object to publish is called **URL traversal**. Zope will start at the **application root** – the root node in the ZODB, normally the place where a Plone site lives – and look for an item matching the first part of the URL, in this case an object called `guitars`. Zope will then look at the next part of the URL – `fender` – and try to find it, using the following logic:

1. If `fender` is an attribute on the `guitars` object, traversal will continue from this attribute.

2. If `fender` can be looked up as a view that is registered for `guitars`, this will be used instead.

3. If `guitars` supports the Python dictionary interface and `fender` is a valid key in it, the value at that key will be used.

4. If `fender` cannot be found, a `NotFound` exception is raised, which in Plone will result in an error page and a 404 response.

When an object is found, Zope will attempt to call it and render it as a stream of data that will be sent to the browser. Page templates and other items implement the `__call__()` method to render themselves. Some objects implement an `index_html()` method instead, which will be used in preference over `__call__()`.

Plone has some additional logic that determines the default view for a content object when the URL does not explicitly include the name of a page template, script, or method alias to use. It works as follows:

1. If an object provides the Plone-specific `IBrowserDefault` interface (normally using `Products.CMFDynamicViewFTI.browserdefault. BrowserDefaultMixin` as a base class), then the currently selected **layout** (as managed by the **Display** menu in Plone) or, if applicable, the current **default page** (an object set as the default view of a folder, also from the display menu) will be used.

2. If there is a `(Default)` **method alias** for the content type of the object that is being displayed, this will be queried to find a page template or view to display. Method aliases are defined in the **Factory Type Information (FTI)** of an object, as found in `portal_types` in the ZMI.

3. If there is no `(Default)` alias, but there is a `view` action in the FTI (this is the action that gets rendered as the **View** tab on the object when viewed in Plone), this will be resolved to find out which page template to display.

Because this logic is already in place for the base classes used by virtually all content objects in Plone, you will rarely need to worry about the details, but it is important to understand how attributes and containment can be used to influence what will be displayed.

Containment and URLs

URL traversal thus normally walks the **containment hierarchy**, also known as the **object graph**, in the ZODB. Each object has exactly one parent, and everything is ultimately a child of the **application root**. Three methods, available on all regular content objects, are used to reference the containment hierarchy:

- `absolute_url()` returns an absolute URL to an object, which can be safely rendered as a link to the user. It will take into account the actual URL (including the server name) that the server has assumed, including any virtual hosting setup.

- `absolute_url_path()` returns the path segment of `absolute_url()`, that is, without the hostname and protocol.

- `getPhysicalPath()` returns a tuple that includes each element of the path, all the way to the application root.

Note that in most hosting scenarios, the application is hosted in such a way that the Plone site appears to be the root of the server, even though to Zope, it lives one level down, inside the Zope application root. Therefore, it is not safe to construct URLs manually from physical paths or to persist URLs as returned by `absolute_url()`. However, physical paths are useful as unique identifiers of objects (at least until those objects are moved by the user), and are frequently used when constructing catalog searches. A common construct for converting the physical path tuple to a /-separated string is `'/'.join(context.getPhysicalPath())`. In particular, this is what we pass to the catalog when searching its `path` index.

Hence, if an object called `taylor` is found inside a Plone site called `guitarsrus`, in a folder called `acoustic`, its absolute URL could be `http://localhost:8080/guitarsrus/acoustic/taylor`. As we will learn in *Chapter 17, Setting up a Production Server*, it could also be exposed using **virtual hosting**, for example assuming the URL `http://example.org/acoustic/taylor`. In both cases, the physical path would be `/guitarsrus/acoustic/taylor`, so `taylor.getPhysicalPath()` would return a tuple `('', 'guitarsrus', 'acoustic', 'taylor')`.

In the ZODB object graph, nodes (or rather, objects capable of acting as containers) are known as **folderish** objects and leaves are called **non-folderish** objects. A **folderish** object has the special attribute `isPrinicipiaFolderish` set to `True`; non-folderish objects have this set to `False`.

 Why `isPrincipiaFolderish`? A long, long time ago, Zope was known as *Principia*.

Plone also introduces the concept of a **non-structural folder**, which is just a folderish object that does not appear to be a folder in Plone's user interface. Non-structural folders are distinguished by providing the interface `Products.CMFPlone.interfaces.INonStructuralFolder`. You will sometimes see the term **structural folder** used to refer to 'real' folders.

Recall that traversal checks for attributes before anything else. In Zope 2, folderish objects, specifically those that derive from `OFS.ObjectManager`, implement `__getattr_()` in such a way that any attempt to get an attribute that is not directly found on the folderish object itself will result in an attempt to retrieve a contained object. Each containable object has an ID that is unique in its folder. This can be obtained by calling `getId()` on the contained object.

As you may have guessed, this sometimes leads to naming conflicts between contained objects and methods and attributes on folders. In Plone, names that would lead to conflicts are treated as 'reserved' and any object that is added will be renamed to create an unambiguous name. In newer code, the preference is to use mapping semantics, that is, `__getitem__()`, instead of attribute semantics, to model containment.

Here is an example of using mapping semantics and `getId()` to retrieve an object from its container. We first create a document with ID `guitars` inside the portal, and then obtain it as an attribute on that folder. The `invokeFactory()` method, available on any standard folder, comes from `Products.CMFCore.PortalFolder` and takes as arguments a portal type name (as found in the `portal_types` tool) and an ID, as well as any initial properties, passed as keyword parameters.

```
>>> name = self.folder.invokeFactory('Document', 'favorites',
...                                  title=u"Favorite Guitars")
>>> obj = portal[name]
>>> obj.getId()
'favorites'
```

To discover the parent of an object, we can use the `aq_parent()` function:

```
>>> from Acquisition import aq_parent
>>> aq_parent(obj) is portal
True
>>> obj.aq_parent is portal
True
```

Acquisition chains

As you may have guessed from the previous examples, containment hierarchies are linked to Zope **acquisition**. Recall from *Chapter 4, Basics of Customization*, how acquisition allows attributes on objects to come from parents – normally through the containment hierarchy – in what is known as an **acquisition chain**. It is possible for an object to have more than one acquisition chain, for example if it is being explicitly 'wrapped' into a new chain as we will see in a moment. Hence, it is normally safer to ask for the innermost chain when we want to walk the containment hierarchy:

```
>>> from Acquisition import aq_parent, aq_inner
>>> containment_parent = aq_parent(aq_inner(obj))
```

There are two base classes that signal an object's participation in acquisition. Most content objects inherit `Acquisition.Implicit`, which means that `_getattr_()` is implemented in such a way that if an attribute is not found on the object, the parents in the (outermost) acquisition chain will be queried. This is the type of acquisition we saw in *Chapter 4, Basics of Customization*. Bear in mind that this applies both to containment and to attributes defined in code. Using **implicit acquisition** (for example, during URL traversal), an object contained in a parent folder may be returned if it matches the name of the requested attribute.

If we need to temporarily 'turn off' implicit acquisition, we can use the `aq_explicit` attribute, which is provided by `Acquisition.Implicit`. Use the `aq_base` function to discard the **acquisition wrapper** and get the raw object when testing object reference equivalence. Without `aq_base`, we would be comparing the object references of the acquisition wrappers themselves, not the objects they wrap.

```
>>> from Acquisition import aq_base
>>> favorites = folder['favorites']

>>> acquiring = folder.favorites
>>> aq_base(acquiring) is aq_base(favorites)
True

>>> non_acquiring = getattr(folder.aq_explicit, 'favorites', None)
>>> non_acquiring is None
True
```

The other type of acquisition is **explicit acquisition**, provided by the `Acquisition.Explicit` base class. Here, attributes are not acquired from parents in the chain implicitly as they are with `Acquisition.Implicit`. Explicit acquisition still maintains an acquisition chain, which is crucial for Zope security and containment. Methods such as `absolute_url()` and `getPhysicalPath()`, which rely on acquisition to construct a path, continue to work.

An object's **acquisition chain** is constructed dynamically, during traversal or inspection from code. If an attribute on an acquisition-aware object returns another acquisition-aware object, then the former object is the immediate acquisition chain parent of the returned object. The acquisition chain can be inspected using the `aq_chain()` function:

```
>>> from Acquisition import aq_chain, aq_inner
>>> aq_chain(portal.favorites) # doctest: +ELLIPSIS
[<ATDocument at /plone/favorites>, <PloneSite at /plone>, <Application
at >, <ZPublisher.BaseRequest.RequestContainer object at ...>]

>>> aq_chain(folder.favorites) # doctest: +ELLIPSIS
[<ATDocument at /plone/favorites used for /plone/folder>, <ATFolder at
/plone/folder>, <PloneSite at /plone>, <Application at >, <ZPublisher.
BaseRequest.RequestContainer object at ...>]
```

Notice how the acquisition chain for `favorites` is different depending on whether it was acquired from `portal` (which also happens to be its containment parent) or `folder` (via implicit acquisition). We can explicitly request the innermost chain, which is normally the containment chain:

```
>>> aq_chain(aq_inner(portal.favorites)) # doctest: +ELLIPSIS
[<ATDocument at /plone/favorites>, <PloneSite at /plone>, <Application
at >, <ZPublisher.BaseRequest.RequestContainer object at ...>]
```

Also, notice how the final parent in the acquisition chain that results from URL traversal is a special **request container** object. You will sometimes see this:

```
request = context.REQUEST
```

Here, the `REQUEST` variable is implicitly acquired from the context. The preceding construct will be deprecated over time, however, in favor of using `aq_get()`:

```
from Acquisition import aq_get
request = aq_get(context, 'REQUEST')
```

This achieves the same thing, but is explicit about invoking acquisition. It works for both implicit and explicit acquisition-aware objects.

Sometimes we need to control the acquisition chain directly. This generally occurs when we are trying to make an object appear as if it came from somewhere other than where it was originally stored, either as part of a security scheme, or to fool implicit acquisition. To do so, we can use the __of__() method, which is part of any acquisition-aware object.

In the following example, we instantiate a content object in memory, without connecting it to the containment hierarchy, and then wrap it in the acquisition context of the portal:

```
>>> from Products.ATContentTypes.content.document import ATDocument
>>> temp_document = ATDocument('temp_document')
>>> aq_chain(temp_document)
[<ATDocument at temp_document>]
>>> aq_chain(temp_document.__of__(portal)) # doctest: +ELLIPSIS
[<ATDocument at /plone/temp_document>, <PloneSite at /plone>,
<Application at >, <ZPublisher.BaseRequest.RequestContainer object at
...>]
```

 Manual acquisition wrapping with _of_() is an advanced concept, and one you are likely to use rarely, if at all.

Path traversal

In page templates or actions (that is, places where **TALES expressions** are used), you will sometimes see expressions such as context/guitars/fender. This is using **path traversal** relative to a particular object, employing a similar heuristic to the one described for URL traversal. Acquisition is taken into account here too.

Path traversal can be invoked from Python code relative to a content object, using this syntax:

```
>>> setRoles(portal, TEST_USER_NAME, ('Manager',))

>>> guitarsId = portal.invokeFactory('Folder', 'guitars')
>>> fenderId = portal[name].invokeFactory('Document', 'fender')

>>> portal.unrestrictedTraverse('guitars/fender')
<ATDocument at /plone/guitars/fender>

>>> fenderPath = \
...     '/'.join(portal[guitarsId][fenderId].getPhysicalPath())
>>> fenderPath
'/plone/guitars/fender'
```

```
>>> portal.unrestrictedTraverse(fenderPath)
<ATDocument at /plone/guitars/fender>
```

There is also a `restrictedTraverse()` method, which has the same semantics, but performs security checks for each traversal step, in the same way as skin layer page templates and scripts are subject to 'untrusted code' security checks as explained in *Chapter 6, Security and Workflow*.

 Path expressions in page templates can also 'traverse' to elements inside dictionaries and lists. This does not apply to the `restrictedTraverse()`/`unrestrictedTraverse()` methods.

Persistence in the ZODB

When working with Zope, developers are largely free from having to worry about persistence. Zope begins a new transaction for each request. If an error occurs (that is, an uncaught exception is raised), the transaction is rolled back and no changes are written. If no error occurs, the transaction is committed and any changes to objects connected to the ZODB object graph are saved.

Transactions

Transactions are managed by the `transaction` module. It is possible to manually begin and end transactions, but in practice the only operation we are likely to perform outside of tests is to set a **savepoint**. A savepoint is like a sub-transaction. It is required before certain operations, but it also helps to free up memory by writing the partial transaction to a disk cache.

 A very small number of functions require a savepoint to run in combination. Most commonly, if you need to use the `manage_cutObjects()` and `manage_pasteObjects()` methods from `OFS.CopySupport` in the same transaction, you may need to place a savepoint between them.

To set a savepoint, use:

```
import transaction
savepoint = transaction.savepoint()
```

It is now possible to call `savepoint.rollback()` to roll back this sub-transaction. If we are only interested in freeing up memory, we can use an **optimistic savepoint**:

```
transaction.savepoint(optimistic=True)
```

This still returns a value, but rolling back an optimistic savepoint will result in an error.

If we need to abort a transaction, we can raise an unhandled exception. Note that the ZODB error handling machinery uses a special exception called a `ConflictError` to deal with write conflicts when multiple threads attempt to modify the same object. A conflicted transaction can almost always be resolved automatically, but we must let this exception go uncaught, allowing Zope to **retry** the failed transaction.

 Do not use a bare `try...except` clause around code that could cause a ZODB write, and thus could raise a `ConflictError`. Always let a `ConflictError` go unhandled. Of course, you should try to avoid bare excepts in any case.

To ensure `ConflictErrors` are not swallowed, we will sometimes use code like this:

```
from ZODB.POSException import ConflictError

try:
    # some unpredictable operation that may cause a write
except ConflictError:
    raise
except Exception:
    # Swallow other errors or handle in some other way
```

Object persistence

For an object to be persisted, it must either be a **primitive** (for example, an integer or string) or of a class deriving from `persistence.Persistent`. All Plone content types ultimately derive from this base class. The base classes we will use in *Chapter 10, Custom Content Types* to build new content types properly derive from `Persistent` as well.

To be saved, an object must be connected to the ZODB object graph, by being set as an attribute of another persistent object or placed into a persistent mapping. This is what happens when a content object is added to a folderish parent in Plone, for example. When an attribute or mapping value is accessed later, the ZODB will transparently load the associated object from the disk if necessary.

The ZODB will automatically detect when a persisted object has been changed. Those changes will be saved when the transaction is committed. The exception is that if an object has a Python list or dict as an attribute, and a value in that list or dict is changed, Zope will not be able to detect it. If no other changes took place for that object, the changes may be lost.

To explicitly tell the ZODB to persist an object, we can set the _p_changed property to True:

```
>>> someobj.somedict['key1'] = "new value"
>>> someobj._p_changed = True
```

Alternatively, we can use the classes persistent.mapping.PersistentMapping or persistent.list.PersistentList. These act exactly like standard dicts and lists, but derive from Persistent and will set _p_changed as necessary:

```
>>> from persistent.mapping import PersistentMapping
>>> someobj.somedict = PersistentMapping()
>>> someobj.somedict['key1'] = "new value"
```

The PersistentMapping and PersistentList types are not recommended for large data sets (hundreds of items or more). This is because each time the ZODB saves an object, it will essentially write out a new copy of it. Every time an item in one of these data structures is changed, the entire dict or list is versioned.

At least with the default ZODB FileStorage, which stores the database in the Data.fs file. This is what allows the **Undo** tab in the ZMI to work. It also makes the ZODB very fast. On frequently changing sites, the ZODB should be **packed** regularly. You can do so from the **Maintenance** control panel in Plone, or the **Control_Panel** in the ZMI. In *Chapter 17, Setting up a Production Server*, we will look at how to automate this process.

For large data sets, the BTrees module provides several optimized data structures, which do not suffer from this problem. They come in sets (IOSet, OOSet, OISet, IISet), sorted sets (IOTreeSet, OOTreeSet, OITreeSet, IITreeSet) and mappings (IOBTree, OOBTree, OIBTree, IIBTree), designed for integer or object keys or values. For example, BTrees.IOBTree.IOSet is an unordered set with integer keys, while BTrees.OIBTree.OIBTree is a mapping with object keys and integer values. See the BTrees.Interfaces module for more information.

The most common type of object key in an OIBTree or OOBTree is a string. For example, Plone's *Folder* type stores its children in an OOBTree with strings keys and content object values. It is generally advisable to stick to using primitives as object keys.

Finally, it is possible to use **volatile attributes**, which are never saved. They will only remain as long as the object is in memory. Since there is no guarantee of how long an object will remain in memory until it is **ghosted** by the ZODB, we can never rely on volatile attributes being there (or rely on when they are removed), but they are sometimes useful as a simple cache.

Volatile attributes have names beginning with _v_. They must be used defensively:

```
>>> someobj._v_saved = expensive_operation()
>>> # do something else for a while
>>> saved = getattr(someobj, '_v_saved', None)
>>> if saved is None: # in case we lost it ...
>>>     saved = expensive_operation()
```

ZODB BLOBs

The ZODB has supported **Binary Large Objects (BLOBs)** since version 3.8. BLOBs are used to efficiently store, manage, and serve up large chunks of data, such as files uploaded to a Plone site. When a BLOB resource is requested (for example, if a user wants to download a file from a Plone site), Zope will stream its data to the client using a separate thread that reads directly from disk, freeing up the main Zope threads to handle new requests. Plone 4's *Image* and *File* content types now store their data in BLOBs.

When using the default `FileStorage` ZODB backend, BLOBs are stored in files in a directory managed by Zope. In a standard Plone buildout, this is usually found under `var/blobstorage/`.

It is easy to use BLOBs in custom content types, as we will see in the next chapter.

 In Plone development, it is relatively uncommon to use BLOB objects directly. At a high level, you store a `ZODB.blob.Blob` object in the ZODB like any other persistent object, and feed it data using the `consumeFile()` method. To read the BLOB's data, use the `open()` method, which returns a file-like object. Take a look at `ZODB.interfaces.IBlob` for more details.

Searching for objects using the catalog

So far, we have discussed the object graph of the ZODB. We can walk this graph, using the `dict` protocol to retrieve acquisition-wrapped objects, and we can scan folderish objects using methods such as `keys()`, which returns a list of all the IDs in that container, and `values()` which returns a list of contained objects.

Walking the entire ZODB every time we want to find an object is not ideal. In particular, functions such as `values()` should be avoided if possible, because they can **wake up** a large number of objects from the ZODB – reading them from disk and swapping them into the ZODB cache. This can have a major performance impact for large data sets.

Zope mitigates this problem with `ZCatalogs`, relational database-like tables of objects. In Plone, there is a `ZCatalog` called `portal_catalog` in the root of the site which indexes all content objects. We can get hold of it as follows:

```
>>> from Products.CMFCore.utils import getToolByName
>>> catalog = getToolByName(context, 'portal_catalog')
```

Here, `context` must be an object inside the Plone site or the Plone site root itself.

The catalog is configured with **indexes** – which can be used to search various attributes of indexed objects – and **metadata** – copies of certain attributes which can be examined without fetching the underlying content object. Sometimes, the same attribute is used both in an index and as metadata. You can think of an index as something you use to find an object, and a metadata item as something you use to inspect the search results.

Where an object does not provide a particular attribute, the value of any corresponding metadata item may be `Missing.Value` (or it could be acquired from a parent).

> If too many attributes are listed in the metadata table, the catalog will grow in size and become slower, counteracting the efficiency benefits of using metadata instead of fetching full objects.

To see the complete list of metadata columns, look at `portal_catalog` in the ZMI, under the **Metadata** tab. Indexes are listed on the **Indexes** tab. We will see an example of adding additional indexes and metadata columns via the `catalog.xml` import step in the next chapter.

Plone's catalog applies an implicit search parameter which ensures that only those content objects that are viewable by the current user are returned, and since non-content objects (for example, CMF tools found in the portal root) are not indexed, they will not be found when searching the catalog.

> If you want to find objects which are not viewable by the current user, you can use the `unrestrictedSearchResults()` function of `portal_catalog`. In Restricted Python (see next), use of this function is usually restricted to the Manager role.

When we search the catalog, it returns a lazy list of items known as catalog brains. **Catalog brains** have attributes consisting of the values of the various columns in the metadata table. Brains also contain a few useful methods for inspecting the object that was cataloged. Most importantly, retrieving a catalog brain does not wake up the indexed content object itself. To get the full object, we can use the `getObject()` method on the brain.

For further information about `ZCatalogs`, see the *Searching and Categorizing Content* chapter of the Zope Book, which can be found at `http://docs.zope.org/zope2/ zope2book/`. You will find examples of using the catalog in the subsequent chapters, and throughout Plone's source code. The following are a few examples of common catalog usage.

To retrieve all published news items in the site, use:

```
>>> for brain in catalog(
...     {'portal_type': 'News Item', 'review_state': 'published'}
... ):
...     print(brain.getPath())
/plone/folder/guitars/strat
/plone/folder/guitars/lp
```

Here, we call the catalog object directly to execute a query. For the purposes of testing, we simply print the path, as returned by the brain-specific `getPath()` function. This is equivalent to using `'/'.join(obj.getPhysicalPath())` on a regular object.

To prove this, we will use `getObject()` to retrieve such an object. Note that normally, we would try not to do this to avoid a performance hit:

```
>>> for brain in catalog.searchResults(
...     {'portal_type' : 'News Item', 'review_state' : 'published'}
.. ):
...     print('/'.join(brain.getObject().getPhysicalPath()))
/plone/folder/guitars/strat
/plone/folder/guitars/lp
```

Here we also use the `searchResults()` method, which is equivalent to calling the catalog object.

The `getURL()` method of a brain is complementary to `getPath()`. It returns the referenced object's URL. As with the `absolute_url()` method on a regular object, this takes into account the current server URL (which may be different from the server URL at the time that the object was indexed):

```
>>> for brain in catalog(
...     {'portal_type': 'News Item', 'review_state': 'published'}
```

```
... ):
...         print brain.getURL() == brain.getObject().absolute_url()
True
True
```

Different types of indexes accept different types of search parameters. The most common kinds are the `FieldIndex`, which indexes a single field, and the `KeywordIndex`, used when a field contains a list of values and we would like to be able to search for a subset of them. For example, the `Subject` index refers to the Dublin Core *subject* (a.k.a. keywords) field. To find any documents (pages) or news items that refer to *Guitars* or *Fender*, we could write:

```
>>> results = catalog(
...     {'portal_type': ('Document', 'News Item',),
...      'Subject': ('Guitars', 'Fender',)}
... )
>>> sorted([r.getId for r in results])
['fender', 'lp', 'tele']
```

Here, there are three objects, `fender`, `lp`, and `tele`, which match the given criteria. We also make use of the `getId` metadata attribute (which stores the return value of the method with the same name) and reduce the lazy list of results to a sorted list of string IDs for the purposes of validating the output reliably.

The `path` index can be used to search for objects by location. By default, it will match the specified path and all sub-paths. By passing a dictionary with keys `query` and `depth` to the index, we can search either for just a specific path (depth `0`) or just sub-paths of specified path (depth `1`):

```
>>> guitarsPath = '/'.join(folder['guitars'].getPhysicalPath())
>>> results = catalog({'path': guitarsPath})
>>> sorted([r.getId for r in results])
['basses', 'fender', 'guitars', 'jagstang', 'lp', 'pbass', 'strat',
'tele']

>>> results = catalog({'path': {'query': guitarsPath, 'depth': 0}})
>>> sorted([r.getId for r in results])
['guitars']

>>> results = catalog({'path': {'query': guitarsPath, 'depth': 1}})
>>> sorted([r.getId for r in results])
['basses', 'fender', 'jagstang', 'lp', 'strat', 'tele']
```

In these examples, pbass is a child of basses, which is why it shows up when searching for all items under guitars, but not when searching for only those objects directly inside guitars. Also notice that with no depth restriction, the guitars folder is included in the search results, but it is excluded when searching for items at depth 1 (that is, those objects that are directly inside the folder folder).

We can control the order of the returned items using the special sort_on and sort_order parameters, and the maximum number of returned objects using sort_limit. When using sort_limit, we could potentially get a few more items back – it is only a hint to the search algorithms, and the lazy nature of the returned list makes it possible that complex searches will cause them to overshoot a little. Therefore, we normally also explicitly limit the number of items we iterate over:

```
>>> results = catalog(
...     {'portal_type': 'Document', 'sort_on': 'sortable_title'}
... )
>>> [r.Title for r in results]
['Favorite guitars', 'Fender', 'Precision bass']

>>> results = catalog(
...     {'portal_type': 'Document', 'sort_on': 'sortable_title',
...      'sort_order': 'descending'}
...)
>>> [r.Title for r in results]
['Precision bass', 'Fender', 'Favorite guitars']

>>> limit = 5
>>> results = catalog(
...     {'portal_type': 'Document', 'sort_on': 'sortable_title',
...      'sort_limit': limit}
... )[:limit]
>>> [r.Title for r in results]
['Favorite guitars', 'Fender', 'Precision bass']
```

This returns the last five published objects, sorted on title. The sort_order parameter can be "ascending" or "descending", with "reverse" being an alias for "descending". The sortable_title index is a special version of the Title index which uses some clever string manipulation to make sure that titles will sort the way people normally expect them to.

When objects change, they need to be reindexed for the catalog to be updated. This is done automatically when content is manipulated through the Plone user interface. However, when making changes in code, we sometimes need to reindex manually.

```
>>> folder['favorites'].setDescription("Contains a list of favorites")
>>> len(catalog({'Description': "list of favorites"}))
0
>>> folder['favorites'].reindexObject(idxs=['Description'])
>>> len(catalog({'Description': "list of favorites"}))
1
>>> folder['favorites'].setDescription("My favorites!")
>>> folder['favorites'].setTitle("My favorite guitars")
>>> folder['favorites'].reindexObject()
>>> len(catalog({'Title': "My favorite guitars"}))
1
```

The `reindexObject()` function comes from the `CMFCatalogAware` mix-in class, used in nearly all content objects. It tells the catalog to reindex the given object. Without parameters, it reindexes all indexes, but we can save a bit of processing by passing a list of indexes to reindex if we are certain nothing else has changed. There is also `reindexObjectSecurity()`, which will automatically refresh the permission-related indexes for the current object and any children they may have.

Describing functionality with interfaces

Thus far, we have described the core concepts of traditional Zope 2 programming. The remainder of this chapter will focus on concepts that come with the Zope Toolkit: interfaces, utilities, adapters, views, and events.

Interfaces are a key part of most Zope Toolkit techniques. They are best thought of as verifiable documentation – descriptions of components and their behavior which can be inspected at run-time. The simplest form of an interface – known as a **marker interface** – is one that describes the type of a component without promising any methods or attributes.

Because Python does not have a language construct for interfaces, we define them using classes inheriting from `zope.interface.Interface`:

```
>>> from zope.interface import Interface
>>> class IBelievable(Interface):
...     """An item which can be believed
...     """
```

Often, reading a package's interfaces is the best way of understanding how the components of that package are meant to fit together. By convention, interfaces are found in a module called `interfaces` (usually in a `interfaces.py` file), and have names starting with the letter `I`. Interfaces should always include a meaningful docstring.

Software design can be modeled using interfaces, using constructs such as specialization (inheritance) and association (composition). For example, here is a specialization of the `IBelievable` interface:

```
>>> class IUndeniable(IBelievable):
...      """Something that is so believable it cannot be denied
...      """
```

Interfaces can also describe methods and attributes. Note that methods in interfaces do not have the `self` parameter, nor do they have method bodies, although they do have docstrings; again, they serve as documentation. Of course, if the interface is implemented by a class, that class will use the self parameter and have a method body, as we will see further. However, interfaces can also be used to describe functions in a module.

Attributes can be described using `zope.interface.Attribute`. We can also make more precise statements about the valid contents of attributes using `zope.schema`, which we will cover in *Chapter 11, Standalone Views and Forms*, when we look at how Zope can auto-generate forms from this information. In modern code, there is usually a preference for using attributes and Python properties over separate get and set methods when modeling attributes of an object.

Note that if you are using the Python `property` syntax, you will not have an acquisition context. Since property getters and setters tend to be simple, this is not usually a problem, but if you find yourself needing one, look at Zope 2's `ComputedAttribute` class.

```
>>> from zope.interface import Attribute

>>> class IMessage(Interface):
...      """A message being communicated
...      """
...
...      def shout(noise_level=5):
...          """Shout the message
...          """
...
...      content = Attribute("The actual text of the message")
```

Interfaces are typically **implemented** by classes. Objects of these classes are then said to **provide** those interfaces. This implies that the object exposes all the methods and attributes promised by the interface (though this is not strictly enforced).

```
>>> from zope.interface import implements

>>> class StandardMessage(object):
...         implements(IMessage)
...
...         def __init__(self, content):
...             self.content = content
...
...         def shout(self, noise_level=5):
...             print self.content * noise_level

>>> class StrongMessage(StandardMessage):
...         implements(IBelievable)
```

Interfaces are inherited from base classes, and a class can implement multiple interfaces by passing several parameters to `implements()`. We can use `implementsOnly()` in lieu of `implements()` to disable interface inheritance.

The `zope.interface` package contains methods for manipulating interfaces on classes and objects. Interfaces themselves contain methods which can be used to verify their relevance to classes and objects.

```
>>> IMessage.implementedBy(StandardMessage)
True
>>> IMessage.implementedBy(StrongMessage)
True

>>> IBelievable.implementedBy(StandardMessage)
False
>>> IBelievable.implementedBy(StrongMessage)
True
```

Here, the `implementedBy()` method is used to determine if objects of a particular class will comply with the given interface. More commonly, we inspect objects directly, using the `providedBy()` method:

```
>>> fender = StandardMessage("All Fender guitars rock")
>>> strats = StrongMessage("Stratocasters are great!")
>>> telecaster = StrongMessage("Telecasters are awesome!")

>>> IMessage.providedBy(fender)
True
```

```
>>> IMessage.providedBy(strats)
True

>>> IBelievable.providedBy(fender)
False
>>> IBelievable.providedBy(strats)
True
```

We can also apply interfaces directly to objects. Here, the `IUndeniable` interface is being applied selectively to messages using `alsoProvides()`:

```
>>> from zope.interface import alsoProvides
>>> alsoProvides(telecaster, IUndeniable)

>>> IUndeniable.providedBy(fender)
False
>>> IUndeniable.providedBy(telecaster)
True
```

We can use `noLongerProvides()` to take a directly provided interface away:

```
>>> from zope.interface import noLongerProvides
>>> noLongerProvides(telecaster, IUndeniable)
>>> IUndeniable.providedBy(telecaster)
False
```

It is also possible to let a class object provide (as opposed to implement) an interface, in which case we are making a statement about the type of the class, rather than the type of object created by that class. We can even apply interfaces to interfaces to group them logically, or apply interfaces to modules, to describe their public functions and variables. In normal programming, these constructs are rarely needed, but you may come across them in framework code.

Here, we describe mechanisms for creating messages as 'communication factories'. Because we are applying the interface to the class object, there is no notion of inheritance between the `StrongMessage` and the `StandardMessage` declarations – we have to declare the interface on both classes explicitly.

```
>>> class ICommunicationFactory(Interface):
...     """A Python callable (e.g. classes) which is able to produce
...     communication devices (e.g. messages).
...     """

>>> alsoProvides(StandardMessage, ICommunicationFactory)
>>> alsoProvides(StrongMessage, ICommunicationFactory)
```

```
>>> ICommunicationFactory.implementedBy(StandardMessage)
False

>>> ICommunicationFactory.providedBy(StandardMessage)
True
>>> ICommunicationFactory.providedBy(StrongMessage)
True
```

The documentation in `zope.interface.interfaces` describes in detail the various ways in which interfaces can be applied, inspected, and manipulated.

Using interfaces in catalog searches

In the previous section, we demonstrated how to use the catalog to search for objects by their `portal_type`, a string. This pattern is quite common, but has a few drawbacks:

- There can only ever be one content type installed with a given `portal_type` name. We can search for multiple portal types, but the code that searches needs to be aware of all such types in advance.

- Although it is uncommon, `portal_type` names can be changed.

Interfaces are a better way to describe the semantic type of a content object. The `object_provides` catalog index can be used to search for objects providing a particular interface. This takes into account interfaces inherited from parent objects, as well as generalizations of specific interfaces provided.

```
>>> from Products.ATContentTypes.interfaces import ITextContent
>>> results = catalog(
...     {'object_provides': ITextContent.__identifier__}
... )
>>> sorted([r.getId for r in results])
['favorites', 'fender', 'lp', 'pbass', 'strat', 'tele']
```

Note that the `object_provides` index only stores the names of the interfaces an object held when it was being cataloged. Changes in code or ZCML may mean that an object's interfaces change after it has been indexed, in which case the catalog would not be aware of this until the object is reindexed.

In this example, we search for all standard 'text content'. Interfaces for Plone's standard content types can be found in `Products.ATContentTypes.interfaces`.

Component configuration with ZCML or Grokkers

ZCML (Zope Component Meta-Language) is an XML format used by Zope to configure components such as utilities, adapters, and views. We have already seen ZCML files in the `optilux.policy` package, and they are found throughout Zope and Plone.

ZCML files are rooted in a `<configure />` node and include directives from one of several XML namespaces, including `zope`, for core component configuration, `browser`, for configuration of views and browser resources, and `plone`, for directives specific to Plone.

```
<configure
    xmlns="http://namespaces.zope.org/zope"
    xmlns:browser="http://namespaces.zope.org/browser"
    xmlns:plone="http://namespaces.plone.org/plone">

    ...

</configure>
```

We will normally describe specific ZCML directives alongside the concepts that they relate to. One important generic directive, however, is `<include />`. This can be used to trigger processing of other ZCML files, and allows us to manage interdependencies between packages' configuration or split long ZCML files into more manageable chunks. Common examples include:

```
<include package="zope.annotation" />
<include package=".browser" />
<include file="permissions.zcml" />
```

The first example will cause the ZCML parser to proceed to the `configure.zcml` file in the `zope.annotation` package if it has not been processed already. The second includes the browser sub-package inside the current package, again looking for a `configure.zcml` file there. The third example includes a file called `permissions.zcml` in the same directory as the current file. Relative paths are also allowed.

We commonly want to load any ZCML configuration, including any `meta.zcml` files that define new ZCML directives, for each package that we depend on. To make this easier, we can use the following directive:

```
<includeDependencies package="." />
```

This will scan through all dependencies listed in `install_requires` (and any enabled extras) in `setup.py` and include their ZCML configuration, if any.

ZCML files are loaded at Zope startup, according to the following rules:

1. The `etc/site.zcml` file in the **instance home** (usually `parts/instance` or a similar directory inside a Plone buildout) is read first. This file is usually generated by the buildout recipe `plone.recipe.zope2instance`.

2. During processing of `etc/site.zcml`, all top level `meta.zcml` and `configure.zcml` files in old-style products (that is, packages in the `Products.*` namespace) are loaded.

3. Next, any `*-meta.zcml` and `*-configure.zcml` files in `etc/package-includes` inside the instance home are loaded. These files are known as **ZCML slugs**, and are usually used to include the configuration of packages that are installed in the Zope instance. ZCML slugs can be generated by listing packages under the `zcml` option to `plone.recipe.zope2instance` in the buildout configuration.

4. Finally, any `overrides.zcml` files in old-style products and any `*-overrides.zcml` files in `etc/package-includes` are loaded. These can be used to override configuration from earlier packages without causing a configuration conflict.

ZCML slugs have become less common since the introduction of `z3c.autoinclude` in Plone 3.3. In *Chapter 5, Developing a Site Strategy*, we learned how to add a `z3c.autoinclude` entry point to our distribution's `setup.py`:

```
entry_points="""
# -*- Entry points: -*-
[z3c.autoinclude.plugin]
target = plone
""",
```

In `Products.CMFPlone`'s `configure.zcml`, `meta.zcml`, and `overrides.zcml`, you will find statements like:

```
<includePlugins package="plone" file="configure.zcml" />
```

This tells Zope to load the configuration (from `configure.zcml` in this case) from all distributions that use a `z3c.autoinclude.plugin` entry point with the target `plone`. Since `Products.CMFPlone` is an old-style product that is loaded automatically on startup, this means all distributions that register themselves with an entry point like the one above are loaded automatically as well, without ZCML slugs.

Python directives and grokkers

ZCML configuration allows very precise control over the components that are registered and used in a Zope application. Some ZCML directives are used purely for configuration, such as:

- The `<include />` and `<includeDependencies />` directives seen previously.

- The `<permission />` directive, seen in *Chapter 6, Security and Workflow*, which is used to create new permissions.

- The `<browser:resource />`, `<browser:resourceDirectory />` and `<plone:static />` directives, used to allow publication of static file resources such as images and stylesheets in various ways.

- The `<z3c:jbot />` directive seen in *Chapter 8, Creating a Custom Theme*, used to register `z3c.jbot` template overrides.

However, most other directives, are used to configure components that are written in Python. Some developers find it cumbersome to separate the Python implementation from component configuration in ZCML. Instead, they prefer to use **convention-over-configuration** to register components. This usually means using a specific base class for the relevant component and adding some **Python directives** into the class body. A component called a **grokker** scans the source code in a given package for these special code constructs and performs the required configuration.

 Why the name *grokker*? This style of configuration originated from **Grok** (see `http://grok.zope.org`), a standalone web framework using the Zope Toolkit and convention-over-configuration.

Grokkers are built with the `martian` library (`http://pypi.python.org/pypi/martian`). The most important grokkers can be found with the packages `grokcore.component` and `grokcore.view`. To use these in Zope 2, however, we employ an integration package called `five.grok`.

We will show examples of registering standard components with `five.grok` in the next several sections. Grokking can be enabled with the `<grok:grok />` ZCML directive:

```
<configure
    xmlns="http://namespaces.zope.org/zope"
    xmlns:grok="http://namespaces.zope.org/grok">
    <includeDependencies package="." />
    <grok:grok package="." />
</configure>
```

This will scan all modules in the current package and its sub-packages for grok-aware base classes and directives and configure the components using them accordingly.

The `<includeDependencies />` line will ensure the standard grokkers are available, assuming we have listed `five.grok` as a dependency in `setup.py`. We should also make sure we used an appropriate known good set of packages for `five.grok`. Known good sets can be found at `http://good-py.appspot.com/release/five.grok`, although the Dexterity known good set that we will show in the next chapter also includes `five.grok` and its dependencies.

To learn more about grokkers and `five.grok`, take a look at `http://plone.org/products/dexterity/documentation/manual/five.grok`. Further examples will follow in the remainder of this chapter.

 Please be aware that at the time of writing, core Plone packages are required to use ZCML configuration only, to avoid an explicit dependency on `five.grok` in Plone itself.

Component registries using utilities

The Zope Component Architecture can be seen as a collection of registries. Code in one component can look up other components by interface and possibly a name, and use them to perform some function. Interfaces are thus the main contract between components, and the Component Architecture is responsible for locating an appropriate implementation of a particular interface for a particular purpose.

Broadly, there are two main types of components:

- **Utilities**, which are context-less. Utilities can either act as singletons, looked up by interface, or as registries of similar components, looked up by interface and name.

- **Adapters**, which are contextual. Adapters allow code expecting components providing a particular interface to adapt objects of some other type to this interface. Seen differently, adapters are used to provide a particular aspect of an object without modifying the original object itself.

Global utilities

The simplest type of component is a global **unnamed utility**. Such utilities act as **singletons** – components which are instantiated exactly once and reused wherever they are needed.

Consider a broadcaster of music, which we want to use in various parts in some program:

```
>>> from zope.interface import Interface
>>> class IBroadcaster(Interface):
...        """A component capable of broadcasting a message to the world
...        """
...
...        def __call__(message):
...            """Broadcast the given message
...            """

>>> from zope.interface import implements
>>> class RadioBroadcaster(object):
...        implements(IBroadcaster)
...
...        def __call__(self, message):
...            print("And now for a special announcement:", message)
```

We could of course instantiate a `RadioBroadcaster` each time we wanted to broadcast something, but this would mean a hard dependency on this specific implementation. Really, all we are interested in is something that complies with the `IBroadcaster` interface, and we can leave it up to application configuration to decide which specific implementation is appropriate. Such configuration is done in ZCML like this:

```
<utility factory=".broadcaster.RadioBroadcaster" />
```

Alternatively, we could explicitly specify the provided interface. This is necessary if the class does not have an `implements()` declaration, or if the class implements more than one interface.

```
<utility
    provides=".interfaces.IBroadcaster"
    factory=".broadcaster.RadioBroadcaster"
    />
```

The ZCML examples in this chapter are hypothetical only, but here we pretend that `IBroadcaster` is in a module called `interfaces` in the current package, and the implementation is in a module called `broadcaster`.

To use a grokker to register the utility instead, we would change our code to use the `grok.GlobalUtility` base class:

```
>>> from five import grok
>>> from zope.interface import implements
```

```
>>> class RadioBroadcaster(grok.GlobalUtility):
...      implements(IBroadcaster)
...
...      def __call__(self, message):
...          print("And now for a special announcement:", message)
```

Assuming the <grok:grok /> directive is enabled in configure.zcml, this will register an unnamed utility providing IBroadcaster.

> In the doctests, we use a Python API to register the utilities instead of ZCML, and we define all the interfaces and classes as part of the test. The Python API for component registrations is found in zope.component. See zope.component.interfaces for more detail.

With utility registered, we can write:

```
>>> from zope.component import getUtility
>>> broadcaster = getUtility(IBroadcaster)
>>> broadcaster("Jimi Hendrix played a Stratocaster")
And now for a special announcement: Jimi Hendrix played a Stratocaster
```

We could also have used zope.component.queryUtility, which is similar to getUtility(), but will return None if no suitable utility can be found, whereas getUtility() will raise a zope.component.interfaces.ComponentLookupError.

Common uses for unnamed utilities include:

- Providing services through singletons. This is analogous to the classic **Service Locator pattern**.

- Providing access to commonly used utility functionality in a more formalized, implementation-exchangeable way.

- Storing policy decisions or global configuration settings in such a way that they can be overridden, for example using overrides.zcml or local utilities (see further).

> For settings that are specific to a Plone site or need to be changeable by a site administrator, use plone.app.registry instead.

Named utilities

An unnamed utility is actually a special case of a **named utility**, having the name u"" (an empty unicode string). Named utilities allow us to use the utility registry as a general registry for any kind of homogenous components. Here, "homogenous" just means "provide the same interface".

For example, suppose we needed an abstraction for a channel used to transmit a message:

```
>>> class IChannel(Interface):
...     """A channel through which a message could be transmitted
...     """
...
...     def transmit(source, destination, message):
...         """Transmit a message between two destinations
...         """
```

There could be a number of different types of channels, such as FTP or HTTP, each with different configurations. Let us assume that we do not want the application to make a single decision in this case, but rather allow the choice to be made at runtime. To achieve this, we could register the various types of channels as named utilities.

```
>>> class Channel(object):
...     implements(IChannel)
...
...     def __init__(self, port):
...         self.port = port
...
...     def transmit(self, source, destination, message):
...         print "Sending", message, "from", source, \
...               "to", destination, "on", self.port

>>> http = Channel(80)
>>> ftp = Channel(21)
```

In this example, we are actually instantiating objects to act as utilities, rather than providing a factory to let the Component Architecture instantiate it for itself. It would be perfectly feasible to write different factories (for example, different classes) and register a utility for each one, but we can save some code by using a parameterized class instead.

To register these objects in ZCML, we could use something like:

```
<utility
    provides=".interfaces.IChannel"
```

```
        component=".channel.http"
        name="http"
        />

    <utility
        provides=".interfaces.IChannel"
        component=".channel.ftp"
        name="ftp"
        />
```

If we wanted to use `five.grok` configuration, we would add the following at module level:

```
>>> grok.global_utility(http,
...     provides=IChannel, name='http', direct=True)
>>> grok.global_utility(ftp,
...     provides=IChannel, name='ftp', direct=True)
```

 To provide a name for a utility defined only with a factory class deriving from `grok.GlobalUtility`, we would use the `grok.name()` directive in the class body.

To look up these utilities, we still use `getUtility()` or `queryUtility()`, but this time we provide an additional `name` parameter:

```
>>> from zope.component import queryUtility
>>> chosen_channel = u"ftp" # perhaps selected by the user
>>> channel = queryUtility(IChannel, name=chosen_channel)
```

Named utilities can be used when:

- We need a registry of similar components (providing a particular interface) identifiable by name. This saves us from writing a custom registry, ties the component lookup explicitly to a formalized interface, and allows us to use a standard API to enumerate or access the registry. See `zope.component.interfaces` for a list of functions that can be used to locate and iterate over registered utilities.

- We want other packages and applications to be able to "plug in" new components. For example, the list of addable portlets in Plone is constructed by querying the utility registry for named utilities providing `IPortletType`. This allows third party packages to tell Plone about a new portlet simply by registering a utility carrying the necessary information. Here, the name of each utility needs only be unique – the framework code is more interested in the interface. To get back a list of name-utility pairs for all utilities providing a particular interface, use `zope.component.getUtilitiesFor()`.

- We require the user to choose among a number of possible components, say to influence the policy used by a particular process. The user's choice is then translated to a utility name and an appropriate utility is found.

Local utilities

A **component site manager** keeps track of component registrations. The default site manager, which is what we have been using until now, is known as the **global site manager**. Components in the global site manager are usually configured with ZCML.

Any folder in the containment hierarchy may have its own **local site manager**, where **local components** are persisted. When a local site manager is active, it will take precedence over the global site manager or a local site manager further up in the containment hierarchy, but will fall back on a parent or the global site manager if it does not have an appropriate registration for some requested component. This is similar to how Zope 2 acquisition allows local overrides, except that it pertains only to component registrations.

The Plone site root is also a component site with its own local site manager. During URL traversal, this is activated so that whenever a component is looked up by code invoked inside the Plone site, local components are allowed to override global ones. This is purely a configuration issue – the code performing the component lookup will use the same APIs, such as `getUtility()` and `queryUtility()`.

Unlike global utilities, local utilities are stored in the ZODB and thus can be used to persist state. However, it is generally better to use a dedicated storage such as the one provided by `plone.app.registry` (which itself is looked up via a utility), as this is easier to manage and less likely to cause problems if a package is removed from the Zope instance.

The easiest way of registering a local utility is to use the `componentregistry.xml` import step with GenericSetup. Plone's version of this file is a good point of reference. Following is a short extract:

```
<componentregistry>
  ...
```

```
<utilities>
 <utility
    interface="five.customerize.interfaces.IViewTemplateContainer"
    object="/portal_view_customizations"/>
 <utility
    interface="plone.app.redirector.interfaces.IRedirectionStorage"
    factory="plone.app.redirector.storage.RedirectionStorage"/>
</utilities>
 ...
</componentregistry>
```

In the first example, we register an object that is already in the ZODB (in the portal root) as a local utility. This is done because the `portal_view_customizations` tool should be navigable from the ZMI. In the second example, we register a new utility implemented by the class `RedirectionStorage`, allowing the site manager to instantiate it for itself using the supplied factory.

Remember that unlike ZCML directives or grokkers, which are processed every time Zope is started, a GenericSetup profile is only run when applied. Thus, while global components are created and kept in volatile memory, local components are instantiated once and persisted.

To access the redirection storage, we would use exactly the same syntax as if we were accessing a global utility:

```
>>> from plone.app.redirector.interfaces import IRedirectionStorage
>>> redirector = getUtility(IRedirectionStorage)
```

This would work so long as we were in a view or other object being executed as a result of Zope traversing to some object inside Plone site, thus activating the local component registry.

When programming for Plone, this is almost always the case. One exception is in a general event handler for an `IObjectMovedEvent` or a sub-type which may be invoked when the portal object itself is renamed or deleted. In this case, we are operating from outside the Plone site, in the ZMI root, and the local registry is not activated. In these cases, it may be safer to use `queryUtility()` and check for a `None` return value. You may also encounter this problem from code that is executed outside the Plone site, for example during a `./bin/ zopectl debug` session. If you need to, you can call `zope.site.hooks.setHooks()` followed by `zope.site.hooks.setSite()` to explicitly set the current component site. See `zope.site` for details.

Tools

CMF tools were the precursors to local utilities. They are persistent objects, typically deriving from OFS.SimpleItem.SimpleItem, a common base class for non-folderish plain-Zope objects. Tools are by convention stored in the root of the Plone site, and have names beginning with portal_, such as portal_membership or portal_types. They are used to store configuration information or expose common utility methods. Use the **Doc** tab in the ZMI (which is installed by Products.DocFinderTab) or see the relevant interfaces to find out more about what each tool does.

Because they are persisted in the root of the site, tools may be acquired as attributes of any object inside the portal or obtained using URL or path traversal. The safest way to obtain tools, however, is to use the getToolByName() function. This is especially true as some tools are being refactored into more appropriate components such as local utilities and views. As this happens, getToolByName() may be used to provide backwards compatibility.

```
>>> from Products.CMFCore.utils import getToolByName
>>> membership_tool = getToolByName(context, 'portal_membership')
```

Here, context must be an object inside the Plone site (or the site itself). Sometimes, we do not have an appropriate context to acquire the tools from. In that case, we can use this trick:

```
>>> from zope.site.hooks import getSite
>>> site = getSite()
>>> from Products.CMFCore.utils import getToolByName
>>> types_tool = getToolByName(site, 'portal_types')
```

This works because the getSite() method returns the current component registry site, which should be the Plone site root or an object inside it.

The standard tools are crucial to Plone, but they are largely being superseded by utilities, which do not need to live in 'content space', and which can be looked up more easily using getUtility() and similar APIs, rather than being acquired from a context. Moreover, some tools were written mainly to provide view logic to be called from a page template that needed to be executed as trusted filesystem code. Such tools are now better implemented using template-less Zope browser views with appropriate security declarations.

Modelling component aspects with adapters

When modeling design with interfaces, we should always endeavor to adhere to the principle of **separation of concerns**. A component, as described by an interface, should do one thing and one thing only, providing the minimum necessary operations (methods) and attributes (properties) to support that function.

In complex systems such as Plone, we often need to provide general functionality that can act on different types of objects. Continuing with our earlier examples, consider an instrument that is playable.

```
>>> class IPlayable(Interface):
...     """An instrument that can be played
...     """
...
...     def __call__(tune):
...         """Play that tune!
...         """
```

We may write some general code that expects an IPlayable. An object-oriented programming approach could be to use a mix-in or base class and rely on polymorphism:

```
>>> class PlayableMixin(object):
....    implements(IPlayable)
...     def __call__(self, tune):
...         print "Strumming along to", tune

>>> class BassGuitar(PlayableMixin):
...     pass

>>> class ClassicalGuitar(PlayableMixin):
...     pass
```

This will work, but with multiple aspects of instruments in general and guitars in particular to model, we would quickly end up with a large number of mix-in classes, bloating the APIs of the subclasses and incurring the risk of naming conflicts. Furthermore, if we needed to model some new aspect of an instrument, we could end up having to modify several classes to use a new mix-in. By tightly weaving a number of application-specific classes into the inheritance hierarchy, this approach also makes reuse much more difficult.

Zope 2, alas, suffers from all of these problems. Just take a look at the number of base classes on a typical content item, which support aspects such as local role support, persistent properties, or WebDAV publishing.

With the Zope Component Architecture, different aspects of an object are provided by different **adapters**. For example:

```
>>> from zope.interface import Interface, Attribute
>>> class IGuitar(Interface):
...     """A guitar
...     """
...
...     strings = Attribute("Number of strings")
>>> class IBass(IGuitar):
...     """A bass guitar
...     """
>>> class IElectric(IGuitar):
...     """An electric guitar
...     """
>>> from zope.interface import implements
>>> class Bass(object):
...     implements(IBass)
...     strings = 4
>>> class Electric(object):
...     implements(IElectric)
...     strings = 6
>>> pbass = Bass()
>>> tele = Electric()
```

Here, we are explicitly modeling different types of guitars. We will make use of this level of granularity later, but let us first provide a simple adapter from IGuitar to IPlayable:

```
>>> from zope.component import adapts
>>> class GuitarPlayer(object):
...     implements(IPlayable)
...     adapts(IGuitar)
...
...     def __init__(self, context):
...         self.context = context
...
...     def __call__(self, tune):
...         print "Strumming along to", tune
```

The __init__() method takes a parameter conventionally called context. This is the object being adapted, in this case an IGuitar. The adapter itself provides IPlayable, and fully implements this interface by defining a __call__() method.

We now have a means of turning any IGuitar into an IPlayable. Before we can use the adapter, however, we must register it using ZCML:

```
<adapter factory=".players.GuitarPlayer" />
```

This shorthand version inspects the class for implements() and adapts() declarations. To be more explicit, or if these were omitted or ambiguous, we could use:

```
<adapter
    provides=".interfaces.IPlayable"
    for=".interfaces.IGuitar"
    factory=".players.GuitarPlayer"
    />
```

If we wanted to use five.grok to configure this instead, we would use the grok.Adapter base class and the grok.context() and grok.provides() directives:

```
>>> from five import grok
>>> class GuitarPlayer(grok.Adapter):
...         grok.provides(IPlayable)
...         grok.context(IGuitar)
...
...         def __call__(self, tune):
...             print "Strumming along to", tune
```

With this base class, we can also omit the constructor, as the base class provides one that sets self.context for us.

The simplest way of looking up an adapter is by "calling" the interface we want to get an adapter to:

```
>>> tele_player = IPlayable(tele)
>>> tele_player("Toxic Girl")
Strumming along to Toxic Girl
```

When the Component Architecture is looking for an appropriate adapter from the tele object to an IPlayable, it performs a search of the registered adapters against the interfaces provided by the context object (tele). If the object provides the desired interface itself, it will be returned as-is (known as a **null-adapter**). Otherwise, the **most specific** adapter available will be instantiated and returned.

A 'more specific' adapter is one registered for a more specific interface. For example, an adapter matching an interface directly implemented by the object's class is more specific than one matching an interface implemented by a base class, or a parent interface of an interface provided by the object. Although this sounds complicated, the Component Architecture tends to find the adapter we would expect it to find, given a number of general and specific adapter registrations.

Let us look at an example. If we tried to adapt the pbass object, we would get the same general IGuitar adapter:

```
>>> pbass_player = IPlayable(pbass)
>>> pbass_player("Como Ves")
Strumming along to Como Ves
```

We could register a more specific adapter for IBass, however:

```
>>> class BassPlayer(object):
...     implements(IPlayable)
...     adapts(IBass)
...
...     def __init__(self, context):
...         self.context = context
...
...     def __call__(self, tune):
...         print "Slappin' it to", tune
```

And in ZCML:

```
<adapter factory=".players.BassPlayer" />
```

Or, using five.grok:

```
>>> class BassPlayer(grok.Adapter):
...     grok.provides(IPlayable)
...     grok.context(IBass)
...
...     def __call__(self, tune):
...         print "Slappin' it to", tune
```

Now, we will get the new, more specific adapter for pbass, but not for tele:

```
>>> tele_player = IPlayable(tele)
>>> tele_player("Toxic Girl")
Strumming along to Toxic Girl

>>> pbass_player = IPlayable(pbass)
>>> pbass_player("Como Ves")
Slappin' it to Como Ves
```

This is a very powerful concept. For example, imagine that Plone comes with some standard functionality, written as an adapter for, say, `Products.CMFCore.interfaces.IContentish`, which applies to most if not all content items. Content types with particular needs can then provide a more specific adapter by registering it for a more specific interface. Any code that is written to look up adapters when working with a particular aspect of an object will be extensible in this way.

Furthermore, recall from the discussion of interfaces earlier in this chapter that specific objects can be marked with an interface using `alsoProvides()`. An interface provided directly by an object is more specific still than one implemented by its class. Therefore, we could register an adapter for an interface which is conditionally applied to objects and expect conditional behavior accordingly.

Plone's content staging solution, `plone.app.iterate`, uses this technique. It marks working copies with an `IWorkingCopy` marker interface when they are checked out and uses various adapters registered for this interface to override more general adapters which apply to base copies. When a working copy is checked back in again, the marker interface is removed (using `noLongerProvides()` from `zope.interface`) and the behavior reverts to normal.

The most general adapter is one registered for `Interface`. This can sometimes be useful when constructing global fallback adapters. In ZCML, we can express this with:

```
<adapter
    for="*"
    provides=".interfaces.IPlayable"
    factory=".players.FallbackPlayer"
    />
```

With `five.grok` configuration, we would use `grok.context(Interface)` to achieve the same thing.

With no such general fallback, we would get a `TypeError` when trying to look up an adapter for which no registration is found. This can happen legitimately if, for example, we are depending on other packages to provide appropriate adapters, or if some aspect of an object is deemed optional. We can write more defensive code by using:

```
>>> possibly_playable = IPlayable(some_object, None)
```

If no adapter is found, this will return `None`, or whatever else is passed as the second parameter.

Multi-adapters

So far, we have seen adapters that vary by a single interface, adapting a single context. It is also possible to register adapters that adapt multiple objects, and thus can be specialized on any one or more of their interfaces. These are known as **multi-adapters**.

Suppose we were dealing not only with guitars, but also with amplifiers:

```
>>> class IAmp(Interface):
...      """An amplifier
...      """
...
...      goes_up_to = Attribute("How far up does it go?")
>>> class ElevenAmp(object):
...      implements(IAmp)
...      goes_up_to = 11 # This one goes to eleven!
>>> vox = ElevenAmp()
```

To do a gig, we would need both a guitar and an appropriate amp. We will model this by adapting the guitar and the amp to an IGiggable interface. Notice how the __init__() method now takes two parameters, since there are two objects being adapted:

```
>>> class IGiggable(Interface):
...      """A setup which can be gigged
...      """
...
...      def __call__(stage_set):
...          """Gig a particular set
...          """
>>> class GigRig(object):
...      implements(IGiggable)
...      adapts(IElectric, IAmp)
...
...      def __init__(self, guitar, amp):
...          self.guitar = guitar
...          self.amp = amp
...
...      def __call__(self, stage_set):
...          print "Setting volume to", self.amp.goes_up_to
...          playable = IPlayable(self.guitar)
...          for song in stage_set:
...              playable(song)
```

To register this adapter, we use the same ZCML directive as before:

```
<adapter factory=".gig.GigRig" />
```

If we omitted the `adapts()` declaration, we would need to specify the two adapted interfaces in the for attribute, separated by whitespace:

```
<adapter
    provides=".interfaces.IGiggable"
    for=".interfaces.IElectric .interfaces.IAmp"
    factory=".gig.GigRig"
    />
```

Alternatively, using `five.grok` configuration:

```
>>> class GigRig(grok.MultiAdapter):
...     grok.provides(IGiggable)
...     grok.adapts(IElectric, IAmp)
...
...     def __init__(self, guitar, amp):
...         self.guitar = guitar
...         self.amp = amp
...
...     def __call__(self, stage_set):
...         print "Setting volume to", self.amp.goes_up_to
...         playable = IPlayable(self.guitar)
...         for song in stage_set:
...             playable(song)
```

 Note that for multi-adapters, there is no default constructor. Also note that we use `grok.context()` for single adapters, but `grok.adapts()` for multi-adapters.

To look up a multi-adapter, we cannot use an interface on its own, since that only takes a single context parameter. Instead, we do:

```
>>> from zope.component import getMultiAdapter
>>> gig = getMultiAdapter((tele, vox,), IGiggable)
>>> gig(["Foxxy Lady", "Voodoo Chile",])
Setting volume to 11
Strumming along to Foxxy Lady
Strumming along to Voodoo Chile
```

There is also `zope.component.queryMultiAdapter()`, which will return `None` if the adapter lookup fails.

Multi-adapters are written less commonly than regular adapters. If we have an adapter where most methods take the same parameter, it may be a sign that we really want a multi-adapter. Being able to specialize based on multiple dimensions (that is, the different interfaces being adapted) can add a lot of flexibility, possibly at the cost of additional complexity. Internally in Zope, multi-adapters are used all the time – more on that when we get to views in a moment.

Named adapters

Like utilities, adapters can be named, with unnamed adapters really just being **named adapters** called u"". Named single-adapters are not particularly common, but can make sense if behavior needs to vary not just based on the type of object being adapted, but also based on user input or other runtime configuration.

Suppose that we wanted to let the user pick the style in which a guitar was played:

```
>>> class StyledGuitarPlayer(object):
...     implements(IPlayable)
...
...     def __init__(self, context, style):
...         self.context = context
...         self.style = style
...
...     def __call__(self, tune):
...         print self.style, "to", tune
>>> from zope.component import adapter
>>> from zope.interface import implementer

>>> @implementer(IPlayable)
... @adapter(IGuitar)
... def fingerpicked_guitar(context):
...     return StyledGuitarPlayer(context, 'Picking away')

>>> @implementer(IPlayable)
... @adapter(IGuitar)
... def strummed_guitar(context):
...     return StyledGuitarPlayer(context, 'Strumming away')
```

And in ZCML:

```
<adapter
  factory=".styles.fingerpicked_guitar"
  name="fingerpick"
  />

<adapter
```

```
factory=".styles.strummed_guitar"
name="strum"
/>
```

If we wanted to use `five.grok` instead, we would do:

```
>>> from five import grok
>>> @grok.implementer(IPlayable)
... @grok.adapter(IGuitar, name="fingerpick")
... def fingerpicked_guitar(context):
...     return StyledGuitarPlayer(context, 'Picking away')
```

 As with utilities, we can use `grok.name()` in the class body to register a named adapter from a factory. This also applies to multi-adapters.

To look up a named adapter, we need to use `getAdapter()` or `queryAdapter()`, like this:

```
>>> from zope.component import getAdapter
>>> preferred_style = u"fingerpick"
>>> playable = getAdapter(tele, IPlayable, name=preferred_style)
>>> playable("Like a Hurricane")
Picking away to Like a Hurricane
```

The other main use case for named adapters is to allow multiple adapters to be registered simultaneously, for use with framework code that looks up and operations on all adapter implementations. Here is an example based on code in the `borg.localrole` package that ships with Plone:

```
for count, a in enumerate(
    (a[1] for a in getAdapters((obj,), ILocalRoleProvider))
):
    for pid in principal_ids:
        roles.update(a.getRoles(pid))
```

See `zope.component.getAdapters()` for more details.

With this pattern, it is still possible to override an adapter by registering one with the same name for a more specific interface.

Adapter factories

In the preceding example, we are doing something a little different to what we did in earlier examples – using a function (`strummed_guitar()`) that returns an object as the adapter factory, rather than a class. Zope only requires those factories are callables that take the appropriate number of arguments and return an object providing the desired interface, which the `strummed_guitar()` function does. The `@adapter` and `@implementer` function decorators are analogous to using `adapts()` and `implements()` for a class, alleviating the need to specify the `for` and `provides` attribute in the `<adapter />` ZCML directive.

This pattern can also be useful if we want to return an adapter that is not a class referencing the adapted object. For example, in `plone.contentrules`, there is an adapter factory which allows us to write code like:

```
assignable = IRuleAssignmentManager(context)
assignable['key'] = assignment
```

Here, the `context` could be a content object, and `assignable` is a container object that stores assignments of rules to that context. The adapter factory, which can be found in `plone.contentrules.engine.assignments`, retrieves a persistent instance of the container that is stored in an annotation on the context. The calling code, of course, does not care where the adapter came from, only that it correctly implements `IRuleAssignmentManager` and pertains to the particular context.

 An annotation is a general way to store additional meta-data on an object, using a dictionary-like syntax. See `zope.annotation.interfaces` for more.

Views and other presentation components

A Zope browser view is a component which can be found during URL traversal and (usually) asked to render itself. When Zope traverses a URL such as `http://example.org/guitars/@@list-guitars` it will first find the `guitars` object, using the rules outlined in the description of object publishing at the beginning of this chapter, and then do something akin to:

```
view = getMultiAdapter((guitars, request), name="list-guitars")
```

That is, a **view** is simply a named multi-adapter of some context and the current request. The name is usually disambiguated from content objects and attributes by prefixing it with @@, although this is optional. To render the view object, Zope will call it, which normally results in a page template being invoked, although some views will simply construct a string and return it.

In Zope 2, views commonly inherit from `Products.Five.browser.BrowserView`, although as of Zope 2.12 (and Plone 4) this is no longer a requirement for participation with Zope 2 security. Therefore, it is now preferable to inherit from `zope.publisher.browser.BrowserView`, which is more general.

 Unlike page templates in skin layers, views (including their templates) execute in unprotected filesystem code and are not subject to additional through-the-web security restrictions.

Views are often located in a `browser` module. For larger packages, `browser` is often a package with its own `configure.zcml` file, included from the main ZCML file using:

```
<include package=".browser" />
```

Here is an example consisting of a class `GuitarsListing` and a **template** (not shown) in the file `guitarlisting.pt`. The base class `__init__()` method (acting as the multi-adapter's factory) will assign `self.context` and `self.request` appropriately.

```
from zope.publisher.browser import BrowserView

class GuitarListing(BrowserView):
    """List guitars found in the current context
    """

    def list_guitars(self):
        ...
```

In ZCML, we would register this with:

```
<browser:page
    name="list-guitars"
    class=".listing.GuitarListing"
    template="guitarlisting.pt"
    for="..interfaces.IGuitarFolder"
    permission="zope2.View"
    />
```

Here, the `for` attribute refers to the type of context for which the view is available (the `request` part of the multi-adapter is implied, but can be specialized with the `layer` attribute, as we saw in *Chapter 8, Creating a Custom Theme*). The `permission` attribute is required. `zope.Public` can be used to define a view that is available to anyone. Other standard permissions, including the CMF core permissions described in *Chapter 6, Security and Workflow*, can be used as well, as shown here.

Inside a view page template, the implicit variables `context`, `request`, and `view` will refer to the context object (`guitars`), the request and the view instance itself, respectively. This allows us to put all the display logic inside the view class, exemplified by `list_guitars()`, and use simple TAL constructs like `view/list_guitars` in the template.

 Refer to `http://plone.org/documentation/manual/theme-reference/buildingblocks/skin/templates` or `http://docs.zope.org/zope2/zope2book/` for more details about the TAL syntax.

The `class` attribute of the ZCML directive could be omitted if we had no need for a class to manage display logic, so long as we provided a `template`. Conversely, we could implement a view without a template by supplying a `class` that implements the `__call__()` method to return a unicode string.

For example, here is a sketch of a view that returns CSV data as an attachment, allowing the user to download it:

```
import csv
from StringIO import StringIO
from zope.publisher.browser import BrowserView

class CSVData(BrowserView):

    def _getData(self):
        # return a list of 3-item lists here

    def __call__(self):
        out = StringIO()

        writer = csv.writer(out)

        # Write header
        writer.writerow(["Item", "Price", "Quantity"])

        # Write data
        for row in self._getData():
            writer.writerow(row)

        response = self.request.response
        response.setHeader('Content-Type', 'text/csv')
```

```
response.setHeader('Content-Disposition',
    'attachment; filename="data.csv"'
)
return out.getvalue()
```

Other times, we want to choose between multiple templates. In this case, we can explicitly declare our templates in code using the `ViewPageTemplateFile` class. Here is a sketch of a view that looks for a request variable to determine which page template to render:

```
import csv
from StringIO import StringIO
from zope.publisher.browser import BrowserView

from Products.Five.browser.pagetemplatefile import \
    ViewPageTemplateFile

class MultiPageView(BrowserView):

    template1 = ViewPageTemplateFile('template1.pt')
    template2 = ViewPageTemplateFile('template2.pt')

    def __call__(self):
        form = self.request.form

        if form.get('page') == 'page2':
            return self.template2()
        else:
            return self.template1()
```

 A page template referenced with the `template` ZCML attribute is available to the relevant `class` under the variable `self.index`.

Sometimes, we have nothing to render at all. This can be the case if we are defining a view for some shared utility functions which is looked up by other views or templates, but never rendered on its own. In this case, we omit both the `__call__()` method and the `template` ZCML attribute. If we had a view called `@@guitar_utils`, we could look it up in a page template with:

```
<tal:block define="utils_view context/@@guitar_utils">
```

Or, in Python from another view class:

```
utils_view = getMultiAdapter((self.context, self.request,),
    name="guitar_utils")
```

As we saw in *Chapter 8, Creating a Custom Theme*, it is possible to register a view for a particular **browser layer**. During traversal, Plone sets a marker interface on the request to indicate the current skin and any activated browser layers (via `browserlayer.xml`). Since the view is a multi-adapter on the context and the request, a view for a particular browser layer is a more specific adapter on the request, compared to a view not registered for a layer. The default layer is `zope.publisher.interfaces.browser.IDefaultBrowserLayer`.

```
<browser:page
    name="list-guitars"
    class=".listing.GuitarsListing"
    template="guitarlisting.pt"
    for=".interfaces.IGuitarsFolder"
    layer=".interfaces.IThemeSpecific"
    permission="zope2.View"
    />
```

It is also possible to define views using a grokker, through the `grok.View` base class. For example:

```
from five import grok
class GuitarListing(grok.View):
    """List guitars found in the current context
    """
    grok.name('list-guitars')
    grok.context(IGuitarFolder)
    grok.require('zope2.View')

    def list_guitars(self):
        ...
```

The `grok.View` base class adds some features beyond the standard `BrowserView` base class which you should be aware of:

- You can override the `update()` method to prepare any information for the view. If this results in a redirect (using `self.request.response.redirect()`), the view will not be rendered.

- You can override the `render()` method if you want to manually construct a response. If you do not, a template must be associated with the view.

- You should normally *not* override `__call__()`, since the base class version of this is responsible for calling `update()` and `render()` at the appropriate times.

- A template is automatically associated with the view by looking for a file `${modulename}_templates/${viewname}.pt`. For example, if the view `GuitarListing` was found in the module `listing.py`, `five.grok` would look for a page template in `listing_templates/guitarlisting.pt`. If no template is found and the `render()` method is not defined, a configuration exception will be raised on startup.

- The view name defaults to the class name all in lowercase if the `grok.name()` directive is not used. In this case, the default name would be `guitarlisting`.

- The view defaults to being public if the `grok.require()` directive is not used to indicate the name of a required permission.

- A browser layer interface can be specified using `grok.layer()`.

In the next chapter, we will see several examples of views used to render custom content types, and in *Chapter 11, Standalone Views and Forms*, we will cover standalone views and auto-generated forms.

Content providers and viewlets

When building pages with page templates, we can use METAL macros to include other pages. However, you may also see statements such as:

```
<div tal:replace="structure provider:guitars.header" />
```

The `provider:` expression type comes from `zope.contentprovider` (with some overrides in `Products.Five.viewlet` to support Zope 2). It will perform an operation analogous to:

```
provider = getMultiAdapter((context, request, view,),
                           name="guitars.header")
return provider()
```

That is, the content provider is a named multi-adapter of the context, request and the current view instance. For skin layer templates (which are not Zope browser views), Plone's `main_template` will define the default view to be the `@@plone` view, which is described in the interface `Products.CMFPlone.browser.interfaces.IPlone`.

Content providers are rarely used directly, but they are the building blocks for **viewlets**. A **viewlet manager** is a content provider which, when rendered, will locate any number of viewlets appropriate for the current context, request, and view that are registered to the particular viewlet manager. As you may have guessed, there are some named multi-adapters involved under the hood. However, unlike raw content providers, there are ZCML directives to make things easier.

To create a new viewlet manager, we must first define a marker interface for it:

```
from zope.viewlet.interfaces import IViewletManager
class IGuitarsHeader(IViewletManager):
    """A viewlet manager that is put at the head of a guitar listing
    """
```

Then we register it in ZCML with:

```
<browser:viewletManager
    name="guitars.header"
    provides=".interfaces.IGuitarsHeader"
    permission="zope2.View"
    />
```

The name should be unique. The convention is to use a dotted name prefixed with the package name.

It is possible to specify a custom implementation of the viewlet manager, which allows us to control the rendering of viewlets more precisely. In Plone, we normally use the implementation from `plone.app.viewletmanager`, to gain support for the `@@manage-viewlets` screen and viewlet reordering using the `viewlets.xml` GenericSetup syntax:

```
<browser:viewletManager
    name="guitars.header"
    provides=".interfaces.IGuitarsHeader"
    permission="zope2.View"
    class="plone.app.viewletmanager.manager.OrderedViewletManager"
    />
```

We can now register any number of viewlets for this viewlet manager.

```
<browser:viewlet
    name="guitars.headers.adbanner"
    manager=".interfaces.IGuitarsHeader"
    class=".ads.GuitarAds"
    permission="zope2.View"
    />
```

We can also use the attributes `layer` and `view` to reference specific interfaces for the request (browser layer) and view. The latter allows us to have a viewlet in a general viewlet manager (say, one defined in `main_template`) that is shown on one particular view but not all views.

As an example, here is a viewlet that is only shown on the main view of an object, but not on any other tabs or templates. This works because `IViewView` is a marker interface applied to the view instance during page construction when Plone renders the default view of a content item:

```
<browser:viewlet
    name="guitars.headers.adbanner"
    manager="plone.app.layout.viewlets.interfaces.IAboveContent"
    view="plone.app.layout.globals.interfaces.IViewView"
    class=".ads.GuitarAds"
    permission="zope2.View"
    />
```

Because viewlets are multi-adapters, the usual rules about overrides apply. We could have a general viewlet for all views, and a more specific one with the same name for a particular type of context, request and/or view.

Unlike views, viewlets (actually content providers) are not rendered by being called. Instead, they must provide the methods `update()` and `render()`. During rendering, `update()` is called on all the viewlets in a viewlet manager, before `render()` is called on each viewlet in turn. The results of the `render()` calls are concatenated and then inserted into the output stream. The `update()` method should be used to update state from the request, potentially allowing viewlets to communicate with each other prior to final rendering.

Here is an example, again using a page template for rendering. As with views, the implicit `view` variable can be used in the template to reference methods on the viewlet class:

```
from zope.interface import implements
from zope.viewlet.interfaces import IViewlet
from zope.publisher.browser import BrowserView
from Products.Five.browser.pagetemplatefile import \
    ViewPageTemplateFile

class GuitarAds(BrowserView):
    """Rotating ads for new guitars
    """
    implements(IViewlet)

    def __init__(self, context, request, view, manager):
        self.context = context
        self.request = request
        self.__parent__ = view # from IContentProvider
        self.manager = manager # from IViewlet
```

```
def update(self):
  pass

render = ViewPageTemplateFile("rotating_ads.pt")
```

Plone inserts a number of viewlet managers in `main_template` and the standard content type views, offering third party components various places to plug into the general user interface. These are defined in `plone.app.layout.viewlets` and use the viewlet manager implementation from `plone.app.viewletmanager`.

Again, it is possible to use `five.grok` to register a viewlet. The syntax is:

```
from five import grok
from plone.app.layout.viewlets.interfaces import IAboveContent
from plone.app.layout.globals.interfaces import IViewView

class GuitarAds(grok.Viewlet):

    grok.name('guitars.headers.adbanner")
    grok.require('zope2.View')
    grok.viewletmanager(IAboveContent)
    grok.view(IViewView)

    ...
```

A specific context may be set using `grok.context()`, and the viewlet can be restricted to a particular browser layer using `grok.layer()`. As with views, a template will be automatically associated based on the module and class name, unless the `render()` method is implemented.

 In a template for viewlet registered with `five.grok`, the viewlet class instance will be available as the variable `viewlet`, not `view`. `view` will refer to the current view instance wherein the viewlet is rendered instead.

Synchronous events

Zope Component Architecture events allow us to easily emit events and register subscribers for those events from elsewhere. Events are synchronous – emitting code will block until all event handlers have completed – and unordered – there are no guarantees about the sequence in which event handlers are called.

To define a new type of event, all we need is an interface that identifies the event, and a concrete class implementing it.

```
>>> from zope.interface import Interface, Attribute
```

```
>>> class INewGigEvent(Interface):
...     """An event signaling that there's a new gig in town
...     """
...
...     band = Attribute("Name of the band")

>>> from zope.interface import implements
>>> class NewGigEvent(object):
...     implements(INewGigEvent)
...
...     def __init__(self, band):
...         self.band = band
```

Elsewhere, we would then define a subscriber for this event. This is simply a callable, which will be passed the event when invoked:

```
>>> from zope.component import adapter
>>> @adapter(INewGigEvent)
... def invite_friends(new_gig):
...     print "Hey guys, let's go see", new_gig.band
```

The @adapter decorator is used to identify the type of event being handled. This has to do with the fact that events are really just a special case of **subscription adapters**. Unlike regular adapters, there can be multiple subscription adapters adapting an object to a particular interface. They are not used very often, except in situations like object validation.

Event subscribers are registered with ZCML:

```
<subscriber handler=".events.invite_friends" />
```

If we did not use the @adapter decorator, we could specify the type of event explicitly:

```
<subscriber
    for=".interfaces.INewGigEvent"
    handler=".events.invite_friends"
    />
```

If we were using five.grok configuration instead, we would do:

```
>>> from five import grok
>>> @grok.subscribe(INewGigEvent)
... def invite_friends(new_gig):
...     print "Hey guys, let's go see", new_gig.band
```

Triggering the event, and thus calling all appropriate event subscribers, is as simple as:

```
>>> from zope.event import notify
>>> notify(NewGigEvent("The Gypsy Sun and Rainbow Band"))
Hey guys, let's go see The Gypsy Sun and Rainbow Band
```

There is no need to explicitly register the event type, because event subscribers are found based on the interface(s) provided by the event object. This also means that if an event object provides an interface that has a base interface, and there is a more general subscriber for the base interface, this subscriber will be called as well.

Object events

Zope and Plone emit a few generic events, known as **object events**, when items are added to, removed from, or moved in containers, as well as when they are first created, modified or copied. These events all derive from `zope.component.interfaces.IObjectEvent` and are defined in `zope.lifecycleevent`.

We can register subscribers for object events just like any other type of event, but we are usually only interested in handling an object event for a particular type of object. Therefore, we will register an event subscriber for both the object type and the event type:

```
>>> class IBand(Interface):
...       """A band
...       """
...
...       name = Attribute("The name of the band")
>>> class Band(object):
...       implements(IBand)
...
...       def __init__(self, name):
...           self.name = name
>>> from zope.lifecycleevent.interfaces import IObjectModifiedEvent
>>> @adapter(IBand, IObjectModifiedEvent)
... def band_changed(band, event):
...       assert band == event.object # At least normally, see below
...       print "Changes to the lineup in", band.name
```

And in ZCML:

```
<subscriber handler=".events.band_changed" />
```

Or, if we did not use the `@adapter` decorator, separating the interfaces by whitespace:

```
<subscriber
    for=".interfaces.IBand
         zope.lifecycleevent.interfaces.IObjectModifiedEvent"
    handler=".events.band_changed"
    />
```

Or, with `five.grok`:

```
>>> @grok.subscribe(IBand, IObjectModifiedEvent)
... def band_changed(band, event):
...     assert band == event.object # At least normally, see below
...     print "Changes to the lineup in", band.name
```

There is no difference in the way that an object event is emitted, although we must ensure that we construct the object event instance properly, so that `event.object` references the right object:

```
>>> from zope.lifecycleevent import ObjectModifiedEvent
>>> beatles = Band("The Beatles")
>>> notify(ObjectModifiedEvent(beatles))
Changes to the lineup in The Beatles
```

Because we are now relying on two interfaces, the subscriber is passed two objects: the object and the event. In most cases, as asserted in the code example, the object passed as the first parameter and `event.object` will be the same.

There is one exception: **container events** are re-dispatched to items inside the container recursively. For example, if a folder is moved or deleted, items inside that folder will be notified with the appropriate event. In this case `event.object` will refer to the folder the event originated from, whilst the object passed as the first parameter will be the child object currently being processed.

Container events, emitted largely from `OFS.ObjectManager`, are a little tricky, because they all provide `IObjectMovedEvent`. This specifies attributes `oldParent`, `oldName`, `newParent` and `newName` referring to where the object used to be and what it was called, and where it is now located and what it is now called. In an `IObjectAddedEvent`, `oldParent` and `oldName` are both `None` – the object moved in from the great unknown. In an `IObjectRemovedEvent`, the reverse is true – the object moved away into the ether. This means that if we register a subscriber for `IObjectMovedEvent`, it will be called when objects are renamed, moved, added or removed. In this case, we may need to explicitly check whether any of the aforementioned four variables are `None` if we want to react only when objects are actually moved.

Given the generic and object-centric nature of the Plone user interface, it is no surprise that object events are everywhere. A few of the more commonly used types of object events include:

- The aforementioned three container events in `zope.lifecycleevent.interfaces` - `IObjectAddedEvent`, `IObjectRemovedEvent` and the more general `IObjectMovedEvent`. (Note that these events used to live in `zope.app.container.interfaces` before being moved to `zope.lifecycleevent`.)

- The lifecycle events `IObjectCreatedEvent` and `IObjectModifiedEvent` from `zope.lifecycleevent.interfaces`, which are emitted from view code when objects are first created and subsequently modified.

- Archetypes-specific events in `Products.Archetypes.interfaces` including `IObjectInitializedEvent` and `IObjectEditedEvent`, both of which inherit from `IObjectModifiedEvent`. These deal with the fact that Archetypes objects are created in the ZODB before they are first populated with real data. You can think of these as "safe" versions of `IObjectCreatedEvent` and `IObjectModifiedEvent` for Archetypes content objects.

- Workflow events like `Products.CMFCore.interfaces.IActionSucceededEvent` and the more low-level `Products.DCWorkflow.IAfterTransitionEvent`.

You can create your own object events by inheriting from and fulfilling `zope.component.interfaces.IObjectEvent`. If you are curious about how the re-dispatching of object events work, take a look at `zope.component.event`, in particular the `objectEventNotify()` function.

Summary

In this chapter, we have taken a high-level look at Zope programming concepts, including:

- Zope as an object publisher
- Traversal of object graphs
- Automatic ZODB persistence
- Zope 2's concept of "acquisition"
- Using the catalog to search for objects in the ZODB
- Describing components with interfaces
- Using the utility registry to look up singletons
- Using the utility registry as a general registry of homogenous components

- Using adapters to model different aspects of objects independently of class inheritance hierarchies
- Zope browser style views
- Zope's synchronous events system

Don't worry if this is all a bit much to take in on the first reading. Take a look at the `optilux.codeexamples` package that can be found on the book's accompanying website (`https://www.packtpub.com/professional-plone-4-development/book`), and play with the examples there. If you want to explore the namespace at a particular point of a doctest interactively, remember that you can add this line to enter the debugger:

```
>>> import pdb; pdb.set_trace()
```

In the remainder of Part 3, we will put the concepts from this chapter to use when creating content types, building forms and interactive functionality, talking to relational databases, and managing users and groups. You may find it useful to come back to this chapter from time to time when you see Zope programming concepts demonstrated as part of the examples we will present later in the book.

10
Custom Content Types

Plone is a content management system, so it is not surprising that programming for Plone usually revolves around content. Although it is possible to employ traditional web development techniques such as using standalone forms to populate a database, Plone is most powerful as a platform when solutions can be modeled in terms of hierarchical, semi-structured content types.

In this chapter, we will cover:

- Design patterns that allow us to model problems in terms of content types and content hierarchies
- The Dexterity content type framework, and how it relates to the Archetypes framework
- Creating a distribution containing Dexterity content types
- Content schemata, fields, and widgets
- Vocabularies and validation
- Content item security
- Indexing fields in the catalog
- Creating views for content items
- Using the Archetypes schema extender to modify existing types
- Creating portlets using our custom content types

Content-centric design

Let us revisit the requirements from *Chapter 2, Introduction to the Case Study*, which relate to cinemas and films. We will delay considering the actual screening of a film at a particular cinema until *Chapter 12, Relational Databases*, when we show how to connect to an external database. We will also delay reporting on cinemas and films until the next chapter, when we look at creating standalone forms and dynamic pages.

Requirement	Importance
The site should show information about all of Optilux's cinemas.	High
Non-technical cinema staff should be able to update information about each cinema.	High
The site should allow staff to highlight promotions and special events. These may apply to one or more cinemas.	High
Cinema staff should be able to publish information about new films. It should be possible to update this information after publication.	High

The nouns in these requirements, together with the information architecture proposed in *Chapter 5, Developing a Site Strategy*, suggest that we need five content types — *Cinema Folder, Cinema, Film Folder, Film*, and *Promotion*. These are represented in the following class diagram, which is a more detailed version of the relevant parts of the high-level initial class diagram presented in *Chapter 2, Introduction to the Case Study*.

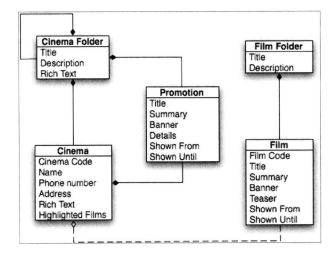

This shows that films are contained within film folders—for example, to group similar films—and cinemas are created within cinema folders—for example, to group cinemas by geographical location. Cinema folders may contain other cinema folders, allowing arbitrary nesting.

Promotions are permitted inside both cinema folders and cinemas, to allow promotions specific to one cinema or to a group of cinemas in the same folder. We will not show promotions in regular content listings, but rather through a custom portlet displayed when viewing a cinema folder or cinema. Alongside specific promotions, we allow the manager of a cinema to select one or more "highlighted films" from across the site to display next to that cinema.

Notice the inclusion of the **Film Code** and **Cinema Code** fields. These will be simple strings for now and are not shown to the user. When we connect cinemas and films to the external database system which manages film screenings and custom bookings, these will act as keys in its tables.

There are other legitimate ways in which we could have modeled these particular requirements. For example, we could have done away with the *Cinema Folder* and *Film Folder* types and let *Cinema* and *Film* be first-order content types, or we could have required all promotions to live in a separate *Promotion Folder*. However, some general concepts usually apply:

- Plone provides a rich user interface for managing content items. It is usually a good idea to leverage this by conceptualizing problems as content types with fields for the data items we need to manage.

- If we need a one-to-many relationship, it is often easiest to model the "one" as a container (folder) and the "many" as children inside that container, as we have done with *Cinema* and *Promotion*.

- If it is impractical to have the "many" part of the relationship live inside the "one", we can use reference fields instead. For many-to-many type relationships, such as the "related items" field found on most standard content types, you will need to use references as well.

- Most users are accustomed to thinking in terms of folders and files. By allowing a *Promotion* to sit inside a *Cinema* as well as a higher-level *Cinema Folder*, we can easily and naturally manage promotions relative to specific cinemas or cinema folders at any depth.

- Where possible, we should avoid the need for complicated or composite content edit forms. The edit form found on the **Edit** tabs of Plone's standard content types is generated from content type schemata. It is perfectly possible to write our own edit form if the standard one is too limiting, but it can be a laborious process.

- If we find ourselves with dozens (or even hundreds) of content types, or write types with a huge number of fields, something is wrong. Neither Plone nor our users will be particularly pleased about having to navigate a maze of content types or lengthy edit forms.

Choosing a content type framework

Recall from *Chapter 1, Plone in Context*, that Plone is built atop the CMF, which provides the fundamental components to manage content types and items. It is possible to create content types using the facilities of the CMF alone, but this can be quite cumbersome. A higher-level framework can help us make types that are consistent and powerful by providing a number of features, such as:

- Automatic generation of add and edit forms from a declarative schema

- Control over validation and error handling to ensure content items are always in a consistent state

- Standard views, which may suffice for simple types, but which we will often override to control how a content item of a given type appears to the end user

- Management of the permissions and security declarations that control who can add, edit, and view content items of a given type

There are two Plone content type frameworks in common use today: Archetypes and Dexterity.

Archetypes is the older of the two, and has been part of Plone since version 2.1. It has been enormously beneficial to Plone developers' productivity and is used not only by Plone's core content types, but also by a huge number of add-ons. However, some aspects of its design are showing their age. For example:

- Archetypes uses its own schemata syntax instead of the one provided by `zope.schema` that is used everywhere else in the Zope Toolkit (which, admittedly, Archetypes predates).

- Archetypes relies on code generation (the so-called Class Generator) to allow dynamic calculation of field values, resulting in methods like `getFoo()` and `setFoo()` instead of the more modern pattern of having a `property` called `foo`.

- Archetypes does not support true add forms, resulting in the need to create temporary objects during initialization using the `portal_factory` tool, which leads to all kinds of complex workarounds in the codebase.

Dexterity is a newer, simpler framework based on modern Zope Toolkit design principles. It employs commonly used technologies such as `zope.schema` for defining schemata and `z3c.form` for generating forms.

Working with Dexterity, we can write less boilerplate and integrate our content type code more seamlessly with the rest of our application. It is even possible to define basic Dexterity types through the web, using point-and-click only.

The examples in this chapter will use Dexterity. We will focus on filesystem development and schemata defined in Python. For more information and documentation about Dexterity, see `http://plone.org/products/dexterity`.

That said, Archetypes is still a good deal more widely used than Dexterity, and will continue to be a part of Plone for the foreseeable future. For some use cases—most notably support for multilingual content and translation workflows—Archetypes still has the edge.

 The first edition of this book covered Archetypes exclusively. The Archetypes chapter was updated for Plone 4 before it was decided that the book should cover Dexterity instead. You can find the (unedited) Archetypes draft online at `https://www.packtpub.com/professional-plone-4-development/book`.

Creating a distribution

Our new content types will be contained in a new distribution, called `optilux.cinemacontent`, containing a package with the same name.

1. As before, we will create a skeleton using ZopeSkel and register the new package with our project's buildout environment. In the `src/` directory, we run the following command:

   ```
   $ ../bin/zopeskel plone optilux.cinemacontent
   ```

   Again, we stick with "easy" mode and answer `True` when asked to create a GenericSetup profile.

2. We then edit the generated `setup.py` file. We first update the `install_requires` line to add a few dependencies and add an `extras_require` line to enable the `[test]` extra:

   ```
   install_requires=[
       'setuptools',
       'Products.CMFPlone',
       'plone.app.dexterity [grok]',
   ```

```
        'plone.app.referenceablebehavior',
        'plone.app.relationfield',
        'plone.namedfile [blobs]',
    ],
    extras_require={
        'test': ['plone.app.testing',]
    },
```

We depend on `plone.app.dexterity` for the basic content type framework
and include the `[grok]` extra to be able to use Grok-style convention-over-
configuration as we saw in *Chapter 9, Nine Core Concepts of Zope Programming*.
We also depend on `plone.app.referenceablebehavior`, which will allow
us to make our Dexterity items referenceable from Archetypes reference
fields such as the standard Plone "related items" fields, `plone.app.`
`relationfield` to be able to use reference fields, and `plone.namedfile` with
the `[blobs]` extra, which will allow us to use ZODB BLOBs for storing files
and images. More on all of these later in the chapter.

3. As in *Chapter 5, Developing a Site Strategy*, we can also comment out or
    remove the `setup_requires` and `paster_plugins` lines.

4. Next, we edit `packages.cfg` in the top level buildout directory to register the
    new distribution and include the Dexterity Known Good Set of versions:

```
[buildout]
extensions = mr.developer buildout.dumppickedversions
extends =
# Known good sets of eggs we may be using
    http://dist.plone.org/release/4.1/versions.cfg
    http://good-py.appspot.com/release/plone.app.
theming/1.0b8?plone=4.1rc2
    http://good-py.appspot.com/release/dexterity/1.0.1?plone=4.1
    versions.cfg


...


[eggs]
main =
    optilux.policy
test =
    optilux.policy [test]
    optilux.theme [test]
    optilux.cinemacontent [test]
devtools =
    bpython
    plone.reload
```

```
Products.PDBDebugMode
Products.PrintingMailHost
Products.DocFinderTab
[sources]
optilux.policy = fs optilux.policy
optilux.theme  = fs optilux.theme
optilux.cinemacontent = fs optilux.cinemacontent
```

Here, we are using version 1.0.1 of the Dexterity framework. A newer version may be available by the time you read this, so check `http://plone.org/products/dexterity`.

 In a future version of Plone, possibly as early as 4.3, the Dexterity Known Good Set may be merged into the Plone Known Good Set. When that happens, it will no longer be necessary to include the version set explicitly as shown previously.

5. We then update the `optilux.policy` package to ensure `optilux.cinemacontent` is installed as a dependency. First, we edit the `install_requires` parameter in `src/optilux.policy/setup.py`:

```
install_requires=[
        'setuptools',
        'Plone',
        'Products.PloneFormGen',
        'optilux.theme',
        'optilux.cinemacontent',
    ],
```

6. Finally, we edit `profiles/default/metadata.xml` in the same package to add:

```
<dependencies>
    <dependency>profile-Products.PloneFormGen:default</dependency>
    <dependency>profile-optilux.theme:default</dependency>
    <dependency>profile-optilux.cinemacontent:default</dependency>
</dependencies>
```

With this in place, we should be able to run buildout again and see our new distribution installed. As before, we run:

```
$ bin/buildout
```

Contents of the distribution

The complete `optilux.cinemacontent` package is part of the source code which accompanies this book. You are encouraged to browse the code as you read this chapter, and to borrow from it in your own code as much as you would like.

For the sake of brevity, we will not reproduce every line of code here, usually where code for the different content types is conceptually similar. To provide additional guidance, the source code contains plenty of inline comments, although these are taken out of the code listings in this chapter.

The package follows generally accepted conventions for code layout. Under `src/optilux.cinemacontent/optilux/cinemacontent`, you will find the following files and directories pertaining to our content types:

File	Purpose
`__init__.py`	Registers a message factory for internationalization of strings.
`configure.zcml`	Basic component configuration, including grokking of the package (see *Chapter 9, Nine Core Concepts of Zope Programming*) and registration of the GenericSetup extension profile to install and configure our new content types.
`permissions.zcml`	Defines custom add permissions: one for each content type. This file is included from `configure.zcml`.
`interfaces.py`	Contains the interfaces describing shared components. Note that we will follow Dexterity conventions and keep the content type schemata interfaces in their respective modules alongside any custom logic or views for each content type.
`cinema_templates/ view.pt`	The page template for the default view (`@@view`) of the *Cinema* content type, following `five.grok` conventions (see *Chapter 9, Nine Core Concepts of Zope Programming*).
`cinemafolder.py`	Definition of the *Cinema Folder* content type schema and view.

File	Purpose
`cinemafolder_templates/view.pt`	The page template for the default view (`@@view`) of the *Cinema Folder* content type, as per `five.grok` conventions (see *Chapter 9, Nine Core Concepts of Zope Programming*).
`film.py`	Definition of the *Film* content type schema, validators and view.
`film_templates/view.pt`	The page template for the default view (`@@view`) of the *Film* content type, as per `five.grok` conventions (see *Chapter 9, Nine Core Concepts of Zope Programming*).
`filmfolder.py`	The schema of the *Film Folder* content type, which does not have its own view (it uses the standard folder listing view instead).
`promotion.py`	Definition of the *Promotion* content type schema and view.
`promotion_templates/view.pt`	The page template for the default view (`@@view`) of the *Promotion* content type, as per `five.grok` conventions (see *Chapter 9, Nine Core Concepts of Zope Programming*).
`profiles/`	Contains the GenericSetup extension profile used to install the product.
`static/`	Icons and stylesheets used by the content types.
`testing.py`	Test layer setup.
`tests/`	Test suites that exercise the various content types and other code.

Using the Dexterity framework

We will not provide a comprehensive reference to all of Dexterity in this chapter because such a guide already exists. Instead, we will show the key techniques of modern Dexterity development and reference other documentation where necessary.

 Detailed Dexterity documentation can be found in the Dexterity Developer's Manual found at `http://plone.org/products/dexterity/documentation/manual/developer-manual`.

What is in a content type?

Before we show the code behind the various content types in `optilux.cinemacontent`, it is helpful to understand the components that make up a content type in Plone:

Component	Purpose	Example
Schema	Defines the fields of the content type, and is the basis for generating add and edit forms, automatic validation, and other types of introspection. The fields in a schema describe properties that can be set or read on the content object.	`ICinema` in `cinema.py`.
Class	Python class used for instances of the type. Dexterity provides two standard classes: `Item` and `Container`. It is possible to extend these, but most types will not need to do so.	`optilux.CinemaFolder.xml` in `profiles/default/types` declares that the *Cinema Folder* type uses the `Container` class, whilst `optilux.Cinema.xml` configures *Cinema* to use the `Item` class.
Factory	Responsible for creating new instances of a type. Dexterity provides a default factory that is rarely overridden.	N/A
Factory Type Information (FTI)	A persistent object in the `portal_types` tool in the ZMI that defines how a given type may be used, for example, where it can be added and what items can be added inside it. References the schema and various views (in the form of **actions**). Usually configured with GenericSetup, but may be created or cloned through the web. Dexterity FTIs may be looked up as a named utility providing `IDexterityFTI`, where the name matches the content type name.	`optilux.CinemaFolder.xml` in `profiles/default/types`.

Component	Purpose	Example
View	In this context, the default view used for the type. Conventionally called `@@ view` and mapped to the `(Default)` method alias, ensuring that this view is rendered when a request is made for the content item itself with no explicit view at the end of the URL.	The class `View` in `cinemafolder.py`, which has an (automatically) associated template in `cinemafolder_templates/ view.pt`.
Add form	A form used to create a new instance of the type. By default, Dexterity generates one based on the schema and any schema fields provided by enabled behaviors. See the Dexterity Developer's Manual for details about overriding the add form.	N/A
Edit form	A form used to edit existing instances of the type. By default, Dexterity generates one based on the schema and any schema fields provided by enabled behaviors. See the Dexterity Developer's Manual for details about overriding the edit form.	N/A
Behaviors	Reusable components that can be enabled on a per-type basis through enumeration in the FTI. May confer additional schema fields, apply interfaces dynamically or enable adapters that provide specific functionality. See the Dexterity documentation for details about writing new behaviors.	`optilux.CinemaFolder. xml` in `profiles/default/ types` enables several behaviors: `INameFromTitle`, which generates a content item id from the title entered by the user on the add form, `IReferenceable`, which makes it possible to reference a content item from an Archetypes content item, and `IDublinCore`, which adds the default metadata fields expected of most Plone content items.

Basic configuration

As in most Zope packages, we have an _init_.py file that defines a message factory used for internationalization of strings:

```
from zope.i18nmessageid import MessageFactory
CinemaMessageFactory = MessageFactory('optilux.cinemacontent')
```

We also have a configure.zcml file where we include our dependencies, opt into grokking of this package (see *Chapter 9, Nine Core Concepts of Zope Programming*) and register a GenericSetup extension profile:

```
<configure
    xmlns="http://namespaces.zope.org/zope"
    xmlns:i18n="http://namespaces.zope.org/i18n"
    xmlns:grok="http://namespaces.zope.org/grok"
    xmlns:genericsetup="http://namespaces.zope.org/genericsetup"
    i18n_domain="optilux.cinemacontent">

  <includeDependencies package="." />
  <include file="permissions.zcml" />

  <grok:grok package="." />

  <genericsetup:registerProfile
      name="default"
      title="Optilux content types"
      directory="profiles/default"
      description="Installs the optilux.cinemacontent package"
      provides="Products.GenericSetup.interfaces.EXTENSION"
      />

</configure>
```

We will come back to the extension profile and the included permissions.zcml later in this chapter.

Schemata and fields

The schema is usually the first part of a content type that we write. A schema is an interface that defines fields, most of which are found in the package zope.schema. Most Dexterity schemata derive from the class plone.directives.form.Schema, which allows certain convention-over-configuration directives to be applied, to supply hints to the standard add and edit forms, for example to hide certain fields or override the default widget used for a particular field.

For example, take the schema in `cinema.py`.

We begin with some imports:

```
from five import grok
from zope import schema
from plone.directives import form

from zope.interface import Invalid

from plone.app.textfield import RichText

from z3c.relationfield.schema import RelationList, RelationChoice
from plone.formwidget.contenttree import ObjPathSourceBinder

from optilux.cinemacontent import CinemaMessageFactory as _
from optilux.cinemacontent.film import IFilm

...
```

The standard field types are found in `zope.schema`, but we will also use fields from `plone.app.textfield` (rich text with a WYSIWYG editor) and `z3c.relationfield` (content references).

Next, we define a constraint function, which will be called to validate the value of the cinema code. It should return `True` if all is well, and raise an `Invalid` exception with an appropriate error message otherwise:

```
def cinemaCodeIsValid(value):
    """Contraint function to make sure the given cinema code is valid
    """
    if value:
        if len(value) < 4 or len(value) > 6 or \
                not value.startswith('C'):
            raise Invalid(
                _(u"The cinema code is not of the correct format")
                )
    return True
```

We then define the schema itself. `plone.directives.form.Schema` is simply a subclass of `zope.interface.Interface`, which acts as a marker to various grokkers that can operate on any directives in the schema.

```
class ICinema(form.Schema):
    """A cinema
    """
```

We list the fields of the content type in the body of the schema. Note that standard fields such as the content's title, description, creation date, and so on are supplied by a behavior (`IDublinCore`), which is listed in the GenericSetup file that creates the FTI. We will show this later in this chapter.

```
cinemaCode = schema.ASCIILine(
        title=_(u"Cinema code"),
        description=_(u"Code used in the bookings database"),
        constraint=cinemaCodeIsValid,
    )

phone = schema.TextLine(
        title=_(u"Phone number"),
      description=_(u"Please enter as the customer should dial"),
    )

text = RichText(
        title=_(u"Details"),
        description=_(u"Description of the cinema"),
    )

highlightedFilms = RelationList(
        title=_(u"Highlighted films"),
        description=_(u"Films to highlight for this cinema"),
        value_type=RelationChoice(
                source=ObjPathSourceBinder(
                        object_provides=IFilm.__identifier__
                ),
            ),
        required=False,
    )
```

For a full list of fields and their associated properties, see the reference at `http://plone.org/products/dexterity/documentation/manual/developer-manual/reference/fields`.

Form hints in the schema

By default, the generated add and edit forms will show, in order, each field from the schema and the schemata provided by any enabled behaviors, using the default widget for each field. We can supply hints to the forms (which use base classes provided by the `plone.autoform` package) to exert some more control over how the forms are rendered, without having to override them wholesale.

For example, consider this schema, adapted from the Dexterity Developer's Manual:

```
from five import grok
from zope import schema

from plone.directives import form, dexterity

from z3c.relationfield.schema import RelationChoice
from plone.formwidget.contenttree import ObjPathSourceBinder

from plone.formwidget.autocomplete import AutocompleteFieldWidget

from example.conference import _
from example.conference.presenter import IPresenter

class ISession(form.Schema):

    ...

    form.widget(presenter=AutocompleteFieldWidget)
    presenter = RelationChoice(
            title=_(u"Presenter"),
            source=ObjPathSourceBinder(
                    object_provides=IPresenter.__identifier__
                ),
            required=False,
        )
```

Here, we have specified an alternative widget for the `RelationChoice` field. The `AutocompleteFieldWidget` from `plone.formwidget.autocomplete` provides a 'search-as-you-type' auto-completion widget using the specified source (more on sources shortly). The Dexterity Developer's Manual contains an overview of the commonly used widgets.

> It is conventional to place a form directive immediately above the field it pertains to. However, the link between the field and the directive is made in arguments passed to the directive, not the placement of the directive relative to a field. In fact, most directives can optionally be passed several fields to configure at once.

Other directives can be used to omit fields from the forms entirely, make hidden fields, create tabbed field sets, or order fields relative to one another. These constructs are most useful when writing behaviors or other reusable schemata, but can sometimes be useful if fine-grained control over the rendering of forms is required. See the Dexterity Developer's Manual and the documentation for details.

> For forms that deviate significantly from the default, it is usually easiest to register custom add and edit forms. The Dexterity Developer's Manual contains examples of both.

Validation

The `constraint` set for the `cinemaCode` field provides simple validation of the value entered by the user when the add or edit form is submitted. Furthermore, each field has intrinsic type validation: an `Int` field, for instance, will show an error if a non-integer value is entered.

Some fields also have basic validation properties. For example, numeric fields types have `min` and `max` properties that can be used to control the minimum and maximum allowable values, while text fields generally support `min_length` and `max_length`. Finally, all fields are required (cannot be left blank) unless `required=False` is set. Refer to the Dexterity Developer's Manual for details about the specific validation properties available for each field type.

For more complicated validation, we can use a `z3c.form` field validator, which will execute as the add or edit form is saved. In `cinema.py`, we register such a validator to ensure each cinema code is unique across the site:

```
from z3c.form import validator
from plone.uuid.interfaces import IUUID
from Products.CMFCore.utils import getToolByName


...


class ValidateCinemaCodeUniqueness(validator.SimpleFieldValidator):
    """Validate site-wide uniqueness of cinema codes.
    """
```

The `validate()` function will be called to validate the form field for which the validator is registered. We call the base class validation first: without this, the field's intrinsic validation would be ignored.

```
def validate(self, value):
    super(ValidateCinemaCodeUniqueness, self).validate(value)
```

We then perform a catalog search to find any items with the same cinema code. We will show how to add the `cinemaCode` catalog index later in this section.

```
if value is not None:
```

```
catalog = getToolByName(self.context, 'portal_catalog')
results = catalog({'cinemaCode': value,
                   'object_provides': ICinema.__identifier__})
```

Finally, we compare the unique identifier (more on those in a moment) of the current item with the unique IDs of any returned results: without this check, we would get a validation error if we tried to save an item without changing its code.

```
contextUUID = IUUID(self.context, None)
for result in results:
    if result.UID != contextUUID:
        raise Invalid(
            _(u"The cinema code is already in use"))
```

The validator is registered as a multi-adapter with many discriminators. To avoid having to declare each one, we use a helper function from z3c.form to ensure this adapter is specific to a particular field in the ICinema schema:

```
validator.WidgetValidatorDiscriminators(
        ValidateCinemaCodeUniqueness,
        field=ICinema['cinemaCode'],
    )
```

Finally, we register the adapter. We've opted to use the five.grok approach here. See *Chapter 9, Nine Core Concepts of Zope Programming*, for details about the alternative ZCML syntax.

```
grok.global_adapter(ValidateCinemaCodeUniqueness)
```

While this is more cumbersome than registering a constraint, it allows access to the context (self.context) and request (self.request). It is also possible to provide different validators for different forms or contexts.

> If you do not require access to the context, you can use the @validator decorator from plone.directives.form to turn a simple function into a field validator discriminated by context, request, form, or field instance. See the http://pypi.python.org/pypi/plone.directives.form for details.

Refer to the Dexterity Developer's Manual for further examples and more advanced validation techniques.

Vocabularies

It is quite common to need a field from which the user chooses from a predefined list of values. We call this list a **vocabulary**. For single selection, we can use a Choice field; for multi-selection, we can use a Tuple, List, or Set field with a Choice as the value_type.

The simplest approach is to have a choice between several hardcoded values, for example:

```
gender = schema.Choice(
       title=_(u"Gender"),
       values=(u"Male", u"Female",)
   )
```

Here, the field gender will be a drop-down list where the user can choose either *Male* or *Female*.

For more advanced vocabularies, we can use a **source**, which is a named utility that provides a **vocabulary factory**, a callable (for example, a function) that is able to return a vocabulary. A vocabulary consists of **terms** with up to three properties:

- A value, which is what is stored on the underlying object. May be of any type.
- A token, which must be an ASCII string with a one-to-one mapping to the vocabularies items. This is the string that is passed between the user's browser and the server. By default, the token is calculated by calling str() on the value.
- A title, which should be a unicode string or message object that is shown to the user in the selection list.

The package plone.app.vocabularies that ships with Plone contains several useful sources. Here is an implementation from this package that provides a vocabulary of all currently available workflows:

```
from zope.i18n import translate
from zope.i18nmessageid import MessageFactory
from zope.interface import implements
from zope.schema.interfaces import IVocabularyFactory
from zope.schema.vocabulary import SimpleTerm
from zope.schema.vocabulary import SimpleVocabulary
from zope.site.hooks import getSite

from Acquisition import aq_get
from Products.CMFCore.utils import getToolByName
```

```
_ = MessageFactory('plone')

class WorkflowsVocabulary(object):
    implements(IVocabularyFactory)

    def __call__(self, context):
        items = []
        site = getSite()
        wtool = getToolByName(site, 'portal_workflow', None)
        if wtool is not None:
            items = [(w.title, w.id) for w in wtool.values()]
            items.sort()
            # initialize with value, token, title
            items = [SimpleTerm(i[1], i[1], i[0]) for i in items]
        return SimpleVocabulary(items)

WorkflowsVocabularyFactory = WorkflowsVocabulary()
```

This is registered in ZCML as:

```
<utility
    component=".workflow.WorkflowsVocabularyFactory"
    name="plone.app.vocabularies.Workflows"
    />
```

See *Chapter 9, Nine Core Concepts of Zope Programming* for the alternative
`five.grok` syntax (using `grok.global_utility`).

To use this (and illustrate a multi-select list), we could do:

```
workflows = schema.Tuple(
        title=_(u"Workflows"),
        value_type=schema.Choice(
            source="plone.app.vocabularies.Workflows",
        ),
    )
```

Rich text fields

The simplest way to store a block of text is to use `zope.schema.Text`, which will
store a unicode string and present an HTML `<textarea />` as the default widget. To
use a WYSIWYG text editor that renders HTML and strips out potentially dangerous
tags (as a security measure to guard against cross-site request forgery and cross-site
scripting attacks in case of untrusted editors), we can use a `RichText` field from
`plone.app.textfield` instead.

We have already seen an example of one in `cinema.py`:

```
from five import grok
from zope import schema
from plone.directives import form

from plone.app.textfield import RichText

...

class ICinema(form.Schema):

    ...

    text = RichText(
            title=_(u"Details"),
            description=_(u"Description of the cinema"),
        )
```

This field stores a `RichTextValue` object, which contains the source text, its MIME type and a cache of the final output text, usually in HTML. To render this in a page template, we can use the following syntax:

```
<div tal:replace="structure context/text/output" />
```

Please refer to the Dexterity Developer's Manual if you need to know how to manipulate `RichTextValue` objects programmatically.

Files, images, and BLOBs

The `plone.namedfile` package, which is a dependency of Dexterity, provides fields and helpers for working with file and image fields. In the browser, these render as file upload fields. On the server, they may be stored in one of the following two ways:

- As byte strings
- As BLOBs

The former is fine for small files, but can be inefficient for larger ones. As discussed in *Chapter 9, Nine Core Concepts of Zope Programming*, BLOBs can help reduce the size of the primary ZODB storage, improve the efficiency of the ZODB cache, and greatly improve the efficiency with which Zope can accept and serve large files.

 To ensure all dependencies required to work with BLOBs are included, make sure you depend on `plone.namedfile [blobs]` in your package.

The IFilm schema in film.py contains an example of a field containing an image BLOB:

```python
from five import grok
from zope import schema
from plone.directives import form

from zope.interface import Invalid

from plone.namedfile.interfaces import IImageScaleTraversable
from plone.namedfile.field import NamedBlobImage

from plone.app.textfield import RichText

from optilux.cinemacontent import CinemaMessageFactory as _

...

class IFilm(form.Schema, IImageScaleTraversable):
    filmCode = schema.ASCIILine(
            title=_(u"Film code"),
            description=_(u"Code used in the bookings database"),
            constraint=filmCodeIsValid,
        )

    image = NamedBlobImage(
            title=_(u"Banner image"),
            description=_(u"An image used to highlight this film"),
        )

    teaser = RichText(
            title=_(u"Teaser"),
            description=_(u"Information about the film"),
        )

    startDate = schema.Date(
            title=_(u'Start date'),
            description=_(u"First date that the film is showing"),
        )

    endDate = schema.Date(
            title=_(u'End date'),
            description=_(u"Last date that the film is showing"),
            required=True
        )
```

For non-image content, we would use NamedBlobFile as the field type instead of NamedBlobImage. The non-BLOB versions of the fields are called NamedFile and NamedImage.

To render an image in a page template, we can use the special `@@images` helper view. The simplest version is:

```
<img tal:replace="structure context/@@images/image" />
```

Note that this will only work if context provides `IImageScaleTraversable`. We ensure this is the case by mixing this into the `IFilm` schema interface.

The final path element (`/image`) refers to the name of the field, which must exist on the content. This will render the image exactly as uploaded.

Plone also supports image scaling to predefined sizes, which are managed in the **Image Handling** control panel under Plone's **Site Setup**.

 Use the `propertiestool.xml` import step to manage image scale dimensions with GenericSetup.

Knowing that one of the available sizes is `thumb`, we can scale the image to the dimensions defined for this size using:

```
<img tal:replace="structure context/@@images/image/thumb" />
```

In Python code, we could obtain the tag with:

```
scales = getMultiAdapter((context, request), name='images')
scale = scales.scale('image', scale='thumb')
imageTag = scale.tag()
```

For files, we may want to provide a link to download the file with the correct filename and MIME type. For this, we can use a construct like this in a page template:

```
<a tal:attributes="
   href string:${context/absolute_url}/@@download/fileField">Click here
to download</a>
```

The `@@download` view will ensure the correct response headers are set to download the file stored under the field named `fileField`.

Content reference fields

In the preceding ICinema schema, we saw an example of a relation field, also known as a reference field:

```
from z3c.relationfield.schema import RelationList, RelationChoice
from plone.formwidget.contenttree import ObjPathSourceBinder
```

```
. . .

class ICinema(form.Schema):

    . . .

    highlightedFilms = RelationList(
            title=_(u"Highlighted films"),
            description=_(u"Films to highlight for this cinema"),
            value_type=RelationChoice(
                    source=ObjPathSourceBinder(
                            object_provides=IFilm.__identifier__
                        ),
                ),
            required=False,
        )
```

This is a multi-valued reference. A single-valued reference would simply use a `RelationChoice` without a `RelationList` wrapper.

> To use relation fields, it is best to explicitly depend on `plone.app.relationfield` as shown earlier in this chapter. Future versions of Dexterity (probably from version 2.0) may ship with a simpler reference field implementation, relegating `plone.app.relationfield` to an optional installation.
>
> The reason for this is that some users with large, multi-database Plone installations have found it difficult to mange the integer ID storage mechanism that underpins the relationship catalog. They have had more success with storages based on sets of unique IDs, which, while not as powerful, are much simpler. Work is underway to develop a generic solution based on this approach, but is not generally available at the time of writing.

The `source` that is set for the relation choice field here is a special object known as a source binder. The source binder `ObjPathSourceBinder` can be passed a set of catalog query parameters as keyword arguments (but not as a dictionary), which are used to constrain what types of content items can be selected. Here, we are restricting the relationship to only allow references to objects that provide the `IFilm` schema.

Relation fields store `RelationValue` objects (or lists of such objects). These allow lazy loading of referenced objects using the property `to_object`. Here is an extract from the view of the *Cinema* type that uses the field above:

```
films = []

if self.context.highlightedFilms is not None:
```

```
for ref in self.context.highlightedFilms:
    obj = ref.to_object
    scales = getMultiAdapter((obj, self.request),
                                name='images')
    scale = scales.scale('image', scale='thumb')
    imageTag = None
    if scale is not None:
        imageTag = scale.tag()

    films.append({
            'url': obj.absolute_url(),
            'title': obj.title,
            'summary': obj.description,
            'imageTag': imageTag,
    })

return films
```

The relation engine is very powerful. For example, it is possible to do more advanced searches across content references. See the Dexterity Developer's Manual for more details.

Unique content identifiers

Since Plone 4.1, a package called `plone.uuid` provides a unified interface to obtain a **universally unique identifier (UUID)** for any type of object, including Archetypes and Dexterity content objects.

In Dexterity 1.0, you should enable the `plone.app.referenceablebehavior.referenceable.IReferenceable` behavior to ensure your types have UUIDs. In Dexterity 2.0, all types will have UUIDs by default.

The standard way to look up a UUID on an object (not a catalog brain!) is:

```
>>> from plone.uuid.interfaces import IUUID
>>> film1_uid = IUUID(film1)
```

Here, `IUUID` is an adapter interface, so we are in effect adapting an object (`film1`) to a UUID string.

Note that UUIDs are indexed in the catalog under the UID index and metadata column (note the single U — a historical accident). We saw an example of using this earlier when we showed the cinema code uniqueness validator.

Indexers

In *Chapter 9, Nine Core Concepts of Zope Programming*, we learned about how we can use the indexes in the catalog to search for content, and how to access information about search results through metadata columns.

To create an index for a custom field, we can often just register an index for the name of the field. This will cause the catalog to attempt to index an attribute with this name on any content item — possibly acquiring an index value from an acquisition parent.

Sometimes, we want to have more control, for example to calculate the value stored in the index or use a name that does not match the name of an existing attribute. Enter custom indexers: named adapters that can be used to calculate a value for indexing purposes.

Here is an example from `film.py`, which registers an indexer for the `start` index that is already part of Plone and used for things like the calendar. We use this to index the value of the `startDate` field.

```
from five import grok
from plone.indexer import indexer

...

@grok.adapter(IFilm, name='start')
@indexer(IFilm)
def filmStartIndexer(context):
    return context.startDate
```

The `@indexer` decorator from `plone.indexer` is used to turn the function into an indexer, and to limit it so that it only operates on objects providing `IFilm`. We then use `five.grok` to register it as a named adapter from `IFilm` with the name `"start"`. The adapter name matches the catalog index.

For some more advanced examples of custom indexers, see `Products.CMFPlone.CatalogTool`.

Content security

As we learned in *Chapter 6, Security and Workflow*, content security is primarily controlled by workflow. Dexterity's views employ the standard CMF permissions: the user must have the *Add portal content* permission to access the add form, *Modify portal content* to be able to edit a content item, and *View* to see the content item in folder listings or traverse to it. If we register custom views or forms, we can protect them with these or our own permissions.

Add permissions

Dexterity content types can also have a specific **add permission**, which will be required in addition to *Add portal content* to be allowed to add content. Per-type add permissions are usually a good idea, as they allow fine-grained control over what can be added where. At times, it is preferable to define one or two permissions per package, and let these be shared among multiple, related content types.

We have opted to define one add permission for each of our new types. In `permissions.zcml`, we have:

```
<configure
    xmlns="http://namespaces.zope.org/zope"
    xmlns:i18n="http://namespaces.zope.org/i18n"
    i18n_domain="optilux.cinemacontent">

<permission
    id="optilux.AddCinemaFolder"
    title="Optilux: Add Cinema Folder"
    />

<permission
    id="optilux.AddCinema"
    title="Optilux: Add Cinema"
    />

<permission
    id="optilux.AddFilmFolder"
    title="Optilux: Add Film Folder"
    />

<permission
```

```
        id="optilux.AddFilm"
        title="Optilux: Add Film"
        />
    <permission
        id="optilux.AddPromotion"
        title="Optilux: Add Promotion"
        />

</configure>
```

Note the naming convention where the title is prefixed by a shared name. This makes it easy to see the permissions in one place on the **Security** tab in the ZMI.

These permissions are assigned to roles in the `rolemap.xml` import step. It is conventional to assign add permissions to the roles *Owner*, *Manager*, *Site Administrator*, and *Contributor* in most cases. Refer to *Chapter 6, Security and Workflow*, for more details.

Dexterity add permissions are associated with types through the `add_permission` property in the FTI. We will show the configuration of the various FTIs with GenericSetup later in this chapter.

Schema permissions

Occasionally, it may be useful to control security on a per-field basis. Dexterity allows us to assign a read permission and/or a write permission to each field using form schema hints. These mainly affect the add and edit forms, as well as the default view generated by Dexterity: if a user does not have a field's read permission, the field will not be shown in the default view; if he or she does not have the relevant write permission, the field will not be shown on the add or edit forms.

The following is an example of setting a write permission, adapted from the Dexterity Developer's Manual examples:

```
from five import grok
from zope import schema

from plone.directives import form
from example.conference import _

class ISession(form.Schema):

    ...

    form.write_permission(track='example.conference.ModifyTrack')
    track = schema.Choice(
            title=_(u"Track"),
            source=possibleTracks,
```

```
              required=False,
       )
```

The `form.write_permission()` directive can be passed a number of fields and their corresponding write permission IDs as keyword arguments. To set a read permission, use `form.read_permission()`, which works analogously.

Please see the `plone.directives.form` documentation at `http://pypi.python.org/pypi/plone.directives.form` or the Dexterity Developer's Manual for more details and examples.

Views and browser resources

Having created the content types and their schemata, we will now turn to the user interface, and create views for our types.

Icons and stylesheets

Each type has its own icon, a 16x16 pixel image file. We will also register a stylesheet specific to our package. Since we have opted to grok the `optilux.cinemacontent` package, we can place all static resources in a top-level directory `static/`. When the package is grokked, this will be registered as a **browser resource directory** with the name `++resource++optilux.cinemacontent/`.

We will use this GenericSetup configuration for each FTI and the `cssregistry.xml` import step to register the stylesheet shortly.

Main content views

The view for each content type is registered using `five.grok` semantics the respective module where each schema and related logic is defined. (See *Chapter 9, Nine Core Concepts of Zope Programming*, for details about the difference between this style of configuration and configuration using ZCML.)

By convention, the default view of a type is called `@@view`. Because we register it for a particular content type's interface, there are no clashes even though several content types use the same name.

Let us have a look at the view for the *Cinema* type in `cinema.py`:

```
from five import grok
from zope.component import getMultiAdapter
from plone.memoize.instance import memoize

...
```

```
class View(grok.View):
    grok.context(ICinema)
    grok.require('zope2.View')
    grok.name('view')
```

Here, we register the view, ensuring it has the name @@view; is available for any context providing the ICinema schema interface defined earlier in the same module; and requires the *View* permission (with id *zope2.View*) to be renderable. Please refer to *Chapter 9, Nine Core Concepts of Zope Programming,* for more details.

We then define some helpers. In update(), which is called prior to rendering of the page template associated with the view, we store a Boolean to indicate whether we have any highlighted films:

```
def update(self):
    self.haveHighlightedFilms = len(self.highlightedFilms()) > 0
```

The list of highlighted films is prepared in its own method. We **memoize** this using an instance memo from plone.memoize to ensure that it is only executed once, even if it is called several times. It may be called at least twice—once in update(), and once from the page template.

```
@memoize
def highlightedFilms(self):

    films = []

    if self.context.highlightedFilms is not None:
        for ref in self.context.highlightedFilms:
            obj = ref.to_object
            scales = getMultiAdapter((obj, self.request),
                                     name='images')
            scale = scales.scale('image', scale='thumb')
            imageTag = None
            if scale is not None:
                imageTag = scale.tag()

            films.append({
                    'url': obj.absolute_url(),
                    'title': obj.title,
                    'summary': obj.description,
                    'imageTag': imageTag,
                })

    return films
```

The automatically associated template is found in `cinema_templates/view.pt`. (Recall from *Chapter 9, Nine Core Concepts of Zope Programming*, that the convention is `${modulename}_templates/${viewname}.pt`):

```
<html xmlns="http://www.w3.org/1999/xhtml" xml:lang="en"
      xmlns:tal="http://xml.zope.org/namespaces/tal"
      xmlns:metal="http://xml.zope.org/namespaces/metal"
      xmlns:i18n="http://xml.zope.org/namespaces/i18n"
      lang="en"
      metal:use-macro="context/main_template/macros/master"
      i18n:domain="optilux.cinemacontent">
<body>

<metal:content-core fill-slot="content-core">
    <metal:content-core define-macro="content-core">

        <label for="phoneNumber"
               i18n:translate="label_cinema_phone_number">
            Phone number:
        </label>
        <span id="phoneNumber" tal:content="context/phone" />

        <div class="highlighted-films"
             tal:condition="view/haveHighlightedFilms">
            <h3 i18n:translate="heading_featured_films">
                Featured films:
            </h3>
            <div tal:repeat="film view/highlightedFilms">
                <a tal:attributes="href film/url;
                                   title film/summary">
                    <img tal:replace="structure film/imageTag" />
                    <div tal:content="film/title" />
                </a>
            </div>
        </div>

        <div tal:replace="structure context/text/output" />

    </metal:content-core>
</metal:content-core>

</body>
</html>
```

Here, we fill the `content-core` slot in the `master` macro of `main_template`. This lets Plone render the title, description, and common visual elements in their standard locations, and should be used for standard content views.

For templates not used to render a standard content item, you may want to fill the `main` slot instead. In this case, you probably want to output a title using an `<h1 class="documentFirstHeading" />` at the top of the page.

In this example, we render each field's corresponding attribute using a simple TALES expression:

```
<span id="phoneNumber" tal:content="context/phone" />
```

For rich text fields such as the `text` field, however, this would escape HTML characters (using *<* for <, for example), because Zope treats any string as potentially tainted: a string that could have come from the user may contain malicious HTML or JavaScript code that could be a security issue. In this case, we know the text is safe, because it has been passed through Plone's safe HTML filter by virtue of using the `text/x-html-safe` output mime type (the default output MIME type for `RichText` fields). Therefore, we can use the `structure` keyword to turn off HTML escaping:

```
<div tal:replace="structure context/text/output" />
```

We also did this for the film tag as returned by the view, since this also contains (safe) HTML.

The other types contain equivalent views, several of them even simpler. The *Film Folder* does not have a view at all: Instead, we will use the standard `folder_summary_view` to provide a folder listing.

Installing and registering types

With the content types and their views created, all that remains is to write the installation code. We do this with a GenericSetup extension profile in the `optilux.cinemacontent` product. Recall from the beginning of this chapter that in the package's main `configure.zcml` file, we have:

```
<genericsetup:registerProfile
    name="default"
    title="Optilux content types"
    directory="profiles/default"
    description="Installs the optilux.cinemacontent package"
    provides="Products.GenericSetup.interfaces.EXTENSION"
    />
```

As usual, we also have a `metadata.xml` file in `profiles/default`. This will ensure `plone.app.dexterity` is installed and configured:

```
<metadata>
    <version>1</version>
    <dependencies>
        <dependency>profile-plone.app.dexterity:default</dependency>
    </dependencies>
</metadata>
```

The import step `profiles/default/types.xml` registers the content types:

```
<object name="portal_types">

 <object name="optilux.CinemaFolder" meta_type="Dexterity FTI"/>
 <object name="optilux.Cinema"       meta_type="Dexterity FTI"/>
 <object name="optilux.FilmFolder"   meta_type="Dexterity FTI"/>
 <object name="optilux.Film"         meta_type="Dexterity FTI"/>
 <object name="optilux.Promotion"    meta_type="Dexterity FTI"/>

</object>
```

This will cause various **factory-based type information** objects (**FTIs**) to be created in the `portal_types` tool. We use the `Dexterity FTI` type as required for all Dexterity content types.

Each FTI is configured in more detail in corresponding file in `profiles/default/types/`. The filename must match the portal type name, though any spaces are converted to underscores. For Dexterity types, the convention is to use dotted names with no spaces, as shown previously.

Let us go through the configuration for *Cinema*, found in `profiles/default/types/optilux.Cinema.xml`.

The first few lines give the content type a name, description, and icon, which will be shown in the Plone user interface. The icon references the browser resource described previously.

```
<?xml version="1.0"?>
<object name="optilux.Cinema" meta_type="Dexterity FTI"
    xmlns:i18n="http://xml.zope.org/namespaces/i18n"
    i18n:domain="optilux.cinemacontent">

    <property name="title" i18n:translate="">Cinema</property>
    <property name="description" i18n:translate="">A description of a
cinema</property>
    <property name="content_icon">++resource++optilux.cinemacontent/
cinema_icon.gif</property>
```

Next, we turn off commenting (discussion) by setting `allow_discussion` to `False`:

```
<property name="allow_discussion">False</property>
```

The next few properties control the relationship between containers and their children:

```
<property name="global_allow">False</property>
<property name="filter_content_types">True</property>
<property name="allowed_content_types">
    <element value="Document" />
    <element value="Image" />
    <element value="optilux.Promotion" />
</property>
```

We set `filter_content_types` to `True` and specify a list of types allowable inside *Cinema*s with `allowed_content_types`. Similarly, *Cinema Folder* specifies *Cinema* as an allowed type. Generic folder types would set `filter_content_types` to `False`. In this case, all types that are globally addable—those which (unlike *Cinema*) have `global_allow` set to `True`—would be allowed in these containers.

We then tie the FTI to the content type schema, class, and add permission:

```
<property name="schema">optilux.cinemacontent.cinema.ICinema</
property>
<property name="klass">plone.dexterity.content.Container</
property>
<property name="add_permission">optilux.AddCinema</property>
```

For a non-container type such as *Promotion*, we can use `plone.dexterity.content.Item` instead of `Container`. It is also possible to specify a custom class here, though such a class would normally derive from one of these two. The add permission is a permission ID, and must refer to a permission that already exists. We created `optilux.AddCinema` in `permissions.zcml` above.

Next, we list the behaviors that should be enabled on instances of this type:

```
<property name="behaviors">
    <element value="plone.app.content.interfaces.INameFromTitle"
/>
    <element value="plone.app.referenceablebehavior.referenceable.
IReferenceable" />
    <element value="plone.app.dexterity.behaviors.metadata.
IDublinCore" />
</property>
```

`INameFromTitle` will cause the ID of each content item to be a normalized version of its title. `IReferenceable` allows Dexterity types to be referenced from Archetypes content items (including the standard Plone 4 content types), and `IDublinCore` provides a number of standard metadata fields, such as title, description, and creation date. For a list of commonly used behaviors, see the Dexterity Developer's Manual.

We then configure the default view and any alternative views for the type:

```
<property name="default_view">view</property>
<property name="default_view_fallback">False</property>
<property name="view_methods">
    <element value="view"/>
</property>
```

These properties relate to Plone's **Display** menu. They specify which view is used by default, and the full list of available `view` methods for objects of this type. *Cinema Folder* and *Film Folder* both allow a few of the standard Plone folder listings to be selected as alternatives to their own standard views.

This is followed by:

```
<alias from="(Default)" to="(selected layout)"/>
<alias from="edit" to="@@edit"/>
<alias from="sharing" to="@@sharing"/>
<alias from="view" to="@@view"/>
```

These specify the method aliases for our content type. By convention, most Plone content types use these four aliases. We can use the special targets (dynamic view) and (selected layout) — here we have opted for the latter. They both relate to the currently selected view method, but the former also supports a default page content item selection. This should never be used for the `view` alias, because the user should always be able to append `/view` to a URL and see the exact object at this location, regardless of any default page.

Finally, we define the content object's actions:

```
<action title="View" action_id="view" category="object"
    condition_expr=""
    url_expr="string:${folder_url}/" visible="True">
    <permission value="View"/>
</action>
<action title="Edit" action_id="edit" category="object"
    condition_expr=""
    url_expr="string:${object_url}/edit" visible="True">
    <permission value="Modify portal content"/>
</action>
</object>
```

These, by virtue of being in the `object` category, are displayed as tabs on the content item. Notice how they reference the preceding method aliases. For the sake of URL consistency across content types, they are almost always the two shown previously — **view** and **edit** — pointing to their respective method aliases. Note that container types will use `string:${folder_url}/` as the view action, whereas non-container items such as *Film* or *Promotion* use `string:${object_url}` (note the lack of a trailing slash).

Add permissions

Earlier, we defined several new add permissions, which are associated with types in the Dexterity FTI. We will now set the roles for each of the new permissions. As before, we use a `rolemap.xml` import step:

```
<rolemap>
  <permissions>
    <permission name="Optilux: Add Cinema Folder" acquire="False">
        <role name="Manager" />
        <role name="Site Administrator" />
    </permission>
    <permission name="Optilux: Add Cinema" acquire="False">
        <role name="Manager" />
        <role name="Site Administrator" />
        <role name="Owner" />
        <role name="Contributor" />
    </permission>
    <permission name="Optilux: Add Film Folder" acquire="False">
        <role name="Manager" />
        <role name="Site Administrator" />
    </permission>
    <permission name="Optilux: Add Film" acquire="False">
        <role name="Manager" />
      <role name="Site Administrator" />
        <role name="Owner" />
        <role name="Contributor" />
    </permission>
    <permission name="Optilux: Add Promotion" acquire="False">
        <role name="Manager" />
        <role name="Site Administrator" />
        <role name="Owner" />
        <role name="Contributor" />
    </permission>
  </permissions>
</rolemap>
```

Notice that we do not use the StaffMember role here. This is because StaffMember is a feature of our site policy product, and depending on it in the more general optilux.cinemacontent product would make it harder to reuse and test the latter. Therefore, we let optilux.policy make the necessary adjustments for the StaffMember role after it has installed optilux.cinemacontent, as shown in a moment.

Adding catalog indexes and metadata columns

When we defined validators for film and cinema code, we made use of two new catalog indexes, filmCode and cinemaCode. We can now add the indexes to the catalog with the catalog.xml import step:

```
<object name="portal_catalog">
    <index name="filmCode" meta_type="FieldIndex">
        <indexed_attr value="filmCode"/>
    </index>
    <index name="cinemaCode" meta_type="FieldIndex">
        <indexed_attr value="cinemaCode"/>
    </index>

    <column value="filmCode"/>
    <column value="cinemaCode"/>
</object>
```

 Be aware that the catalog.xml import step will delete and recreate the index if the profile is later re-applied in full, requiring a reindex that can be very slow on large sites.

Adding the stylesheet

Finally, we add our new stylesheet to the portal_css registry, using cssregistry.xml:

```
<?xml version="1.0"?>
<object name="portal_css">
    <stylesheet
        id="++resource++optilux.cinemacontent/cinemacontent.css" />
</object>
```

Here, we let Plone decide the best default settings. See *Chapter 8, Creating a Custom Theme*, for details about the other options supported here.

Integration tests

As always, we must add tests for our code. We use a `testing.py` module similar to the one we have seen before to define a test layer:

```python
from plone.app.testing import PloneSandboxLayer
from plone.app.testing import applyProfile
from plone.app.testing import PLONE_FIXTURE
from plone.app.testing import IntegrationTesting

from zope.configuration import xmlconfig

class OptiluxCinemaContent(PloneSandboxLayer):

    defaultBases = (PLONE_FIXTURE,)

    def setUpZope(self, app, configurationContext):
        # Load ZCML
        import optilux.cinemacontent
        xmlconfig.file('configure.zcml', optilux.cinemacontent,
                       context=configurationContext)

    def setUpPloneSite(self, portal):
        applyProfile(portal, 'optilux.cinemacontent:default')

OPTILUX_CINEMACONTENT_FIXTURE = OptiluxCinemaContent()
OPTILUX_CINEMACONTENT_INTEGRATION_TESTING = IntegrationTesting(
        bases=(OPTILUX_CINEMACONTENT_FIXTURE,),
        name="OptiluxCinemaContent:Integration"
    )
```

For this package, we will turn the `tests` module into a package, so we create a `tests/` folder with an empty `__init__.py` file. For now, this will contain a single module called `test_content.py`. This begins with the usual class declaration:

```python
import unittest2 as unittest

from plone.app.testing import TEST_USER_ID
from plone.app.testing import setRoles

from optilux.cinemacontent.testing import \
    OPTILUX_CINEMACONTENT_INTEGRATION_TESTING

from Products.CMFCore.utils import getToolByName

...

class TestContent(unittest.TestCase):

    layer = OPTILUX_CINEMACONTENT_INTEGRATION_TESTING
```

First, we test that we can create the various types in the right hierarchy. Here, we are mainly just looking for `Unauthorized` errors, which would be raised if we configured permissions or allowable content types incorrectly.

```
def test_hierarchy(self):
    portal = self.layer['portal']

    setRoles(portal, TEST_USER_ID, ('Manager',))

    portal.invokeFactory('optilux.CinemaFolder', 'cf1',
                        title=u"Cinema folder")
    portal.invokeFactory('optilux.FilmFolder', 'ff1',
                        title=u"Film folder")

    setRoles(portal, TEST_USER_ID, ('Member',))

    portal['cf1'].invokeFactory('optilux.Cinema', 'c1',
                        title=u"Cinema")
    portal['cf1']['c1'].invokeFactory('optilux.Promotion', 'p1',
                        title=u"Promotion")

    portal['ff1'].invokeFactory('optilux.Film', 'f1',
                        title=u"Film")
```

We also test the uniqueness validators and indexers for cinema and film codes, the films vocabulary, catalog indexing, and the highlighted films calculations in the cinema view. We will not list the full tests here, but you are encouraged to read the code and make sure you understand how the tests work, and what they are testing.

Installation and configuration in the policy package

Finally, we will amend the optilux.policy product to install and configure optilux.cinemacontent according to our other policy decisions. We already saw how the optilux.cinemacontent package is included as a dependency of optilux.policy in its setup.py and configured from optilux.policy's main configure.zcml file.

We also make sure the new product gets installed when the policy product itself is installed. In optilux.policy's profiles/default/metadata.xml, we now have:

```
<metadata>
    <version>1</version>
    <dependencies>
        <dependency>profile-Products.PloneFormGen:default</dependency>
        <dependency>profile-optilux.theme:default</dependency>
        <dependency>profile-optilux.cinemacontent:default</dependency>
    </dependencies>
</metadata>
```

Adjusting the security policy

We want to allow staff members to add promotions by default. Therefore, we amend `rolemap.xml` as follows:

```
<rolemap>
  ...
  <permissions>
    ...
    <permission name="Optilux: Add Promotion" acquire="False">
        <role name="Manager" />
        <role name="Site Administrator" />
        <role name="Owner" />
        <role name="Editor" />
        <role name="StaffMember" />
    </permission>
  </permissions>
</rolemap>
```

Adjusting navigation tree properties

Because promotions are intended to be shown using the promotions portlet, we do not want them to show up in the navigation tree under cinemas and cinema folders. Thus, we hide the *Promotion* type from the navigation tree by adding it to the `metaTypesNotToList` property in the `navtree_properties` property sheet. This in turn stores several of the settings managed through Plone's **Navigation** control panel.

To change this, we use `propertiestool.xml`:

```
<?xml version="1.0"?>
<object name="portal_properties">
    <object name="navtree_properties">
        <property name="metaTypesNotToList" type="lines"
            purge="false">
            <element value="Promotion"/>
        </property>

    </object>
</object>
```

Enabling content object versioning

Finally, we want to make sure certain content types can be versioned. This can be done using the `repositorytool.xml` import step:

```xml
<?xml version="1.0"?>
<repositorytool>
    <policymap>
        <type name="optilux.Film">
            <policy name="at_edit_autoversion"/>
            <policy name="version_on_revert"/>
        </type>
        <type name="optilux.Cinema">
            <policy name="at_edit_autoversion"/>
            <policy name="version_on_revert"/>
        </type>
        <type name="optilux.Promotion">
            <policy name="at_edit_autoversion"/>
            <policy name="version_on_revert"/>
        </type>
    </policymap>
</repositorytool>
```

Here, we have enabled two versioning policies for each of the *Film*, *Cinema*, and *Promotion* types: `at_edit_autoversion`, which will create a new version each time an object is edited (and which, despite its name, works for non-Archetypes content); and `version_on_revert` which will create a new version each time the user reverts to an older version (to allow the reversion to be undone).

Site policy tests

Of course, we must not forget the tests, which go in `tests.py` in `optilux.policy`:

```python
def test_cinemacontent_installed(self):
    portal = self.layer['portal']
    portal_types = getToolByName(portal, 'portal_types')

    self.assertTrue('optilux.Cinema' in portal_types)

def test_metaTypesNotToList_configured(self):
    portal = self.layer['portal']
    portal_properties = getToolByName(portal,
                                      'portal_properties')
    navtree_properties = portal_properties['navtree_properties']
    metaTypesNotToList = navtree_properties.getProperty(
            'metaTypesNotToList'
```

```
            )
        self.assertTrue("Promotion" in metaTypesNotToList)
        self.assertTrue("Discussion Item" in metaTypesNotToList)
        self.assertFalse("Cinema" in metaTypesNotToList)
    def test_add_promotion_permission_for_staffmember(self):
        portal = self.layer['portal']

        self.assertTrue('Optilux: Add Promotion' in
                         [r['name'] for r in
                           portal.permissionsOfRole('StaffMember')
                            if r['selected']])
```

These tests verify that the dependency has been installed, that the `portal_ properties` tool has been updated, and that the `StaffMember` role has been granted the permission to add promotions.

Using the schema extender

Let us imagine that a new requirement has just come in: Optilux Cinemas has acquired a Digital Asset Management (DAM) system for keeping track of their various images and files, including those used on their website. For audit purposes, they must allow a "DAM code" to be selected against each file or image used on the website. The list of allowable DAM code should be maintainable by an administrator.

We could address this requirement by replacing the core *File* and *Image* types, but since these types are so widely used, we would need to change many of Plone's defaults, such as the types used for user uploads through the visual editor, which is cumbersome. As a more elegant solution, we can use the **Archetypes schema extender**, which allows us to modify one or more existing types, to add a new field to the standard *File* and *Image* types.

 This technique requires some understanding of Archetypes schemata. Please refer to the Archetypes chapter of the Plone Developer Manual at `http://plone.org/documentation/manual/developer- manual/archetypes`.

To use the schema extender, we must write a new adapter. To make it easy to apply this adapter to the types we want declaratively (using ZCML), we will define a marker interface (`IHasDAMCode`) and use this as the adaptation context.

To store the DAM code vocabulary, we can use the registry from `plone.registry`. We will define a schema interface (`IOptiluxSettings`) to contain settings related to our package, and install its fields into the registry, allowing the administrator to manage the vocabulary through the web.

In the next chapter, we will show how we can use the new field in custom views that allows the user to find content associated with a particular DAM code.

Adding the schema extender and registry

Before we can begin, we must add the relevant dependencies to `optilux.cinemacontent`'s `setup.py`:

```
install_requires=[
    'setuptools',
    'Products.CMFPlone',
    'plone.app.dexterity [grok]',
    'plone.app.referenceablebehavior',
    'plone.app.relationfield',
    'plone.namedfile [blobs]',
    'archetypes.schemaextender',
    'plone.app.registry',
],
```

Since we use `<includeDependencies />` in our `configure.zcml`, we do not need to explicitly configure these new packages.

Next, we update `optilux.cinemacontent`'s `profiles/default/metadata.xml` as follows to ensure `plone.app.registry` is properly configured in the Plone site before we use it:

```
<metadata>
    <version>1</version>
    <dependencies>
        <dependency>profile-plone.app.registry:default</dependency>
        <dependency>profile-plone.app.dexterity:default</dependency>
    </dependencies>
</metadata>
```

With this in place, we can rerun buildout:

```
$ bin/buildout
```

Defining the registry settings

Before we define the schema extender, we will configure the registry so that we have somewhere to look up valid DAM code values from. The easiest way to create new registry records is to define a schema interface to describe them, and then use GenericSetup to install the fields from this schema into the registry.

We start with the schema, in `interfaces.py`:

```
class IOptiluxSettings(Interface):
    """Describes registry records
    """

    damCodes = schema.Tuple(
        title=_(u"Digital Asset Management codes"),
        description=_(u"Allowable values for the DAM code field"),
        value_type=schema.TextLine(),
    )
```

This defines a single field containing a tuple of unicode strings. The title and description are used in the configuration registry user interface.

Next, we install this in the Plone site through `profiles/default/registry.xml`:

```
<registry>
    <records
        interface="optilux.cinemacontent.interfaces.IOptiluxSettings"
        />
</registry>
```

With this in place, we should be able to restart Zope, reinstall `optilux.cinemacontent` through Plone's **Add-ons** control panel, and find the new record under the **Configuration registry** control panel installed by `plone.app.registry`. Feel free to add some values here, too.

> See `http://pypi.python.org/pypi/plone.app.registry` for more details about the registry configuration syntax, and `http://pypi.python.org/pypi/plone.registry` for information about how to use the registry from code.

Creating the schema extender, vocabulary, and indexer

We can now create the extender itself. First, we create the marker interface for types that have this field, in `interfaces.py`:

```
class IHasDAMCode(Interface):
    """Marker interface for content with the DAM code field, which is
    enabled via a schema extender.

    This is applied to relevant types in content/configure.zcml.
    """
```

We apply this marker interface to the *File* and *Image* types in `content/configure.zcml`, by specifying that their common base class (`ATBlob` from `plone.app.blob`) implements our interface:

```
<class class="plone.app.blob.content.ATBlob">
    <implements interface="..interfaces.IHasDAMCode" />
</class>
```

This is the ZCML equivalent of adding a new interface to the `implements()` directive on the class, but can be done without modifying the original source code.

We can then write the schema extender itself, in `content/dam.py`. First, we have to define a custom field type for the extended field, by mixing together the `ExtensionField` base class from `archetypes.schemaextender`, and the standard `StringField` from Archetypes:

```
from five import grok
from zope.component import queryUtility
from zope.schema.interfaces import IVocabularyFactory
from zope.schema.vocabulary import SimpleVocabulary
from plone.registry.interfaces import IRegistry
from plone.indexer import indexer
from archetypes.schemaextender.interfaces import ISchemaExtender
from archetypes.schemaextender.field import ExtensionField
from Products.Archetypes import atapi
from optilux.cinemacontent import CinemaMessageFactory as _
from optilux.cinemacontent.interfaces import IOptiluxSettings
from optilux.cinemacontent.interfaces import IHasDAMCode
class DAMCodeField(ExtensionField, atapi.StringField):
    """Field for holding the DAM code
    """
```

We are happy with the default semantics for fields here, but it is possible to override the field's behavior if necessary. For example, we could override the `set()`, `get()`, and `getRaw()` methods, which are used when the field is set, read, or read for the edit form, respectively.

Next, we define the extender itself. This is a uniquely named adapter that is queried for the fields to add when the schema is composed. We will use `five.grok` semantics to configure it:

```
class DAMCodeExtender(grok.Adapter):
    """An adapter that extends the schema of any object marked with
    IHasDAMCode.
    """

    grok.provides(ISchemaExtender)
    grok.context(IHasDAMCode)
    grok.name("optilux.cinemacontent.DAMCodeExtender")

    fields = [
            DAMCodeField("damCode",
                vocabulary_factory=u"optilux.cinemacontent.DAMCodes",
                widget=atapi.SelectionWidget(
                    label=_(u"DAM code"),
                    description=_(u"Please select from the list"),
                ),
            ),
        ]

    def getFields(self):
        return self.fields
```

Notice how we define the field in a class variable and then return it in a list of one element from `getFields()`, which is expected to return a list of fields to add to the schema. This is more efficient than constructing the field inside `getFields()`, which may be called many times, even in a single request.

Next, we define the vocabulary factory we referenced in the field and register this as a named source. This uses the `plone.registry` API to look up the fields for our interface. The `check=False` parameter ensures that we do not get errors if the interface has not been installed already.

```
def DAMCodesVocabularyFactory(context):
    """Vocabulary factory for available DAM codes
    """
```

```
registry = queryUtility(IRegistry)
if registry is None:
    return SimpleVocabulary()

settings = registry.forInterface(IOptiluxSettings, check=False)
return SimpleVocabulary.fromValues(settings.damCodes or ())

grok.global_utility(DAMCodesVocabularyFactory,
        provides=IVocabularyFactory,
        name="optilux.cinemacontent.DAMCodes",
        direct=True,
    )
```

Finally, we add a catalog indexer for the new field, which we will use in the next chapter to allow the user to search by DAM code

```
@grok.adapter(IHasDAMCode, name='damCode')
@indexer(IHasDAMCode)
def damCodeIndexer(context):
    """Create a catalogue indexer, registered as an adapter
    """
    return context.getField('damCode').get(context)
```

The indexer just reads the value of the field, but it cannot use an accessor method (getDamCode()). This is because fields added with the schema extender are not a part of the schema when the Archetypes class generator is run, so there is no generated accessor to call. Instead, we use the low-level field API to obtain the field from the context and then use the field's get() method to get the value from the context instance.

We add the following to profiles/default/catalog.xml to let the damCode field be indexed (there is no metadata column here):

```
<index name="damCode" meta_type="FieldIndex">
    <indexed_attr value="damCode"/>
</index>
```

With this in place, we should be able to restart Zope, reinstall our add-on, and see the new field appear on the edit form for *File* and *Image* objects.

Adding tests

We can test the schema extender like any other field, with the previously mentioned caveat that there are no generated accessor and mutators, so we must use the field `get()` and `set()` methods that take the instance as their first argument. The tests in `tests/test_content.py` contain three new tests.

First, we check that the field has been installed and can be found in the schema of a newly created image:

```python
def test_dam_field(self):
    portal = self.layer['portal']

    setRoles(portal, TEST_USER_ID, ('Manager',))
    portal.invokeFactory('Image', 'i1', title=u"Image 1")
    setRoles(portal, TEST_USER_ID, ('Member',))

    i1 = portal['i1']

    self.assertTrue('damCode' in i1.Schema())
```

Next, we verify that the indexer works, by setting a DAM code on an image, reindexing the content object, and searching for it again:

```python
def test_dam_field_indexer(self):
    portal = self.layer['portal']

    setRoles(portal, TEST_USER_ID, ('Manager',))
    portal.invokeFactory('Image', 'i1', title=u"Image 1")
    portal.invokeFactory('Image', 'i2', title=u"Image 2")
    setRoles(portal, TEST_USER_ID, ('Member',))

    i1 = portal['i1']
    i1.getField('damCode').set(i1, u'One')
    i1.reindexObject()

    i2 = portal['i2']
    i2.getField('damCode').set(i2, u'Two')
    i2.reindexObject()

    catalog = getToolByName(portal, 'portal_catalog')
    results = catalog({'damCode': u"Two"})

    self.assertEqual(1, len(results))
    self.assertEqual(results[0].getURL(), i2.absolute_url())
```

Finally, we test the vocabulary by looking it up as a named source and invoking the vocabulary factory explicitly:

```python
def test_dam_vocabulary(self):
    from optilux.cinemacontent.interfaces import IOptiluxSettings
```

```
portal = self.layer['portal']

registry = getUtility(IRegistry)
settings = registry.forInterface(IOptiluxSettings)
settings.damCodes = (u"One", u"Two", u"Three",)

# Look for them in the vocabulary
vocabularyFactory = getUtility(IVocabularyFactory,
        name=u"optilux.cinemacontent.DAMCodes"
    )

vocabulary = vocabularyFactory(portal)
terms = list(vocabulary)

self.assertEqual(3, len(terms))
tokens = [term.token for term in terms]

self.assertTrue('One' in tokens)
self.assertTrue('Two' in tokens)
self.assertTrue('Three' in tokens)
```

Using portlets

With the content types in place, we now have a flexible system for managing cinema content. The site administrator can create the basic site structure with standard folders and pages as well as the more specific *Cinema Folder* and *Film Folder* types. Inside these, staff can describe *Cinemas* and *Films* in some detail, and add promotions for cinemas and groups of cinemas. However, we have not yet explained how promotions are shown to the user, which we will do using a new type of portlet.

Creating a new portlet

The portlet is found in the `portlets` sub-package. The files here follow the conventions established in `plone.app.portlets`. For the promotions portlet, there is a page template called `promotions.pt` and a Python module called `promotions.py`.

Starting with the template, it looks like this:

```
<dl class="portlet portletPromotions"
    i18n:domain="optilux.cinemacontent">
    <dt class="portletHeader">
        <span class="portletTopLeft"></span>
        Promotions
        <span class="portletTopRight"></span>
    </dt>
    <tal:items tal:repeat="promotion view/promotions">
```

```
        <dd class="portletItem"
            tal:define="oddrow repeat/promotion/odd;"
            tal:attributes="class python:oddrow and 'portletItem even'
or 'portletItem odd'">
            <a href=""
                tal:attributes="href promotion/url;
                                title promotion/title;">
                <img tal:replace="structure promotion/image_tag" />
                <tal:title content="promotion/title">
                    Title
                </tal:title>
                <span class="portletItemDetails"
                        tal:content="promotion/summary"
                        >Promotion summary</span>
            </a>
        </dd>
    </tal:items>
    <dd class="portletFooter">
        <span class="portletBottomLeft"></span>
        <span class="portletBottomRight"></span>
    </dd>
</dl>
```

This employs the styling used by most of the standard Plone portlets. As is good practice, all the logic for determining which promotions to show is delegated to a view—or rather, a portlet renderer—found in `promotions.py`.

Let us now look at `promotions.py`. Again, this follows the conventions and structure of Plone's standard portlets. First, a few imports:

```
import random
from zope import schema
from zope.formlib import form
from zope.interface import implements
from zope.component import getMultiAdapter

from plone.app.portlets.portlets import base
from plone.memoize.instance import memoize
from plone.portlets.interfaces import IPortletDataProvider

from DateTime import DateTime
from Products.Five.browser.pagetemplatefile import \
    ViewPageTemplateFile

from Products.CMFCore.utils import getToolByName

from optilux.cinemacontent.promotion import IPromotion
from optilux.cinemacontent import CinemaMessageFactory as _
```

Notice the `base` module imported from `plone.app.portlets`. This contains various base classes which make the task of creating new portlet components easier.

```
class IPromotionsPortlet(IPortletDataProvider):

    count = schema.Int(
            title=_(u"Number of promotions to display"),
            description=_(u"Maximum number of promotions to show"),
            required=True,
            default=5,
        )

    randomize = schema.Bool(
            title=_(u"Randomize promotions"),
            description=_(u"If enabled, promotions to show will"
                          "be picked randomly. If disabled, newer "
                          "promotions will be preferred."),
            default=False,
        )

    sitewide = schema.Bool(
            title=_(u"Sitewide promotions"),
            description=_(u"If enabled, promotions from across the "
                          "site will be found. If disabled, only "
                          "promotions in this folder and its "
                          "subfolders are eligible."),
            default=False,
        )
```

This interface defines the configurable aspects of the portlet type, much like the schemata we saw earlier defined the fields of a content type. (Note that we do not derive from `form.Schema` when defining portlet schemata.) The schema is implemented by the following class:

```
class Assignment(base.Assignment):
    implements(IPromotionsPortlet)

    def __init__(self, count=5, randomize=False, sitewide=False):
        self.count = count
        self.randomize = randomize
        self.sitewide = sitewide

    title = _(u"Promotions")
```

This, the portlet assignment class, defines a persistent object which manages the *configuration* of an instance of this portlet. The `title` property is defined in `plone.portlets.interfaces.IPortletAssignment`, declared by `base.Assignment`. It will be shown in Plone's portlet management user interface. It is possible to use a dynamic `@property` for this if required.

Most of the logic of the portlet is found in the portlet renderer. This class is akin to a view, except that it only renders part of a page. It is initialized with various parameters. In the base class, you will find:

```
def __init__(self, context, request, view, manager, data):
    self.context = context
    self.request = request
    self.view = view
    self.manager = manager
    self.data = data
```

The `context` and `request` are passed in as they are for regular views. The current `view` which the portlet is being rendered within is also provided. `manager` refers to the portlet manager (such as the left column or right column), which is just a named utility providing `plone.portlets.interfaces.IPortletManager`. Finally, `data` is the portlet data provider, which in most cases is the same object as the portlet assignment (notice how we derived `IPromotionsPortlet` from `IPortletDataProvider`). Thus, we can access the configuration properties of the `Assignment` through `self.data`:

```
class Renderer(base.Renderer):

    render = ViewPageTemplateFile('promotions.pt')

    @property
    def available(self):
        return len(self._data()) > 0

    def promotions(self):
        for brain in self._data():
            promotion = brain.getObject()
            scales = getMultiAdapter((promotion, self.request),
                                     name='images')
            scale = scales.scale('image', scale='thumb')
            imageTag = None
            if scale is not None:
                imageTag = scale.tag()

            yield dict(title=promotion.Title(),
                       summary=promotion.Description(),
                       url=brain.getURL(),
                       imageTag=imageTag)
```

```
@memoize
def _data(self):
    limit = self.data.count
    query = dict(object_provides=IPromotion.__identifier__)
    if not self.data.sitewide:
        query['path'] = '/'.join(self.context.getPhysicalPath())
    if not self.data.randomize:
        query['sort_on'] = 'modified'
        query['sort_order'] = 'reverse'
        query['sort_limit'] = limit
    query['effectiveRange'] = DateTime()
    catalog = getToolByName(self.context, 'portal_catalog')
    results = catalog(query)
    promotions = []
    if self.data.randomize:
        promotions = list(results)
        promotions.sort(
            lambda x,y: cmp(random.randint(0,200),100))
        promotions = promotions[:limit]
    else:
        promotions = results[:limit]
    return promotions
```

Portlet renderers, being cousins of viewlets (see *Chapter 9, Nine Core Concepts of Zope Programming*), are a special kind of content provider. Therefore, they have `update()` and `render()` methods. An empty `update()` method is defined in the base class, and the `render` callable is set to the page template shown above. We also define the `available` property. If this is `False`, the portlet will not be displayed. If all portlets in a column are unavailable, the entire column will be hidden (as opposed to showing an empty column).

The rest of the class is providing display logic specific to the promotions portlet. It searches for promotions in the current context (a *Cinema Folder* or *Cinema*), using the settings in the portlet assignment to control how the list is constructed. It returns a simplified list of dicts for the template to loop over and render.

Finally, we must define the add- and edit-forms for this new portlet type, which allow the user to create and modify promotions portlet assignments.

```
class AddForm(base.AddForm):
    form_fields = form.Fields(IPromotionsPortlet)
    label = _(u"Add Promotions portlet")
    description = _(u"This portlet displays cinema promotions.")
```

```
    def create(self, data):
        assignment = Assignment()
        form.applyChanges(assignment, self.form_fields, data)
        return assignment
class EditForm(base.EditForm):
    form_fields = form.Fields(IPromotionsPortlet)
    label = _(u"Edit Promotions portlet")
    description = _(u"This portlet displays cinema promotions.")
```

These classes use `zope.formlib` (a precursor to `z3c.form`) to generate a series of form widgets (held in the `form_fields` class variable) from the interface defined at the beginning of the file. The add-form additionally implements a `create()` method, which is required to construct a new assignment instance and apply the submitted form data to it.

There is no reason we could not use `z3c.form` to define the portlet add and edit forms, and future versions of Plone may make this the default approach. At the time of writing, however, all the convenience base classes for creating portlet forms are based on `zope.formlib`, so it would be a good deal more work to use `z3c.form`.

Configuring and registering new portlet types

To configure the new portlet type, we add the following to `portlets/configure.zcml`:

```
<configure
    xmlns="http://namespaces.zope.org/zope"
    xmlns:plone="http://namespaces.plone.org/plone">

    <include package="plone.app.portlets" />

    <plone:portlet
        name="optilux.Promotions"
        interface=".promotions.IPromotionsPortlet"
        assignment=".promotions.Assignment"
        renderer=".promotions.Renderer"
        addview=".promotions.AddForm"
        editview=".promotions.EditForm"
        />

</configure>
```

Behind the scenes, this statement registers a few utilities, adapters and browser views. Note that if there is nothing to edit, you can skip the `editview` attribute. In this case, you may also want to use `plone.app.portlets.portlets.base.NullAddForm` as a base class for the add form class, which in effect skips the add form.

Finally, we must register the new portlet type when the product is installed, so that it may be added from the portlet management screen. This is done using GenericSetup, with the `portlets.xml` import step.

```
<portlets>
    <portlet
        addview="optilux.Promotions"
        title="Promotions"
        description="A portlet which can show current promotions."
        />
</portlets>
```

The `addview` defined here must match the `name` of the portlet as defined in `portlets/configure.zcml`.

Naturally, we have also written tests for the portlet. `plone.app.portlets.tests` establishes a convention for portlet tests. Please see `tests/test_portlet_promotions.py`. This contains two test cases: `TestPortlet`, which ensures the portlet is properly registered and installed and is mostly boilerplate; and `TestRenderer`, which exercises view logic in the `Renderer` class above.

Assigning portlets automatically

Because our new portlet is the primary way in which promotions are viewed, we will ensure that it is added to all new top-level *Cinema Folders*. In `cinemafolder.py`, we define an event subscribe for the `IObjectAddedEvent` using `five.grok` semantics. (See *Chapter 9, Nine Core Concepts of Zope Programming,* for more details about the events system.)

```
from five import grok
from zope import schema
from plone.directives import form

from plone.app.textfield import RichText

from optilux.cinemacontent import CinemaMessageFactory as _

...

from zope.component import getUtility
from zope.component import getMultiAdapter
```

```
from zope.container.interfaces import INameChooser

from zope.lifecycleevent.interfaces import IObjectAddedEvent

from plone.portlets.interfaces import IPortletManager
from plone.portlets.interfaces import IPortletAssignmentMapping

from optilux.cinemacontent.interfaces import \
        PROMOTIONS_PORTLET_COLUMN
from optilux.cinemacontent.portlets import promotions

from Acquisition import aq_parent

...

@grok.subscribe(ICinemaFolder, IObjectAddedEvent)
def addPromotionsPortlet(obj, event):
    parent = aq_parent(obj)
    if ICinemaFolder.providedBy(parent):
        return

    column = getUtility(IPortletManager,
                    name=PROMOTIONS_PORTLET_COLUMN)
    manager = getMultiAdapter((obj, column,),
                        IPortletAssignmentMapping)
    assignment = promotions.Assignment()
    chooser = INameChooser(manager)
    manager[chooser.chooseName(None, assignment)] = assignment
```

This event handler will be invoked when a *Cinema Folder* is first saved. First, we make sure the portlet is only added to a top-level *Cinema Folder*, since children will by default acquire the portlet from their parent. Then, we look up the portlet manager (column) we wish to modify. The name of the portlet manager is held in a constant in `interfaces.py`:

```
PROMOTIONS_PORTLET_COLUMN = u"plone.rightcolumn"
```

The portlet manager is multi-adapted alongside the context object to `IPortletAssignmentMapping`, which provides an ordered container of portlet assignments for the given context and portlet manager. It has a dict-like interface, with string keys. To make sure we get a unique and proper key, we rely upon a name chooser adapter.

Summary

In this chapter, we have learned about:

- Expressing requirements in terms of content types
- Modeling these content types using interfaces
- Using Dexterity to create new content types
- Creating custom views for our content types
- Installing and configuring the new content types
- Using the Archetypes schema extender to modify existing content types
- Creating and installing a new type of portlet

You are encouraged to read the source code of the `optilux.cinemacontent` package and borrow from it freely. The code contains copious amounts of comments to explain what is going on at each step.

In the next chapter, we will move on to create a few pages which are not connected to content types directly, and learn more about generating forms with `z3c.form`.

11
Standalone Views and Forms

In the previous chapter, we learned how to create content types with custom views. When rendering a view, the current content item was accessed through the `context` variable. Because of the way that the views were registered, they could make the assumption that their context provided a particular interface, through which it could be inspected or modified.

Not all pages in an application will be tied to a specific content type, however in this chapter, we will learn about:

- Templates and forms more generally
- Creating views that are not registered for a particular type of context, but are available either everywhere or on the portal root
- Handling form submissions in views that submit to themselves
- Auto-generating forms using the `z3c.form` library
- Writing viewlets
- Creating a control panel form
- Using the global helper functions Plone makes available to all views

Pages without a specific context

As it happens, there is no such thing as a truly context-less template or view. In *Chapter 9, Nine Core Concepts of Zope Programming*, we learned how views are initialized with a context and a request, which are also available in page templates. Even though the view may not directly access properties of its context, it may still use the context as the starting point for looking up other views or tools. At the very least, Zope's security machinery needs to know the context to determine the user's current roles.

Templates in skin layers

Chapter 4, Basics of Customization introduced templates in skin layers in the `portal_
skins` tool. Unlike browser views, these can be invoked in any context. Take for
example the `document_view` template in the `plone_content` layer. This assumes its
context is a **Page** (internally called **Document**), but Zope will still attempt to invoke
the template if we call it on a different type of object, for example with an URL like:

```
http://mysite.com/news/some-news-item/document_view
```

Of course, we may get an `AttributeError` if the context does not provide an
attribute that the view is expecting to find.

Some templates are intended to be generic. For example, the `content_status_
history` template, found in the `plone_forms` skin layer and linked to from the
workflow State drop-down menu, works on all workflow-aware content types.

Finally, consider the search template, also found in `plone_forms`. It is invoked when
a user performs a search from the quick-search box found on every page. It is always
invoked in the context of the portal root—in `searchbox.pt` of the `plone.app.
layout.viewlets` you will find:

```
<form name="searchform"
      action="search"
      tal:attributes="action string:${navigation_root_url}/search">
```

Here, `navigation_root_url` is a variable that refers to the root of the Plone site.
There is no reason why the `search` form action could not be invoked in other
contexts, but also no reason why it should—it behaves the same regardless of
context. In this case, it is better for web spiders and cache servers if the URL is
always the same.

Views available on all objects

With browser views, we can be a little more formal. In the previous chapter, we
registered the main view for each new content type, using the name `@@view` and
tying it to a type-specific interface:

```
class View(grok.View):
    grok.context(IFilm)
    grok.require('zope2.View')
    grok.name('view')

    . . .
```

With ZCML configuration, this would have been:

```
<browser:page
    for=".film.IFilm"
    name="view"
    class=".film.View"
    permission="zope2.View"
    />
```

Please refer to *Chapter 9, Nine Core Concepts of Zope Programming*, for more details about the differences between these two styles of configuration, and the associated view base class requirements.

> To use `five.grok` configuration for views, you should make sure you use an appropriate known good set of packages in your buildout configuration, and depend on `five.grok` in your `setup.py install_requires`, either directly or transitively. In the previous chapter, we saw how to include the Dexterity known good set, which also includes `five.grok` and `plone.directives.form` (described in the following sections). If you would like to use `five.grok` without Dexterity, you can find known good sets at `http://good-py.appspot.com/release/five.grok`. For `plone.directives.form`, it is currently best to use the Dexterity known good set.

Sometimes, we may want a general view available for all content types. In this case, we could register it for a generic interface such as `Products.CMFCore.interfaces.IContentish`. However, it may be more appropriate to specify that a view is simply available for any type of context. For example, in `plone.app.workflow`, we have:

```
<browser:page
    name="sharing"
    for="*"
    class=".sharing.SharingView"
    permission="cmf.ChangeLocalRoles"
    />
```

Recall from *Chapter 9, Nine Core Concepts of Zope Programming*, that views are multi-adapters on a context and a request. The `for` attribute of the `<browser:page />` directive specifies what type the context must be for the adapter lookup to succeed, and the `for="*"` idiom is equivalent to saying `for="zope.interface.Interface"` — in other words, this view is registered for the most general of all interfaces. (With `five.grok` configuration, we would simply do `grok.context(Interface)`).

Generic views can also be useful as a default option when there are more specific registrations available. For example, here is a pair of registrations from `Products.CMFPlone.browser`:

```
<browser:page
    for="*"
    name="breadcrumbs_view"
    class=".navigation.PhysicalNavigationBreadcrumbs"
    permission="zope.Public"
    allowed_attributes="breadcrumbs"
    />

<browser:page
    for="plone.app.layout.navigation.interfaces.INavigationRoot"
    name="breadcrumbs_view"
    class=".navigation.RootPhysicalNavigationBreadcrumbs"
    permission="zope.Public"
    allowed_attributes="breadcrumbs"
    />
```

The `breadcrumbs_view` is used to construct the **You are here** breadcrumbs across the top of the site. The former, more general view will look up the `breadcrumbs_view` recursively on its parent. When it reaches the navigation root (normally the portal root), it will find the latter view, which is responsible for rendering the first element in the breadcrumb list and does not try to look further up the chain.

Views on the navigation root

For views which do not make direct use of their context, the navigation root is normally the most appropriate context.

> Avoid using for="*" unless there is a compelling reason to do so, to reduce the risk of name clashes, that is, two views with the same name being available in the same context. If this does happen, recall from *Chapter 9, Nine Core Concepts of Zope Programming* that the one with the most specific registration will be used.

In the `optilux.cinemacontent` package, we have added a view which allows site administrators to find content related to the "DAM code" that we added to File and Image objects in the previous chapter. It can be found in the module `dam.py`:

```
from five import grok
from plone.app.layout.navigation.interfaces import INavigationRoot

...
```

```
class DAMReport(grok.View):
    """View for showing content related to a particular DAM code
    """

    grok.context(INavigationRoot)
    grok.name('dam-report')
    grok.require('optilux.ViewReports')
```

We could have used ZCML configuration instead, in which case it would look something like the following screenshot:

```
<browser:page
    for="plone.app.layout.navigation.interfaces.INavigationRoot"
    name="dam-report"
    class=".dam.DAMReport"
    template="dam_templates/damreport.pt"
    permission="optilux.ViewReports"
    />
```

This ensures that if we try to traverse to /@@dam-report anywhere other than the site root, we will get a NotFound exception and a 404 error message.

optilux.ViewReports is a custom permission defined in permissions.zcml in optilux.cinemacontent:

```
<permission
    id="optilux.ViewReports"
    title="Optilux: View Reports"
    />
```

When creating custom permissions for use in a view like this, make sure they are defined in ZCML before they are used.

The new permission is granted the StaffMember role in rolemap.xml in optilux.policy:

```
<permission name="Optilux: View Reports" acquire="False">
    <role name="Manager" />
    <role name="StaffMember" />
</permission>
```

The view class is implemented much as the views we created in *Chapter 10, Custom content types* with an `update()` method preparing information for the template.

```
from five import grok
from plone.app.layout.navigation.interfaces import INavigationRoot

...

class DAMReport(grok.View):
    grok.context(INavigationRoot)
    grok.name('dam-report')
    grok.require('optilux.ViewReports')

    def update(self):
        # Hide the editable-object border
        self.request.set('disable_border', True)

        ...
```

 If you are not using the `grok.View` base class (that is, you are using ZCML-based configuration), there is no `update()` method to override. Instead, you can override `__call__()`. If you have associated a template in ZCML, you can render this by writing `return self.index()` at the end of the `__call__()` method.

Notice how we set `disable_border` in the request before rendering the template. This causes Plone to hide the (green) **editable border**, which normally does not apply to standalone views.

The template, which is automatically associated as per `grok.View` semantics, is found in `dam_templates/damreport.pt` (see *Chapter 9, Nine Core Concepts of Zope Programming*). This time, we fill the `main` slot instead of `content-core` and output our own title and description instead of using the context's Dublin Core values, which would not be appropriate for the standalone view:

```
<html xmlns="http://www.w3.org/1999/xhtml" xml:lang="en"
      xmlns:tal="http://xml.zope.org/namespaces/tal"
      xmlns:metal="http://xml.zope.org/namespaces/metal"
      xmlns:i18n="http://xml.zope.org/namespaces/i18n"
      lang="en"
      metal:use-macro="context/main_template/macros/master"
      i18n:domain="optilux.cinemacontent">
<body>

<metal:main fill-slot="main">
    <metal:main define-macro="main">
```

```
        <h1 class="documentFirstHeading"
            i18n:translate="header_recent_dam_report">
          DAM report
        </h1>

        <p class="documentDescription" i18n:translate="description_
recent_dam_report">
            This report shows content associated with DAM codes
        </p>

        ...

    </metal:main>
  </metal:main>

  </body>
</html>
```

We will discuss the rest of the implementation of this view shortly, when we look at how to use HTML forms in views.

Invoking standalone pages

When we created views for content types in the previous chapter, we made use of actions and aliases in the FTI that we installed in the `portal_types` tool. Plone renders the actions in the `object` category as tabs on the object (so long as the 'editable border' is visible), making it easy to assign a custom view to the **View** tab of a content type.

When we create standalone pages such as the one shown in the previous code example, we need to decide how they will be invoked. (Some developers assume that they should be shown in the navigation tree, but this is really about navigating site content, and templates are definitely not content.)

One option is to render a link from another template. For example, we could have a statement like this in a customized template forming part of our custom theme:

```
<a tal:attributes="href string:${portal_url}/@@dam-report"
   tal:condition="python:checkPermission('Optilux: View Reports',
context)">
  View recent activity report
</a>
```

Another option would be to use an `action` in a category which is displayed independently of the context. For example, the `site_actions` category refers to the `Site Map`, `Contact` and related links normally found near the very top of the site. The `portal_tabs` category can be used to add additional static tabs next to `Home` in the main site navigation, before the tabs generated from the content in the root of the site. To see the full list of available actions and their contents, take a look at the `portal_actions` tool in the ZMI or the GenericSetup import step that creates them in `CMFPlone/profiles/default/actions.xml`.

For the purposes of our case study, we have opted to add another link in the `site_ actions` category. As this is a policy decision, we do this in the GenericSetup profile of the `optilux.policy` product. The file `profiles/default/actions.xml` contains:

```xml
<?xml version="1.0"?>
<object name="portal_actions"
    xmlns:i18n="http://xml.zope.org/namespaces/i18n">
 <object name="site_actions">
  <object name="dam-report" meta_type="CMF Action"
          i18n:domain="optilux.cinemacontent">
   <property name="title" i18n:translate="">DAM report</property>
   <property name="description" i18n:translate=""></property>
   <property name="url_expr">string:$portal_url/@@dam-report</property>
   <property name="icon_expr"></property>
   <property name="available_expr"></property>
   <property name="permissions">
    <element value="Optilux: View reports"/>
   </property>
   <property name="visible">True</property>
  </object>
 </object>
</object>
```

There are plenty of other examples in Plone's own `actions.xml`.

Writing custom forms

So far, we have only created views to present information already in the ZODB. The only forms we have needed have been taken care of by **Dexterity**. Letting Dexterity provide edit forms and validation for content objects is a good idea, but we often need an ad-hoc form as well. `PloneFormGen`, which we installed in *Chapter 7, Using Add-ons* is useful when we want site administrators to create forms through the web, but we frequently need to create custom forms in our own views, just as in the DAM report example.

There is nothing magical about `forms` in Zope. Form actions resolve to resources such as browser views, which may inspect the request and take some action. A common pattern is to create self-submitting forms—those where a page has a form that submits back to the same view and use the view class to process any incoming request parameters.

Let us take a look at the body of `dam_templates/damreport.pt` in some more detail.

```
As usual, we invoke the master macro in main_template, before filling
the main slot:
<html xmlns="http://www.w3.org/1999/xhtml" xml:lang="en"
      xmlns:tal="http://xml.zope.org/namespaces/tal"
      xmlns:metal="http://xml.zope.org/namespaces/metal"
      xmlns:i18n="http://xml.zope.org/namespaces/i18n"
      lang="en"
      metal:use-macro="context/main_template/macros/master"
      i18n:domain="optilux.cinemacontent">
<body>

<metal:main fill-slot="main">
```

Next, we define some variables that will be used later. We will display search results in batches of 10, using Plone's **batching** support. This requires that we define:

- A batch size, here hardcoded to `10` as `b_size`.
- An orphan threshold—in effect, the minimum size of a page. Here we hardcode `b_orphan` to `1`, which means that if the last page in the batch would have only one element, the `orphan` element is added to the previous page instead.
- A batch start index, `b_start`, which is taken from the request if present, but defaults to `0`.

We use these parameters to call the `relatedContent()` method on the view, which returns a list of values to display in batch, storing the results in the variable `content`. We will show the implementation of this method shortly.

Finally, we record the current selection as calculated in the view's `update()` method in the variable `currentSelection`.

```
<metal:main define-macro="main"
       tal:define="b_size    python:10;
                    b_orphan python:1;
                    b_start   request/b_start | python:0;
                    content   python:view.relatedContent(
                       start=b_start, size=b_size+b_orphan);
                    currentSelection view/selectedDAMCode">
```

Following this, we render the document title and description, using Plone's standard CSS classes:

```
<h1 class="documentFirstHeading"
    i18n:translate="header_recent_dam_report">
  DAM report
</h1>
<p class="documentDescription" i18n:translate="description_
recent_dam_report">
      This report shows content associated with DAM codes
  </p>
```

Next, we create the search form. We construct the form action using the context URL and view name to ensure that we submit back to this view. Of course, we could just as easily have constructed an expression submitting to some other view.

```
<form method="get" tal:attributes="action string:${context/
absolute_url}/${view/__name__}">
```

Immediately inside the form, we invoke Plone's `@@authenticator` view to render a **Cross-Site Request Forgery (CSRF)** protection token. This renders a hidden input field with an automatically generated one-time token. In the following view implementation, we will check that this token is valid to guard against potential security vulnerabilities.

```
<span
tal:replace="structure context/@@authenticator/authenticator" />
```

 You should always include this authenticator in your forms. To learn more about CSRF attacks, see `http://en.wikipedia.org/wiki/Cross-site_request_forgery`.

Next, we output the remaining form fields. The damCodes view instance variable, prepared in the view's update() method, is used to provide a vocabulary of values to select from in an HTML <select /> element. The selected attribute will be set to "selected" for the one <option /> element where the vocabulary value matches currentSelection, which we defined at the top of the template.

```
<fieldset>
        <legend i18n:translate="fieldset_legend_search">Search
parameters</legend>
                <div i18n:translate="dam_report_code">
                    Select a code

                    <select name="damCode" size="1">
                        <option value="">Please select</option>
                        <option
                            tal:repeat="code view/damCodes"
                            tal:attributes="value code;
  selected python:currentSelection == code and 'selected' or None"
                            tal:content="code"
                            />
                    </select>

                    <input type="submit" class="context"
name="form.button.Search"
                        value="Search"
                        i18n:name="submit_button"
                        i18n:attributes="value" />
                </div>
        </fieldset>
    </form>
```

We display the search results below the search form. First, we handle the case where there are no results:

```
    <h2 i18n:translate="heading_search_results">Search
results</h2>

    <p tal:condition="not:content" i18n:translate="description_no_
content_found">
        No content found
    </p>
```

If there are results, we output them in a table. Here, we use Plone's `Batch` class and the `batch_macros` template to output the results in an appropriate batch and render the batch navigation controls. The `Batch` instance is passed a catalog result (the `content` variable). When we loop over the search results, we will be returned with catalog brains, on which we look up metadata values. We call the `localize()` on the view (shown later) to prepare an appropriately formatted and localized modification date:

```
<tal:block condition="content"
      define="Batch python:modules['Products.CMFPlone'].Batch;
            batch python:Batch(content, b_size,
                    int(b_start), orphan=int(b_orphan));">
    <table class="listing">
        <thead>
            <tr>
          <th i18n:translate="column_label_title">Title</th>
          <th i18n:translate="column_label_modified">Modified</th>
            </tr>
        </thead>
        <tbody>
            <tr tal:repeat="item batch">
                <td>
                    <a
                      tal:attributes="title item/Description;
                                    href item/getUrl"
                        tal:content="item/Title" />
                </td>
        <td tal:content="python:view.localize(item.modified)" />
            </tr>
        </tbody>
    </table>

    <div metal:use-macro="context/batch_macros/macros/
navigation" />
    </tal:block>


    </metal:main>
</metal:main>

</body>
</html>
```

Why did we not prepare the modification date in a list of dictionaries in the `relatedContent()` method and keep the template to simply outputting values? For the batching support to work reliably and efficiently in conjunction with a catalog query, it needs to be passed to the lazy catalog result set directory.

Let us now look at the full implementation of the view in `dam.py`. The class, view directives, and beginning of the `update()` method were explained previously:

```python
from five import grok

from zope.component import getMultiAdapter
from zope.component import getUtility

from plone.memoize.instance import memoize

from plone.registry.interfaces import IRegistry

from plone.app.layout.navigation.interfaces import INavigationRoot
from Products.CMFCore.utils import getToolByName

from zExceptions import Forbidden

...

class DAMReport(grok.View):
    grok.context(INavigationRoot)
    grok.name('dam-report')
    grok.require('optilux.ViewReports')

    def update(self):
        # Hide the editable-object border
        self.request.set('disable_border', True)
```

Next, we check the CSRF token using the `authenticator` view, as long as something was submitted (that is, not the first time the view is rendered):

```python
if 'damCode' in self.request.form:
    authenticator = getMultiAdapter(
        (self.context, self.request), name=u"authenticator")
    if not authenticator.verify():
        raise Forbidden()
```

 When using the `@@authenticator` view to generate a CSRF protection token, always call `authenticator.verify()` (as shown in the previous code example) before trusting any form input.

Presuming this does not raise a security exception, we continue to calculate the available DAM codes by looking up the IOptiluxSettings configuration registry records that we installed in the previous chapter. These are saved in the view instance variable damCodes, which we used earlier to enumerate the options in the select list in the form:

```
registry = getUtility(IRegistry)
settings = registry.forInterface(IOptiluxSettings)
self.damCodes = settings.damCodes or ()
```

At the end of the update() method, we store the currently selected code from the request in the variable selectedDAMCode, which is used in the template to determine which option to preselect:

```
self.selectedDAMCode = self.request.form.get('damCode') or \
    None
```

Next, we implement the selectedContent() method. This is passed to the batch start and size from the template, although we also define default values here for convenience. It constructs a catalog search looking for all content items marked with IHasDAMCode where the damCode catalog index matches the selected code. We also pass the b_start and b_size parameters to the catalog, which allows the catalog to optimize its query based on the intended batch size:

```
def relatedContent(self, start=0, size=11):
    catalog = getToolByName(self.context, 'portal_catalog')
    return catalog({
        'object_provides': IHasDAMCode.__identifier__,
        'damCode': self.selectedDAMCode,
        'sort_on': 'modified',
        'sort_order': 'reverse',
        'b_start': start,
        'b_size': size,
    })
```

The optimization made possible by the b_start and b_size catalog query parameters is only supported in Plone 4.1 and later. The query and template syntax shown here should work on earlier versions of Plone, too, but the query will be less efficient.

Finally, we implement the localize() function, which uses Plone's time localization features to render an appropriately formatted date and time. It is called from the template when outputting the modification time. We **memoize** (cache) the lookup of the time localization function itself from the translation_service tool, to avoid having to look up the tool once for each item in the batch.

```
def localize(self, time):
    return self._time_localizer()(time, None, self.context,
                                 domain='plonelocales')


@memoize
def _time_localizer(self):
    translation_service = getToolByName(self.context,
                                       'translation_service')
    return translation_service.ulocalized_time
```

Processing form actions

In this example, we let the template "pull" values from the view, which looks them up as necessary. In some cases, we simply need to perform some processing when the form is submitted, perhaps taking the user to another view with a redirect at the end. In this case, we can put logic into the __call__() method, inspecting `self. request.form` for form values to act upon.

> To ensure you only process POST requests, you can use a check such as, `self.request.get('REQUEST_METHOD', 'GET').upper() != 'POST':` . . . to test the request method.

Checking form submit buttons

When processing forms in this way, it is usually important to check whether a particular button was pressed and take different actions depending on which button, if any, is present in the request. Browsers will only send the button that was clicked as a request parameter (the value of that parameter is the button's label, which is not at all that useful), so we can check for the existence of such a key in the request to determine whether a particular button was clicked.

> In Internet Explorer, if the user clicks *Enter* in a form field, the form will be submitted with no button in the request. Other browsers tend to submit the button defined first in the form instead.

Here is an example adapted from `plone.app.workflow.browser.sharing`:

```
class SharingView(BrowserView):

    # Actions

    template = ViewPageTemplateFile('sharing.pt')
```

```
def __call__(self):
    """Perform the update and redirect if necessary, or
    render the page
    """

    postback = True

    form = self.request.form

    # Make sure we had a proper form submit, not just a
    # GET request
    submitted = form.get('form.submitted', False)

    saveButton = form.get('form.button.Save') is not None
    cancelButton = form.get('form.button.Cancel') is not None

    if submitted and not cancelButton:

        # Update the acquire-roles setting

        ...

    # Other buttons return to the sharing page
    if saveButton or cancelButton:
        postback = False

    if postback:
        return self.template()
    else:
        self.request.response.redirect(
            self.context.absolute_url())
        return u""
```

Notice how we check for the **save** and **cancel** buttons in the request. In the `sharing.pt` template, you will find these buttons again:

```
<input class="context" type="submit" name="form.button.Save"
value="Save" />
<input class="standalone" type="submit" name="form.button.Cancel"
value="Cancel" />
```

Performing redirects

In certain circumstances, the view in `sharing.py` will call:

```
self.request.response.redirect(self.context.absolute_url())
```

This tells the browser to perform a redirect (using HTTP status code `302`), here returning to the default view of the context, leaving the current template. The `redirect()` method should be passed a full URL.

If you want to issue a redirect with status code `301` instead ("moved permanently"), you can use:

```
self.request.response.redirect(url, status=301)
```

Redirects are the easiest way to control the flow between pages in response to form input or other conditions. When performing a redirect, the view does not need to render anything. In fact, it would be a waste of server resources to do so, as the browser is not going to display the page anyway. The view should, however, return an empty string.

Form input converters

The `sharing.pt` template also demonstrates marshaling of form fields into Python types other than strings. It contains form fields such as:

```
<input
    type="hidden"
    name="entries.id:records"
    tal:attributes="value entry/id"
    />
<input
    type="hidden"
    name="entries.type:records"
    tal:attributes="value entry/type"
    />
```

These are being rendered inside a `tal:repeat` loop. Notice the `:records` part of the name. When the form is submitted, the view will receive a single form variable called `entries`, containing a list of dictionaries, with keys 'id' and 'type'. Here are the various types of marshaling directives available:

Converter	Example	Result
`boolean, int, long, float, string, date`	`<input type="hidden" name="limit:int" value="10" />`	Cast the variable to the appropriate Python type. `date` results in a Zope DateTime. `string` is the default and therefore a little superfluous. Note that these are normally only useful in hidden fields – if the user enters a value which cannot be converted, the resulting error message is not very friendly.

Converter	Example	Result
text	`<textarea name="message:text" />`	Convert to a `string` with normalized line breaks appropriate for the server platform.

list, tuple	`<input type="checkbox" name="selection:list" value="1"/>`
	
	`<input type="checkbox" name="selection:list" value="2"/>`
		Produce a list or a tuple from multiple fields with the same name, or from a multi-selection list box. This can be combined with other converters. such as, `:int:list` will result in a list of integers.

tokens, lines	`<input type="text" name="keywords:tokens" />`	Turn a space-separated (tokens) or newline-separated (lines) string into a list.

record, records	`<input type="text" name="data.id:record" />`
	
	`<input type="text" name="data.val:record" />`
		Produce a dictionary (record) or list of dictionaries (records). The name before the . (dot) is the variable name, and the name after the . (dot) is the key. In the example, we would get `data['id']` and `data['val']`.

required	`<input type="text" name="name:required" />`	Raise an exception if the field is not filled in. Again, this is rarely used, because the error message is not very friendly.
ignore_empty	`<input type="text" name="id:ignore_empty" />`	Omit the variable from the request, if no value was entered. Can be combined with other converters.

default	`<input type="hidden" name="accept:boolean:default" value="True" />`
	
	`<input type="checkbox" name="accept:boolean:default" value="False" />`
		Give a default value if no other field with the same name was submitted. This is very useful for checkboxes, which are omitted from the request unless they were checked. Can be combined with other converters.

Form input converters are often used in hidden fields that are used to carry state between templates, for example if a single form has been broken down into multiple steps.

Generating forms automatically

It is not terribly difficult to create forms manually, even if we want basic validation and a standardized look-and-feel.

 `skins/plone_forms/search_form.pt` of `Products.CMFPlone` contains a good example of the usual form markup and patterns.

However, creating forms from scratch can be quite time-consuming. Luckily, there are ways to automatically create forms.

In Plone 3 (and the previous edition of this book), the most advanced form library available was called **formlib**, contained in the `zope.formlib` package. This is still used for portlet add and edit forms and some of Plone's control panels, but it is now largely superseded by `z3c.form`, a more powerful and flexible forms library.

To demonstrate the use of `z3c.form`, we will create a page form containing an enquiries page for the Optilux website. A page form is a full-page form in its own view. `z3c.form` also supports add forms and edit forms for editing content (which are used by Dexterity for its add and edit forms), user preferences or indeed anything else, and sub-forms, which can be used to compose a single form from multiple component forms.

As with other views, we can choose to use ZCML configuration or convention-over-configuration a la Grok. ZCML registration works just like any other view. For Grok-style configuration, however, we will usually use the `plone.directives.form` package, which provides base classes that mix `grok.View` semantics into the standard `z3c.form` base classes.

For the sake of convenience, we will keep this in the `optilux.cinemacontent` package. The form is defined in `enquiry.py`. There is no corresponding template, as `z3c.form` takes care of the visuals for us.

 Unlike views derived from `grok.View`, forms using the `plone.directives.form` base classes are not required to override `render()` if no associated template is found. The usual semantics for associating a template apply, but the template is optional.

First we define an interface which describes the form fields:

```
import re

from five import grok
from plone.directives import form
```

```
from zope.interface import Interface
from zope.interface import Invalid
from zope import schema

from z3c.form import field, button

from Products.statusmessages.interfaces import IStatusMessage

from Products.CMFCore.interfaces import ISiteRoot
from Products.CMFCore.utils import getToolByName

from optilux.cinemacontent import CinemaMessageFactory as _

checkEmail = re.compile(
    r"[a-zA-Z0-9._%-]+@([a-zA-Z0-9-]+\.)*[a-zA-Z]{2,4}").match
def validateEmail(value):
    if not checkEmail(value):
        raise Invalid(_(u"Invalid email address"))
    return True

MESSAGE_TEMPLATE = """\
Enquiry from: %(name)s <%(emailAddress)s>

%(message)s
"""

class IEnquiryForm(Interface):
    """Define the fields of our form
    """

    subject = schema.TextLine(
            title=_(u"Subject"),
        )

    name = schema.TextLine(
            title=_(u"Your name"),
        )

    emailAddress = schema.ASCIILine(
            title=_(u"Your email address"),
    description=_(u"We will use this to contact you if you request it"),
            constraint=validateEmail
        )

    message = schema.Text(
            title=_(u"Message"),
            description=_(u"Please keep to 1,000 characters"),
            max_length=1000
        )
```

See the interfaces in `zope.schema` for more information about which fields and options are available.

Note the constraint property of the `email_address` field. This is a callable constraint, which should return `True` if the value entered is valid. When it is not, we raise an `Invalid` exception with an error message.

The form view class itself derives from one of `plone.directives.form` base classes:

```
class EnquiryForm(form.Form):
    grok.context(ISiteRoot)
    grok.name('make-an-enquiry')
    grok.require('zope2.View')

    fields = field.Fields(IEnquiryForm)

    label = _(u"Make an enquiry")
    description = _(u"Got a question or comment? " +
                    u"Please submit it using the form below!")

    ignoreContext = True
```

If we had wanted to use ZCML registration instead, we would have omitted the `grok.*` directives, of course, and used `z3c.form.form..Form` as a base class, instead of `plone.directives.form.form`. The names of the base classes in `plone.directives.form` match those in `z3c.form.form`. See http://pypi.python.org/pypi/plone.directives.form for more information.

The `fields` variable contains the fields to be rendered here built from the fields in the schema interface. It is possible to assign custom widgets, change field properties or add and omit fields from this list see the `z3c.form` documentation for details.

The `label` and `description` will be rendered at the top of the page in Plone.

We set `ignoreContext` to `True`, so that `z3c.form` does not attempt to read the current value of any of the fields from the context the Plone site root, which would result in an error.

Reading the context makes more sense for edit forms. Sometimes, you may want to create a page form with some defaults calculated at runtime (that is, they cannot be set in a form schema interface). In this case, you can add a method `getContent()` to the form class and return from it a dictionary with keys and values corresponding to the fields in the form's schema. Alternatively, you can provide an adapter from the context to the form's schema interface, to allow the form to read and set the various field values. See the `z3c.form` documentation for more details.

Next, we make use of the same trick as before to hide the editable border when the form is displayed. We do this in the `update()` method, which is called before the form is rendered or the submitted form processed, taking care to call the base class version to allow the usual processing.

 The base class version of `update()` in a `grok.View` does nothing, so we usually do not bother calling it. When using `z3c.form`, however, we must call the base class `update()` method.

```
# Hide the editable border and tabs
def update(self):
    self.request.set('disable_border', True)
    return super(EnquiryForm, self).update()
```

Next, we define the form's primary button using the `@button.buttonAndHandler()` decorator, which takes the button's label as an argument. When the user clicks this button, `z3c.form` will call the decorated function.

```
@button.buttonAndHandler(_(u"Send"))
def sendMail(self, action):
    data, errors = self.extractData()
    if errors:
        self.status = self.formErrorsMessage
        return


    . . .
```

The first few lines here are found at the top of most form button handlers. We first extract the submitted form data and any validation errors, and abort if there are any problems. This will cause the form to be rendered again with validation error messages output next to the relevant fields.

The remainder of `sendMail()` sends the email and then redirects to the portal front page with a status message. The status message is queued up by adapting the request to `IStatusMessage` from `Products.statusmessages.interfaces`, and calling the adapter's `add()` method:

```
mailhost = getToolByName(self.context, 'MailHost')
urltool = getToolByName(self.context, 'portal_url')

portal = urltool.getPortalObject()

toAddress = portal.getProperty('email_from_address')
source = "%s <%s>" % (data['name'], data['emailAddress'])
subject = data['subject']
message = MESSAGE_TEMPLATE % data

mailhost.send(message, mto=toAddress, mfrom=str(source),
              subject=subject)

confirm = _(u"Thank you! Your enquiry has been received " +
            u"and we will respond as soon as possible")
IStatusMessage(self.request).add(confirm, type='info')

self.request.response.redirect(portal.absolute_url())
return u''
```

 Do not forget to configure a mail host in Plone's control panel before testing this, or you will get an error.

Finally, we have a **Cancel** button.

```
@button.buttonAndHandler(_(u"Cancel"))
def cancelForm(self, action):
    urltool = getToolByName(self.context, 'portal_url')
    portal = urltool.getPortalObject()
    self.request.response.redirect(portal.absolute_url())
    return u''
```

In this case, we do not care about the submitted data or any validation errors.

As before, we will add this as a site action, using `actions.xml` in optilux.policy:

```
<object name="enquiry" meta_type="CMF Action"
        i18n:domain="optilux.cinemacontent">
  <property name="title" i18n:translate="">Contact us</property>
  <property name="description" i18n:translate=""></property>
  <property name="url_expr">string:$portal_url/@@make-an-enquiry</
property>
  <property name="icon_expr"></property>
```

```
<property name="available_expr"></property>
<property name="permissions">
 <element value="View"/>
</property>
<property name="visible">True</property>
</object>

<object name="contact">
  <property name="visible">False</property>
</object>
```

Here, we also hide the default `contact` action by setting its `visible` property to `False`.

 To learn more about `z3c.form`, take a look at its documentation at `http://packages.python.org/z3c.form`. See `http://pypi.python.org/pypi/plone.directives.form` for more information about Grok-style configuration for forms.

Creating a control panel view

In the previous chapter, we used the registry to store values for the vocabulary of available 'DAM codes'. These can be edited through the generic Configuration registry control panel. However, to provide a better user experience for site administrators, we may want to create our own control panel for our custom settings. Luckily, `plone.app.registry` contains some helpers, based on `z3c.form`, which can be used to easily construct control panel forms from the type of settings schema we created with `IOptiluxSettings`.

The control panel view can be found in `controlpanel.py`, and contains:

```python
from plone.z3cform import layout

from plone.app.registry.browser.controlpanel import RegistryEditForm
from plone.app.registry.browser.controlpanel import \
    ControlPanelFormWrapper
from optilux.cinemacontent.interfaces import IOptiluxSettings
from optilux.cinemacontent import CinemaMessageFactory as _

class OptiluxControlPanelForm(RegistryEditForm):
    schema = IOptiluxSettings

    label = _(u"Optilux control panel")

OptiluxControlPanelView = layout.wrap_form(OptiluxControlPanelForm,
                                        ControlPanelFormWrapper)
```

Here, we are creating a standalone form class and then wrapping it into a browser view. This pattern allows `plone.app.registry` to control the page template surrounding the form. This view is registered in `configure.zcml` (there are no standard grokkers for the `RegistryEditForm` base class):

```
<browser:page
    for="plone.app.layout.navigation.interfaces.INavigationRoot"
    name="optilux-controlpanel"
    class=".controlpanel.OptiluxControlPanelView"
    permission="cmf.ManagePortal"
    />
```

We can install this into the control panel using GenericSetup. In `profiles/default/controlpanel.xml`, we have:

```
<?xml version="1.0"?>
<object
    name="portal_controlpanel"
    xmlns:i18n="http://xml.zope.org/namespaces/i18n"
    i18n:domain="optilux.cinemacontent ">

    <configlet
        title="Optilux settings"
        action_id="optilux"
        appId="optilux"
        category="Products"
        condition_expr=""
        url_expr="string:${portal_url}/@@optilux-controlpanel"
        icon_expr="string:$portal_url/++resource++film_icon.gif"
        visible="True"
        i18n:attributes="title">
            <permission>Manage portal</permission>
    </configlet>
</object>
```

Notice how we reference the view name in `url_expr` property. We have also reused the Film type's icon as the control panel's icon.

The form controller tool

At the time of writing, many of Plone's default forms use the `form controller` tool to orchestrate page flow. This allows a collection of skin layer page templates and untrusted code, and Python scripts to be used to build forms with validation and actions.

Unfortunately, the form controller is quite cumbersome to use, as it requires the registration of skin layers and relies on multiple files. You are therefore not recommended to use it for new code.

For more information about the form controller, refer to the **Documentation** tab of the `portal_form_controller` tool in the ZMI.

Writing new viewlets

Up to now, our views have all been of the full page variety, filling either the `main` or content-core slots in `main_template` master macro. Occasionally, however, we only want to provide snippets of HTML to be rendered on existing views, above or below the content. To achieve this, we can write a viewlet.

As we learned in *Chapter 9, Nine core concepts of Zope Programming*, viewlets are similar to views, but are registered not just for a context and request, but also, optionally, for a type of view, and associated with a viewlet manager that defines the region on the page where viewlets may be rendered.

 To see which viewlet managers are available, you can append `/@@manage-viewlets` to the end of the URL of a Plone site, and make a note of the viewlet name and interface for the manager you would like to use.

In *Chapter 9, Nine core concepts of Zope Programming*, we showed a simple, fictitious viewlet registration. As a more interesting example, let us consider how to use forms in a generic viewlet. In *Chapter 2, Introduction to the Case Study*, we presented the requirement to allow users to rate films. To manage film ratings, we have added an `IRatings` interface to `interfaces.py` in `optilux.cinemacontent`:

```
class IRatings(Interface):
    """An object which can be rated
    """

    score = schema.Int(title=_(u"A score from 1-100"),
                        readonly=True)

    def available(user_token):
        """Whether or not rating is available for the given user
        """

    def rate(user_token, positive):
        """Give a positive (True) or negative (False) vote.
        """
```

In `ratings.py`, there is an adapter from `IFilm` to `IRatings` which stores ratings in annotations on a Film object. We will not reproduce that code here, but take a look at the class and its doctest to understand how it works.

The viewlet itself is found further down in `ratings.py`, and is registered by using the `grok.Viewlet` base class:

```
from five import grok

from optilux.cinemacontent.film import IFilm
from zope.component import getMultiAdapter
from plone.app.layout.globals.interfaces import IViewView
from plone.app.layout.viewlets.interfaces import IBelowContentTitle
from zExceptions import Forbidden

...

class RatingsViewlet(grok.Viewlet):
    grok.context(IFilm)
    grok.view(IViewView)
    grok.viewletmanager(IBelowContentTitle)
    grok.name('optilux.cinemacontent.ratings')
    grok.require('zope2.View')


    ...
```

The equivalent ZCML registration would have been:

```
<browser:viewlet
    name="optilux.cinemacontent.ratings"
    for="optilux.cinemacontent.interfaces.IFilm"
    view="plone.app.layout.globals.interfaces.IViewView"
    manager="plone.app.layout.viewlets.interfaces.IBelowContentTitle"
    class=".ratings.RatingsViewlet"
    template="ratings_templates/ratingsviewlet.pt"
    permission="zope2.View"
    />
```

We choose to render it in the area below the content title. (See `plone.app.layout.viewlets` for other possible viewlet managers.) We also choose to only show the viewlet on the canonical view (that is, the **View** tab) of an `IFilm` object, as formalized by the `IViewView` marker interface. This is applied to the view automatically during traversal, if appropriate.

The automatically associated template can be found in `ratings_templates/`
`ratingsviewlet.pt`. It defines a simple form with two buttons, and outputs the
current rating:

```
<dl class="portalMessage info" i18n:domain="optilux.cinemacontent">
    <dt i18n:translate="">
        Ratings
    </dt>
    <dd>
        <div i18n:translate="info_film_rating" tal:condition="viewlet/
haveScore">
            <span i18n:name="rating" tal:replace="viewlet/score" />%
of those who voted liked this film.
        </div>
        <div i18n:translate="info_film_rating_none"
tal:condition="not:viewlet/haveScore">
            No-one has voted yet
        </div>
        <form method="get" tal:attributes="action context/absolute_
url" tal:condition="viewlet/available">

            <span tal:replace="structure context/@@authenticator/
authenticator"/>

            <div i18n:translate="vote_film_rating">
                Did you like this film?
                <input
                    type="submit"
                    name="optilux.cinemacontent.ratings.VotePositive"
                    value="Yes"
                    i18n:attributes="value button_yes"
                    i18n:name="yes_button"
                    />
                <input
                    type="submit"
                    name="optilux.cinemacontent.ratings.VoteNegative"
                    value="No"
                    i18n:attributes="value button_no"
                    i18n:name="no_button"
                    />
            </div>
        </form>
    </dd>
</dl>
```

Notice the fairly long names for the form buttons. We have opted to let the form submit to the current context's default view, as part of which the viewlet will be rendered. However, we cannot be sure what that view is, or what it would do with a particular request parameter. By using a very specific name, we reduce the risk that it could be interpreted incorrectly by the view or another viewlet.

Also notice the presence of the CSRF authenticator, and the reference to the `haveScore()` and `available()` methods on the `viewlet` object. We will show how these are implemented shortly.

 When not using `grok.Viewlet` as a base class (that is, when using ZCML configuration), be aware that the viewlet instance is made available to the template using the variable name `view`, not `viewlet` as shown earlier.

When submitted, the form will be processed in the `update()` method of the viewlet. This is guaranteed to be called before the `render()` method, indeed before any viewlet in this viewlet manager is rendered. Here is the remainder of the viewlet implementation:

```
def update(self):
    self.ratings = IRatings(self.context)
    self.portal_state = getMultiAdapter(
        (self.context, self.request), name=u"plone_portal_state")

    form = self.request.form

    vote = None
    if 'optilux.cinemacontent.ratings.VotePositive' in form:
        vote = True
    elif 'optilux.cinemacontent.ratings.VoteNegative' in form:
        vote = False

    if vote is None or self.portal_state.anonymous():
        return

    # Perform CSRF check (see plone.protect)
    authenticator = getMultiAdapter(
        (self.context, self.request), name=u"authenticator")
    if not authenticator.verify():
        raise Forbidden()

    userToken = self.portal_state.member().getId()
    if userToken is not None and \
            self.ratings.available(userToken):
        self.ratings.rate(userToken, vote)

def haveScore(self):
```

```
            return self.score() is not None
    def available(self):
        if self.portal_state.anonymous():
            return False
        return self.ratings.available(
            self.portal_state.member().getId())
    def score(self):
        return self.ratings.score
```

Here, we inspect the request looking for the relevant request keys, perform CSRF validation if required, and then use the `IRatings` adapter to record the user's vote.

> The ratings example encompasses several of the techniques we covered in *Chapter 9, Nine Core Concepts of Zope Programming*, including adapters, annotations, and viewlets. You may find it useful to study it in more detail through the book's source code (available from `https://www.packtpub.com/professional-plone-4-development/book`), and think about why we designed it as we did.

Global template variables and helper views

You may have noticed a few template variables that we did not define explicitly, such as `portal_url` or `checkPermission`. These are defined at the top of `main_template` and so inherited by any template that fills its main slots.

The standard variables are:

Global template variable	Purpose
portal_url	The URL of the Plone site root.
checkPermission	A function used to check whether the current user has a permission in the current context, for example: It is used as `python:checkPermission('Modify portal content', context)`.
portal_state	The `@@plone_portal_state` view
context_state	The `@@plone_context_state` view

There are three 'helper' views in `plone.app.layout.globals` which can be used to access commonly used information. These are:

- * `@@plone_portal_state`, which contains information about the portal in general, such as the portal root URL, the current user (member), and whether that user is anonymous or logged in

- * `@@plone_context_state`, which contains information specific to the current context, such as its URL, its path, whether it is a folder, its workflow state, and whether it is editable

- * `@@plone_tools`, which gives access to the most commonly used CMF tools

In all of these views, the various methods are cached so that, for a given request, they will only calculate their return values the first time they are called. They can be looked up in Python code, not just in templates. In fact, we saw this in the viewlet earlier:

```
self.portal_state = getMultiAdapter((self.context, self.request),
                            name=u"plone_portal_state")
...
if self.portal_state.anonymous():
    return False
```

In a template, we could do something like:

```
<div tal:define="context_state context/@@plone_context_state">
    ...
    <div tal:condition="context_state/is_view_template"> ... </div>
</div>
```

Here, we have redefined the `context_state` variable. This is only necessary when not filling a macro slot in `main_template`, such as when writing a viewlet or portlet, but it is always safe to do the explicit lookup.

You should aim to use these views in your own views and templates if possible, rather than perform potentially expensive calculations which may have been performed already and cached. Take a look at `plone.app.layout.globals.interfaces` to see the full list of methods available.

Functional testing of views

We have not yet shown any tests for the code we have presented in this chapter. Rest assured they are there. There are two general approaches to testing view components such as views and viewlets:

- Instantiate or traverse to view instances (such as using `unrestrictedTraverse()`) and call the view's helper methods, making assertions on the output
- Use the test browser to simulate the user's interactions with views and viewlets, to test page flow and make assertions about the HTML markup generated by a view

The latter is known as **functional testing**. It works best when there are also tests for more detailed functionality (such as the `IRatings` adapter in the `viewlet` example mentioned earlier), as functional tests are by definition coarse-grained and somewhat brittle to cosmetic changes in markup or text. However, it is useful to have basic functional test coverage over the major page flows in the application, as detailed unit tests cannot always alert us to mistakes in ZCML registrations, URL construction or the integration of user interface components.

To use functional tests, we must define a `FunctionalTesting` layer, which we do in `testing.py`. We can use the same fixture layer we used previously for our integration tests, wrapping it in the `FunctionalTesting` layer lifecycle class:

```
OPTILUX_CINEMACONTENT_FIXTURE = OptiluxCinemaContent()
OPTILUX_CINEMACONTENT_INTEGRATION_TESTING = \
    IntegrationTesting(bases=(OPTILUX_CINEMACONTENT_FIXTURE,),
                       name="OptiluxCinemaContent:Integration")
OPTILUX_CINEMACONTENT_FUNCTIONAL_TESTING = \
    FunctionalTesting(bases=(OPTILUX_CINEMACONTENT_FIXTURE,),
                      name="OptiluxCinemaContent:Functional")
```

 The difference between the integration and functional testing layers is that the functional testing layer sets up a temporary copy of the ZODB for each test, which means that it is safe for the code under test to commit changes, as happens when the test browser completes a request. As an optimization, the integration testing lifecycle relies on being able to roll back the database transaction at the end of each test.

There are several functional tests in the book's accompanying source code, in `tests/test_controlpanel.py`, `tests/test_damreport.py`, `tests/test_enquiry.py`, and `tests/test_ratings_viewlet.py`. Here is the first test in `test_ratings_viewlet.py`.

First, we import the layer and complete the test fixture with a new film:

```
import datetime
import unittest2 as unittest

from plone.testing.z2 import Browser
from plone.app.testing import TEST_USER_ID, TEST_USER_NAME, \
    TEST_USER_PASSWORD
from plone.app.testing import setRoles

from optilux.cinemacontent.testing import \
    OPTILUX_CINEMACONTENT_FUNCTIONAL_TESTING

class TestRatingsViewlet(unittest.TestCase):

    layer = OPTILUX_CINEMACONTENT_FUNCTIONAL_TESTING

    def test_vote_negative(self):
        app = self.layer['app']
        portal = self.layer['portal']

        setRoles(portal, TEST_USER_ID, ('Manager',))
        portal.invokeFactory('Film Folder', 'ff1',
                             title=u"Film folder")
        setRoles(portal, TEST_USER_ID, ('Member',))
        portal['ff1'].invokeFactory('optilux.Film', 'f1',
                title=u"Film",
                startDate=datetime.date.today(),
                endDate=datetime.date.today()
            )

        f1 = portal['ff1']['f1']

        import transaction; transaction.commit()
```

Notice how we commit the transaction when we are done constructing the fixture. Without this, the test browser will not 'see' the changes we have made.

We can now instantiate the test browser. We tell it not to handle errors itself, so that we can see error pages output from Plone if necessary.

```
        browser = Browser(app)
        browser.handleErrors = False
```

We can then use the `browser` instance to open pages, click buttons, and make assertions about the page returned by Plone.

```
browser.open(f1.absolute_url())

self.assertTrue("Ratings" in browser.contents)
self.assertTrue("No-one has voted yet" in browser.contents)
self.assertFalse(
    u"optilux.cinemacontent.ratings.VotePositive" in
    browser.contents)
```

> When debugging tests, it can be useful to put a break point (`import pdb; pdb.set_trace()`) after opening a page, and then printing the browser contents to see the HTML rendered by Plone using `print(browser.contents)`. Another useful technique is to write the raw HTML to a temporary file, such as `open('/tmp/test.html', 'w').write(browser.contents)`, and then opening this file in a browser. Stylesheets, images, and other referenced resources will not be found, but you can use tools like Firebug to inspect the rendered page this way.

Next, we want to test as a logged-in user. We could use the test browser to navigate to the login view and fill in the test user's details, but for simplicity's sake, we use HTTP Basic authentication instead by setting the Authorization header:

```
browser.addHeader('Authorization',
        'Basic %s:%s' % (TEST_USER_NAME, TEST_USER_PASSWORD,)
    )
browser.open(f1.absolute_url())
self.assertTrue("Ratings" in browser.contents)
self.assertTrue("No-one has voted yet" in browser.contents)
self.assertTrue("optilux.cinemacontent.ratings.VotePositive"
                in browser.contents)
browser.getControl(
   name='optilux.cinemacontent.ratings.VotePositive').click()
self.assertTrue("Ratings" in browser.contents)
self.assertTrue("100% of those who voted liked this film" in
                browser.contents)
```

This is only a short example of what the test browser can do. Please see `http://pypi.python.org/pypi/plone.app.testing` and `http://pypi.python.org/pypi/zope.testbrowser` for more details about how to use the test browser. Also take a closer look at the remaining tests in the book's accompanying source code, available from `https://www.packtpub.com/professional-plone-4-development/book`.

Summary

In this chapter, we have covered:

- The fact that no view or template in Zope is entirely context-free
- Views available on all types of context
- Registering a general view to only be available at the portal root
- A few suggestions for how the user may be directed to a standalone view
- Processing forms submitted by the user
- The pattern of letting views have forms which submit to the view itself
- Creating forms with a standard layout automatically from an interface, using `z3c.form`
- Creating a control panel form
- Writing viewlets
- Using forms in viewlets
- The standard helper views and global template variables which may be useful in your own views
- Writing functional tests for visual components using the test browser

In the next chapter, we will create some more advanced forms and views, this time linked to an external relational database.

12
Relational Databases

Until now, all our content and persistent configuration have been managed in the ZODB. The ZODB is an efficient and convenient data store for Plone content, but many organizations have existing relational databases that they want to integrate into a Plone website. Furthermore, certain kinds of data may be more appropriately managed using an RDBMS.

In this chapter, we will cover:

- The role of relational databases in Zope and Plone
- Modeling solutions that rely on data in a relational database
- Using the SQLAlchemy library to interact with relational databases

Relational databases versus the ZODB

Some customers are uncomfortable with the ZODB. It feels opaque and unfamiliar. They worry about performance and resilience. And surely, it cannot integrate into their existing IT environment.

In fact, the ZODB is a proven data store that scales well and is easily backed up. It is well-documented, and provides low-level tools to extract data if necessary. As we learned in *Chapter 9, Nine Core Concepts of Zope Programming*, it also largely frees developers from worrying about persistence, improving their productivity.

Relational databases, relying on normalized database schemata, are not terribly good at storing hierarchical, semi-structured content, possibly with binary attachments and unpredictable field lengths—precisely the kind of thing users may create in a CMS. On the other hand, relational databases are hard to beat for storing large amounts of homogenous data, like payment or customer records. Such data is also typically easier to query using SQL than the Zope catalog and custom Python code.

When developing with Plone, the default position should always be to use the ZODB. Certainly, you cannot do without it completely, nor would you want to. However, you should know when to consider moving aspects of your application to a relational database, and how to use existing databases when appropriate.

Modeling screenings and reservations

In our example application, we have used Plone content types to represent *Films* and *Cinemas*. However, we have not yet connected the two. We could have modeled a *Screening* of a particular film at a particular cinema as a content type, but given that screenings recur frequently over time and could cover lots of different combinations of films and cinemas, we would end up with a large number of *Screening* objects. The ZODB could handle this without problem, but we would probably need to develop a custom user interface to populate and manage them, since Plone's UI paradigms are not really geared towards managing large numbers of similar objects in bulk. It is also unclear whether a screening would best be modeled as a child of a *Film* or *Cinema* (or neither).

A *Screening* is just a relationship (between a *Cinema* and a *Film*) with a single piece of metadata — the scheduled date/time. We will almost certainly need to perform queries across different dimensions on this relationship, such as finding all films showing at a given cinema, or all screenings of a particular film in a particular time period. With many cinemas and films, there will likely be a large number of scheduled screenings. Thus, screenings appear to be a good candidate for a relational model. Besides, the requirements in *Chapter 2, Introduction to the Case Study*, already hinted that this data was to be found in an existing SQL database.

We will also use this relational database to hold ticket *Reservations*. To keep things simple, we will not concern ourselves with taking payments, but merely allow customers to reserve a number of tickets in their name. The database schema will be restricted to two tables:

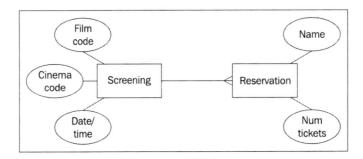

Recall from *Chapter 10, Custom Content Types,* that the *Film* and *Cinema* content types have `filmCode` and `cinemaCode` fields, respectively, and that we index these in the catalog. We will use these fields in our code to bridge the content items in the ZODB and the records in the relational database.

Although they are not stored in the ZODB, we will use *Screening* and *Reservation* entities in Python code. Therefore, we define interfaces for them, much like we defined schema interfaces for our content types in *Chapter 10, Custom Content Types.*

First, in `screening.py`:

```
from five import grok
from zope.interface import Interface
from zope import schema
from optilux.cinemacontent import CinemaMessageFactory as _

...

class IScreening(Interface):
    """A screening of a film at a particular cinema
    """

    screeningId = schema.Int(
            title=_(u"Screening identifier"),
        )

    cinemaCode = schema.TextLine(
            title=_(u"Cinema code"),
        )

    filmCode = schema.TextLine(
            title=_(u"Film code"),
        )

    showTime = schema.Datetime(
            title=_(u"Show time"),
        )

    remainingTickets = schema.Int(
            title=_(u"Remaining tickets"),
        )
```

And in `reservation.py`:

```
from five import grok
from zope import schema
from zope.interface import Interface
from optilux.cinemacontent import CinemaMessageFactory as _

...

class IReservation(Interface):
```

```
    """A ticket reservation for a particular screening
    """

    reservationId = schema.Int(
            title=_(u"Reservation identifier"),
        )

    screening = schema.Object(
            title=_(u"Screening"),
            schema=IScreening,
        )

    numTickets = schema.Int(
            title=_(u"Number of tickets"),
            description=_(u"Number of tickets to reserve"),
            min=1,
        )

    customerName = schema.TextLine(
            title=_(u"Customer name"),
    description=_(u"The name of the customer making the reservation"),
        )
```

These interfaces will be implemented by our domain classes, which represent the
database tables. The screening attribute of IReservation here represents the
relationship between the two relations.

Screening query and reservation services

Later in this chapter, we will add listings of *Screenings* to the views of the *Cinema* and
Film content types. Logged-in users will be able to click on a particular screening and
make a ticket reservation.

This suggests that we need tools to query the database for screenings by cinema,
film, and time. We will also need a way to make a reservation. However, we do not
want the view code to deal with the database directly.

To keep our code clean, testable, and maintainable, we will generally
abstract database operations into simple domain classes and general
utilities. This also makes it easier to provide alternative storage
implementations, for example, for testing.

With this in mind, we will add interfaces describing two new utilities to
interfaces.py:

```
class IScreeningLocator(Interface):
    """A utility used to locate appropriate screenings based on
```

```
    search criteria
    """


    def filmsAtCinema(cinemaCode, fromDate, toDate):
        """Return a list of all films screening at the particular
        cinema between the specified dates.

        Returns a list of dictionaries with keys 'filmCode',
        'url', 'title' and 'summary'.
        """


    def cinemasForFilm(filmCode, fromDate, toDate):
        """Return a list of all cinemas screening the given film
        between the specified dates.

        Returns a list of dictionaries with keys 'cinemaCode',
        'url', 'name'  and 'address'.
        """


    def screenings(filmCode, cinemaCode, fromDate, toDate):
        """Return all screenings of the given film, at the given
        cinema, between the given dates

        Returns a list of IScreening objects.
        """


    def screeningById(screeningId):
        """Get an IScreening from a screening id
        """


class ITicketReserver(Interface):
    """A utility capable of making reservations
    """


    def __call__(reservation):
        """Make a reservation
        """
```

We also define an exception type for reservation errors:

```
class ReservationError(Exception):
    """Exception raised if there is an error making a reservation
    """
```

We will spend the rest of this chapter implementing these utilities and the views that use them.

Setting up the database

The examples in this book use MySQL 5.1, but the concepts we describe should apply equally to other databases. We chose MySQL because it is free and relatively easy to set up. You can download MySQL from `http://mysql.org`.

The table definitions, as well as some sample data, are provided with the book, in the `sql` package inside `optilux.cinemacontent`. The scripts create a database instance, `optilux`, and insert some test data to simulate upcoming screenings. The following is the code which sets up the main database, in `init.sql`:

```
create database if not exists optilux;
use optilux;

create table if not exists screening (
    screeningId integer unsigned not null auto_increment primary key,
    cinemaCode char(4) not null,
    filmCode char(4) not null,
    showTime datetime not null,
    remainingTickets integer unsigned not null,
    index showing_cinemaCode(cinemaCode),
    index showing_filmCode(filmCode),
    index showing_showTime(showTime),
    index showing_remainingTickets(remainingTickets)
) engine=InnoDB;

create table if not exists reservation (
    reservationId integer unsigned not null auto_increment primary
key,
    screeningId integer unsigned not null,
    numTickets tinyint unsigned not null,
    customerName varchar(64) not null,
    index reservation_numTickets(numTickets),
    foreign key(screeningId)
        references screening(screeningId)
            on update restrict
            on delete restrict
) engine=InnoDB;
```

We will refer to this database as the reservations database.

We use MySQL's `InnoDB` table engine here because it has better support for foreign key constraints, which will allow our tools to make inferences against the database.

You will also need to set up an appropriate database user. For testing purposes, the default super-user account in MySQL, called *root* with no password will suffice, but obviously this is not a good idea for production systems.

Database connectivity in Zope

Over the years, the Zope community has developed several approaches for integrating Zope 2 and relational databases. Let us briefly look at the most important ones:

- **ZSQL methods** are akin to *Script (Python)*'s or *DTML* templates and can be created through-the-web or in a skin layer. They are essentially a way of parameterizing SQL queries and retrieving the results for processing in a page template. ZSQL methods are quite simple, but can be awkward to use with component-based program designs because they are used through skin layers only and use the now-defunct DTML syntax.

- Archetypes **SQLStorage** and its derivatives are a valiant attempt to let Archetypes content objects store their actual data in a relational database. A ZODB stub is still required. Unfortunately, it is difficult to map Archetypes schemas onto existing (or even well-normalized) data models using this storage, and there are intrinsic performance issues related to the way Archetypes uses its storage abstraction layer.

- **RelStorage** is a low-level ZODB backend that stores the ZODB's binary "pickles" in a relational database, rather than on the filesystem. This can give some performance and resilience benefits, but has nothing to do with accessing relational data models. We will look at RelStorage further in the final part of this book.

More recently, attention has shifted away from Zope-specific solutions to third-party Python libraries dedicated to relational database integration. The most popular of these is **SQLAlchemy** — a powerful, flexible, well-supported, and well-documented package that supports a multitude of databases. It offers low-level connection management, a Python API for constructing SQL queries, and advanced Object/ Relational Mapping (ORM) functionality.

SQLAlchemy basics

We will use SQLAlchemy to implement our two database utilities, demonstrating ORM mapping as well as query building. We will use a Zope integration package called `z3c.saconfig` to connect to the database and integrate database transactions with Zope's transaction machinery. This way, if a Zope transaction is rolled back, so will the database one be.

When dealing with SQLAlchemy, we need to be familiar with a few terms:

Component	Purpose
Engine	Manages database connections and various database-specific details. We will configure the engine using a ZCML directive provided by `z3c.saconfig`.
Table	Represents a table in the database. A *Table* must be bound to the Metadata of an Engine for SQLAlchemy to be aware of it. We will make use of the Declarative Extension for SQLAlchemy to define our tables based on a simple Python class syntax.
Metadata	Binds a collection of *Tables* to a specific *Engine*.
Mapper	Represents an entity in the database (as described by a Table) as a Python class. When using the Declarative Extension, the mapper and table are defined together using Python `class` definitions.
Session	Manages instances of Mapper classes. The Session can load new instances from the database, save changes to objects or add new objects as records in the database. We will rely on `z3c.saconfig` to obtain a valid session in our code and tests.
Connection	Allows the execution of SQL queries, either constructed with Python statements or passed as strings.

We will not cover SQLAlchemy itself in great detail in this book, concentrating only on what we need to support the case study and showing how the Zope integration works. To learn more, you should consult `http://sqlalchemy.org`, where you will find SQLAlchemy's excellent documentation, including several in-depth tutorials and an API reference.

Managing database connections

SQLAlchemy provides a standard interaction pattern for creating engines, metadata, tables, and mappers. However, in the context of a Plone application, we have some particular requirements:

- Zope is a multi-threaded server. We need to ensure that any shared database resources are thread-safe.

- Database transactions need to be synchronized with Zope transactions. If one fails and rolls back, so should the other.

- Data source names (DSNs) may need to be externalized into the build configuration.

Luckily, all of this is taken care of by the z3c.saconfig package. It provides simple API for defining database engines and obtaining sessions.

We declare z3c.saconfig as a dependency in setup.py file of optilux.cinemacontent, alongside our database driver, which in this case is MySQL-python:

```
install_requires=[
    'setuptools',
    'Products.ATContentTypes',
    'Products.Archetypes',
    'archetypes.schemaextender',
    'plone.app.registry',
    'plone.app.z3cform',
    'z3c.saconfig',
    'MySQL-python',
],
```

The easiest way to set up a database connection with z3c.saconfig is to use a pair of ZCML directives to define an engine and a default session. We could do this in our package's configure.zcml, but we will typically want to be able to control our database connection details from the build so that it can be easily changed between environments. Therefore, we will put the relevant configuration into our (development) buildout.cfg, making use of the zcml-additional option to plone.recipe.zope2instance:

```
[instance]
recipe = plone.recipe.zope2instance
http-address = 8080
user = admin:admin
verbose-security = on
eggs =
    ${eggs:main}
```

```
      ${eggs:devtools}
zcml-additional =
    <configure xmlns="http://namespaces.zope.org/zope"
               xmlns:db="http://namespaces.zope.org/db">
       <include package="z3c.saconfig" file="meta.zcml" />
       <db:engine name="optilux"
                  url="mysql://root@localhost/optilux" />
       <db:session engine="optilux" />
    </configure>
```

If we now rerun `./bin/buildout`, it should install `z3c.saconfig`, which in turn will install the latest supported version of `SQLAlchemy` and `MySQL-python`. We should copy the relevant versions to our `versions.cfg` file as well, to pin them down for future deployments.

Working with the database

We will place all our database-related code in the `optilux.cinemacontent` package, reflecting the close integration between our custom content types (cinemas, films) and database entities (screenings, reservations).

Mapping the database tables

First, we will map the database tables to SQLAlchemy ORM models. SQLAlchemy offers three approaches here:

- Build a relational model in Python and ask SQLAlchemy to create the corresponding tables in the database.
- Automatically generate tables and mappers by introspecting an existing database schema. ORM attributes will be added to classes at runtime.
- Define tables and mappers in Python that match an existing relational database schema.

The first approach can be useful if the relational database is specific to your application and you are using a relational database as a tactical data management choice. The second approach is convenient, but does not allow precise control over tables and mappers, and does not allow us to use the **SQLAlchemy Declarative Extension**, which makes our code readable and easy to test. Therefore, we will use the third approach here.

To use the SQLAlchemy Declarative Extension, we must first create a suitable base class. In `__init__.py` of `optilux.cinemacontent`, we add:

```
from sqlalchemy.ext import declarative
...
ORMBase = declarative.declarative_base()
```

We use this first in `screening.py`, where we also defined the `IScreening` interface:

```
import sqlalchemy.types
import sqlalchemy.schema
from zope.interface import implements
from optilux.cinemacontent import ORMBase
...

class Screening(ORMBase):
    """Database-backed implementation of IScreening
    """

    implements(IScreening)

    __tablename__ = 'screening'

    screeningId = sqlalchemy.schema.Column(
            sqlalchemy.types.Integer(),
            primary_key=True,
            autoincrement=True,
        )
    cinemaCode = sqlalchemy.schema.Column(
            sqlalchemy.types.String(4),
            nullable=False,
        )
    filmCode = sqlalchemy.schema.Column(
            sqlalchemy.types.String(4),
            nullable=False,
        )
    showTime = sqlalchemy.schema.Column(
            sqlalchemy.types.DateTime(),
            nullable=False,
        )
    remainingTickets = sqlalchemy.schema.Column(
            sqlalchemy.types.Integer(),
            nullable=False,
        )
```

Here, `__tablename__` specifies the table name to map this class to. The remaining attributes define the mapped database schema. Please refer to the SQLAlchemy documentation for more details.

Note carefully that we use `sqlalchemy.schema` here, not `zope.schema` as we use in interfaces. SQLAlchemy has its own, database-specific notion of a schema that we use to define the types of columns. There is obviously a correlation with the generic interface attributes we defined for `IScreening`, but the two ways of describing schemata should not be confused. SQLAlchemy knows nothing about `zope.schema` and vice versa.

In `reservation.py`, we have:

```
import sqlalchemy.types
import sqlalchemy.orm
import sqlalchemy.schema

from zope.interface import implements

from optilux.cinemacontent.screening import Screening
from optilux.cinemacontent import ORMBase

...

class Reservation(ORMBase):
    """A reservation for a particular screening by a particular
    customer
    """

    implements(IReservation)

    __tablename__ = 'reservation'

    reservationId = sqlalchemy.schema.Column(
            sqlalchemy.types.Integer(),
            primary_key=True,
            autoincrement=True,
        )

    screeningId = sqlalchemy.schema.Column(
            sqlalchemy.types.Integer(),
            sqlalchemy.schema.ForeignKey('screening.screeningId'),
            nullable=False,
        )

    numTickets = sqlalchemy.schema.Column(
            sqlalchemy.types.Integer(),
            nullable=False,
        )

    customerName = sqlalchemy.schema.Column(
            sqlalchemy.types.String(64),
            nullable=False,
        )
```

```
screening = sqlalchemy.orm.relation(Screening,
        primaryjoin=Screening.screeningId==screeningId,
    )
```

Here, `screening` is an `orm.relation`, which describes to SQLAlchemy that there is a many-to-one relationship between screenings and reservations joined on the column called `screeningId` in both tables. Please refer to the SQLAlchemy documentation for more details about how to model various types of relationships.

Querying the database

Now that we have the means to access the database, and the full power of SQLAlchemy at our fingertips, implementing the utilities that perform database operations is easy.

The `IScreeningLocator` utility, found in `screening.py`, is implemented as follows:

First, some imports and the class definition. We use `five.grok.GlobalUtility` to configure the utility (see *Chapter 9, Nine Core Concepts of Zope Programming*, for the alternative ZCML configuration syntax).

```
from five import grok

from z3c.saconfig import Session

from zope.interface import implements
from zope.site.hooks import getSite

from Products.CMFCore.utils import getToolByName
from optilux.cinemacontent.interfaces import IScreeningLocator

...

class ScreeningLocator(grok.GlobalUtility):
    implements(IScreeningLocator)
```

Next, the `filmsAtCinema()` function queries the database for film code matching its parameters, and then looks up the corresponding *Film* content items using the catalog.

We access the SQLAlchemy session by importing the global `Session` object from `z3c.saconfig`, which is thread-safe and transaction aware. We then use standard SQLAlchemy query syntax to search the database for screenings (all the database-related code is highlighted).

Since the utility does not have access to an acquisition context, we use the `getSite()` trick described in *Chapter 9, Nine Core Concepts of Zope Programming*, to obtain the `portal_catalog` tool.

```
def filmsAtCinema(self, cinemaCode, fromDate, toDate):
    # Avoid circular import
    from optilux.cinemacontent.film import IFilm

    results = Session.query(Screening) \
        .filter(Screening.cinemaCode==cinemaCode) \
        .filter(Screening.showTime.between(fromDate, toDate))

    filmCodes = [row.filmCode for row in results]

    site = getSite()
    catalog = getToolByName(site, 'portal_catalog')

    return [ dict(filmCode=film.filmCode,
                  url=film.getURL(),
                  name=film.Title,
                  summary=film.Description,)
             for film in
                 catalog({'object_provides': IFilm.__identifier__,
                          'filmCode': filmCodes,
                          'sort_on': 'sortable_title'})
           ]
```

The cinemasForFilm() method is very similar, searching instead for *Cinema* objects matching the passed-in film code and dates.

```
def cinemasForFilm(self, filmCode, fromDate, toDate):
    # Avoid circular import
    from optilux.cinemacontent.cinema import ICinema

    results = Session.query(Screening) \
        .filter(Screening.filmCode==filmCode) \
        .filter(Screening.showTime.between(fromDate, toDate))

    cinemaCodes = [row.cinemaCode for row in results]

    site = getSite()
    catalog = getToolByName(site, 'portal_catalog')

    return [ dict(cinemaCode=cinema.cinemaCode,
                  url=cinema.getURL(),
                  name=cinema.Title,
                  address=cinema.Description,)
             for cinema in
```

```
catalog({'object_provides':
         ICinema.__identifier__,
         'cinemaCode': cinemaCodes,
         'sort_on': 'sortable_title'})
    ]
```

The final two methods return screening objects, which exist in the database only and so do not need to be correlated to content objects:

```
def screenings(self, filmCode, cinemaCode, fromDate, toDate):
    screenings = Session.query(Screening) \
        .filter(Screening.filmCode==filmCode) \
        .filter(Screening.cinemaCode==cinemaCode) \
        .filter(Screening.showTime.between(fromDate, toDate)) \
        .order_by(Screening.showTime)

    return screenings.all()

def screeningById(self, screeningId):
    return Session.query(Screening).get(screeningId)
```

Notice that we have had to import ICinema and IFilm in the methods that use them instead of importing them at module scope. This is because we will shortly place some code in cinema.py and film.py that import symbols from this module. With two modules importing symbols from one another at module level, we'd end up with circular imports and "undefined symbol" exceptions.

Another way to address this problem would have been to move all the interfaces into the shared interfaces.py module. The author prefers to put schemata for content types (for example, ICinema) and database entities (for example, IScreening) in the same module as related code (for example, views, utilities), and put shared services (such as IScreeningLocator) in a top-level interfaces.py for easier code inspection. There is of course nothing wrong with putting all interfaces in interfaces.py, and many developers prefer this as a default position, not at least because it makes circular import problems less common.

Updating and inserting records

Whereas the `IScreeningLocator` utility only queries the database, the
`ITicketReservations` utility needs to insert new records. In `reservation.py`, we
have:

```
from five import grok

from z3c.saconfig import Session

from zope.interface import implements
from zope.interface import Interface

from optilux.cinemacontent.interfaces import ITicketReserver
from optilux.cinemacontent.interfaces import ReservationError

from optilux.cinemacontent import CinemaMessageFactory as _

...

class TicketReserver(grok.GlobalUtility):
    implements(ITicketReserver)

    def __call__(self, reservation):
        # Make sure there are still seats available
        screening = reservation.screening

        if screening.remainingTickets <= 0:
            raise ReservationError(
                _(u"This screening is sold out!"))
        elif screening.remainingTickets < reservation.numTickets:
            raise ReservationError(
                _(u"Not enough tickets remaining!"))

        # Otherwise, we can save the reservation
        screening.remainingTickets -= reservation.numTickets

        Session.add(reservation)
```

This is a perfect example of the natural flow of the SQLAlchemy ORM API. We
first check that there are remaining tickets, in case a concurrent transaction may
have grabbed the remaining tickets. Then we update the count of remaining
tickets, and insert a new reservation. If the requested screening fills up, we raise a
`ReservationError`. We will see in a moment how this is caught in the user interface
in order to display a sensible error message to the user.

We have opted to keep things simple here. If this were a real reservation
system, we would also need to implement some kind of locking so that
concurrent transactions cannot lay claim to the same tickets.

Testing the database

When working with external systems such as databases, we must ensure our unit tests cannot accidentally write to the external system, and that we can easily maintain isolation between tests.

For the purposes of our tests, we will set up a database connection using **sqlite**, a minimalist, embedded SQL database that ships with Python (version 2.5 and later). This does mean that we will need to perform some manual integration tests against the real database (we could of course automate this into a separate test layer with a bit more effort), but it makes it easy and safe to test our main Python logic.

To set up a `sqllite` connection we will add the following to `testing.py`:

```
import os
import tempfile

import sqlalchemy

...

from zope.component import provideUtility

from z3c.saconfig.utility import EngineFactory
from z3c.saconfig.utility import GloballyScopedSession

class OptiluxCinemaContent(PloneSandboxLayer):

    defaultBases = (PLONE_FIXTURE,)

    def setUpZope(self, app, configurationContext):
        # Load ZCML
        import optilux.cinemacontent
        xmlconfig.file('configure.zcml', optilux.cinemacontent,
                       context=configurationContext)

        # Make sure initialize() is called
        z2.installProduct(app, 'optilux.cinemacontent')

        # Create database in a temporary file
        fileno, self.dbFileName = tempfile.mkstemp(suffix='.db')
        dbURI = 'sqlite:///%s' % self.dbFileName
        dbEngine = sqlalchemy.create_engine(dbURI)
        optilux.cinemacontent.ORMBase.metadata.create_all(dbEngine)

        # Register z3c.saconfig utilities for testing
        engine = EngineFactory(dbURI, echo=False,
                               convert_unicode=False)
        provideUtility(engine, name=u"ftesting")

        session = GloballyScopedSession(engine=u"ftesting",
                                        twophase=False)
        provideUtility(session)
```

```
def tearDownZope(self, app):
    # Uninstall products installed above
    z2.uninstallProduct(app, 'optilux.cinemacontent')

    # Clean up the database
    os.unlink(self.dbFileName)

def setUpPloneSite(self, portal):
    applyProfile(portal, 'optilux.cinemacontent:default')
```

Here, we create a temporary file for our database (we could also have used an in-memory `sqllite` database, but this does not play well with functional testing using the test browser), and ask SQLAlchemy to create in it the tables we defined based on `ORMBase`.

We then register an engine and default session in a way that is analogous to how the ZCML directives work. On tear-down, we remove the temporary file (the standard component architecture teardown provided by `plone.app.testing` takes care of the utilities).

The tests themselves, in `tests/test_db.py`, make use of the SQLAlchemy API to exercise the `IScreeningLocator` and `ITicketReserver` utilities. Here is a short extract:

```
import datetime
import unittest2 as unittest

from plone.app.testing import TEST_USER_ID
from plone.app.testing import setRoles

from optilux.cinemacontent.testing import \
    OPTILUX_CINEMACONTENT_INTEGRATION_TESTING

class TestReservationsDatabase(unittest.TestCase):

    layer = OPTILUX_CINEMACONTENT_INTEGRATION_TESTING

    ...

        def test_ticket_reserver(self):
        from optilux.cinemacontent.screening import Screening
        from optilux.cinemacontent.reservation import Reservation
        from optilux.cinemacontent.interfaces import ITicketReserver
        from z3c.saconfig import Session
        from zope.component import getUtility

        screening = Screening()
        screening.cinemaCode = u"ABC1"
        screening.filmCode = u"DEF1"
        screening.showTime = datetime.datetime(2011, 1, 1, 12, 0, 0)
```

```
        screening.remainingTickets = 10
        Session.add(screening)
        Session.flush()

        reservation = Reservation()
        reservation.numTickets = 2
        reservation.customerName = u"John Smith"
        reservation.screening = screening

        reserver = getUtility(ITicketReserver)
        reserver(reservation)

        Session.flush()

        self.assertTrue(reservation.reservationId is not None)
        self.assertEqual(screening.remainingTickets, 8)
    ...
```

Please refer to the book's accompanying source code for the full listing.

Adding the user interface

All that remains now is to add the view code which uses these utilities to present information to the user. We will first update the *Film* and *Cinema* views with information about screenings, and then add two new views—a view to show screenings of a particular film at a particular cinema, and a form, using z3c.form, to allow the user to make a reservation.

Updating the Film and Cinema views

The changes to film.py and film_templates/view.pt are simple. In the View class:

```
    @memoize
    def cinemas(self, days=14):
        locator = getUtility(IScreeningLocator)

        fromDate = datetime.now()
        toDate = fromDate + timedelta(days)
        return locator.cinemasForFilm(self.context.filmCode,
                fromDate, toDate,
            )
```

And in the template:

```
    <h2 i18n:translate="title_film_showing_at">Now showing at</h2>
    <dl>
```

```
<tal:block repeat="cinema view/cinemas">
    <dt>
        <a tal:attributes="href cinema/url"
            tal:content="cinema/name" />
    </dt>
    <dd tal:content="cinema/address" />
</tal:block>
</dl>
```

The view in `cinema.py` contains very similar code for listing the films shown at a cinema:

```
@memoize
def films(self, days=14):
    locator = getUtility(IScreeningLocator)

    fromDate = datetime.now()
    toDate = fromDate + timedelta(days)

    return locator.filmsAtCinema(self.context.cinemaCode,
            fromDate, toDate,
        )
```

In the `cinema_templates/view.pt` template, we also link to the new `@@screenings` view, which shows a listing of all dates and times at which a particular film is screened at a particular cinema:

```
<h2 i18n:translate="title_cinema_now_showing">Now showing</h2>
<dl>
    <tal:block repeat="film view/films">
        <dt>
            <a tal:attributes="href film/url"
                tal:content="film/name" />
            <a tal:attributes="href string:${context/absolute_url}/@@
screenings/${film/filmCode}"
                i18n:translate="label_view_screenings">
                (show times)
            </a>
        </dt>
        <dd tal:content="film/summary" />
    </tal:block>
</dl>
```

Custom traversal

You may have noticed something a little unusual about the way we construct the link to the preceding @@screenings view: we have included the film code in a separate path element after the @@screenings view name. The full URL generated may be something similar to the following:

```
http://optilux-cinemas.com/cinemas/cinema-1/@@screenings/ABC1
```

With this construct, the view will know which cinema to show screenings for by virtue of its context, and the film code by virtue of its **traversal sub-path**, that is, the subsequent URL path segments.

 Another option would have been to pass the film code as a query string parameter (../@@screenings?filmCode=ABC1), and use self.request.form to extract it. This is a little easier to implement, but also makes for less meaningful URLs.

Recall from *Chapter 9, Nine Core Concepts of Zope Programming*, that we call the process of resolving a URL to a view or other resource to render **URL traversal**. To implement the @@screenings view, we need to implement **custom URL traversal** logic, which we can do by implementing IPublishTraverse in our view.

 IPublishTraverse cannot be used to implement path traversal. That is, we cannot use a TAL path expression or a function such as restrictedTraverse() to traverse to a path like context/@@screenings/ABC1 if we implement the film code lookup using IPublishTraverse.

Implementing the screening view

Since the screenings view is a separate view on a cinema object, we will put its implementation in cinema.py. As before, we will use five.grok for configuration:

```python
from five import grok

from zope.interface import implements
from zope.publisher.interfaces import IPublishTraverse
from optilux.cinemacontent.interfaces import \
    MAKE_RESERVATION_PERMISSION
from AccessControl import getSecurityManager
from zExceptions import NotFound

...
```

```
class Screenings(grok.View):
    implements(IPublishTraverse)

    grok.context(ICinema)
    grok.name('screenings')
    grok.require('zope2.View')

    filmCode = None
```

We implement `IPublishTraverse` and the method it promises, `publishTraverse()`. When Zope traverses to a resource that provides (or is adaptable to) `IPublishTraverse`, it will call the `publishTraverse()` method with the current request and the next name in the traversal stack, expecting to get back another object from which URL traversal and publication can continue:

```
def publishTraverse(self, request, name):
    if self.filmCode is None:
        self.filmCode = name
        return self
    else:
        raise NotFound()
```

We expect the name on the traversal sub-path to be the film code. We store this in an instance variable, `self.fimCode`, and return the *same* view instance (`self`) that was traversed to previously. If there are any further names to traverse to (that is, there are further path segments in the URL), we consider this a *404 Not Found* error and raise the corresponding exception.

> It is possible to let `publishTraverse()` return some other object than
> `self`, for example by looking up another view. In this case, you must
> take care that it has its __parent__ set to the current view instance
> (`self`), otherwise you may get security exceptions.

At this point, we have a view instance with the `filmCode` variable set. Zope will invoke this view much like any other, which will cause our template to be rendered. As in *Chapter 11, Standalone Views and Forms*, we override `update()` from `grok.View` to hide the editable border:

```
def update(self):
    self.request.set('disable_border', True)
```

The template will make use of various other view instance methods:

```
@memoize
def upcomingScreenings(self, days=14):
```

```
    cinema = self.context
    locator = getUtility(IScreeningLocator)

    fromDate = datetime.now()
    toDate = fromDate + timedelta(days)

    canReserve = getSecurityManager().checkPermission(
            MAKE_RESERVATION_PERMISSION, cinema
        )

    film = self.film()
    return [dict(screeningId=screening.screeningId,
                showTime=self.localize(screening.showTime),
                remainingTickets=screening.remainingTickets,
                canReserve=(canReserve and
                        screening.remainingTickets > 0))
            for screening in
                locator.screenings(
                        film.filmCode,
                        cinema.cinemaCode,
                        fromDate,
                        toDate,
                    )]

@memoize
def film(self):
    catalog = getToolByName(self.context, 'portal_catalog')
    return catalog({'filmCode': self.filmCode})[0].getObject()

def localize(self, time):
    return self._time_localizer()(time.isoformat(),
                                    long_format=True,
                                    context=self.context,
                                    domain='plonelocales')

@memoize
def _time_localizer(self):
    translation_service = getToolByName(
            self.context, 'translation_service'
        )
    return translation_service.ulocalized_time
```

The template fills the `main` slot and outputs some basic information. It then loops over the films to reserve, outputting them in a table:

```
<tr tal:repeat="screening view/upcomingScreenings">
<tal:block define="reserveURL string:${cinemaURL}/
    @@reserve/${screening/screeningId}">
    <td>
```

```
            <a tal:attributes="href reserveURL"
               tal:omit-tag="not:screening/canReserve">
               <tal:block content="screening/showTime" />
            </a>
         </td>
         <td>
            <a tal:attributes="href reserveURL"
               tal:omit-tag="not:screening/canReserve">
               <tal:block content="screening/remainingTickets" />
            </a>
         </td>
      </tal:block>
   </tr>
```

Please refer to the book's source code for the full listing.

Implementing the reservations form

The keen-eyed reader will have noticed that we repeated the traversal sub-path trick for the @@reserve view, which implements the form used to reserve tickets. This is found further down cinema.py. It uses plone.directives.form to implement a form, as we learned in the previous chapter, and implements IPublishTraverse in a way that is analogous to the preceding example:

```
from five import grok
from plone.directives import form

from zope.interface import implements
from zope.publisher.interfaces import IPublishTraverse
from optilux.cinemacontent.interfaces import \
    MAKE_RESERVATION_PERMISSION
from AccessControl import getSecurityManager
from zExceptions import NotFound

from z3c.form import field, button
from Products.statusmessages.interfaces import IStatusMessage
from optilux.cinemacontent.interfaces import ReservationError
from optilux.cinemacontent.interfaces import ITicketReserver
from optilux.cinemacontent.reservation import IReservation
from optilux.cinemacontent.reservation import Reservation

...

class Reserve(form.Form):
    implements(IPublishTraverse)

    grok.context(ICinema)
    grok.name('reserve')
```

```
grok.require('optilux.MakeReservation')
label = _(u"Reserve tickets")
fields = field.Fields(IReservation) \
            .omit('screening', 'reservationId')
ignoreContext = True

screeningId = None

def publishTraverse(self, request, name):
    if self.screeningId is None:
        self.screeningId = int(name)
        return self
    else:
        raise NotFound()
```

Notice here how we omit the `screening` and `reservationId` fields from the form using `Fields.omit()`, since these fields would not make much sense to the user.

The `update()` method hides the editable border and then prepares some information for the custom for template that we will define in a moment:

```
def update(self):
    self.request.set('disable_border', True)
    # Get the real screening object
    locator = getUtility(IScreeningLocator)
    self.screening = locator.screeningById(self.screeningId)
    # Localise the screening time
    self.screeningTime = self.localize(self.screening.showTime)
    # Get the film title
    catalog = getToolByName(self.context, 'portal_catalog')
    film = catalog({
                'object_provides': IFilm.__identifier__,
                'filmCode': self.screening.filmCode,
            })[0]
    self.filmTitle = film.Title

    # Let z3c.form do its magic
    super(Reserve, self).update()
```

We also add some helper methods similar to the ones we have used before for time localization:

```
def localize(self, time):
    return self._time_localizer()(
        time, None, self.context, domain='plonelocales')
```

```
    @memoize
def _time_localizer(self):
    translation_service = getToolByName(self.context,
                                        'translation_service')
    return translation_service.ulocalized_time
```

Next, we define the main button handler, which uses the `ITicketReserver` utility to make a reservation:

```
    @button.buttonAndHandler(_(u"Reserve"))
def reserve(self, action):
    data, errors = self.extractData()
    if errors:
        self.status = self.formErrorsMessage
        return

    reserver = getUtility(ITicketReserver)
    reservation = Reservation(
                    screeningId=self.screeningId,
                    screening=self.screening,
                    numTickets=data['numTickets'],
                    customerName=data['customerName'],
                )
    try:
        reserver(reservation)
    except ReservationError, e:
        IStatusMessage(self.request).add(str(e), type='error')
    else:
        confirm = _(u"Thank you! Your tickets will be ready " +
                    u"for collection at the front desk.")
        IStatusMessage(self.request).add(confirm, type='info')
        self.request.response.redirect(
            self.context.absolute_url())
```

Finally, we have a cancellation button:

```
    @button.buttonAndHandler(_(u"Cancel"))
def cancel(self, action):
    confirm = _(u"Reservation cancelled.")
    IStatusMessage(self.request).add(confirm, type='info')

    self.request.response.redirect(self.context.absolute_url())
```

Finally, let us take a look at the template. We create this as `cinema_templates/reserve.pt`, which means that `plone.directives.form` will automatically associate it with our view.

> If you are using ZCML configuration and the standard `z3c.form.form` base classes, and you wish to use a custom template, you can set a class variable `template` on the form view class to an instance of `Products.Five.browser.pagetemplatefile.ViewPageTemplateFile`, passing the template file name as the sole constructor argument.

We begin with the usual preamble, filling the `main` slot:

```
<html xmlns="http://www.w3.org/1999/xhtml" xml:lang="en"
      xmlns:tal="http://xml.zope.org/namespaces/tal"
      xmlns:metal="http://xml.zope.org/namespaces/metal"
      xmlns:i18n="http://xml.zope.org/namespaces/i18n"
      lang="en"
      metal:use-macro="context/main_template/macros/master"
      i18n:domain="optilux.cinemacontent">
<body>

<metal:main fill-slot="main">
    <tal:main-macro metal:define-macro="main">

        <h1 class="documentFirstHeading"
            tal:content="view/label | nothing" />

        <div id="content-core">
```

Next, we define a table of information about the screening for which a reservation is being made:

```
<table class="listing vertical reservation-info">
    <tr>
      <th i18n:translate="label_reservation_cinema">
          Cinema
      </th>
      <td tal:content="context/Title" />
    </tr>
    <tr>
      <th i18n:translate="label_reservation_film">
          Film
      </th>
      <td tal:content="view/filmTitle" />
    </tr>
    <tr>
```

```
                       <th i18n:translate="label_reservation_screening">
                           Screening
                       </th>
                       <td tal:content="view/screeningTime" />
                   </tr>
                   <tr>
                       <th i18n:translate="label_reservation_remaining">
                           Tickets remaining
                       </th>
                       <td
                        tal:content="view/screening/remainingTickets" />
                   </tr>
               </table>

               <p i18n:translate="description_reservations">
                   Please enter your name and the number of tickets
                   you would like to reserve.
               </p>

               <div class="divider"><!-- --></div>
```

Notice how we extract the cinema's title from the context, and the rest of the information from the view as prepared in update().

Finally, we include a macro from plone.app.z3cform which contains the form itself as generated by z3c.form:

```
                   <metal:block
                       use-macro="context/@@ploneform-macros/titlelessform"
                       />
               </div>

           </tal:main-macro>
       </metal:main>
       </body>
       </html>
```

Take a look at the plone.app.z3cform documentation at http://pypi.python.org/pypi/plone.app.z3cform for more details about the macros and slots in the @@ploneform-macros view.

Tests

Having tested the database-related logic in `tests/test_db.py`, all that remains is to add some functional tests using the test browser to exercise the views. You can find these in `tests/test_reservations.py` in the book's accompanying source code, omitted here for brevity as these are similar to the tests in *Chapter 11, Standalone Views and Forms*.

Summary

In this chapter, we have covered:

- A few rules of thumb about when to consider using a relational database instead of the ZODB
- How to connect to a relational database using the SQLAlchemy library
- A few design principles for abstracting database operations into utilities
- A few tips for testing database operations
- A few examples of how to integrate database-backed views and forms into the Plone user interface

We have just scratched the surface of what SQLAlchemy can do. You are encouraged to read its documentation, found at `http://sqlalchemy.org`.

In the next chapter, we enable members of the public to make ticket reservations using the views created in this chapter, when we design the user management policy of the site.

Users and their Permissions

13

So far, we have focused on building functionality. Although we have introduced new permissions where appropriate, we have not yet considered user and role management in detail. It is now time to define exactly who can do what, when, and where in the site.

In this chapter, we will cover:

- Defining a security policy for our application
- Attaching additional metadata to a user
- Reading and changing user metadata
- Customizing Plone's security infrastructure using the Pluggable Authentication Service API
- Integrating Plone with Facebook's authentication service

Defining a membership policy

Let us take a look at the requirements from *Chapter 2, Introduction to the Case Study*, which relate to user management.

Requirement	Importance
Customers should not need to log in to use the site, but a username and password should be required when they wish to reserve tickets.	Medium
Logged-in customers should have easy access to their preferred cinema or cinemas, for example, those in their area.	Medium
Customers should be able to log in using their Facebook account.	Medium

In addition, other requirements make it clear that staff members will need to be distinguished from customers. These users may have elevated permissions in certain parts of the site, for example to update Cinema information or add new Films and Promotions.

As usual, the best place to start is Plone's built-in functionality. Through the **Users and Groups** control panel, we can define new **groups**, create new **users** (also sometimes known as **members**), assign users to groups, and give roles to individuals and groups.

When they are first created, users are given the global `Member` role. Through the Sharing tab, which is available on most content objects, we can give **local roles** – those which apply only to a particular folder of the site – to specific users or groups. These roles include `Editor` (can edit content), `Reader` (can view private content) and `Contributor` (can add new items to folders).

By default, users must be added by administrators, and passwords are generated and emailed for newly created accounts. Both of these policies can be changed in the **Security** control panel.

In *Chapter 6, Security and Workflow*, we anticipated the need to separate staff users from users representing members of the public. Thus, we created the `StaffMember` role and granted it to a new group called `Staff`. We can use this pair in two different ways:

- By granting permissions to the `StaffMember` role, either site-wide or as part of a workflow, we can let staff users perform tasks which regular members cannot.

- By assigning local roles to the `Staff` group, we can give staff special privileges in a particular area of the site. For example, a private folder could be invisible to regular users, but available to all staff by granting the `Reader` local role to the `Staff` group.

We can refine this policy by adding additional groups. For example, the site administrator could decide to delegate responsibility for managing all cinemas in a 'northern region' to a particular group of employees. He/she could hence create a new group called `Northern Region` and grant this group the `Editor` local role, using the **Sharing** tab, in a particular `Cinema Folder` containing all northern region cinemas.

While staff users can be managed explicitly, members of the public are likely to want to sign up to the site themselves. They will not be given the chance to add any content, but will be granted permissions for activities such as rating movies and reserving tickets. Since these are the most common type of user (or perhaps, the least controllable), it makes sense to manage them using the default `Member` role.

Updating the site policy product

To support our use case, we need only to make minor changes to Plone's out-of-the-box membership functionality:

- Add the `StaffMember` role and `Staff` group.
- Disable the personal **Dashboard** for regular members – they should not need to have personalized portlets.
- Ensure that anonymous users can register themselves as site members.

We already added the `StaffMember` role and `Staff` group in *Chapter 6, Security and Workflow*. The last two points can be achieved by adding the following to `profiles/default/rolemap.xml` in the `optilux.policy` package:

```
<permissions>
    ...
    <!-- This disables the dashboard for regular members -->
    <permission name="Portlets: Manage own portlets" acquire="False">
        <role name="Manager" />
        <role name="StaffMember" />
    </permission>
    <!-- This allows anonymous visitors to register for the site  -->
    <permission name="Add portal member" acquire="False">
        <role name="Manager" />
        <role name="Anonymous" />
    </permission>
</permissions>
```

The first stanza ensures that the `Member` role cannot manage personal portlets, which in turn disables the dashboard. The second allows `Anonymous` users to create new members for themselves, which enables the **Register** personal action. (This is the permission that is changed when using the **Security** control panel to allow users to register themselves.)

Of course, there are corresponding tests in `tests.py`:

```
    def test_manage_own_portlets_permission(self):
        portal = self.layer['portal']
        self.assertTrue('Portlets: Manage own portlets' in
                [r['name'] for r in
                    portal.permissionsOfRole('StaffMember')
                        if r['selected']])
        self.assertFalse('Portlets: Manage own portlets' in
                [r['name'] for r in
```

```
                    portal.permissionsOfRole('Member')
                        if r['selected']])
    def test_add_portal_member_permission(self):
        portal = self.layer['portal']
        self.assertTrue('Add portal member' in
                [r['name'] for r in
                    portal.permissionsOfRole('Anonymous')
                    if r['selected']])
```

We will not encode other policy decisions relating to specific content items, users, or local roles in the policy product. These are better left to site administrators, who may use techniques such as those outlined previously to set up an appropriate site structure.

We have been implying other aspects of the member policy throughout the book. For example, when we built the ticket reservation functionality in the previous chapter, we ensured that the relevant permissions were only granted to the Member role. When we built an administrator's report in *Chapter 11, Standalone Views and Forms*, we restricted it to the Manager and StaffMember roles. The choices here were mostly obvious from the requirements, and easily implemented by relying on Plone's standard roles.

Always protect views and other functionality with appropriate permissions, and create new permissions when none of the standard ones are a good match. Assign sensible default roles to new permissions, and attempt to model your site membership policy as much as possible on standard roles such as Member, Reviewer, Site Administrator, and Manager.

Managing user metadata

Beyond considering the permissions we grant to different types of users in the site, we often want to manage some additional **user metadata**.

Plone's standard member profile information, which can be accessed from the **Personal Preferences** form, covers the basics, but it is not difficult to add new member properties. In this case, we want to store one or more 'home' cinemas for each site user.

The portal_memberdata tool keeps track of which user properties are available. We can use GenericSetup to add a new property. In optilux.cinemacontent's profiles/ default folder, we have a new file called memberdata_properties.xml:

```
<?xml version="1.0"?>
<object name="portal_memberdata" meta_type="Plone Memberdata Tool">
    <property name="homeCinemas" type="lines"></property>
</object>
```

As with all Zope **property sheets**, a `lines` property contains a list of strings, delimited by newlines when edited through the Zope Management Interface. We can set a default value inside the `<property />` tag, though in this case we want the default to be an empty list.

To allow users to add or remove cinemas from this list, we will register a new viewlet on the main view of a `Cinema`. This is similar to the film ratings viewlet we added in *Chapter 11, Standalone Views and Forms*. It can be found in `mycinema.py`:

```
from five import grok

from zExceptions import Forbidden
from zope.component import getMultiAdapter

from plone.app.layout.globals.interfaces import IViewView
from plone.app.layout.viewlets.interfaces import IBelowContentBody

from optilux.cinemacontent.cinema import ICinema

class MyCinema(grok.Viewlet):
    grok.context(ICinema)
    grok.name('optilux.cinemacontent.mycinema')
    grok.view(IViewView)
    grok.viewletmanager(IBelowContentBody)
    grok.require('zope2.View')

    def update(self):
        self.portal_state = getMultiAdapter(
                (self.context, self.request),
                name=u"plone_portal_state",
            )

        if not self.available():
            self.isHome = False
        else:
            member = self.portal_state.member()
            cinemaCode = self.context.cinemaCode
            homeCinemas = list(member.getProperty('homeCinemas', []))

            if 'optilux.cinemacontent.mycinema.Toggle' in \
                    self.request.form:
                authenticator = getMultiAdapter(
                        (self.context, self.request),
                        name=u"authenticator",
```

```
            )
            if not authenticator.verify():
                raise Forbidden()

            if cinemaCode in homeCinemas:
                homeCinemas.remove(cinemaCode)
            else:
                homeCinemas.append(cinemaCode)
            member.setProperties(homeCinemas=homeCinemas)

        self.isHome = (cinemaCode in homeCinemas)

    def available(self):
        return not self.portal_state.anonymous()
```

Here, we obtain a member object using the `plone_portal_state` helper view. We
then use `getProperty()` to read a property, and `setProperties()` to set a property.

 `setProperties()` can take an arbitrary number of keyword arguments,
allowing you to set multiple properties at the same time.

Everything else in the preceding code listing is just logic to determine how to
render the viewlet and react to form input. The template in `mycinema_templates/`
`mycinema.pt` is trivial, containing only a toggle button and a form authentication to
guard against cross-site request forgery, as seen in *Chapter 11, Standalone Views and
Forms.* Refer to the book's accompanying source code for details.

To give the user quick access to their 'home' cinema or cinemas, we will add a new
portlet. This is similar to the portlet we created for promotions in *Chapter 10, Custom
Content Types.* In `portlets/mycinemas.py`, we have:

```python
from zope.component import getMultiAdapter
from zope.interface import implements

from plone.app.portlets.portlets import base
from plone.memoize.instance import memoize
from plone.portlets.interfaces import IPortletDataProvider

from Products.Five.browser.pagetemplatefile import \
    ViewPageTemplateFile

from Acquisition import aq_inner
from Products.CMFCore.utils import getToolByName

from optilux.cinemacontent.interfaces import ICinema
from optilux.cinemacontent import CinemaMessageFactory as _

class IMyCinemasPortlet(IPortletDataProvider):
    pass
```

```
class Assignment(base.Assignment):
    implements(IMyCinemasPortlet)

    title = _(u"My cinema")

class Renderer(base.Renderer):

    render = ViewPageTemplateFile('mycinemas.pt')

    @property
    def available(self):
        return len(self._cinemaCodes()) > 0

    def cinemas(self):
        context = aq_inner(self.context)
        cinemaCodes = self._cinemaCodes()

        if cinemaCodes:
            catalog = getToolByName(context, 'portal_catalog')
            for brain in catalog({
                        'cinemaCode': cinemaCodes,
                        'object_provides': ICinema.__identifier__}
                ):
                    yield dict(title=brain.Title,
                               address=brain.Description,
                               url=brain.getURL())

    @memoize
    def _cinemaCodes(self):
        context = aq_inner(self.context)
        portal_state = getMultiAdapter(
                (context, self.request),
                name="plone_portal_state",
            )
        if portal_state.anonymous():
            return []
        return portal_state.member().getProperty('homeCinemas', [])

class AddForm(base.NullAddForm):

    def create(self):
        return Assignment()
```

Again, we use `getProperty()` to access member data. There is also an associated template in `portlets/mycinemas.pt`, the appropriate component registration in `portlets/configure.zcml`, installation instructions in `profiles/default/portlets.xml` and tests in `tests/test_portlet_mycinemas.py`.

Of course, these are just two examples of using custom member data. Another interesting option may be to create a custom form to make a particular set of member properties editable. This could use `z3c.form` as we learned in *Chapter 11, Standalone Views and Forms*. An interface representing the member schema could be used to create form fields. The action handler would use the syntax we have seen in this chapter to set member properties for the currently authenticated member. The form itself could be made available via an action, installed with an `actions.xml` import step as we learned in *Chapter 11, Standalone Views and Forms*.

Collaborative workspaces

Many sites require some form of **collaboration** and sharing of content among a subset of users. For example, you could want to set up a **workspace** for a particular project or team.

Collaborative workspaces in Plone can be as simple as appropriately configured folders:

- A workspace folder could be private and thus invisible to regular members.
- A particular group could be given the `Reader` local role on the **Sharing** tab. They would thus be able to view the folder's contents.
- The same group could be given the `Contributor` local role, allowing them to create new content items.
- The **Restrict...** option in the **Add** menu could be used to restrict which content types these users would be allowed to add.
- If applicable, a section-specific workflow policy could be installed, using **placeful workflow**, which ships with Plone, but is not installed by default.

The Pluggable Authentication Service

At the root of every Zope instance, there is a **user folder**, called `acl_users`. User folders provide functionality for authenticating, authorizing, finding, and inspecting users. The user folder in the Zope application root typically contains only the main administrator user. There is a more specific user folder inside each Plone site, also called `acl_users`, which manages regular users.

Plone's user folder is powered by **PAS** – the **Pluggable Authentication Service**. This is a very flexible kind of user folder, which delegates responsibility for managing numerous aspects of site membership to different **PAS plugins**. Plugins can perform functions such as extracting user credentials from a request, authenticating these credentials, creating a user object for a particular user ID, providing user properties, assigning global or local roles, and enumerating a user's assigned groups.

This structure affords great flexibility. For example, it is possible to have an extraction plugin looking for a username in a HTTP cookie, an authentication plugin checking an LDAP directory, and a user property plugin reading user data from an SQL database, all working together.

Anatomy of a PAS plugin

A **PAS plugin** is a persistent object that is installed into the `acl_users` folder. Plugins provide one or more **plugin interfaces** (also referred to as **plugin types**), which tell PAS which aspects of authentication the plugin can be used for. A plugin may be **activated** for zero or more of these interfaces at any given time through the **plugin registry** found in the ZMI at `acl_users/plugins` inside a Plone.

More than one plugin can be activated for a given interface at the same time. Plugins are then invoked in the order they are listed under the given plugin type in the registry. For most plugin types, the first plugin to return a valid response will be used, allowing us to maintain precedence among plugins through their ordering. In some cases, such as for user properties, enumeration, or the resetting of credentials, plugins are additive, in that all plugins are always given an opportunity to provide a response.

Most plugin interfaces are defined in `Products.PluggableAuthService.` `interfaces.plugins`. These include:

Interface	Purpose
IExtractionPlugin	Extracts a user's credentials (for example, login name and password) from a request. This returns a dictionary, which is then passed to the active authentication plugins.
IAuthenticationPlugin	Given the credentials extracted by an extraction plugin, authenticates the given user if possible. If this returns a tuple `(userid, loginname)`, the user will be deemed authenticated. The user ID is a unique, never-changing key for the user. The login name is usually the name the user entered during the login process. The two are often, but not always the same.
IChallengePlugin	If a user is not logged in and attempts to access a resource not accessible to `Anonymous`, the active challenge plugins are given an opportunity to challenge the user to log in, for example by redirecting him or her to a login page.

Interface	Purpose
ICredentialsUpdatePlugin	Called when the user has asked to change his or her password.
ICredentialsResetPlugin	Called when the user has logged out.
IUserAdderPlugin	Called when a new user is to be added, for example, through the Plone control panel.
IRoleAssignerPlugin	Called when a user is to be granted or denied a particular global role, for example, through the Plone control panel.
IUserFactoryPlugin	Used to create a new (transient) user object, which is then stored in the request's security manager. This is the object returned by getSecurityManager().getUser().
IAnonymousUserFactoryPlugin	Used to create a new (transient) user object for the anonymous user.
IPropertiesPlugin	Used to obtain properties for a given user.
IGroupsPlugin	Used to enumerate the groups that a given principal (user or other group) belongs to.
IRolesPlugin	Used to enumerate the roles that a given principal (user or group) belongs to.
IUpdatePlugin	Used to update a user's properties.
IValidationPlugin	Used to validate properties before they are set on a given user.
IUserEnumerationPlugin	Used to search for users by various criteria.
IGroupEnumerationPlugin	Used to search for groups by various criteria.
IRoleEnumerationPlugin	Used to search for available roles by various criteria.

In addition, Plone ships with `Products.PlonePAS`, which adds some Plone-specific plugins. Their interfaces are found in `Products.PlonePAS.interfaces.plugins`:

Interface	Purpose
IUserIntrospection	Used to get a list of users. Rarely used – the IUserEnumerationPlugin is normally a better choice.
ILocalRolesPlugin	Used to list the roles a given principal has in a particular context. (For a simpler way to provide local roles dynamically, see the borg.localrole package, which ships with Plone.)
IUserManagement	Used by Plone to modify or delete users.
IMutablePropertiesPlugin	Used by Plone to set user properties, for example, when the user changes his or her preferences.
ISchemaMutablePropertiesPlugin	Used when the administrator adds new properties to a user to indicate the types of those properties.

 Please refer to the docstrings on the various interfaces themselves for more detail.

In addition to the plugin itself, a PAS plugin needs a ZMI add form, and some ZCML registrations to add security declarations for its methods and inform PAS of its existence.

A Facebook authentication plugin

As an illustration of a custom PAS plugin, we will show how to integrate Plone with Facebook's authentication API, to allow users to log in with their Facebook account details. Our basic design is as follows:

- A simple login view uses the **Facebook authentication API (OAuth** 2.0) to authenticate the user via a series of redirects between Plone and Facebook. Note that this view has no associated template—all it does is orchestrate OAuth redirects.

- An action in the `user` category, shown for anonymous users, is used to let the user access this view.

- If login succeeds, we store authentication details in a secure **session**. We will use the **Beaker** framework, through the `collective.beaker` integration package, to manage our sessions. Beaker provides a flexible session and caching implementation, which can use a variety of storage mechanisms, including files on disk or **memcached**, a fast and scalable cache server. See `http://pypi.python.org/pypi/collective.beaker` for details about Beaker and its integration into Plone.

- A PAS plugin will interact with Plone's security infrastructure, relying on the information in the session to identify a user. It will use the following PAS interfaces:

  - `IExtractionPlugin`, to extract credentials from the session. If no session details are found, the plugin will do nothing, allowing Plone's standard extraction and authentication plugins to take over.

  - `IAuthenticationPlugin`, to authenticate users. Since we will have already authenticated the user through the login view, this simply trusts that if a user was extracted from the session by the plugin itself, the user remains authenticated.

  - `ICredentialsResetPlugin`, to destroy the session when the user logs out.

  - `IPropertiesPlugin`, to set the `fullname` property to the user's name as returned by Facebook. We would normally also set at least the `email` property, but Facebook will not always return a user's e-mail address for privacy reasons, so we skip it here.

  - `IRolesPlugin`, to grant users authenticated by this plugin the `Member` role.

  - `IUserEnumerationPlugin`, to allow a currently authenticated user to show up in searches. Plone expects this as a minimum. In other scenarios, we may have implemented some kind of user search and enumeration here, but searching all of Facebook's 600 million users (and counting) could prove a little tricky.

- We will also need some setup code to correctly register the PAS plugin during installation of the policy product.

For more details about the Facebook authentication API, see `http://developers.facebook.com/docs/authentication`. For the purposes of this example, we have registered an application with Facebook called `Optilux Cinemas` and obtained an associated application ID and secret. We have set the site URL to be `http://localhost:8080`, to allow us to test with a Plone site running locally on that port. If you are testing with Plone running on any other domain name or port, Facebook will refuse authentication. For a real-world application, we would of course use a public domain name instead.

Facebook authentication is a nice, reusable chunk of functionality. As such, we will put it in its own distribution, `optilux.facebookauth`. We can create this and add it to the build in the same way that we created `optilux.policy` (*Chapter 5, Developing a Site Strategy*), `optilux.theme` (*Chapter 8, Creating a Custom Theme*) and `optilux.cinemacontent` (*Chapter 10, Custom Content Types*), using ZopeSkel.

Next, we can add `optilux.facebookauth` as a dependency of `optilux.policy` so that it is installed appropriately. In the latter's `setup.py`, we add:

```
install_requires=[
    'setuptools',
    'Plone',
    'Products.PloneFormGen',
    'optilux.theme',
    'optilux.cinemacontent',
    'optilux.facebookauth',
]
```

Since we use `<includeDependencies />` in optilux.policy's `configure.zcml`, we do not need to include optilux.facebookauth's configuration. However, we will preemptively add a GenericSetup profile dependency in optilux.policy's `metadata.xml`:

```
<metadata>
    <version>1</version>
    <dependencies>
      <dependency>profile-Products.PloneFormGen:default</dependency>
      <dependency>profile-optilux.theme:default</dependency>
      <dependency>profile-optilux.cinemacontent:default</dependency>
      <dependency>profile-optilux.facebookauth:default</dependency>
    </dependencies>
</metadata>
```

Package configuration

We can now build `optilux.facebookauth`. Since there are only a few components to install, and to keep it as reusable and dependency-free as possible, we will use ZCML-based configuration and explicitly manage all ZCML dependencies.

In `setup.py`, we list the following dependencies:

```
install_requires=[
    'setuptools',
    'zope.interface',
    'zope.publisher',
    'zope.i18nmessageid',
    'five.globalrequest',
    'collective.beaker',
    'Products.PluggableAuthService',
    'Products.PlonePAS',
    'Products.statusmessages',
],
extras_require={
    'test': ['plone.app.testing',]
},
```

We can also comment out the `z3c.autoinclude` entry point (since we want to explicitly configure this component from `optilux.policy`) and the `setup_requires` and `paster_plugins` lines:

```
# entry_points="""
# # -*- Entry points: -*-
#
# [z3c.autoinclude.plugin]
# target = plone
# """,
# setup_requires=["PasteScript"],
# paster_plugins=["ZopeSkel"],
```

In `configure.zcml`, we first include the minimum set of dependencies we need to configure, and then register our installation profile and a custom import step to configure the plugin imperatively:

```
<configure
    xmlns="http://namespaces.zope.org/zope"
    xmlns:genericsetup="http://namespaces.zope.org/genericsetup"
    xmlns:pas="http://namespaces.zope.org/pluggableauthservice"
    xmlns:five="http://namespaces.zope.org/five"
    xmlns:browser="http://namespaces.zope.org/browser"
```

```
xmlns:i18n="http://namespaces.zope.org/i18n"
i18n_domain="optilux.facebookauth">

<include package="collective.beaker" />
<include package="five.globalrequest" />

<genericsetup:registerProfile
    name="default"
    title="Optilux Facebook authentication"
    directory="profiles/default"
    description="Allows customers to log in with Facebook"
    provides="Products.GenericSetup.interfaces.EXTENSION"
    />

<genericsetup:importStep
    name="optilux-facebookauth-various"
    title="Additional Optilux Facebook Authentication setup"
    description="PAS plugin installer"
    handler="optilux.facebookauth.setuphandlers.importVarious">
    <depends name="rolemap"/>
</genericsetup:importStep>
```

Next, we register the PAS plugin, including an add view that can be used to create an instance of the plugin in the ZMI. Notice how the add view name is referenced in the <five:registerClass /> directive, and how the registered class's meta type is referenced in <pas:registerMultiPlugin />:

```
<five:registerClass
    class=".plugin.OptiluxFacebookUsers"
    meta_type="OptiluxFacebookUsers"
    permission="zope2.ViewManagementScreens"
    addview="optilux-facebook-users"
    />

<pas:registerMultiPlugin
    meta_type="OptiluxFacebookUsers"
    />

<browser:page
    name="optilux-facebook-users"
    for="zope.browser.interfaces.IAdding"
    class=".plugin.AddForm"
    permission="zope2.ViewManagementScreens"
    />
```

Finally, we register the `@@facebook-login` view, which performs the Facebook OAuth orchestration:

```
<browser:page
    name="facebook-login"
    for="Products.CMFCore.interfaces.ISiteRoot"
    class=".login.FacebookLogin"
    permission="zope2.View"
    />

</configure>
```

Before we move on to the code, there is one more level of configuration required — we need to tell Beaker how to store and manage sessions and caches. This is done in `zope.conf`, which is generated by Buildout. We can use the `zope-conf-additional` option for `plone.recipe.zope2instance` to add additional configuration. In `buildout.cfg`, we add:

```
[instance]
recipe = plone.recipe.zope2instance
http-address = 8080
user = admin:admin
verbose-security = on
eggs =
    ${eggs:main}
    ${eggs:devtools}
zcml-additional =
    <configure
            xmlns="http://namespaces.zope.org/zope"
            xmlns:db="http://namespaces.zope.org/db">
        <include package="z3c.saconfig" file="meta.zcml" />
        <db:engine name="optilux"
            url="mysql://root@localhost/optilux" />
        <db:session engine="optilux" />
    </configure>
zope-conf-additional =
    <product-config beaker>
        session.type        file
        session.data_dir    ${buildout:directory}/var/sessions/data
        session.lock_dir    ${buildout:directory}/var/sessions/lock
        session.key         beaker.session
        session.secret      secret
    </product-config>
```

Do not forget to rerun `bin/buildout` after making these changes.

 For a real-world application, you should set `session.secret` to something more secret than the word `secret`. This is used as an encryption key to make it harder to steal someone's session. In a production scenario, you probably also want to set `session.secure` and `session.timeout` to only send session cookies over secure (HTTPS) connections and let sessions time out after a given period of inactivity. Finally, if you are running multiple Zope clients on different machines, you will need to configure a shared `memcached` or database backend for Beaker, or make sessions sticky to a single machine. See `http://beaker.groovie.org/configuration.html` for more details about the various configuration options.

Facebook OAuth authentication

The login view is found in `login.py`. It begins with some imports and constants:

```
import json
import urlparse
import urllib

from zope.publisher.browser import BrowserView

from collective.beaker.interfaces import ISession

from Products.statusmessages.interfaces import IStatusMessage

from optilux.facebookauth import CinemaMessageFactory as _
from optilux.facebookauth.plugin import SessionKeys

FACEBOOK_APP_ID          = "165499400161909"
FACEBOOK_APP_SECRET      = "35477df486f80aaa1bd65d78fe3b2cb8"
FACEBOOK_AUTH_URL        = "https://graph.facebook.com/oauth/
authorize"
FACEBOOK_ACCESS_TOKEN_URL = \
    "https://graph.facebook.com/oauth/access_token"
FACEBOOK_PROFILE_URL     = "https://graph.facebook.com/me"
```

The `CinemaMessageFactory` instance is defined in optilux.facebookauth's `__init__.py` much like the equivalent message factory in `optilux.cinemacontent`:

```
from zope.i18nmessageid import MessageFactory
CinemaMessageFactory = MessageFactory('optilux.facebookauth')
```

The view class itself defines only a `__call__` method that performs the OAuth redirect logic. The view is used both to send the user to Facebook and to receive the response from Facebook in the form of a redirect with embedded query string parameters indicating whether the authentication succeeded or not.

We first check for the scenario where the user has been returned to us with an error code embedded in the request:

```
class FacebookLogin(BrowserView):

    def __call__(self):
        verificationCode = self.request.form.get("code")
        errorReason      = self.request.form.get("error_reason")

        args = {
                'client_id': FACEBOOK_APP_ID,
                'redirect_uri': "%s/%s" %
                    (self.context.absolute_url(), self.__name__,),
            }

        if errorReason is not None:
            IStatusMessage(self.request).add(
                _(u"Facebook authentication denied"), type="error")
            self.request.response.redirect(
                self.context.absolute_url())
            return u""
```

Here, we simply show an error message and redirect the user back to the context's default view (the site's front page).

If there is no error, we consider the scenario where there is no verification code either. In this case, we need to send the user to Facebook for login and possible authorization of the Optilux Cinemas application:

```
        if verificationCode is None:
            self.request.response.redirect(
                "%s?%s" % (FACEBOOK_AUTH_URL,
                            urllib.urlencode(args),)
            )
            return u""
```

The arguments here include our unique application client ID (FACEBOOK_APP_ID), which we obtained when we registered Optilux Cinemas as a Facebook application on the Facebook developer website, and a redirect URL telling Facebook to return to this same view with an error or verification code.

This only leaves the scenario where the user has been verified by Facebook and has authorized our application. We can now use the verification code along with a unique application secret (which we would normally keep more private, of course) to access the Facebook Graph API to obtain an access token. We then use this access token to read the user's profile data, expecting to be returned at least a user ID and a name:

```
args["client_secret"] = FACEBOOK_APP_SECRET
args["code"] = verificationCode
response = urlparse.parse_qs(urllib.urlopen(
        "%s?%s" % (FACEBOOK_ACCESS_TOKEN_URL,
                    urllib.urlencode(args),)
    ).read())
# Load the profile using the access token we just received
accessToken = response["access_token"][-1]
profile = json.load(urllib.urlopen(
        "%s?%s" % (FACEBOOK_PROFILE_URL,
            urllib.urlencode({'access_token': accessToken}),)
    ))
userId = profile.get('id')
name = profile.get('name')
if not userId or not name:
    IStatusMessage(self.request).add(
        _(u"Insufficient information in Facebook profile"),
        type="error")
    self.request.response.redirect(
        self.context.absolute_url())
    return u""
```

If we get this far, we can create a session for the user and save the information that our PAS plugin will expect to find in it. We have put the session keys into a set of constants in the class `SessionKeys` to reduce the risk of typos:

```
session = ISession(self.request)
session[SessionKeys.accessToken] = accessToken
session[SessionKeys.userId]      = userId
session[SessionKeys.userName]    = userId
session[SessionKeys.fullname]    = name

session.save()
```

Finally, we redirect the user back to the portal front page with a success message:

```
IStatusMessage(self.request).add(
    _(u"Welcome. You are now logged in."), type="info")
self.request.response.redirect(self.context.absolute_url())
```

We tell the user here that they are authenticated, which is of course not quite true yet: we are counting on the PAS plugin to extract their credentials from the session and then authenticate them.

Let us have a look at how it does that. The plugin and its add view live in the
`plugin.py` module. This starts with various imports, and then defines the session
keys we saw previously:

```
import logging

from zope.interface import implements
from zope.publisher.browser import BrowserView

from zope.globalrequest import getRequest

from collective.beaker.interfaces import ISession

from Products.PluggableAuthService.plugins.BasePlugin import \
    BasePlugin

from Products.PluggableAuthService.interfaces.plugins import (
        IExtractionPlugin,
        IAuthenticationPlugin,
        ICredentialsResetPlugin,
        IPropertiesPlugin,
        IRolesPlugin,
        IUserEnumerationPlugin
    )

logger = logging.getLogger('optilux.facebookauth')

class SessionKeys:
    """Constants used to look up session keys
    """

    userId      =   "optilux.userId"
    userName    =   "optilux.userName"
    fullname    =   "optilux.fullname"
    accessToken =   "optilux.accessToken"
```

Next, we define the add view to allow the plugin to be added through the ZMI:

```
class AddForm(BrowserView):
    """Add form the PAS plugin
    """

    def __call__(self):
        if 'form.button.Add' in self.request.form:
            name = self.request.form.get('id')
            title = self.request.form.get('title')
            plugin = OptiluxFacebookUsers(name, title)
            self.context.context[name] = plugin
            self.request.response.redirect(
              self.context.absolute_url() +
              '/manage_workspace?manage_tabs_message=Plugin+added.')
```

This is accompanied by a simple template in `addform.pt`. See the book's source code for details.

The plugin itself begins by listing the plugin types it supports, before defining a constructor:

```
class OptiluxFacebookUsers(BasePlugin):

    implements(
            IExtractionPlugin,
            ICredentialsResetPlugin,
            IAuthenticationPlugin,
            IPropertiesPlugin,
            IRolesPlugin,
            IUserEnumerationPlugin,
        )

    def __init__(self, id, title=None):
        self.__name__ = self.id = id
        self.title = title
```

The rest of the class implements the various plugin interfaces' methods, starting with `IExtractionPlugin`:

```
    def extractCredentials(self, request):
        session = ISession(request, None)
        if session is None:
            return None
        if SessionKeys.userId in session:
            return {
                    'src': self.getId(),
                    'userid': session[SessionKeys.userId],
                    'username': session[SessionKeys.userName],
                }
        return None
```

This simply looks for a session that is initialized by the login view. It returns a credentials dictionary that includes the user ID and user name, and sets a key to identify this plugin as the source of those credentials.

 You will notice that the method is written quite defensively. For example, it does not assume that `collective.beaker` is configured to the point where it is possible to adapt the request to its `ISession` interface. Since PAS plugin methods are often called on every request (and sometimes dozens of times during a single request), it is a good idea to be defensive. In the worst case, you could make it impossible to log into your Plone site!

Next, we implement IAuthenticationPlugin:

```
def authenticateCredentials(self, credentials):
    if credentials.get('src', None) != self.getId():
        return

    if (
        'userid' in credentials and
        'username' in credentials
    ):
        return (credentials['userid'], credentials['username'],)

    return None
```

This ignores the credentials provided by any other plugin, but otherwise trusts the credentials entirely. In other scenarios, we may have wanted to check the credentials against a database or applied some other rules to ensure they were valid here.

We do need to be careful that we allow the user to safely log out. We rely on Plone's standard logout mechanism for this, which will invoke every ICredentialsResetPlugin. Our implementation simply destroys the user's session so that authenticateCredentails() will not authenticate the user on the next request:

```
def resetCredentials(self, request, response):
    session = ISession(request, None)
    if session is None:
        return

    session.delete()
```

Next, we implement IPropertiesPlugin. Again, we simply delegate to the session, checking that this is one of 'our' users:

```
def getPropertiesForUser(self, user, request=None):
    if request is None:
        request = getRequest()

    session = ISession(request, None)
    if session is None:
        return {}

    if session.get(SessionKeys.userId, None) != user.getId():
        return {}

    return {
            'fullname': session.get(SessionKeys.fullname),
        }
```

See `portal_memberdata` in the ZMI for other properties that Plone knows about. Custom properties can also be provided here, of course, though they need to be registered with `portal_memberdata` first (alternatively, the method can return a `property sheet` – see the API documentation for details).

The `IRolesPlugin` logic is similar:

```
def getRolesForPrincipal(self, principal, request=None):
    if request is None:
        request = getRequest()
    session = ISession(request, None)
    if session is None:
        return ()
    if session.get(SessionKeys.userId, None) != \
            principal.getId():
        return ()
    return ('Member',)
```

 It is possible to invent and return new roles here. In this case, you should usually also implement `IRoleEnumerationPlugin` so that Plone can list the roles on its various user management screens.

Finally, we implement `IUserEnumerationPlugin`. This can be used for various types of searches – please see the interface's docstring for details – but here we only allow an exact match search against our user ID, which is the minimum that Plone needs for its user management screens:

```
def enumerateUsers(self
                  , id=None
                  , login=None
                  , exact_match=False
                  , sort_by=None
                  , max_results=None
                  , **kw
                  ):
    request = getRequest()
    session = ISession(request, None)
    if session is None:
        return ()

    if exact_match and id == \
            session.get(SessionKeys.userId, None):
        return ({
```

```
                    'id': session[SessionKeys.userId],
                    'login': session[SessionKeys.userName],
                    'pluginid': self.getId(),
               },)

        return ()
```

We have had to resort to `getRequest()` from `zope.globalrequest` (which we enabled previously by depending on and configuring `five.globalrequest`) to get hold of the request so that we can check the session for a user ID, because the request is not passed to this function.

Testing the plugin

Our PAS plugin contains simple methods with few external dependencies. This makes it ideal for unit testing, allowing us to quickly write and execute tests covering a wide range of inputs and expected outputs. Thorough testing is always important, but it is doubly so for security-related code. We have added a large number of tests in `tests.py`. Here is a short extract:

```
import unittest2 as unittest

from plone.testing.zca import UNIT_TESTING
from zope.publisher.browser import TestRequest

from zope.component import provideAdapter

from zope.globalrequest import setRequest

from collective.beaker.interfaces import ISession
from collective.beaker.testing import testingSession

from Products.PlonePAS.plugins.ufactory import PloneUser

class TestPlugin(unittest.TestCase):

    layer = UNIT_TESTING

    def test_extractCredentials_no_session_adapter(self):
        from optilux.facebookauth.plugin import OptiluxFacebookUsers
        request = TestRequest()
        plugin = OptiluxFacebookUsers('optilux')
        creds = plugin.extractCredentials(request)
        self.assertEqual(None, creds)

    def test_extractCredentials_username_in_session(self):
        from optilux.facebookauth.plugin import OptiluxFacebookUsers
        from optilux.facebookauth.plugin import SessionKeys

        provideAdapter(testingSession)

        request = TestRequest()
```

```
        session = ISession(request)

        session[SessionKeys.userName] = 'john@smith.com'
        session[SessionKeys.userId] = '123'

        plugin = OptiluxFacebookUsers('optilux')

        creds = plugin.extractCredentials(request)
        self.assertEqual(creds, {
                'username': 'john@smith.com',
                'src': 'optilux',
                'userid': '123',
            })
    def test_extractCredentials_username_not_in_session(self):
        from optilux.facebookauth.plugin import OptiluxFacebookUsers
        from optilux.facebookauth.plugin import SessionKeys

        provideAdapter(testingSession)

        request = TestRequest()
        session = ISession(request)

        session[SessionKeys.userName] = 'john@smith.com'
        session[SessionKeys.userId] = '123'

        plugin = OptiluxFacebookUsers('optilux')

        creds = plugin.extractCredentials(request)
        self.assertEqual(creds, {
                'username': 'john@smith.com',
                'src': 'optilux',
                'userid': '123',
            })
    ...
```

We use the UNIT_TESTING layer from `plone.testing.zca` to ensure a clean fixture for each test, and the `testingSession` adapter factory from `collective.beaker.testing` to simulate a session in each test. We then simply instantiate the PAS plugin and call the method we want to test with the relevant inputs, before making assertions on its return value.

Installation

Finally, we must install the plugin and register the action that lets the user access the login view.

The action is simple. We add the following in `profiles/default/actions.xml`:

```xml
<?xml version="1.0"?>
<object name="portal_actions"
    xmlns:i18n="http://xml.zope.org/namespaces/i18n">

    <object name="user">

        <object name="facebook-login" meta_type="CMF Action"
                i18n:domain="optilux.cinemacontent">
            <property name="title" i18n:translate="">Login with
Facebook</property>
            <property name="description" i18n:translate=""></property>
            <property name="url_expr">string:$portal_url/@@facebook-
login</property>
            <property name="icon_expr"></property>
            <property name="available_expr">python:member is None</
property>
            <property name="permissions">
                <element value="View"/>
            </property>
            <property name="visible">True</property>
        </object>

        <!-- Disable the built-in login action -->
        <object name="login">
            <property name="visible">False</property>
        </object>

    </object>

</object>
```

Here, we register a new action in the `user` category to be shown only when there is no logged-in user (the condition `member is None`). We also hide the default login action to avoid confusing users. Staff members will now need to access the standard login form (`/login_form`) via a bookmark or similar.

 With this configuration, we would probably also disable user self-registration in the Plone site by removing the section in `rolemap.xml` where we set the `Add portal member` permission. We have kept it in the example code for illustrative purposes, however.

The PAS plugin installation is a little more complicated. There is no simple GenericSetup XML syntax, so we have to use imperative configuration, adding the following to `setuphandlers.py` (recall that we registered its `importVarious` function as a custom import step, analogous to the one we created in `optilux. policy` in *Chapter 6, Security and Workflow*):

```
from StringIO import StringIO
from Products.PlonePAS.Extensions.Install import \
    activatePluginInterfaces

from optilux.facebookauth.plugin import OptiluxFacebookUsers

...

def installPASPlugin(portal, name='optilux-facebook-users'):
    out = StringIO()
    userFolder = portal['acl_users']

    if name not in userFolder:

        plugin = OptiluxFacebookUsers(name, 'Optilux Facebook Users')
        userFolder[name] = plugin

        activatePluginInterfaces(portal, name, out)

        plugins = userFolder['plugins']
        for info in plugins.listPluginTypeInfo():
            interface = info['interface']
            if plugin.testImplements(interface):
                active = list(plugins.listPluginIds(interface))
                if name in active:
                    active.remove(name)
                    active.insert(0, name)
                    plugins._plugins[interface] = tuple(active)

        return out.getvalue()

def importVarious(context):
    if context.readDataFile('optilux.facebookauth-various.txt') \
            is None:
        return

    portal = context.getSite()

    setupGroups(portal)
    setVersionedTypes(portal)
    installPASPlugin(portal)
```

We must also add an empty file in `profiles/default/optilux.facebookauth-various.txt`, as explained in *Chapter 6, Security and Workflow*.

This will create an instance of the plugin and persist it in the `acl_users` folder. It then activates all of the plugin's supported interfaces, and moves the plugin instance to the top of the list of activated plugins for each of the interfaces it supports, thereby ensuring our custom plugin takes precedence over Plone's default plugins.

You are encouraged to browse the configuration for the various plugin types in the ZMI under `acl_users/plugins` inside your Plone site to understand which plugins are activated by default, and what they all do.

Finally, we will add some installation test. We first need an integration testing layer, defined in `testing.py` as normal:

```python
from plone.app.testing import PloneSandboxLayer
from plone.app.testing import applyProfile
from plone.app.testing import PLONE_FIXTURE
from plone.app.testing import IntegrationTesting

from zope.configuration import xmlconfig

class OptiluxFacebookAuth(PloneSandboxLayer):

    defaultBases = (PLONE_FIXTURE,)

    def setUpZope(self, app, configurationContext):
        import optilux.facebookauth
        xmlconfig.file('configure.zcml', optilux.facebookauth,
                    context=configurationContext)

    def setUpPloneSite(self, portal):
        applyProfile(portal, 'optilux.facebookauth:default')

OPTILUX_FACEBOOKAUTH_FIXTURE = OptiluxFacebookAuth()
OPTILUX_FACEBOOKAUTH_INTEGRATION_TESTING = IntegrationTesting(
        bases=(OPTILUX_FACEBOOKAUTH_FIXTURE,),
        name="OptiluxFacebookAuth:Integration",
    )
```

We use this in a separate test class in `tests.py`:

```python
import unittest2 as unittest

from optilux.facebookauth.testing import \
    OPTILUX_FACEBOOKAUTH_INTEGRATION_TESTING

from Products.CMFCore.utils import getToolByName

...

class TestSetup(unittest.TestCase):

    layer = OPTILUX_FACEBOOKAUTH_INTEGRATION_TESTING

    def test_login_action_installed(self):
        portal = self.layer['portal']
        portal_actions = getToolByName(portal, 'portal_actions')

        self.assertTrue('facebook-login' in portal_actions['user'])
        self.assertFalse(portal_actions['user']['login'].visible)
```

```
def test_pas_plugin_installed(self):
    portal = self.layer['portal']
    acl_users = portal['acl_users']

    self.assertTrue('optilux-facebook-users' in acl_users)
```

With this, our Facebook authentication plugin is complete.

 The plugin could be made a little more generic. Right now, we have hardcoded the Facebook keys in `login.py`. It would be relatively easy to move these into `plone.app.registry` keys and look these up in the `@@ facebook-login` view, for example. Consider this an exercise, and an opportunity to create a generally useful component that can be released to the Plone community.

Summary

In this chapter, we have looked at:

- The user and group management features which Plone gives us out of the box
- How we may conceptualize a membership policy for the Optilux website
- Adding and using new user properties
- Writing new plugins for the Pluggable Authentication Service (PAS).

In the next chapter, we will look at how to improve the user experience using the jQuery JavaScript framework.

14
Dynamic User Interfaces with jQuery

Over the past several chapters, we have built the complete Optilux Cinemas website. All the features outlined in *Chapter 2, Introduction to the Case Study*, have been delivered, and the site works well in all major browsers. However, our custom user interface elements are not terribly exciting, and we rely on full-page reloads everywhere.

In this chapter, we will consider how to make our user interface more dynamic. We will cover:

- The roles of Kinetic Style Sheets (KSS) and jQuery in Plone 4
- Installing and managing JavaScript resources
- Using Plone 4's new overlay effect
- Manipulating page structure and submitting background requests in JavaScript

KSS and jQuery in Plone 4

Plone 3 introduced a new JavaScript framework called **KSS**, which stands for **Kinetic Style Sheets**. KSS is based on the premise of a CSS-like 'style sheet' that defines behaviors by linking page elements to one or more client- or server-side plugins.

KSS still exists in Plone 4, but will likely become an optional installation in future versions of Plone. Plone's core JavaScript features now rely on the ubiquitous **jQuery** library (which was not quite so ubiquitous when KSS was chosen for inclusion in Plone 3!), as well as **jQuery Tools**, a collection of useful effects and UI components for use with jQuery.

There are two main reasons for this switch:

1. jQuery and jQuery Tools have a lighter download footprint, thus making Plone page loads a little faster.

2. jQuery is a well-known library, making it easier for people new to Plone to understand its JavaScript architecture.

We will cover the use of jQuery in Plone in this chapter. We will not cover jQuery itself in any depth, however. For jQuery tutorials and reference manuals, please refer to `http://docs.jquery.com`. For details about jQuery Tools, see `http://flowplayer.org/tools`.

 The first edition of this book covered KSS in some detail. The original KSS chapter, which should still be relevant in Plone 4 if you want to use KSS, is available for free on the book's accompanying website: `https://www.packtpub.com/professional-plone-4-development/book`.

Managing JavaScript resources

JavaScript resources in Plone are managed using the `portal_javascripts` tool in the ZMI. Like the `portal_css` tool we saw in *Chapter 8, Creating a Custom Theme*, `portal_javascripts` allows scripts to be included conditionally (for example, to restrict some scripts to authenticated users only) and to be merged and compressed to allow for efficient, low-latency delivery over the Web.

 When using Diazo theming as described in *Chapter 8, Creating a Custom Theme*, you may choose to add JavaScript resources directly into the theme, although this means you will have to forgo the advanced merging and compression tools of `portal_javascripts`.

In this chapter, we will add a small amount of JavaScript to our pages. We will put this in a file called `cinemacontent.js` inside the `static/` directory in `optilux.cinemacontent`. Recall from *Chapter 10, Custom Content Types* that this directory is automatically turned into a resource directory when using `<grok:grok package="." />`. Hence, our JavaScript will be publishable under the URL `../++resource++optilux.cinemacontent/cinemacontent.js`.

To manually register a resource directory, you can use the ZCML directive `<browser:resourceDirectory />`, which takes two attributes: `name`, a unique identifier (used after `++resource++` in the URL) and `directory`, a relative path to a resource directory.

To install this into the registry, we will add a `jsregistry.xml` file to `profiles/default` in `optilux.cinemacontent`, containing:

```xml
<?xml version="1.0"?>
<object name="portal_javascripts">
    <javascript
        id="++resource++optilux.cinemacontent/cinemacontent.js"
        />
</object>
```

This adds our script at the bottom of the registry using defaults for all options. The available options are listed as follows:

Option	Purpose
enabled	Can be set to `True` or `False` to enable or disable a script.
expression	Can be set to a TALES expression that must evaluate to true for the script to be enabled.
authenticated	Can be set to `True` to restrict the script to logged-in users only.
compression	Can be set to `none`, `safe`, or `full` to enable on-the-fly compression of JavaScript files.
inline	Can be set to `True` for the script to be rendered inline in the page instead of fetched as a separate script.
cacheable	Can be set to `True` or `False` to determine whether this script can be cached in the browser.
cookable	Can be set to `True` or `False` to enable or disable resource merging for this resource.
insert-after and insert-before	Can be used to give the ID of a script that this script should be inserted before or after, respectively.
insert-top	Can be used to insert a script at the top of the list.
remove	Can be set to `True` to remove a script installed by a previous profile.

As with stylesheets in `portal_css`, we can use the **Merged JS Composition** tab of `portal_javascripts` in the ZMI to understand how JavaScript resources will be merged when turning off debug mode. Adjacent resources that use the same options will usually be merged, unless `cookable="False"` is set. You can temporarily (until the next restart) turn off debug mode from the main tab of the `portal_javascripts` tool to test resource merging.

Generally, a single, larger resource will result in better overall performance than several smaller resources by reducing latency and server load. A common approach is to aim for one merged resource for anonymous users and two or three resources for authenticated users. To achieve this, you may need to use `insert-before`/ `insert-after` to order resources appropriately. You can of course experiment with changing the order through the Web, too. Bear in mind that a script may sometimes depend on variables defined earlier.

In this example, we have installed a custom script (which is so far empty). However, if you want to use a third-party JavaScript component such as a jQuery plugin, you can add it to a resource directory and register it in much the same way. Typically, you will also want a custom script that makes use of the new component in an application-specific way, for example by binding it to an element on the page. In this case, just put two `<javascript />` lines in `jsregistry.xml`, one for each script.

Overlays

If you have recently upgraded to Plone 4, the new overlays that show up for things such as the contact form and the object delete confirmation page were probably among the first things you noticed. These overlays are made possible by a new package called `plone.app.jquerytools`, which, as its name suggests, integrates jQuery Tools into Plone.

Although we will only show examples of using the overlays here, you have the full power of jQuery Tools at your disposal in Plone 4. You are encouraged to explore the demos and documentation at `http://flowplayer.org/tools`.

In *Chapter 11, Standalone Views and Forms*, we created a custom inquiry form and let it replace Plone's contact form. Alas, with this we lost the overlay effect, so users have to leave the page they are on to load the contact form. Luckily, it is easy to get the overlay back.

Plone's overlay support is implemented purely in JavaScript. The usual pattern is to dynamically replace a link to the relevant page or form with a JavaScript handler that fetches the same URL in the background and displays a portion of the returned page in the overlay. This way, if JavaScript is disabled or the visitor is using an unsupported browser, the link is followed as normal, gracefully degrading to a full-page load.

If the overlay contains a form, a second JavaScript handler can be installed that intercepts the form submission and turns it into a background request. If it then detects that the next page being fetched does not contain the form, it can automatically close the overlay.

To add overlay support for our inquiries form, we can put the following in `cinemacontent.js`:

```
jQuery(function($) {

    // No overlays for IE6
    if (!jQuery.browser.msie ||
        parseInt(jQuery.browser.version, 10) >= 7) {

        // Set up overlays
        $("#siteaction-enquiry > a").prepOverlay({
            subtype: 'ajax',
            filter: '#content>*',
            formselector: '#content-core > form',
            noform: 'close',
            closeselector: '[name=form.buttons.cancel]',
        });

    }

});
```

The first and last lines are jQuery boilerplate that let us use the convention of invoking jQuery operations with the special function $, without polluting the global namespace with this variable (which other JavaScript frameworks sometimes also use), and ensures that our code only executes after the document has finished loading. This is the standard time to register jQuery event handlers and set up plugins.

We then look up the page element for the site action link. With a bit of Firebug introspection, we have determined that this can be matched with the CSS selector `#siteaction-enquiry > a`, reflecting the ID generated automatically by Plone's site actions viewlet. We do not do this for versions of Internet Explorer older than IE 7, since the overlays do not look great in IE 6.

The `prepOverlay()` function, part of `plone.app.jquerytools`, is a wrapper around jQuery Tools' `overlay()` plugin that supports useful Plone semantics and supports the common use case of 'enhancing' a hyperlink to open in an overlay. The options that can be passed to it are as follows:

Option	Purpose
subtype	This should be set to `ajax` for pages fetched in the background. For links to images, you can use `image` instead to automatically scale the overlay to the required image size. If you need to load separate JavaScript in the overlay or fetch something from an external domain, you can use the `iframe` subtype, which loads the content in an `<iframe />` tag, but in this case you cannot use `filter`, `formselector`, or any of the other options that rely on being able to manipulate the fetched content.
filter	This is used to determine which part of the page to include in the overlay. Here, we request that all nodes inside the `#content` div (but not the `#content` element itself) are rendered.
formselector	This indicates which form on the page to install a submission handler for. If this is omitted, no form submission handler will be installed.
noform	This configures what should be done when there is no form matching `formselector` on the fetched page. Usually, this happens when the form is successfully submitted (that is, there are no validation errors). Here, we opt to close the form by passing the string `"close"`. It is also possible to specify `"reload"` to reload the entire page and `"redirect"` to redirect to another page, in conjunction with the separate `redirect` option, which should be used to give an URL to redirect to. Alternatively, you can pass a function that returns one of the strings above.
closeselector	This indicates an element that will cause the overlay to be closed when clicked. Here, we let the `cancel` button simply close the overlay without actually submitting anything.

There are a few other options that can be passed to more closely match URLs and configure the appearance of the overlay in detail. Please see `http://pypi.python.org/pypi/plone.app.jquerytools` for more details.

 The popupforms.js script in Plone's `plone_ecmascript` skin layer also provides a good set of coding examples — this is where Plone's own overlays are defined.

With this in place, we can reapply the `optilux.cinemacontent` extension profile and test our new overlay. It should look something like the following screenshot:

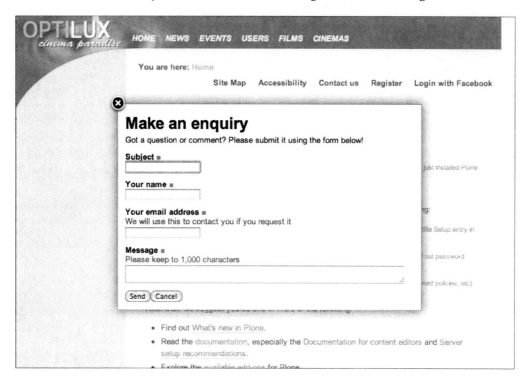

Background requests and DOM manipulation

Overlays are a quick and easy way to simulate dialog boxes and allow users to view ancillary information without leaving the content page they are viewing. Sometimes, we need to be a little more specific, however, changing the page and performing server-side actions in the background. This can be achieved using custom jQuery and **JSON** (JavaScript Object Notation—a convenient way to pass information between the server and the browser).

As an example, we will make the film ratings viewlet a little more dynamic. Instead of reloading the page when the rating buttons are clicked, we will send a background request to the server, and then change the **DOM (Document Object Model** – essentially the HTML being shown to the user) on the client side to reflect the changes.

We will do this through progressive enhancement, without disabling or changing any existing functionality, so that the functionality will still work, albeit a bit more slowly, in browsers with JavaScript disabled.

First, we will write the server-side handler that will receive the background request, update the film's ratings, and return the information needed by the client-side handler to correctly update the page. We can implement this as a view on the film where the viewlet is being rendered.

In `ratings.py`, we first define the updating view, using `five.grok` registration as we have done elsewhere (see *Chapter 9, Nine Core Concepts,* for the ZCML registration equivalent):

```
class UpdateRatings(grok.View):
    """AJAX action for updating ratings.
    """

    grok.context(IFilm)
    grok.name('update-ratings')
    grok.require('zope2.View')
```

The permission and context mirror those of the viewlet itself.

Next, we implement the `update()` method, which receives the request and updates the ratings on the context film object:

```
def update(self):
    self.ratings = IRatings(self.context)
    self.portal_state = getMultiAdapter(
            (self.context, self.request),
            name=u"plone_portal_state"
        )
    self.authenticator = getMultiAdapter(
            (self.context, self.request),
            name=u"authenticator"
        )

    form = self.request.form

    if self.portal_state.anonymous():
        raise Forbidden()

    vote = None
    if 'optilux.cinemacontent.ratings.VotePositive' in form:
        vote = True
```

```
elif 'optilux.cinemacontent.ratings.VoteNegative' in form:
    vote = False

if vote is None:
    return

# Perform CSRF check (see plone.protect)
if not self.authenticator.verify():
    raise Forbidden()

userToken = self.portal_state.member().getId()
if userToken is not None and \
        self.ratings.available(userToken):
    self.ratings.rate(userToken, vote)
```

This implementation is very similar to the code path in the rating viewlet's `update()` method for the case when a form is submitted. Also note that we perform CSRF token validation. See *Chapter 11, Standalone Views and Forms,* for more details.

There is no template for this viewlet. Instead, we will implement a `render()` method that returns a JSON data structure:

```
def render(self):
    score = self.ratings.score

    # Capture a status message and translate it
    translation_service = getToolByName(self.context,
        'translation_service')
    newStatus = translation_service.translate(
                    'score_update_thankyou',
                    domain='optilux.cinemacontent',
                    mapping={'score': score},
                    context=self.context,
                    default=u"Thank you. ${score}% of those " +
                            u"who voted liked this film.")

    data = {
            'score': score,
            'newStatus': newStatus,
        }

    self.request.response.setHeader('Content-Type',
        'application/json')
    return json.dumps(data)
```

Here, we invoke the **translation service** directly to translate a user interface string in the `optilux.cinemacontent` domain. This would normally be done with an `i18n:translate` attribute in a page template as we have seen in our templates so far. Since we are not rendering to a template, however, we have to perform the translation manually. Notice the `${}` delimited variable, which is used as a placeholder and replaced with the value in `mapping` upon translation.

The returned value is a simple mapping with two keys: `score` and `newStatus`. We pass this through the `dumps` (dump string) function in the Python standard library `json` module to produce a JSON string. See the Python documentation for more details about working with JSON data structures.

Before returning a value, we set the response content type to `application/json` so as not to confuse the client.

 The default response content type in Zope is `text/html`.

This view can be tested like any other. We have added a couple of tests to `test_ratings_viewlet.py`. Here is one of them:

```python
def test_ajax_view_positive(self):
    from optilux.cinemacontent.interfaces import IRatings

    portal = self.layer['portal']
    request = self.layer['request']

    # Create a film that can be rated

    setRoles(portal, TEST_USER_ID, ('Manager',))
    portal.invokeFactory('optilux.FilmFolder', 'ff1',
                         title=u"Film folder")
    setRoles(portal, TEST_USER_ID, ('Member',))

    portal['ff1'].invokeFactory('optilux.Film', 'f1',
            title=u"Film",
            startDate=datetime.date.today(),
            endDate=datetime.date.today()
        )

    f1 = portal['ff1']['f1']

    # Simulate an AJAX request

    # This is taken from plone.protect.authenticator and
    # simulates the value created by the @@authenticator view
```

```
keyManager = getUtility(IKeyManager)
secret = keyManager.secret()
auth = hmac.new(secret, TEST_USER_NAME, sha).hexdigest()
request.form = {
    '_authenticator': auth,
    'optilux.cinemacontent.ratings.VotePositive': 'Yes',
}
# Look up and invoke the view via traversal
view = f1.restrictedTraverse('@@update-ratings')
result = view()
self.assertEqual(json.loads(result), {
        u'newStatus': u'Thank you. 100% of those ' +
                        u'who voted liked this film.',
        u'score': 100,
    })
ratings = IRatings(f1)
self.assertEqual(ratings.score, 100)
```

Finally, we can write the client-side JavaScript code. First, we will add a few attributes to the `ratingsviewlet.pt` template to make DOM manipulation a little easier:

```
<dl id="filmRatings"
    class="portalMessage info" i18n:domain="optilux.cinemacontent"
    tal:attributes="data-ajax-target
        string:${context/absolute_url}/@@ update-ratings">
    ...
        <div id="ratingStatus" i18n:translate="info_film_rating"
            tal:condition="viewlet/haveScore">
            <span i18n:name="rating" tal:replace="viewlet/score" />%
of those who voted liked this film.
        </div>
        <div id="ratingStatus" i18n:translate="info_film_rating_none"
            tal:condition="not:viewlet/haveScore">
            No-one has voted yet
        </div>
        <form id="ratingForm" method="get"
            tal:attributes="action context/absolute_url"
            tal:condition="viewlet/available">
        ...
        </form>
    </dd>
</dl>
```

Here, we have added some IDs to make it easier to target the viewlet's markup in jQuery expressions. We have also added an attribute to the outer `<div />` named `data-ajax-target` that contains the correct URL to use when submitting a background request to the `@@update-ratings` view, making sure the current film is used as its context. This URL is easy to calculate on the server at render time, but a little more cumbersome to get right on the client, so we prepare it as a string and store it in the DOM using an HTML5-style **data attribute**.

Finally, here is the jQuery logic to invoke the view when a rating button is clicked and manipulate the page based on the response:

```
jQuery(function($) {

    ...

    // Update film ratings asynchronously
    $("#filmRatings input[type='submit']").click(function() {

        var action = $("#filmRatings").attr('data-ajax-target');
        var token = \
            $("#filmRatings input[name='_authenticator']").val();
        var button = $(this).attr('name');
        var value = $(this).val();

        var data = {'_authenticator': token};
        data[button] = action;

        $.post(action,
            data,
            function(data) {
                var newStatus = data['newStatus'];
                $("#ratingForm").hide();
                $("#ratingStatus").html(newStatus);
            },
            'json');

        return false;
    });

});
```

Notice how we include the CSRF authenticator information in the request, as well as the button name and value. On successful form submission, we hide the rating form and update the rating status display to contain the string returned in the server-side JSON structure.

We have only scratched the surface of what jQuery can do in this example, and we have only showed one of the patterns with which it can be used. Some other common approaches include:

- Let a server-side view render a template and return an HTML fragment in its response. On the client side, use this to replace a part of the page wholesale.

- Build view logic entirely on the client side with jQuery plugins that do anything from displaying slick photo albums from a list of images to sophisticated navigation menus built from nested lists and much more.

- Use a rich widget library such as YUI (`http://developer.yahoo.com/yui`) or jQuery UI (`http://jqueryui.com`) to build browser applications that look and feel more like desktop applications.

- Build advanced, behavior-driven client-side state models with a framework such as Knockout JS (`http://knockoutjs.com`).

Please refer to the jQuery documentation at `http://docs.jquery.com` for more information.

Summary

In this chapter, we have learnt:

- The roles of KSS and jQuery in Plone 4
- How to register new JavaScript resources with `portal_javascripts`
- How to use jQuery Tools overlays in Plone
- How to initiate background requests and manipulate the DOM of the rendered page with jQuery.

In the next chapter, we will review what we have achieved so far and consider a few possible next steps for improving the Optilux application beyond the scope of this book.

15
Summary and Potential Enhancements

We have come far over the past fourteen chapters! The example application is now complete, and sports a wide array of features, bespoke look-and-feel, a powerful user interface and integration with an external database system.

Hopefully, the pieces of the puzzle are now coming together and you feel equipped to tackle your own Plone projects. Feel free to borrow from the example code if it helps you achieve your own ends, and refer to the preceding chapters if you need more clarification. If you are still stuck, take a look at *Chapter 1*, *Plone in Context*, for some tips on how to get help from the Plone community. You may even find the author lurking in the chat room or on the mailing lists.

In this chapter, we will:

- Recap the achievements to date
- Suggest some avenues for further exploration that could improve the Optilux Cinemas example beyond what we have scope to cover in this book

What we have achieved

Let us begin by revisiting the requirements from *Chapter 2, Introduction to the Case Study*:

	Requirement	Status
1	The site should have a look and feel consistent with Optilux's corporate branding.	We built a theme from a static HTML mockup using the Diazo theming engine in *Chapter 8, Creating a Custom Theme.*
2	The site should show information about all of Optilux's cinemas.	Using the Dexterity framework, we defined content types to represent our own data model in *Chapter 10, Custom Content Types.*
3	Non-technical cinema staff should be able to update information about each cinema.	Plone automatically gives us an authoring user interface built from our schema. We defined roles and permissions in *Chapter 6, Security and Workflow* to control who can manage what content.
4	The site should allow staff to highlight promotions and special events. These may apply to one or more cinemas.	We modeled this as a special *Promotion* content type in *Chapter 10, Custom Content Types.*
5	Cinema staff should be able to publish information about new films. It should be possible to update this information after publication.	The *Film* content type in *Chapter 10, Custom Content Types* takes care of this.
6	Customers should be able to find out in which cinemas a particular film is showing, and which films are showing at a particular cinema. Note that the scheduling of films at cinemas is managed in an existing relational database.	In *Chapter 12, Relational Databases* we integrated with the booking database to discover screenings. We used custom publish traversal to construct logical URLs for screenings.
7	Only films that are currently showing or will be shown in the near future should be viewable.	We have assumed this will be managed through content expiry dates.
8	Customers should be able to search and browse films by cinema, location, date/time, or film name.	Plone gives us standard search forms. In *Chapter 11, Standalone Views and Forms*, we learned how to create custom forms that use the catalog to search for content. We could have made a more specific search form had we wanted to.

	Requirement	Status
9	Customers should be able to reserve tickets online. Tickets will be picked up and payment taken at the cinema. Reservations must use Optilux's existing relational database-based ticketing system.	By integrating with the booking database in *Chapter 12, Relational Databases* and using a custom form, we could achieve this in a few dozen lines of code.
10	Any digital assets, such as images or other files, used on the website must be trackable using a special Digital Asset Management Code, which will be used to link the assets to a third party system.	We used the Archetypes schema extender to add a "DAM code" field in *Chapter 10, Custom Content Types,* and built a form in *Chapter 11, Standalone Views and Forms* to enable administrators to search for assets using this code.
11	Customers should not need to log in to use the site, but a username and password should be required when they wish to reserve tickets.	The workflow we defined in *Chapter 6, Security and Workflow* ensures this is the case.
12	Logged-in customers should have easy access to their preferred cinema or cinemas, for example, those in their area.	We built this functionality with a custom viewlet and a new portlet in *Chapter 13, Users and their Permissions*, where we also saw how to store this information against a user's profile.
13	Customers should be able to log in using their Facebook account.	Also in *Chapter 13, Users and their Permissions*, we created a PAS plugin that made use of Facebook's public API to authenticate users against their Facebook accounts.
14	Customers should be able to e-mail enquiries to the site manager if they have questions or feedback.	Plone has its own contact form that would probably have sufficed, but for demonstration purposes, we built a custom form in *Chapter 11, Standalone Views and Forms*, and made it appear in an overlay in *Chapter 14, Dynamic User Interfaces with jQuery*.
15	Customers should be able to discuss and rate movies.	Discussion comes for free with Plone – it only needs to be enabled in the **Types** control panel. We built our own ratings viewlet in *Chapter 11, Standalone Views and Forms* and made it easier to use in *Chapter 14, Dynamic User Interfaces with jQuery* by avoiding the need for a full page refresh.

Of course, when the case study was designed, we picked requirements that we knew we could fulfill over the course of the book. However, if you are developing an application to sit on top of Plone, it is likely that many of your own requirements will reflect those above.

- The first thing customers ask for is usually custom branding. This was covered in *Chapter 8, Creating a Custom Theme*.

- Customers also typically want to turn off a few of Plone's features and change a few defaults. Although this can usually be done by a site administrator through-the-web, we learned in *Chapter 4, Basics of Customization* that customization is better done in a repeatable and testable manner, using filesystem code and GenericSetup profiles as we saw in *Chapter 5, Developing a Site Strategy*.

- There is a plethora of add-on products to be found at `http://plone.org/products` and elsewhere. In *Chapter 7, Using Add-ons*, we looked at how to integrate such components into a Plone deployment.

- Most non-trivial applications end up relying on custom content types to capture and manage domain-specific information. Schema-driven development with Dexterity (or Archetypes) makes it easy to define new content types, which can leverage Plone's standard user interface paradigms. In *Chapter 10, Custom Content Types* we looked at how to model requirements in terms of content objects, and then showed how to construct and install new content types.

- Also in *Chapter 10, Custom Content Types* we learned how to create custom portlets. Portlets are useful for representing additional information which is not tightly linked to the current content object.

- By relying on standard, consistently generated forms to manage content objects, Plone systems tend not to use custom forms for CRUD (create, read, update, delete) operations. Still, there is often a need for bespoke forms and views, as well as reusable snippets. We covered these in *Chapter 11, Standalone Views and Forms*.

- Sometimes, we may want to create general components which augment existing Plone functionality. In *Chapter 11, Standalone Views and Forms*, we saw how to use viewlets to hook into Plone's user interface. The film rating component developed there also demonstrated how to use adapters and annotations to attach additional information to existing content objects.

- Many organizations have existing relational databases which they may need to integrate with Plone, and sometimes relational data models make more sense than Plone's content-centric approach. In *Chapter 12, Relational Databases*, we looked at how to connect to external SQL databases.

- It is quite common to need to capture some additional information about users as part of an application. In *Chapter 13, Users and their Permissions*, we saw how to manage additional member data. We also learned how to use Plone's Pluggable Authentication System to integrate Plone's security infrastructure with external systems.

- In *Chapter 15, Summary and Potential Enhancements*, we learned how to make our user interface more responsive and dynamic using jQuery and jQuery Tools.

Additional functionality

Of course, there are still ways in which the example application could be improved. If it is useful to you, feel free to modify or extend it as you wish. The following suggests a few areas for improvement.

Additional reporting and analytics

We created a report showing the use of 'DAM codes' in *Chapter 11, Standalone Views and Forms*. There may be any number of additional reports that would be useful, but mostly they would work on the same principle: construct a catalog or database query and present the results in a page template.

For usage metrics, you should use external traffic analysis software such as **Google Analytics** or **AWStats**. Plone has a control panel option for pasting in the type of tracking HTML and JavaScript code which these tools use. Furthermore Zope's z2.log file follows the Apache log file conventions and thus can be read by log analysis tools such as AWStats.

 If you are using Google Analytics, take a look at collective. googleanalytics, found at http://pypi.python.org/pypi/ collective.googleanalytics, which can be used to perform detailed page tracking and allows you to bring analytics results into the Plone control panel for easier access.

More advanced ticketing

The ticket reservations system we implemented in *Chapter 12, Relational Databases,* is fairly rudimentary. There is no payment processing, and thus no way to ensure that customers do not reserve tickets that they never pick up.

For real-world usage, we would probably want to integrate with some kind of payment channel. There are various commercial services which can take payments on behalf of other websites, passing back a token to validate a transaction. Designing such a system is beyond the scope of this book, but after reading the preceding chapters, you should have the necessary knowledge to do so yourself. Most likely, a payments solution would involve requests to a remote service to authorize a payment, and one or more views to handle the responses this service would give.

> If the external service uses SOAP **web services**, take a look at the Suds library at `https://fedorahosted.org/suds/`. A common design pattern is to embed a Suds client in a global utility (so that it is instantiated only once, on startup) and use this utility to perform web service calls from view code.

There are also existing e-commerce solutions at `http://plone.org/products` which may provide the necessary infrastructure or be adaptable to a specific use case.

Internationalization

If Optilux expands abroad, we may want to translate the application to different languages. We have been following good practices when defining user interface elements to allow for translation should we need it. However, since most bespoke web applications are monolingual (but not necessarily English!), we have not gone into the details of internationalization.

Translating content

A truly multi-lingual website will offer its content in multiple languages. It is even possible to pick the right language automatically, because web browsers will send a 'preferred' language as part of a request to the server.

Archetypes-based content types can be made translatable using a product called **LinguaPlone**. Content authors can create translated versions of existing content items. Users would browse the site as normal, but only see content in their own language. Please refer to the LinguaPlone documentation for more information.

> At the time of writing, there is no out-of-the-box solution for multilingual content using Dexterity, although work is underway to address this.

Translating user interface strings

As well as translating content, any text which is presented as part of the user interface would need to be translated. Zope and Plone rely on the popular GNU **gettext** system to manage message catalogs – lists of translated messages.

We have been marking strings bound for the user interface so that they can be translated throughout this book. Doing so is good practice. It introduces minimal overhead and makes life much easier should you need to translate some or all of your application in the future.

 Internationalization tools can be used for more than just translating a system from English to Chinese. Sometimes, the differences between for example, American and British English are significant enough to warrant translation. Other times, translation tools can be used to simplify or standardize the terminology used in a third party component without having to customize its code directly.

For example, in page templates, we have used markup such as:

```
<a href="http://plone.org" title="The Plone home page"
  i18n:attributes="title title_plone_homepage;"
  i18n:translate="link_plone_homepage">Visit Plone's home page!</a>
```

The `i18n:translate` attribute specifies that the string inside the tag should be translated by looking up the `link_plone_homepage` message ID. `i18n:attributes` lists which attributes of the tag (in this case, only `title`) need to be translated and the associated message IDs. Multiple attribute-message ID pairs can be specified, separated by semicolons.

Message IDs are optional in both cases. If they are not specified, the full translated string is used. However, this can be more difficult for translators and is generally only useful for short, unambiguous strings of one or two words:

```
<a href="http://plone.org" title="Info"
  i18n:attributes="title"
  i18n:translate="">Info</a>
```

For strings originating from Python code, we have defined message factories and referenced them via the special construct `_()`:

```
from zope.i18nmessageid import MessageFactory
CinemaMessageFactory = MessageFactory('optilux.cinemacontent')

...

from optilux.cinemacontent import CinemaMessageFactory as _
```

```
...
title = schema.TextLine(title=_(u"Title"))
```

Translation extraction tools such as **i18ndude** (`http://plone.org/products/ i18ndude`) will be able to look for these strings in page templates and Python code, as well as in GenericSetup XML files. From these, a message catalog template file is created with the extension `.pot`. Translation tools such as **poEdit** (or indeed, any text editor) can then be used to translate messages into `.po` files, which are placed in the `locales` subdirectory of a package.

Again, the user's web browser will inform Plone which language is preferred. If possible, message strings rendered to page templates will be output in the preferred language, falling back on the default language if necessary.

To learn more about the tools of internationalization – or if you would like to help translate Plone itself – see `http://plone.org/documentation/manual/developer-manual/internationalization-i18n-and-localization-l10n` and `http:// plone.org/documentation/kb/i18n-for-developers`.

Summary

In this chapter, we have recapped on the progress we have made so far in the book, and looked at a few improvements we could want to make to the example application in the future. We have also briefly touched on issues of internationalization.

This concludes Part 3 of the book. In Part 4, we will look at how to deploy the application to a production server and make sure it keeps running smoothly.

Part 4

Real-world Deployments

Zope on the Server 16

Until now, we have been concerned mostly with developing code in a local sandbox. We have filled our development environment with developer tools and turned on debug support in Zope. Now it is time to move our code into a production environment, tighten up security and configure Zope for maximum performance and stability.

In this chapter, we will cover:

- The key configuration differences between a development Zope instance and a production one
- Scaling Zope with multiple instances, using Zope Enterprise Objects or RelStorage
- Managing code and deployment artifacts across environments
- Managing Zope processes and services
- Backup and maintenance

Deployment checklist

We should not expect to change any code to move from a development environment to a test or production server, and configuration changes should be limited to those that directly relate to the target environment. The key tasks are:

1. Remove development and debugging tools from our buildout.
2. Ensure that Zope's "development mode" is turned off.
3. Configure Zope instances for performance and resilience.
4. Ensure that Zope processes are started and stopped at appropriate times, for example during system startup, and in the right order.

5.   Schedule regular backups.

6.   Set up log rotation and regular packing of the ZODB.

We will also normally configure another web server, such as Apache or nginx, and/or a cache proxy, such as Squid or Varnish, in front of Zope. This will be covered in the next chapter.

Scaling Zope

There are three main ways to improve the performance of a Plone website on a given set of hardware:

1.   Make Zope do less work by offloading the serving of static resources (for example, stylesheets, scripts, and images) and unpersonalized or slow-changing web pages to a caching reverse proxy in front of Zope. We will cover this in the next chapter.

2.   Add more Zope instances to handle more requests concurrently.

3.   Tweak the ZODB object cache in each Zope instance to improve the chances that a given object being loaded from the ZODB is found in memory and so does not need to be loaded from disk.

In our development environment, we have a single Zope instance with two threads that manages its own ZODB file storage (in `var/filestorage` and `var/blobstorage`). This is convenient since it allows us to manage everything through a single script: `bin/instance`.

For production deployment, however, a single instance is limiting. With two threads, at most two requests at most can be served simultaneously. We can increase the thread count, but this only marginally improves performance, because Python's **Global Interpreter Lock** (GIL) makes it impossible for Zope to take advantage of multi-core or multi-processor systems to parallelize execution. In fact, excessive thread context switching can be detrimental to performance.

Instead, we will normally add more Zope processes, each running on its own port, and use a load balancer to distribute requests among these instances. (We will cover load balancing in the next chapter).

How many instances to use will depend on the application and the system, but a good rule of thumb is to have twice as many instances as we have CPU cores, each with two threads. Hence, we might have four Zope instances on a dual-core system, or eight on a quad-core system.

Each Zope thread has its own ZODB object cache in memory. This means that increasing the number of Zope instances also increases RAM consumption. The cache size can be tweaked, but a small cache means more time spent reading from disk to load objects from the ZODB. Hence, most Plone sites are either disk or RAM bound, as opposed to CPU bound. At some point, it becomes necessary to add more hardware. For busy or mission critical systems, it is common to distribute Zope processes across at least two physical servers, to provide resilience in case one server fails.

 When investing in a Zope server, most people value RAM and fast disks over CPU. We will consider server characteristics in more detail in the next chapter.

To use more than one Zope instance to serve a single application, we need a shared ZODB. There are two ways to achieve this: **Zope Enterprise Objects** (ZEO) and **RelStorage**.

Zope Enterprise Objects (ZEO)

ZEO is the traditional way to share the ZODB among Zope instances. A separate ZEO server process is used to manage the ZODB storage (that is, the `Data.fs` file and `blobstorage/` directory if using the standard ZODB file storage mechanism). Each Zope instance (**ZEO client**) uses a special **ZEO storage** to connect to this server over a TCP connection instead of managing its own database.

 ZEO is a good choice if you do not want to manage a separate database server, as is required for RelStorage (see below).

The ZEO server can be installed using the `plone.recipe.zeoserver` buildout recipe. The easiest option is to use a single buildout to manage the ZEO server and each of the ZEO client Zope instances that use it. Add `zeo` to the `parts` list in the `[buildout]` section and then add the following section:

```
[zeo]
recipe = plone.recipe.zeoserver
zeo-address = 8100
```

For each Zope instance configured with `plone.recipe.zope2instance`, add the following options:

```
zeo-client  = on
zeo-address = 8100
shared-blob = on
```

The ZEO address can be set to `hostname:port` instead of just a port number for remote addresses. The `shared-blob` option allows the client to read BLOB files directly from the filesystem in `var/blobstorage` instead of streaming files over the ZEO protocol. This provides a sizable performance boost, but requires a shared disk (for example, mounted using NFS) for multi-server setups.

See `http://pypi.python.org/pypi/plone.recipe.zope2instance` and `http://pypi.python.org/pypi/plone.recipe.zeoserver` for more details and options.

RelStorage

RelStorage stores the ZODB in a relational database. At the time of writing, PostgreSQL 8.1 and later, MySQL 5.0 and later, and Oracle 10g and above are supported, provided the relevant database drivers are installed.

RelStorage is a good choice when you already have a relational database server you want to use, either as an enterprise standard, or because you are using a relational database for other purposes, for example, via SQLAlchemy.

Using RelStorage is not quite the same as storing relational data: the tables managed by RelStorage contain binary data specific to the ZODB. However, the reliability, scalability, and replication features of the underlying relational database will still be available and can be administered as normal, which is attractive to many organizations. This is one of the simplest ways to avoid a single point of failure at the ZODB in a Plone deployment.

In this chapter, we will use RelStorage against the MySQL database we configured in *Chapter 12, Relational Databases*. We will show the buildout configuration shortly, but first we need to create the relevant schema and user in MySQL. As the `root` user, we issue the following SQL statements in the `mysql` console:

```
CREATE USER 'zope'@'localhost' IDENTIFIED BY 'secret';
CREATE DATABASE zodb;
GRANT ALL ON zodb.* TO 'zope'@'localhost';
FLUSH PRIVILEGES;
```

If you intend to run any Zope instances on a different server to the one running MySQL, you should change the GRANT statement to allow access from remote hosts. See the MySQL documentation for details.

See `http://pypi.python.org/pypi/RelStorage` for more details and information about configuring other database servers.

A deployment buildout using RelStorage

As with our development environment, we need to ensure we have a repeatable build for each of our deployments. This is especially important for debugging purposes: if something goes wrong in the future, it may be vitally important to be able to rebuild an environment to a specific, previous release that includes all code and configuration exactly as it was.

We will put our deployment buildout in its own file, `deployment.cfg`, and use this instead of `buildout.cfg` via the `-c` option to `bin/buildout`.

For complex setups, it may be preferable to have one top-level `.cfg` file per server, named after the server hostname. We will keep things simple here and assume test and production servers are built identically.

Even when managing multiple servers, it is often possible to stick to a single deployment file by using aliases in `/etc/hosts` to mask the differences in host names and IP addresses across different environments.

This file starts by defining the parts to install and extending `packages.cfg`, which in turn defines known good version sets and distribution working sets.

```
[buildout]
parts =
    instance1
    instance2
    zodbpack
    zodbpack-config
    supervisor

extends =
    packages.cfg
```

Next, we define cache directories for egg distributions, downloaded files and remotely loaded configuration (mainly known good sets) fetched using the `extends` option. This ensures that the buildout directory is completely self-contained, overriding any shared caches defined in `~/.buildout/default.cfg`.

```
eggs-directory  = ${buildout:directory}/var/cache/eggs
download-cache  = ${buildout:directory}/var/cache/downloads
extends-cache   = ${buildout:directory}/var/cache/extends
```

Note that these directories must be created before the buildout is run for the first time.

Next, we need to decide what to do with our custom Python package distributions. The best option is to release and upload these to an internal distribution index. We will discuss how to do this in the next section. We then only need to tell Buildout where to find the index page that lists the eggs on this server, and it will be able to download the relevant eggs. For example:

```
find-links = http://index.example.org/
auto-checkout =
```

If this is not feasible, we can use `mr.developer` to configure development eggs. In this case, it is best to modify the build so that these are loaded from tags, again described in the next section. We take this approach in the book's sample code to make it easy to test locally:

```
auto-checkout =
    optilux.policy
    optilux.theme
    optilux.cinemacontent
always-checkout = false
```

The line `always-checkout = false` makes sure the egg is checked out only once, and not updated each time buildout is run.

Next, we will define a number of constants that we will use in the subsequent configuration. This makes it easy to change things like host names, ports, and user names.

```
[hosts]
instance1  = localhost
instance2  = localhost
syslog     = localhost
database   = localhost
supervisor = localhost

[ports]
instance1  = 8001
instance2  = 8002
syslog     = 543
database   = 3306
supervisor = 9001

[users]
database           = zope
```

```
zope-admin       = admin
zope-process     = nobody
supervisor-admin = admin

[passwords]
database         = secret
zope-admin       = secret
supervisor-admin = secret

[databases]
optilux = optilux
zodb    = zodb
```

> For added flexibility, we could have defined these constants in a separate
> .cfg file and included it via the extends option. This would make it
> possible to change environment-specific properties on each server, and
> means passwords can be kept more confidential by changing this file
> directly on the relevant servers.

In this example, we have decided to create two Zope instances, called instance1 and
instance2. These need to be configured identically, apart from the port they bind to.
Therefore, we will create a template in a section called [instance]. This section is
not in the parts list, but is used to configure [instance1] and [instance2].

We first set up some basic Zope options, disabling debug mode and verbose security
logging:

```
[instance]
recipe = plone.recipe.zope2instance
user = ${users:zope-admin}:${passwords:zope-admin}
debug-mode = off
verbose-security = off
```

Next, we set a Zope **effective user**, which is the system user account that the Zope
process will run under. This user needs to have read access to all source code and
read-write access to the buildout var/ directory for logging and file management.

```
effective-user = ${users:zope-process}
```

We then set some performance-related options. We ensure Zope does not listen to
requests until it is finished starting up, which will make our load balancing more
effective. Then we set the thread count for each Zope instance, and configure the
ZODB cache size:

```
http-fast-listen = off
zserver-threads = 2
zodb-cache-size = 10000
```

How big should the ZODB cache size be?

The answer depends on many factors. A bigger cache reduces communication with the ZEO server or ZODB storage, but more objects in the cache means higher RAM usage per Zope instance, so it is important to strike a balance. A good starting point is to look at the number of objects in the Plone catalog (the `portal_catalog` tool) and have an object cache that is 5,000 objects larger than this figure to allow for some of the fixed objects that Zope and Plone install, but which do not grow in relation to the amount of content managed in Plone.

Next, we configure the working set of distributions Zope has access to at runtime. This uses the working set defined in `packages.cfg`, but we explicitly add `RelStorage`, which is not a dependency of any package since it is a deployment choice only.

```
eggs =
    ${eggs:main}
    RelStorage
```

Note that we do *not* include the `${eggs:devtools}` working set here, since we do not want these enabled in the production environment.

Next, we configure our SQLAlchemy connections as in *Chapter 12, Relational Databases*. You can safely skip this if you do not use SQLAlchemy to connect to any relational databases.

```
zcml-additional =
    <configure xmlns="http://namespaces.zope.org/zope"
               xmlns:db="http://namespaces.zope.org/db">
        <include package="z3c.saconfig" file="meta.zcml" />
        <db:engine
            name="optilux"
        url="mysql://${users:database}:${passwords:database}
@${hosts:database}:${ports:database}/${databases:optilux}"
        />
        <db:session engine="optilux" />
    </configure>
```

In *Chapter 13, Users and Their Permissions*, we opted to use Beaker to manage user sessions for our Facebook-authenticated users. Beaker is configured as in that chapter. Again, you can ignore this if you do not use Beaker sessions.

```
zope-conf-additional =
    <product-config beaker>
```

```
        session.type        file
        session.data_dir    ${buildout:directory}/var/sessions/data
        session.lock_dir    ${buildout:directory}/var/sessions/lock
        session.key         beaker.session
        session.secret      secret
    </product-config>
```

 Note that with this configuration, all Zope instances will share the same session data and lock directories. Beaker handles this well when all processes are on the same server, but if you distribute Zope instances across multiple servers, you will need to use something like the Beaker `memcached` backend instead. More on that in the next chapter.

Next, we configure logging to **syslog**. This allows central log monitoring across all Zope instances on Unix systems. On Windows, you should skip this option:

```
event-log-custom =
    <syslog>
      level all
      format zope[%(process)s]: [%(levelname)s] %(name)s: %(message)s
      facility local1
      address ${hosts:syslog}:${ports:syslog}
    </syslog>
```

 For this to work, syslog must be listening to the relevant TCP port – 543 in this example. Refer to your operating system documentation for more details about using syslog.

Finally, we configure the ZODB RelStorage:

```
rel-storage =
    type mysql
    blob-dir ${buildout:directory}/var/blobstorage
    db ${databases:zodb}
    user ${users:database}
    passwd ${passwords:database}
shared-blob = on
```

We have opted to use shared BLOBs, as described in the section about ZEO previously. See `http://pypi.python.org/pypi/RelStorage` for examples of configuring other database servers.

With the template configured, it is easy to create our two Zope instances:

```
[instance1]
<= instance
http-address = ${hosts:instance1}:${ports:instance1}

[instance2]
<= instance
http-address = ${hosts:instance2}:${ports:instance2}
```

More instances can be added as necessary. Do not forget to add a line to the parts list for each.

We then configure a maintenance script that will enable us to perform regular packaging of the ZODB (more on that below):

```
[zodbpack]
recipe = zc.recipe.egg
eggs =
    RelStorage
    MySQL-python
scripts = zodbpack
```

This script requires a configuration file, which we will generate from a template using collective.recipe.template.

```
[zodbpack-config]
recipe = collective.recipe.template
input = ${buildout:directory}/buildout.d/templates/zodbpack.conf
output = ${buildout:directory}/etc/zodbpack.conf
```

> The collective.recipe.template buildout recipe allows us to use buildout variables in a configuration file template to generate a file specific to a particular environment, perhaps using variables set by other recipes.

The template file in buildout.d/templates/zodbpack.conf contains:

```
<relstorage>
  pack-gc true
  pack-duty-cycle 0.9
  <mysql>
    db ${databases:zodb}
    user ${users:database}
    passwd ${passwords:database}
  </mysql>
</relstorage>
```

This simply configures the database connection used for packaging. See `http://pypi.python.org/pypi/RelStorage` for more details.

Back in `deployment.cfg`, we have one more section to add, which configures **Supervisor**. This is a process management tool that can be used to control and monitor Zope instances. More on that in the *Managing Zope processes* section later in this chapter.

```
[supervisor]
recipe = collective.recipe.supervisor
port = ${ports:supervisor}
user = ${users:supervisor-admin}
password = ${passwords:supervisor-admin}
serverurl = http://${hosts:supervisor}:${ports:supervisor}
programs =
    10 instance1  ${buildout:directory}/bin/instance1 [console] true
${users:zope-process}
    10 instance2  ${buildout:directory}/bin/instance2 [console] true
${users:zope-process}
```

 If you are using ZEO, you should add the `bin/zeo` process to this list, with a lower priority number than the Zope processes.

Moving code, configuration, and data to a server

The buildout configuration above will enable us to build a server provided we have Python, and — when using RelStorage — the relevant database server installed and configured.

 Please refer to *Chapter 3, The Development Environment* for the minimum environment prerequisites that should be installed on any server running Plone, including Python, a C Compiler and PIL.

To have a truly repeatable build process, however, we need a little bit of discipline. We want to avoid a situation where we are deploying point-in-time snapshots of code and configuration, and make it possible to revert to a particular, named version of our deployment easily.

A server deployment consists of four elements:

- Configuration—contained within or managed by a buildout.
- Custom code—in the form of distributions containing Python packages and modules.
- Code dependencies—usually downloaded from PyPI.
- Data—usually a snapshot of the ZODB.

Releasing distributions

In *Chapter 3, The Development Environment*, we learned about known good version sets, and created a `versions.cfg` file to control the versions for distributions we depend on that are not part of the standard known good sets. When preparing for a production deployment, it is vitally important that the version of every package is 'pinned'. In other words, the `buildout.dumppickedversions` extension should not print any picked versions during a deployment buildout run.

 It is possible to tell Buildout to give an error if it picks any unpinned versions, by setting `allow-picked-versions = false` in the main `[buildout]` section.

This is all well and good for publicly released code that can be downloaded from PyPI, but what about our own distributions? Unless they are meant for public consumption, we probably do not want to release them to PyPI. Instead, we can release them to our own **private distribution index**.

The easiest way to create a private distribution index is to set up an internal server running Apache, nginx, IIS, or some other web server capable of rendering an HTML listing of a directory that contains all the eggs we want to make available. This server needs to be reachable from our development environment and from the server where we will run our deployment buildout.

If we do not have a web server handy, we can use the one built into Python by running:

```
$ python -m SimpleHTTPServer 8000
```

This will start a web server on port 8000 providing a directory listing of the current directory.

The index page needs to be added to the buildout configuration using the `find-links` option. For example, if the distribution index is running on a server called `index.example.org` and the index is served on the virtual directory `/distributions`, we could add:

```
find-links = http://index.example.org/distributions/
```

If we were using the `SimpleHTTPServer` as shown previously, running from the directory containing the relevant eggs, we would use:

```
find-links = http://index.example.org:8000/
```

To manually create a distribution, we can use the following command from within the distribution's top-level directory (the one with `setup.py` in it):

```
$ python setup.py sdist
```

This will create a distribution `.tar.gz` file in `dist/`, which we can copy into the directory being used for the index.

In most cases, we will manage each distribution as its own top-level module in our source code repository, pulled into the buildout via the `[sources]` section that is managed by the `mr.developer` extension described in *Chapter 3, The Development Environment*. In this case, we should create a tag for each released version. We should also make sure all locally modified files are properly committed first.

If this sounds cumbersome, there is relief: In *Chapter 3, The Development Environment* we added `jarn.mkrelease` to our development tools. This means we can run the command as the following from our development environment:

```
$ bin/mkrelease -d index.example.org:/srv/eggs src/optilux.policy
```

This will tag and release the current version of `src/optilux.policy`, first committing any unsaved changes (which is often the change to `setup.py` to bump the version number), and then copy the distribution to `/srv/eggs` on `index.example.org` using SCP. This obviously requires that the index server has a running SSH daemon, and that our user has write permissions over the relevant directory.

 Do not forget to update the distribution version in `setup.py` either just before or just after making a new release, so that each release uses a unique version.

`jarn.mkrelease` supports many different ways to package and release distributions, including support making releases to PyPI and PyPI-like indexes such as the one on `http://plone.org/products`. See `http://pypi.python.org/pypi/jarn.mkrelease` for more details and examples.

Once we have made releases of everything, we should update `versions.cfg` to reflect the new version numbers. When using releases, we should not have any packages in the `auto-checkout` list in the active buildout configuration.

 If you prefer, you can remove `mr.developer` entirely from the buildout, although it will not do any harm if left in `packages.cfg` as in the book's example code.

Source distributions from tags

If we are unable to make releases of our custom distributions, we can use tags instead. This means tagging each distribution in our version control system and updating the `[sources]` section in `packages.cfg` to reflect the tags. See `http://pypi.python.org/pypi/mr.developer` for details about how to do this with different version control systems.

With this type of configuration, we need to make sure the `auto-checkout` option lists all the distributions that are managed as tags.

Tagging the build

At this point, we should have a set of buildout configuration files that reflect the code and configuration we want to deploy. We should tag this in our version control system.

 In *Chapter 3, The Development Environment* we outlined which files to check into version control and which ones to ignore. This list obviously applies to tags as well.

Deploying the build

With a tagged build, it is easy to deploy the build to a server. The steps are:

1. Check out the tag of the build into a new directory.

2. Run `python bootstrap.py` to initialize Buildout, as described in *Chapter 3, The Development Environment*.

3. Run `bin/buildout -c deployment.cfg` to build the distribution buildout.

To upgrade a build:

1. Switch to the new tag.
2. Rerun `bin/buildout -c deployment.cfg`.

Some organizations mandate that production servers cannot have internet connections, which stops Buildout from downloading extended files and eggs. In this case, you can use an internet-connected build server to run the buildout, and then copy the entire buildout directory to the target server. This will work so long as:

*   The build server uses the same operating system and processor architecture as the target server

*   Python is installed in the same location

*   The relative path to the buildout is the same on both servers. Depending on the Buildout recipes in use, you may also be able to set `relative-paths = true` in the main `[buildout]` section so that all generated paths be relative.

*   There is no shared egg cache. The buildout configuration described here takes care of this by setting an explicit `eggs-directory`.

Managing data

The **Aspeli Principle of Release Management** states:

> *Code moves forwards, from development to test to production. Data moves backwards, from production to test to development.*

Violate this at your peril. Changing code in a production or test environment and trying to reconcile it back to a development environment is a recipe for disaster.

Similarly, having users edit data in the test environment and then trying to merge it into a live environment that may have evolved in the meantime is a recipe for corrupt databases. This of course applies to persistent configuration as well, which is why we manage all our configuration using GenericSetup or configuration files.

Conversely, it is often useful to copy live data into a test or development environment to make testing more realistic or to diagnose issues.

There is one exception to the rule: The first time a system is deployed, it may be useful to copy data from a test environment. However, this will only work if the two environments use the same processor architecture (for example, both are either 32-bit or 64-bit).

There are three main approaches to copying data between environments:

- Take a backup and restore it. More on that in the *Backups and maintenance* section below.

- Copy `var/filestorage/Data.fs` and the entire `var/blobstorage` directory. This is safe as long as Zope is stopped.

- Create a `.zexp` export in the ZMI in the source environment, copy this to the import directory (which by default can be found in `var/instance/import`, where `instance` is the name of the Zope instance used for the import), and import it from the ZMI in the target environment. This works best when exporting and importing an entire Plone site, and when the site does not contain a lot of data.

Managing Zope processes

With multiple Zope instances come multiple processes (and in the next chapter, we will add a few more for proxies and load balancers in front of Zope). No longer can we simply run `bin/instance fg`. We need to start and stop all processes together and in the right order.

Furthermore, we need to ensure the processes run as **daemons** so that we are not dependent on having a console open for each. There are two common approaches to this:

- Use the `start` and `stop` commands to the instance script (for example, `bin/instance1 start` and `bin/instance2 stop`) to run Zope in daemon mode. Other commands include `restart`, to restart the daemon process, and `status`, to check whether the daemon is currently running.

- Use a parent process that is itself daemonized. In this case, we would use the `console` argument (`bin/instance1 console`) to start Zope in non-debug mode without daemonizing.

When using a ZEO server, the ZEO process can be managed similarly, using the `bin/zeo` script, which accepts the commands `start`, `stop`, `restart`, `status` and `fg`.

Supervisor

To simplify the management of multiple processes, we have opted to use **Supervisor** in our deployment buildout. Together with the `collective.recipe.supervisor` Buildout recipe, this can be used to stop and start multiple processes together. The processes, including command-line options, owning users and options for console output capture are listed in the `programs` option in the buildout. The basic syntax is:

```
priority name binary [arguments] redirect_stderr user
```

For example, to run a process named `instance1` at priority `10` (lower priorities are started earlier) by executing `bin/instance1 console` as the user under `${users:zope-process}`, redirecting stderr to the console, we used:

```
10 instance1 ${buildout:directory}/bin/instance1 [console] true
${users:zope-process}
```

See `http://pypi.python.org/pypi/collective.recipe.supervisor` for details.

With Supervisor installed, we can start all our processes by running:

```
$ bin/supervisord
```

We can monitor and administer processes on the command line using the `bin/supervisorctl` command. In particular, we can shut down all processes with:

```
$ bin/supervisorctl shutdown
```

See `bin/supervisorctl help` for details about other commands.

Finally, we can monitor and administer processes through a web console. In the buildout above, we bound this to port 9001. With `supervisord` running, we can therefore access `http://localhost:9001`, enter the username and password set in the buildout configuration (*admin*/*secret*) to start, stop, restart, and tail processes.

Supervisor supports many other options and usage patterns. See `http://supervisord.org` for detailed documentation.

Unix init scripts

When running Plone on a dedicated server with a UNIX Operating System, it is often desirable to start and stop all the relevant services at system startup and shutdown. This is usually done with a custom **init script** in `/etc/init.d` that runs `supervisord` on startup and `supervisorctl shutdown` on shutdown.

When using RelStorage, this script will normally be configured to start after the script starting the database server to ensure Zope can start up correctly.

Please refer to your operating system documentation for more information about how to write `init` scripts.

Alternatively, we can use `@reboot` entries in the `crontab` of the user owning the Zope process. The following buildout recipe would install such a `crontab`:

```
[supervisor-crontab]
recipe = z3c.recipe.usercrontab
times = @ reboot
command = ${buildout:bin-directory}/supervisord
```

Run `man crontab` in a terminal for more information about `crontab`. See `http://pypi.python.org/pypi/z3c.recipe.usercrontab` for details about the `z3c.recipe.usercrontab` recipe.

Windows services

When deploying on Windows, we will normally forgo Supervisor and install each Zope instance as a **Windows service**. This can be done with the `install` command to the instance script. For example, to install `instance1` and `instance2` as services, we would run:

```
> bin\instance1 install
```

```
> bin\instance2 install
```

The `remove` command can be used to uninstall a service. Zope can now be started and stopped using the *Services* control panel under *Administrative Tools*. When using RelStorage, the database server would normally also be installed as a service, and should be started before Zope.

Errors starting the service will be logged to Windows' *Event Log* viewer, also under *Administrative Tools*.

 At the time of writing, there is no fully functional way to install a ZEO server as a Windows service. However, if you are using RelStorage, there will likely be a way to run your chosen relational database as a service. Please check your database's documentation.

Backups and maintenance

As with any long-running system, Zope requires some regular maintenance. As far as possible, we want to automate this. Maintenance falls into three categories: Backups, database optimization, and log management.

Backups

The importance of **backups** cannot be overstated. There are two types of backups that matter in a Zope context:

- Backups of the deployed code. With a properly isolated and tagged buildout, this may not be required (so long as the version control system itself is backed up), but it is normally prudent to back up the buildout once per deployment anyway, including the cache of downloaded eggs and extended files, in case any downloaded files cannot be downloaded again in the future.

- Backups of the ZODB.

With RelStorage, ZODB backups are done at the database level. Please refer to your chosen database's documentation for details.

With ZEO, you can use `collective.recipe.backup` to install scripts to easily snapshot and restore backups. (These scripts wrap the low-level `repozo` script, which is installed by `plone.recipe.zeoserver`.) See `http://pypi.python.org/pypi/collective.recipe.backup` for more details.

In either case, we will also need to back up the `var/blobstorage` directory to back up BLOB files. This is best done using standard backup solutions such as an atomic copy or `rsync`.

 Make sure you take the main ZODB backup *first* and then the BLOB storage backup immediately after it completes. Also ensure you do not pack the ZODB between making the main backup and backing up the BLOB storage.

Backups should be scheduled regularly, usually nightly, at a time when the server load is expected to be low. On UNIX systems, this normally means using Cron. On Windows, use the Windows task scheduler. Refer to your operating system documentation for more details.

ZODB packing

The Data.fs file that contains the ZODB when using the default file storage backend is **append-only**. This means that the file will not shrink, even as objects are deleted, until it is **packed**. This design brings some performance benefits, and makes it possible to roll the database back to a previous version using the **Undo** tab in the ZMI (at least if there have not been too many complex changes) until a pack is performed, but has obvious disk usage implications.

The ZODB can be packed manually from Plone's **Maintenance** control panel. When packing, we can give a number of days of revision history to keep. Setting this to 0 recovers the most space, but makes it impossible to go back if something goes wrong.

 Note, that when the database is packed from the ZMI, a single backup copy of the database prior to packing is stored as Data.fs.old. You need to remove this (or pack twice) to realize any space savings. This also means you will need at least twice the size of your ZODB in free disk space before attempting to pack the database.

When using RelStorage, we can install a zodbpack script to pack the database, as we did in the buildout earlier in this chapter. Assuming the database is running and the configuration file has been generated in etc/zodbpack.conf, we can pack the database with:

```
$ ./bin/zodbpack -d 7 etc/zodbpack.conf
```

Here, we keep seven days of revision history. Note that with a large database, this can take a long time and negatively impact server performance during the packing process. zodbpack will not create a backup Data.fs.old file.

When using ZEO, we use the zeopack script instead, which is installed by plone.recipe.zeoserver, but is otherwise similar. Assuming ZEO is running, we would pack the database with:

```
$ ./bin/zeopack -d 7
```

As with backups, ZODB packing should be scheduled regularly. Weekly packs are common. Make sure you do not schedule packs at busy times, and try to avoid overlapping the pack time with any scheduled backups.

Log monitoring and rotation

Each Zope instance writes two types of log files by default:

- The **access log**, which uses standard Apache log file format to log every request received. This is useful for analytics and debugging, but can grow very quickly on busy systems. By default, it is written to `var/log/instance-Z2.log`, where `instance` is the name of the Zope instance.

- The **event log**, which is used for log messages output by Python code, for example to signal successful startup or to indicate that an error has occurred. In our buildout above, we redirected this to **syslog**, which means Zope messages can be found in the standard log console or file configure at the operating system level. If we had not configured syslog, each instance would log to its own file in `var/log/instance.log`, where `instance` is the name of the Zope instance.

See `http://pypi.python.org/pypi/plone.recipe.zope2instance` for details about the options that control logging configuration.

Most log files can grow without bound, which means that in time they will fill up the disk. To combat this, we need **log rotation**. On most UNIX Operating Systems, this is done using a daemon called `logrotate`, which can be configured to look for log files matching a given directory/file name pattern and rotate and compress them.

After rotating files, `logrotate` needs to tell Zope to open a new log file. This can be done by sending the USR2 signal to the Zope process. Here is an example using standard `logrotate` syntax that reopens the logs for `instance1` and `instance2`:

```
/path/to/buildout/var/instance*.log {
    rotate 10
    weekly
    compress
    delaycompress
    postrotate
        /sbin/kill -USR2 `cat /path/to/buildout/var/instance1.pid`
        /sbin/kill -USR2 `cat /path/to/buildout/var/instance2.pid`
    endscript
}
```

This would usually go into a directory like `/etc/logrotate.d`. Please refer to your operating system documentation for more details about log rotation.

On Windows, there is no standard log rotation daemon. You may be able to use the `rotatelogs` program that comes with Apache, or rotate logs manually. Alternatively, buy a really big disk.

Summary

In this chapter, we have covered:

- How a "live" server should be configured differently from a development instance.
- Why it is important to use multiple Zope instances to scale Zope.
- Managing multiple instances with RelStorage, ZEO, and Supervisor.
- Moving code and data between developments, staging and live environments.
- Treating Zope as an operating-system level service.
- Regularly packing and backing up the ZODB.

In the next chapter, we will look at how to configure Zope behind a web server, caching proxy and load balancer for resilience and performance.

17
Setting up a Production Server

In the previous chapter we covered how to set up Zope in a server environment. Zope is only one of the services that we commonly deploy to production servers, however, and we have yet to consider hardware or operating system configuration.

In this chapter, we will cover:

- The server components that make up a production-grade Plone deployment: web server, caching reverse proxy, load balancer, Zope instances, and database
- Common configuration and deployment options
- Hardware selection and operating system configuration
- Profiling and deadlock debugging
- Optimization through resource merging
- HTTP caching
- Testing and benchmarking tools

Server components

A Plone deployment usually incorporates the following logical services:

- A web server, responsible for decrypting SSL traffic (if applicable), applying virtual host rewrites (see further) and, sometimes, serving static resources
- A caching reverse proxy, which serves static or shared resources when possible, reducing the load on the backend Zope instances

- A load balancer, responsible for distributing requests among Zope instances.

- The Zope instances themselves, running Plone

- A shared database, either a ZEO server or a relational database if using RelStorage

Some applications will also rely on an external relational database (for example, accessed via SQLAlchemy, as seen in *Chapter 12, Relational Databases*) or a shared application cache such as Memcached (for example, for session or cache storage in Beaker).

For smaller deployments, two or more of these functions will often be handled by a single process running on a single machine. As required, specialized software can be employed for more flexibility and greater scalability. It is important to realize, however, that every situation is different: careful design and testing are key to successful deployments of any system. Moreover, each of the topics covered here could fill a book in its own right, so we can only highlight the most common configurations. You are encouraged to study the relevant documentation and make sure you understand how each component of your deployment works.

Virtual hosting

A Plone site is created as an object that lives inside the ZODB root in a Zope instance. Thus, it is possible to have multiple Plone sites in the same Zope instance. This provides some hosting flexibility, but it means that the Plone site ID is part of the canonical URL; in development, we have used URLs such as `http://localhost:8080/Plone/front-page`.

For deployment, we usually want to drop the Plone site ID from the URL. This is achieved using **virtual hosting**, a feature of Zope whereby URLs rendered as the result of API calls such as `getURL()` (on a catalog brain) or `absolute_url()` (on an object) are changed to reflect the desired 'public' hostname and base path.

Virtual hosting works by inserting some special tokens into the path segment of the URL, normally through a **rewrite rule** in a web server that sits in front of Zope and proxies requests to it. For example, a rewrite rule in the Nginx web server may look like this (Apache configuration is similar):

```
rewrite ^/(.*)$
    /VirtualHostBase/http/example.org:80/Plone/VirtualHostRoot/$1
    break;
```

The first line matches any inbound path and saves it in the variable $1, which is later appended to the end of the URL. The path is then changed to contain the token VirtualHostBase, followed by the protocol, the public-facing host name and port, the Plone site ID, and the end token VirtualHostRoot, before the original path segment.

Hence, if a request is received for http://example.org/front-page and is to be proxied to Zope on localhost:8080, it will be translated to http://localhost:8080/VirtualHostBase/http/example.org:80/Plone/VirtualHostRoot/front-page by the rewrite rule. Zope will then traverse to Plone/front-page as if we had accessed http://localhost:8080/Plone/front-page, but when rendering external links (for example, in Plone's navigation tabs), it will use the public hostname (http://example.org/) and skip the Plone/ prefix.

 For more details about the virtual host monster, see http://docs.zope.org/zope2/zope2book/VirtualHosting.html

Web server

Most websites serve content on port 80 (HTTP) and/or 443 (HTTPS). While it is possible to run a single Zope instance listening on port 80, this is rarely advisable. A dedicated **web server** will be better at receiving a large number of requests, handling spikes in demand and dealing with invalid, potentially malicious requests. Furthermore, Zope does not natively support SSL (HTTPS), which we normally want to mandate for logged-in content authors to reduce the chance of session hijacking or the leaking of sensitive data. Thus, most production Plone deployments employ a web server in front of Zope.

The most popular web servers for use with Zope are:

- **Nginx** (http://wiki.nginx.org), which is fast and easy to configure. This is the author's first choice, and the basis for the examples that come with the book. The *proxy* and *rewrite* modules are used to proxy to Zope and perform rewrites for virtual hosting. The *SSL* module should be enabled for SSL configuration. Nginx runs on most UNIX-like operating systems as well as on Windows, although the Nginx developers warn about performance issues on Windows.

- **Apache** (http://httpd.apache.org/), one of the most popular web servers on the Internet, which often comes pre-installed on Linux and BSD servers, and is also available for Windows. Apache configuration is a little more cumbersome than that for Nginx, and Apache is not as fast in scenarios with very high load, but its ubiquity makes it a default choice for many. The mod_proxy and mod_rewrite modules can be used for proxying and virtual hosting.

- Microsoft **IIS**, which comes pre-installed on Windows servers. With IIS 7, the *URL Rewrite* module can be used for proxying and virtual hosting, but most Windows deployments rely on **Enfold Proxy** (http://www.enfoldsystems.com/software/proxy), which makes Plone configuration easy, works with IIS 6 and later, and includes support for caching.

The web server is configured to proxy to a backend Zope instance (often via a separate caching reverse proxy and/or load balancer – see further), and will usually perform virtual host rewrites. Other common configurations include forcing certain requests to SSL (for example, for logged-in users), setting custom request headers and serving some content statically from disk to bypass Zope entirely.

Caching reverse proxy

Zope and Plone are pretty fast (and Plone 4 much more so than earlier versions), but serving a mix of complex rendered web pages, small static files and larger binaries such as images detracts from perceived user performance. Later in this chapter, we will discuss how to optimize the resources being served from Plone and send cache response headers to instruct caching proxies and browsers how to cache resources. For now, realize that one of the main ways to improve performance and resilience to spikes in demand is to offload the serving of some content – usually static resources, and sometimes web pages that are not personalized and rarely change – to a dedicated **caching reverse proxy** that sits between Zope and the user's web browser.

There are several options for caching:

- **Varnish** (http://www.varnish-cache.org/), a seriously fast, flexible, and powerful caching proxy is usually the weapon of choice for Plone deployments on Linux and BSD. For simpler deployments, Varnish will often listen on port 80 and perform virtual host rewriting, thereby alleviating the need for a separate web server, although a web server is still required for SSL support. The main examples accompanying this chapter use Varnish for caching. Note that Varnish does not work on Windows.

- **Squid** (`http://www.squid-cache.org/`), a general web proxy with cache support that can also be configured as a reverse proxy. Squid used to be the default choice for Plone deployments, but has now largely been superseded by Varnish. There are Windows builds of Squid, but at the time of writing they are not actively maintained.

- **Enfold Proxy** in IIS, which supports caching as well as virtual hosting natively. This is usually the best choice for Windows deployments, although it has a license cost.

- The cache support built into the **Nginx** `Proxy` module. This is less advanced than the dedicated caching reverse proxies, and does not support the *Vary* response header at the time of writing, but is useful for simpler deployments. In the code that accompanies this chapter, there is an example of a minimal configuration that uses Nginx as a web server, cache, and load balancer, which demonstrates how to use this cache.

- Similarly, **Apache**'s `mod_cache` module can be configured for caching. This does support the `Vary` header, but is not as fast or powerful as Varnish.

Cache configuration is an intricate topic. Cache too little, and performance suffers. Cache too much, and users may see 'stale' pages. (This may include scenarios where navigational elements are inconsistent across pages and other potentially confusing behavior.)

The examples that come with the book demonstrate common and safe approaches to caching. If you need to cache more aggressively, you are encouraged first to become very comfortable with the concepts of HTTP caching, and then to spend some quality time with the documentation for your chosen caching proxy. We will discuss how Plone sets caching response headers later in this chapter.

Load balancer

In the previous chapter, we discussed the rationale for distributing load across multiple Zope instances. For this to work, we need a load balancer. Although some organizations will use hardware load balancers, most Plone deployments use a software load balancer to distribute requests.

Again, there are several options:

- **HAProxy** (`http://haproxy.1wt.eu/`), a powerful, flexible, and fast load balancer, is the author's preferred choice and the one demonstrated in the book's accompanying source code. It supports a variety of load balancing algorithms and features a useful status page where all backends can be monitored. HAProxy is not supported on Windows, however.

- **Pound** (http://www.apsis.ch/pound/) is another popular load balancer on UNIX systems, which handles SSL natively.

- **Pen** (http://siag.nu/pen/) is similar to Pound, but also runs on Windows.

- **Nginx**, **Apache**, **Enfold Proxy**, and **Varnish** all support load balancing across backends. They are typically less sophisticated and configurable than a dedicated load balancer, but are often sufficient for simpler setups.

When configuring a load balancer, it is important to consider whether you need **sticky sessions**, which simply means that all requests from a given user are sent to the same backend instance. This obviously makes the load balancing less efficient, and fault tolerance becomes less straightforward. In some systems, sticky sessions are a hard requirement, as session state is maintained in each backend and not shared.

Plone out of the box does not rely on session state, and in our case study, we have used Beaker for our custom session configuration, which uses a shared session storage and so does not require sticky sessions.

There is one reason to sometimes prefer sticky sessions, though: the ZODB cache that is held in each Zope client is more likely to contain the objects a user needs if the user is always accessing the same instance, especially if the cache is small (to conserve memory) and users do not typically access the same objects. Whether there is a performance benefit in practice can only be determined with load testing, however.

Other services

Finally, many deployments will rely on other services, such as:

- A relational database server (for example, when using SQLAlchemy, or for RelStorage).

- A shared application cache, such as **Memcached** (http://memcached.org/). For the Optilux case study, we will build and deploy Memcached as an optimization for RelStorage and as a storage for Beaker sessions.

- A process monitoring and control tool such as **Supervisor**, which we saw in the previous chapter, or **Monit** (http://mmonit.com).

- Server monitoring tools such as Munin (http://munin-monitoring.org/).

- User and group repositories, such as LDAP or Active Directory. We will discuss these in more detail in the next chapter.

Common configurations

As you have probably realized, there are many different ways to configure production servers. The right configuration for you will depend on your circumstances, but further we will outline some of the more common options.

The UNIX versions of these are also included in the book's accompanying source code as buildout configurations (Windows configuration tends to be more manual). There are three top-level buildout files to choose from:

- An expanded `deployment.cfg` based on the code from the previous chapter. This contains the 'maximum flexibility' option, with Nginx, Varnish, HAProxy, and Memcached in addition to the Zope instances and RelStorage configuration from the last chapter.

- An alternative `deployment-minimal.cfg`, which illustrates the 'UNIX with minimal configuration' option. This uses Varnish for caching, virtual hosting, and load balancing, but does not support SSL.

- An alternative `deployment-minimal-ssl.cfg`, which illustrates the 'UNIX with SSL' option. This adds only Nginx configuration to the previous chapter's code, using it for caching, virtual hosting, and load balancing.

All three files have a similar structure:

- Raw build instructions and default configuration for the various server components – Nginx, Varnish, HAProxy, and Memcached – are found in self-contained files in the `buildout.d/` directory, included into the top-level buildout file through the `extends` option and added to the `parts` list explicitly. The idea is that you can copy the `buildout.d/` directory into your own project if you want to reuse the components illustrated here. In `buildout.d/templates/`, you will find commented configuration files for each service, which you may wish to study and adjust as necessary.

- After the global and package configuration from *Chapter 16, Zope on the Server*, you will find a number of configuration options for things such as hosts, ports, system user accounts, and process options that are used by the various recipes and in the configuration file templates in `buildout.d/`. There are comments to explain what each option does.

- The relevant processes are included in the `[supervisor]` configuration started in the previous chapter. This means that the entire stack can be started using `./bin/supervisord` and managed through the Supervisor console, by default running on port *9001*.

Deploying on UNIX with minimal configuration

The simplest production-grade configuration commonly employed uses Varnish in front of Zope to perform virtual hosting, caching, and load balancing. This is very scalable and conserves system resources. The main drawbacks are a lack of SSL support and a relatively simple load balancer.

See `deployment-minimal.cfg` and `buildout.d/templates/varnish-balancer.vcl` for details. Notice the `director {}` section, which defines the upstream Zope instances, and the manipulation of `req.url` to perform virtual hosting.

Refer to `http://varnish-cache.org/docs` for details about VCL syntax.

Deploying on UNIX with SSL

If you require SSL but still want to keep the number of running services to a minimum, you can use Nginx for caching, virtual hosting, and load balancing. As with Varnish, the load balancer is relatively basic. Moreover, the cache is not nearly as flexible or configurable (or, probably, as fast) as Varnish. In particular, there is no support for the `Vary` header (see the discussion of caching basics later in this chapter), which means it is probably not safe to cache any dynamic content pages. Caching static resources should be fine, however, which is usually sufficient.

See `deployment-minimal-ssl.cfg` and `buildout.d/templates/nginx-minimal.conf` for details. Notice the `upstream {}` section which defines the backends, and `proxy_cache_path` and `proxy_temp_path` settings which define the cache. The cache is invoked using `proxy_cache` and related options. For simplicity, we have disabled the cache entirely (using `proxy_cache_bypass`) when Plone's `__ac` cookie is set, that is, for logged in content authors.

Refer to `http://wiki.nginx.org` for more details about Nginx configuration.

Deploying on UNIX with maximum flexibility

This is the full `deployment.cfg` buildout. There is quite a lot going on here, so let us discuss each part in turn.

Nginx is configured from `buildout.d/templates/nginx.conf`:

- There is a single upstream backend, Varnish.

- The main server is defined to listen on port 80.

- The path /_nginx_status_ is configured to show a simple status page, useful for monitoring, and only accessible from localhost.

- Responses are compressed using GZip if the browser supports this, to reduce network overhead.

- The path /system_error (configurable in the buildout) is used to serve the contents of the htdocs/system_error/ directory found in the buildout root. This contains a simple index.html file displaying an outage message. HAProxy will redirect here if all Zope instances are down.

- All other paths are rewritten and proxied. If the __ac cookie signifying a logged-in content author is detected, or if the login form is requested, we redirect the browser to the HTTPS version of the site. Otherwise, we perform virtual host rewrites and proxy upstream.

- An HTTPS server is also defined listening on port 443.

- This references an SSL certificate and key in etc/ in the buildout root. We have created a self-signed certificate using Open SSL, though for public sites you would purchase a certificate from a trusted authority.

- The HTTPS server defines the inverse rewrite of the HTTP one, performing virtual hosting for requests to the login form or where the __ac cookie is set, and forcing the user back to HTTP otherwise.

Varnish is configured from buildout.d/templates/varnish.vcl:

- Most of the file is taken from the default configuration that comes with plone.app.caching (see further).

- We define a backend referencing HAProxy and an access control list for hosts that are allowed to issue PURGE requests.

- For easier debugging, we also set a custom response header, *X-Varnish-Action*, with information about the action Varnish took.

Varnish allows for very detailed control over cache behavior. See http://www.varnish-cache.org/docs for more details about the **Varnish Control Language (VCL)**.

HAProxy is configured from buildout.d/templates/haproxy.conf:

- We log to syslog and limit the number of open connections to match the number of allowed open files, which is determined by the operating system (an open HTTP connection uses a socket, which counts as a file).

- The balancer is then set up for HTTP load balancing.

- A simple monitoring message is made available on the path /_haproxy_
  ping_, which can be used to check whether HAProxy is up.

- HAProxy statistics are served from a dedicated port (8222 by default). This
  provides a very useful overview of the status of all backends and requests at
  any point in time, and is an invaluable debugging tool.

- A single load balancer frontend is then configured. There are two backend
  clusters: default and panic. The access control rule in the frontend makes
  sure that all requests go to the default cluster as long as there is at least one
  backend Zope instance available. If no instances are up, the request is routed
  to the panic cluster.

- The default cluster is set to balance based on which instance currently has
  the fewest active connections. It then lists each Zope instance, providing
  equal weight to each.

- The panic cluster has no backend servers, but redirects the user's browser
  to /system_error after dropping any query string. This is served by Nginx,
  and provides a simple but meaningful error message in case of a fatal (or
  planned) outage.

HAProxy allows very fine-grained tuning of the load balancing algorithm. You may
wish to use multiple backend clusters and access rules to 'ring-fence' resources for
certain types of requests, for example to ensure a spike in anonymous traffic cannot
bring down the instances used for logged-in users.

Refer to the documentation at http://haproxy.1wt.eu/ for more
details.

Memcached has no configuration file, but is included for two purposes:

- In the Beaker configuration in deployment.cfg, we have changed session.
  type from file to ext:memcached, referencing the Memcached server under
  the key session.url. This makes our sessions faster, and makes it easier
  to balance sessions across multiple physical hosts, where filesystem storage
  would require a distributed filesystem or network storage. Note that we will
  lose sessions if Memcached is stopped, so if session permanence is important,
  a file backend may still be preferable. Since Memcached stores all data in
  memory, we may also need to keep an eye on memory usage.

- Also in deployment.cfg, we have added the cache-servers option to the
  rel-storage configuration. This lets RelStorage cache frequently requested
  objects across multiple Zope instances, providing a performance boost.

All of these services are of course managed by a **Supervisor**.

Deploying on Windows

On Windows, the easiest and most common option is to use IIS with Enfold Proxy proxying to multiple Zope instances, performing virtual host rewrites and providing caching.

If you cannot afford the (relatively modest) license cost for Enfold Proxy, you may be able to adapt the minimal Nginx configuration above, but the Nginx documentation indicates that caching does not work on Windows Vista and later. Alternatively, you may be able to configure Apache.

To run the buildout on Windows, you are advised to use the version from the previous chapter, which does not compile any of the UNIX services that are unlikely to build on Windows.

Hardware and operating system concerns

Now that we have covered the logical components, let us consider how to deploy them physically. As always, the right setup will depend on your needs and circumstances, but it is useful to know what kind of choices and tradeoffs are commonly made.

Hardware

Plone deployments tend to be primarily **RAM** bound. With more memory, you can increase the size of the ZODB cache in each Zope instance and/or keep more resources cached in memory in Varnish, leading to big performance improvements. For small deployments, 4-8GB of RAM may be enough, but for bigger sites, you may want 16 or 32GB.

The second most important resource is the number of **CPU cores**. Recall from the previous chapter that Python's **Global Interpreter Lock (GIL)** means it is more effective to have multiple processes with fewer threads than the other way around. More cores means more processes are able to serve requests in parallel. Few operations in Plone are truly CPU bound, so it is usually preferable to have more cores at slightly lower clock speed, instead of the other way around. That said, faster cores would be able to handle each request faster and so become free to serve new requests quicker.

Third comes **disk speed**. While an optimized site should be able to serve most requests from memory (either cached in Varnish or by loading objects from the ZODB cache), disk reads can still be a major performance bottleneck on the server(s) containing the ZODB. Solid State or fast spinning disks are helpful in this regard.

For smaller sites, a single server will suffice. Large and/or mission-critical sites will usually be deployed across multiple servers to improve performance and resilience. It is common to split a deployment into a **web tier**, running the web server and caching reverse proxy, and an **application tier**, running the Zope instances. If you are using a separate software load balancer such as HAProxy, this will often, but not always, sit in the application tier. The database (either the ZEO server or a relational database for RelStorage) may run in the application tier, or on dedicated infrastructure.

Resilience and fault tolerance is a complex topic and outside the scope of this book, but it is worth noting a few things:

- Web servers such as Nginx, caching proxies such as Varnish and load balancers such as HAProxy are stateless and can easily be deployed in an active-active or active-passive configuration.

- Zope instances configured for ZEO or RelStorage are also stateless (provided you use Beaker or ZEO-storage for sessions). For resilience, it is often useful to load balance across two or more physical hosts, each running a number of Zope instances.

- If you are using shared BLOB storage (`shared-blob = on` in the buildout configuration), which is good for performance, the BLOB storage directory (`var/blobstorage`) must be accessible from all Zope instances. If you are running Zope instances on multiple physical hosts, that usually means mounting the BLOB storage on **Network Attached Storage** (**NAS**), for example, via NFS or CIFS, or on a **Storage Area Network** (**SAN**) with a clustered filesystem. Note that SANs can have high disk latency, which can have a negative impact on ZODB performance. You are advised to test carefully.

- The same goes for Beaker sessions using file storage. Memcached storage can be accessed over the network, although you may then want to provide fault tolerance for the Memached daemon itself.

- The database is obviously stateful and fault tolerance needs to be carefully considered. Here, RelStorage is often a big help, as the major databases all have well established failover and redundancy functionality. A simple option, which will work both for a relational database with RelStorage and a ZEO server with file storage, is to use a SAN to store the database files, and maintain a cold standby on a separate physical machine. Failover then involves mounting the SAN virtual disk on the standby machine (only) and starting up the second database server, before failing over the IP address used to access the database server. Note that Zope will probably need to be restarted in the process.

> For more information about high availability and failover on Linux, see the Linux HA project (`http://www.linux-ha.org`). You may also be interested in reading about DRBD (`http://www.drbd.org/`), which provides a cost effective way to synchronize disks for resilience.

When deploying to multiple machines, you may want to create individual top-level buildout configuration files for each node so that only the relevant services are built and configured.

> It is best to avoid hardcoding IP addresses in the buildout configuration, with the possible exception of that for localhost (127.0.0.1). Instead, use logical hostnames and configure the `/etc/hosts` file on each node appropriately. This makes it possible to use the same configuration across multiple environments, for example, for testing or disaster recovery sites.

Buildout or system packages

In the previous examples, we have used various buildout recipes to compile and install local versions of services such as Nginx, Varnish, and HAProxy. On most well-behaved Linux and BSD systems (including Mac OS X), this should work consistently, and provides a simple way to control the exact versions and configurations of the services being used. The Buildout templating system and `collective.recipe.template` also make it easy to define variables for things such as user accounts and hostnames and use them consistently across the configuration files for multiple services.

Some system administrators will prefer to use operating system packages to install the relevant services – as indeed we have opted to do for the database server used in RelStorage – not least because this simplifies upgrades and notification of security patches. In this case, you may still want to use Buildout to generate configuration files. You can edit the `parts` list in the buildout configuration file accordingly.

Operating system configuration

Beyond the services that make up a Plone deployment, a few other operating system configuration tasks are usually required:

- Configure **log rotation** for the log files of all relevant services. These are usually found in the `var/log/` directory inside the buildout root. We showed an example of log rotation in the previous chapter.

- If you are logging to a shared syslog daemon, make sure it is configured to receive log messages over the network.

- If you are expecting a large number of simultaneous requests, make sure that the operating system is configured to allow each process to keep as many files open as necessary (this is known as the **ulimit** on Linux). Bear in mind that each service that keeps an open connection to proxy to another will open a socket requiring a file descriptor, so if you expect 10,000 concurrent requests and are running Nginx, Varnish, and HAProxy on the same machine, they could use up to 30,000 file descriptors between them just to get the requests to Zope.

- You should configure server monitoring so that you are warned of problems or constraints on system resources. **Munin** (`http://munin-monitoring.org/`) is a popular open source monitoring solution with plugins for various services, including Nginx, Varnish, HAProxy, and Zope.

- Finally, you should ensure all relevant services are started automatically if the server is restarted. This usually means creating new startup script in `/etc/init.d` to start `bin/supervisord` in the buildout root and run `bin/supervisorctl shutdown` on system shutdown.

Caching and optimization

With the appropriate services in place, we can now turn our attention to performance optimization. There are two main types of performance problems that can plague Plone sites: slow application code and poor caching.

Application-level problems

Slow application code is usually caused by sloppy programming. Some common problems include:

- Inefficient or redundant loops.
- Poorly constrained catalog queries returning large result sets.

- Unnecessary calls to `getObject()` on catalog brains or walks of the ZODB using functions such as `values()`, `items()`, or `objectValues()` on folders, all of which load objects from the ZODB, possibly from disk, and push other objects out of the ZODB cache.

- Using TALES expressions in page templates that refer to content objects, but forgetting to use the `nocall:` modifier so that the objects are unnecessarily rendered in memory as the expression is evaluated.

- Blocking calls to external systems, including databases, or file operations.

These types of problems can sometimes be detected using **profiling**. Zope has a built-in profiler that can be used to inspect which functions take the longest to execute. To enable it, add the following to the `zope-conf-additional` option in the buildout configuration file and rerun the buildout:

```
zope-conf-additional =
    ...
    publisher-profile-file ${buildout:directory}/var/log/profile.out
```

After restarting Zope, you can go to **Control_Panel** in the root of the ZMI, then click **Debug Information** and finally the **Profiling** tab. Reset the information before executing the requests you intend to profile, then check back to inspect the profile statistics.

You should disable the profiler by removing the `publisher-profile-file` option when you are done, as leaving profiling on will have a performance impact.

Sometimes, truly broken application code, such as infinite loops, can cause Zope to hang, a situation known as a **deadlock**. These types of problems can be difficult to diagnose, but since Zope 2.13, there is a solution (on UNIX-like operating systems at least). If you send signal *USR1* to the Zope process, it will dump a stacktrace of the current point of execution of each thread to the console, allowing you to see where it is hanging.

To do this, you first need to know the process ID (PID) of the Zope process you want to debug. The `ps` command can show you this (as can `bin/supervisorctl status` if you have started Zope using `supervisord`). You then run `kill -USR1 <pid>` to dump the call stack. See the manual pages for `ps` and `kill` for more details.

Optimizing resources

Presuming there are no egregious application performance problems, the next step in optimization is to consider which resources are served by Plone and how they are cached. This will usually have a much bigger impact than any micro-optimization of Python code.

The general aim is to minimize the number of requests served by Plone to render each full page. This lessens the load on the server and improves the perceived performance to the end user as it reduces latency.

We achieve this first by merging related resources, such as stylesheets and JavaScript files, into fewer files, often compressing them in the process. (This can also be done for images using a technique known as **CSS spriting**. Plone's default Sunburst theme uses sprites for its main images.) Second, we want to set appropriate caching response headers on the resources served from Plone to inform the user's browser and any caching proxies (such as Varnish) how content should be cached.

Resource Registries resource merging

Plone's **Resource Registries** – the `portal_css` and `portal_javascripts` tools in the ZMI – support automatic resource merging. When not running in development mode, they will merge any adjacent resources that are registered with the same options and conditions. The merged resource is given a unique URL and cached aggressively. If the composition is changed, the URL is changed so that a new copy will be fetched.

The **Development mode** option in the Resource Registries is on by default when Zope is in debug mode and vice-versa. You can change the setting in the ZMI for testing, but it is reset when the instance is restarted.

You can view how resources are merged in the **Merged CSS Composition** and **Merged JS Composition** tabs of `portal_css` and `portal_javascripts`, respectively, in the ZMI. Move resources up or down and change options as appropriate to reduce the number of distinct resources being served to the browser.

Test carefully and regularly as you proceed: CSS cascading rules and JavaScript dependencies means that it is possible to break the site with careless reordering. Some poorly written JavaScript files may also not handle merging very well.

Once you have an order you are happy with, you can export it via a `portal_setup` snapshot and incorporate it into your policy product. For more fine-grained control, you can use the `insert-after` and `insert-before` attributes in the `cssregistry.xml` and `jsregistry.xml` GenericSetup files to explicitly insert new resources before or after existing resources. Be sure to test your extension profile on a fresh Plone site to ensure it works as expected, in a repeatable manner.

A crash course in caching

The HTTP standard explicitly supports caching, both in proxies and in browsers. A good understanding of web caching concepts is a prerequisite for tuning Plone sites. We will provide an overview here, but you are encouraged to read more about this topic if you are not already familiar with it.

 The tutorial at `http://www.mnot.net/cache_docs/` is a good place to start.

Leaving aside application-specific caching performed in code (for example, using `collective.beaker` or `plone.memoize`), there are two types of caches that matter to web applications. The cache in the user's browser and shared caches managed by caching proxies such as Varnish. A web application – in this case Plone – can set **caching response headers** to instruct these how a given resource (for example, an image, stylesheet, JavaScript file, or web page) may be safely cached (or not). When a request is made, the browser will sometimes include corresponding **caching request headers** to let the web application know what it holds in its cache.

When thinking about caching, we distinguish between **shared resources** and **personalized resources**. A shared resource is one that looks the same to every user, such as an image that is part of the site's theme. A personalized resource may look different to different users. Most web pages in Plone are personalized to some extent, as navigation and portlets may show different content depending on a user's permissions, and because logged-in users see their name on every page. Shared resources are much easier to cache safely. If caching goes wrong, a personalized resource may be cached in a shared way, which can be quite disconcerting; suddenly, the user sees someone else's user name or content!

 If you need to cache aggressively for logged-in users and the username is the only user-specific personalization on most pages, you can customize Plone's `personal_bar.pt` viewlet template (in `plone.app.layout.viewlets`) to render a generic string. If you still want users to see their name, you can fetch it via an asynchronous JavaScript request, cache it in a cookie, and inject it into the DOM on load.

The simplest type of caching is based on modification times. A resource may be returned to the browser with an **Expires** response header indicating a date and time (in GMT) when it expires. Sometimes this is in the past, which is an easy way to tell the browser to always fetch a new version. If it is in the future, most browsers will use a cached copy until it has expired.

Some resources in Plone, such as merged stylesheets and JavaScript files managed by the `portal_css` and `portal_javascripts` tools, are cached 'forever', with an *Expires* header far in the future. This is safe, because the URLs of these resources includes a random string that is changed every time the resources are changed, forcing a new copy to be downloaded and cached.

More fine-grained control can be provided with the **Cache-Control** response header. This may contain a comma-separated list of any of the following tokens:

Token	Purpose
max-age=<seconds>	This is like `Expires`, in that it indicates how long a resource may be cached for, except that it is relative to the current time, not an absolute date and time.
s-maxage=<seconds>	This is like `max-age`, but applies only to caching proxies, not browsers. The `s` stands for 'shared'.
public	This explicitly indicates a response as cacheable, even if HTTP authentication is in use. This is useful for shared resources that have no personalization.
private	This indicates that the content is specific to a given user. A browser may still cache the response, but a shared caching proxy will not.
no-cache	This forces a fresh request each time, even if the cache is configured to sometimes allow stale responses.
no-store	This indicates the response should never be stored. This is useful for sensitive information that should never be cached.
must-revalidate	This forces the cache to respect `Last-Modified` and `ETag` rules (more on this further).
proxy-revalidate	This is like `must-revalidate`, but only applies to caching proxies.

With `Cache-Control`, we can be more precise than simply indicating an expiration time. A static resource such as an image or stylesheet returned by Plone will have a **Last-Modified** header set to a date and time (in GMT) indicating when the resource was last modified. Browsers and caching proxies will remember this date along with a cached copy of the resource. When the resource is requested again, the browser sends the previous `Last-Modified` date and time in a request header called **If-Modified-Since**. If Plone receives this header, it will immediately look up the current last modified time of the given resource. If it has been modified, it is returned as normal with a status code *200 OK*, but if it has not, a body-less response with code `304 NOT MODIFIED` is returned instead. This still involves a request to the server, but by not requiring a full response, a *304* response is significantly faster.

This approach works well for shared resources, but not for personalized web pages, where the response contents may depend on things like the user's roles and other content that is visible in Plone's various navigation aides. Luckily, it is still possible to return a *304* response by using an **Etag**. Instead of returning a `Last-Modified` response header, Plone returns an `Etag` header containing a cache key. To the browser, this is just a string, though in Plone we use a (configurable) pipe-separated list of tokens, usually including things such as the user's roles, the current theme, the user's preferred language and a counter that is incremented each time content is cataloged (that is, when it is created or changed). The browser remembers the Etag when it caches content and sends it back to the server in a request header called **If-None-Match**. Plone then recalculates the Etag and returns a *304* response without rendering the full response if it is still valid. Otherwise, a full response is returned.

Etags work well for personalized resources, but sometimes we have resources that are mostly shared, but may differ slightly depending on the type of request. For example, in a multilingual site, we may have different versions of a given resource (that is, a page on a given URL) depending on the user's preferred language. If we want to cache these pages in a shared caching proxy, we need to tell the proxy to store different versions depending on the language being requested. This can be achieved using the **Vary** response header, which contains a comma-separated list of request header names. The caching proxy will store one copy of a resource for each unique combination of request header values received for these header names. Hence, if Plone returns a response header `Vary: Accept-Language` for a given page, Varnish will cache one copy of the resource for browsers that send `Accept-Language: en` and a different copy for browsers that send `Accept-Language: fr`.

> The `Vary` header can be used with custom headers as well, which can be set in Nginx, Varnish, or another web server, for example based on the value of a cookie or some other information in the request.

Caching configuration and rulesets

The setting of caching response headers and support for `If-Modified-Since` and `If-None-Match` in Plone is handled by the `plone.app.caching` package, which ships with Plone 4.1, superseding the older `CacheFu` product. It is not installed by default, however, so you must enable it through the **Add-ons** control panel, where it is called **HTTP Caching Support**.

In Plone 4.0, you can install `plone.app.caching` by adding it to your buildout and using an appropriate KGS from `http://good-py.appspot.com/release/plone.app.caching`.

`plone.app.caching` works by looking up **caching rulesets** for each resource being published, be it an image, stylesheet, JavaScript file, or view of a content object. Each ruleset is mapped to a **caching operation**, which will set caching response headers and, if appropriate, intercept requests to return *304* responses or responses cached in RAM in Zope. Caching operations can be configured through the **Caching** control panel, where rulesets can be mapped to operations and detailed parameters – such as *max-age* timings, *Vary* headers or *Etag* components – can be changed as required. For even more specific needs, it is possible to write custom operations in Python code, using a library of helper functions. However, the default operations should be sufficient for most deployments.

All the standard resource types and views that come with Plone are handled by `plone.app.caching` out of the box, but we need to declare rulesets for our custom views. This is done in ZCML, using directives from `z3c.caching`, which provides a minimal dependency for packages that need to declare their caching intentions without wanting a dependency on all of `plone.app.caching`.

In `optilux.cinemacontent`, we add the following to `setup.py`:

```
install_requires=[
    'setuptools',
    'Products.CMFPlone',
    'plone.app.dexterity',
    'archetypes.schemaextender',
    'plone.app.registry',
    'plone.app.referenceablebehavior',
    'plone.namedfile [blobs]', # makes sure we get blob support
    'plone.app.z3cform',
    'zope.annotation',
    'z3c.saconfig',
    'MySQL-python',
    'five.globalrequest',
    'collective.beaker',
    'z3c.caching',
],
```

In the main `configure.zcml` file we then add:

```
<!-- Include files -->
<include file="permissions.zcml" />
<include file="caching.zcml" />
```

This new `caching.zcml` file contains the following:

```
<configure
    xmlns="http://namespaces.zope.org/zope"
    xmlns:cache="http://namespaces.zope.org/cache"
    i18n_domain="optilux.cinemacontent">

    <include package="z3c.caching" file="meta.zcml" />

    <cache:ruleset
        for=".cinema.View"
        ruleset="plone.content.folderView"
        />

    <cache:ruleset
        for=".cinema.Screenings"
        ruleset="plone.content.itemView"
        />

    <cache:ruleset
        for=".cinema.Reserve"
        ruleset="plone.content.itemView"
        />

    <cache:ruleset
        for=".cinemafolder.View"
        ruleset="plone.content.folderView"
        />

    <cache:ruleset
        for=".dam.DAMReport"
        ruleset="plone.content.itemView"
        />

    <cache:ruleset
        for=".enquiry.EnquiryForm"
        ruleset="plone.content.itemView"
        />

    <cache:ruleset
        for=".film.View"
        ruleset="plone.content.itemView"
        />

    <cache:ruleset
```

```
        for=".promotion.View"
        ruleset="plone.content.itemView"
        />


</configure>
```

Here, we map each custom view to a ruleset name defined by `plone.app.caching`. `plone.content.itemView` is used for views of content items that are not containers (folders), while `plone.content.folderView` is used for content items that are.

 For the full list of available rulesets, see the `plone.app.caching` documentation. It is also possible to define a custom ruleset type using the `<cache:rulesetType />` directive from `z3c.caching`, which allows you to map specific operations to a subset of views or other resource types. For example, you may wish to declare a custom ruleset for the front page of your site and cache this more aggressively than other views.

With the rulesets in place, we can turn on caching through the **Caching** control panel. We first import a caching profile using the **Import settings** tab. The **With caching proxy** profile is the most appropriate one, provided we are using a caching proxy such as Varnish with a configuration file like the one provided with this chapter. Once imported, we can enable caching using the **Enable** checkbox on the **Change settings** tab.

 If you are using the Nginx configuration from this chapter, do not enable GZip compression in the **Caching** control panel, as it will be handled by Nginx.

There are many more options that can be tweaked in `plone.app.caching`. Chances are that if you observe something untoward in a caching response header in Firebug, there is a setting in the **Caching** control panel to rectify the situation. Please refer to the documentation at `http://pypi.python.org/pypi/plone.app.caching` for more details, including a description of what each of the standard rulesets and operations does.

Testing and benchmarking

When tuning a deployment, you need to be able to test the effects of your changes. There are a number of tools that can help with this, including:

- The venerable **Firebug** plugin for Firefox (http://getfirebug.com/). The **Net** tab in particular lets you view which resources are being requested, the HTTP status code for each request, whether or not a resource was served from the local cache, request and response headers, and timings. The Safari and Chrome developer tools include similar functionality. As a rule of thumb, you should see mostly cached and *304* responses after the initial load of a given page, and you should only see a small number of resources being fetched for each page. Inspect the response headers to understand what cache control is in effect.

- The **Page Speed** plugin for Firefox and Google Chrome (http://code. google.com/speed/page-speed/), which helpfully suggests ways in which your site could be optimized.

- **JMeter** (http://jakarta.apache.org/jmeter/), a graphical tool for building and executing load testing suites.

- **Funkload** (http://funkload.nuxeo.org/), a command line tool based on Python unit test syntax for building and executing load testing suites.

Good load testing in a realistic environment and ongoing monitoring of the live site is essential to proving the performance of a deployment. You should aim to test and optimize realistic user scenarios, not just abstract metrics of such requests per second of the front page. In particular, repeatedly hammering a single page can give skewed benchmarks (unless of course that is what you expect your users to be doing), as that page is likely to be in various caches after the first few requests. Also take the time to learn the intricacies of your load testing tools, so that you are able to properly interpret their outputs.

Summary

In this chapter, we have learned about:

- How and when to deploy with a web server, caching reverse proxy and/or load balancer in front of Zope.
- Common configurations for UNIX (Linux, BSD) and Windows deployments.
- Hardware and operating system considerations.
- Caching and performance optimization.

In the next chapter, we will discuss authentication against an LDAP or Active Directory repository.

18

Authenticating with LDAP or Active Directory

Until now, we have stored users and groups in the ZODB, using Plone's built-in user management functionality. This works well for standalone sites, but many organizations have centralized user databases, usually in LDAP or Microsoft Active Directory repositories. Using an external user database means that site members do not have to be explicitly created in Plone, and that users can keep the same username and password across multiple systems.

In this chapter, we will cover:

- The basics of LDAP and Active Directory
- Setting up a test environment using OpenLDAP
- Connecting Plone to LDAP and Active Directory

LDAP and Active Directory

LDAP is not black magic voodoo, even if it can feel that way sometimes. It is in fact very logical, but it uses unfamiliar terminology and relies on precise specifications of how things are stored and searched. Luckily, it is not very difficult to connect to an existing repository for authentication in Plone, provided its configuration is not too esoteric and you know a few key details about its configuration. The administrator for your organization's LDAP repository should be able to provide this information.

[The tools described in this chapter support both standard LDAP and Active Directory. However, creating users and groups from within Plone is only supported with standard LDAP servers.]

A detailed guide to LDAP is beyond the scope of this book. To learn more, please consult a good LDAP reference or the documentation that comes with OpenLDAP or Active Directory. Before we dive in, however, let us define a few key terms.

LDAP term	Meaning
LDAP	Lightweight Directory Access Protocol. We will focus on LDAP v3, which is the current version.
OpenLDAP	A popular open source LDAP server implementation.
Active Directory	Microsoft's directory tool, which exposes an LDAP interface.
LDAP entry	A record in the LDAP directory, for example representing a user or a group.
LDIF	LDAP Data Interchange Format. LDAP entries can be imported and exported as plain-text files in this format.
Schema	Defines the object classes and permitted attributes for LDAP entries. It is possible to define your own schema, but most implementations will use one of the standard schemata, such as core or cosine.
Attribute	A piece of information about an LDAP entry, such as a line of a user's address, a photo or a telephone number.
Object class	Declares optional and mandatory attributes for an LDAP entry. Each entry has one or more object classes, much like an object in Python is instantiated from a class that may have additional base classes.
Structural object class	The primary (or "core") object class of an entry in the repository. An entry must have exactly one structural object class, but may have additional classes defining secondary attributes.
DN (distinguished name)	A unique, canonical reference to an LDAP entry, for example, a unique specifier for a particular user. A distinguished name consists of several attribute-value pairs. For example, the DN cn=Manager,dc=optilux-cinemas,dc=com means "the object with the common name Manager, under the domain optilux-cinemas.com".
CN (common name)	The common (full) name of a person or group. Can be configured as the login name or user ID, but is most often used as the fullname property in Plone.
UID (user id)	A unique ID for a user. Can be configured as the login name or user ID in Plone.

LDAP term	Meaning
DC (**domain component**)	Part of a domain name, used to specify the domain of a particular resource. For example, the domain `optilux-cinemas.com` would be expressed as `dc=optilux-cinemas,dc=com`.
OU (**organizational unit**)	An organizational unit logically groups entries. In the simple schema we will use below, all users are in an OU called *people* and all groups are in an OU called *groups*. Organizational units may be nested.
Root DN	In OpenLDAP, this is the DN of a user that has overall administrative control.
Relative DN	A single attribute-value pair as used in a DN. When creating new users through Plone, a relative DN is used to construct a proper DN for the new user.

Setting up a test environment

To demonstrate LDAP connectivity, we will create a simple LDAP repository with OpenLDAP. If you already have an LDAP server configured or you are using Active Directory, you can skip this section.

OpenLDAP can be downloaded from `http://openldap.org`. Many operating systems will also have OpenLDAP preinstalled or available as a preconfigured package.

OpenLDAP is configured with a configuration file normally found in `/etc/openldap/slapd.conf`. On the author's test system, it looks similar to the following:

```
include     /etc/openldap/schema/core.schema
include     /etc/openldap/schema/cosine.schema

pidfile     /var/run/slapd.pid
argsfile    /var/run/slapd.args

database    bdb
suffix      "dc=optilux-cinemas,dc=com"
rootdn      "cn=Manager,dc=optilux-cinemas,dc=com"
rootpw      secret
directory   /var/openldap-data
index       objectClass   eq
```

There are many more configuration options, and the preceding settings are not necessarily appropriate for a production system. See the manual page for `slapd.conf` for more details.

The preceding example configuration includes the *core* and *cosine* schemata, which means that we can use object classes and attributes defined in these files. The *cosine* schema is quite extensive and includes several commonly useful attributes. Next, we define some runtime files, and then choose a Berkley DB backend storage. Entries here will be suffixed with the domain components for the `optilux-cinemas.com` domain. The root DN is set to `cn=Manager,dc=optilux-cinemas,dc=com`, with a clear-text password `secret`.

 For production systems, you should not use a clear-text password! See the manual page of `slapd.conf` and the `ldappassword` command for information about how to encrypt the password and otherwise configure access rights to the LDAP repository. Also, the `slapd.conf` file should not be world-readable.

We should also create some entries in the repository. The file `optilux.ldif` found in the `extra` directory in the book's accompanying source code contains a bare-bones repository with one user and one group. It looks like this:

```
version: 1

# Top level - the organization
dn: dc=optilux-cinemas,dc=com
dc: optilux-cinemas
description: Optilux Corporation
objectClass: dcObject
objectClass: organization
o: Optilux Corporation

# Top level - manager
dn: cn=Manager,dc=optilux-cinemas,dc=com
objectclass: organizationalRole
cn: Manager

# Second level - organizational units
dn: ou=people, dc=optilux-cinemas,dc=com
ou: people
description: All people in the organization
objectclass: organizationalunit

dn: ou=groups, dc=optilux-cinemas,dc=com
ou: groups
description: All groups in the organization
objectclass: organizationalunit

# Third level - people
dn: uid=ssmith,ou=people,dc=optilux-cinemas,dc=com
objectClass: pilotPerson
```

```
objectClass: uidObject
uid: ssmith
cn: Susan Smith
sn: Smith
userPassword:: e1NIQX01ZW42RzZNZXpScm9UM1hLcWtkUE9tWS9CZlE9
mail: ssmith@optilux-cinemas.com

# Third level - groups
dn: cn=Staff,ou=groups,dc=optilux-cinemas,dc=com
objectClass: top
objectClass: groupOfUniqueNames
cn: Staff
uniqueMember: uid=ssmith,ou=people,dc=optilux-cinemas,dc=com
```

Here, we define an organization called `Optilux Corporation` corresponding to the domain component `optilux-cinemas` under the domain `optilux-cinemas.com`. This contains two organizational units: `people` and `groups`. We then add one user — `ssmith` — to the `people` OU, and one group — `Staff` — to the `groups` OU. The `userPassword` property is a SHA1 hash (as indicated by the double colons) of the user's password, which happens to also be the string `secret`.

In *Chapter 6, Security and Workflow*, we added code to the `setuphandlers.py` file of the `optilux.policy` product to create a *Staff* group in Plone itself. If the group is coming from LDAP instead, as it is above, we should remove this setup step so that we do not end up with two groups with the same name.

To import the LDIF file, run the following command after starting `slapd`, the LDAP daemon.

```
$ ldapadd -xWD 'cn=Manager,dc=optilux-cinemas,dc=com' -f optilux.ldif
```

You can use the `ldapsearch` command to query the repository. However, it may be easier to use a graphical browser such as the **LDAP Browser/Editor**, available from `http://www.novell.com/coolsolutions/tools/13765.html`.

Connecting Plone to an LDAP repository

To use LDAP from Python, we must first install the `python-ldap` module. Since this contains some operating-system specific code, it is usually easier to install this manually, especially on Windows, for which there is a binary installer. It can be downloaded from `http://pypi.python.org/pypi/python-ldap`, or installed using your operating system's package management tools if applicable.

To use LDAP in Plone, we need to install `plone.app.ldap`. We add this as a dependency to the `setup.py` file of `optilux.policy`. This will pull in a number of dependencies, which we add to our KGS in `versions.cfg`.

With `plone.app.ldap` installed, we can restart Zope and install **LDAP Support** from Plone's **Add-ons** control panel.

 You should not install the `LDAPUserFolder CMF Tools` product. This is a relic of the `LDAPUserFolder` dependency and will not work properly with Plone.

With LDAP support in place, you should see a new **LDAP Connection** control panel under **Site Setup**. It looks as shown in the following screenshot:

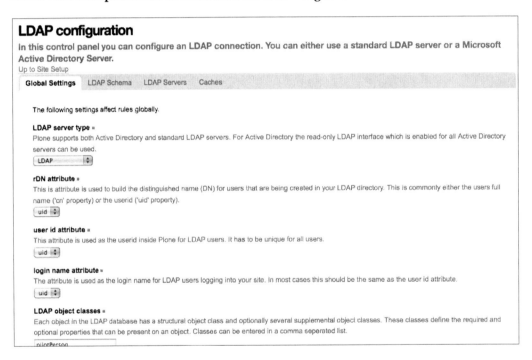

Let us go through the settings we would enter for the example repository we set up earlier, starting with the **Global Settings** tab:

- The **LDAP server type** can be **LDAP** or **Active Directory**. We use the former.

- The **rDN attribute** (relative distinguished name) is used as the first part of the DN for users being created through Plone. It is most commonly the same as the attribute used for the user ID. We will opt for the `uid` attribute here.

- The **user id attribute** gives the attribute used for user IDs in Plone. We will use the `uid` here as well.

- The **login name attribute** is used during authentication. It will normally be the same as the user ID attribute. Again, we will use `uid`.

 With Active Directory, you can use either `userPrincipalName` or `sAMAccountName` as the user ID and login name. (`objectGUID` will not work, as Plone does not support binary user IDs.) The difference between the two is that `userPrincipalName` includes the full domain, while `sAMAccountName` contains the plain username only. The `sAMAccountName` attribute is the best choice if your Active Directory is configured for a single domain only, but may not be unique if you are using multiple domains.

- The **LDAP object classes** field gives the structural object class and any additional object classes (separated by commas) applied to new users created via Plone. We use `pilotPerson, uidObject`, which means that we get a simple user object with a UID.

- The **Bind DN** is the DN used by Plone to access the LDAP repository. We will use the root DN, `cn=Manager,dc=optilux-cinemas,dc=com`.

- The **Bind password** is the password for the user listed under the Bind DN. We set this to the string `secret` in `slapd.conf`.

- The **Base DN for users** gives the location of users in the repository. Recall that we created users under the organizational unit people. Thus, we enter `ou=people,dc=optilux-cinemas,dc=com` here.

- The **Search scope for users** option defines whether users are found directly under the base OU only, or in sub-units as well. For our example, there is only one level anyway, so it does not matter what we choose, but *subtree* is the more common option.

- The **Base DN for groups** tells Plone where in the repository to find groups. Here, we will enter `ou=groups,dc=optilux-cinemas,dc=com`.

- The **Search scope for groups** option is akin to Search scope for users. Again, we choose *subtree*, although it does not make much difference to our example.

- The **User password encryption** option can be used to indicate the method of encryption or hashing used for passwords in the LDAP repository. We will choose **SHA** here.

- The **Default user roles** option indicates the default roles for new users found in the repository. We will set this to the string `Member`.

Do not forget to the save form before moving on to the other tabs.

On the **LDAP Schema** tab, you can map LDAP attributes to Plone member properties. Member properties were described in *Chapter 13, Users and their Permissions*.

By default, the `uid` attribute is defined but not mapped to any Plone properties. This makes it available as a possible user ID, login name, or relative DN under the **Global settings** tab. Similarly, the `sn` (surname) property is entered, but not mapped to a Plone property. We will not use this for anything, but having it here means that it will be entered in the directory with a dummy value when users are created through Plone. This is necessary since the `sn` property is mandatory for the `pilotPerson` structural object class we are using.

The *mail* attribute is mapped to the `email` property and the `cn` attribute is mapped to the `fullname` property. These last two properties are used frequently in the Plone user interface, and should always be mapped.

It is possible to mix standard Plone properties and LDAP-based properties for the same user. When searching for a property value, PAS will look at the available "property sheets" one-by-one, stopping at the first sheet it finds with the required property. With LDAP support installed, the LDAP-backed property sheet comes first, followed by the standard Plone property sheet.

To map a new property, click **Add property** and fill in the required details.

Finally, we must configure one or more servers on the **LDAP Servers** tab. If multiple servers are defined, they will be tried in the order they are listed when attempting to access the repository. Click the **Add LDAP server** button and enter the hostname, connection type, and other options as requested.

If you have followed the examples and are using the example repository from this chapter, you can now test the configuration by logging in as user **ssmith** with password **secret**. You should also be able to create users and groups in Plone and have them appear in the LDAP repository.

Configuring PAS plugins manually

Under the hood, the LDAP configuration is just a PAS plugin which is configured to work through a number of **PAS interfaces**. With LDAP installed and configured, take a look at the `ldap-plugin` object inside `acl_users` in the root of your Plone site in the ZMI (this object is created and managed by the `plone.app.ldap` control panel):

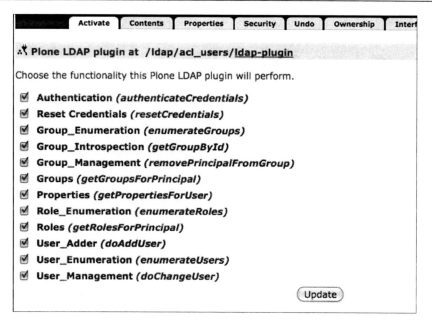

These interfaces perform various functions as part of the user management process. To disable an interface completely, uncheck the corresponding box and click **Update**.

 To learn more about the role played by each PAS interface, look at the `plugins` object inside `acl_users`, or refer to *Chapter 13, Users and their Permissions*.

If you click on an interface, you will be able to configure the active plugins used to perform the relevant task. For example, click on **Properties**, and you will see the following screen:

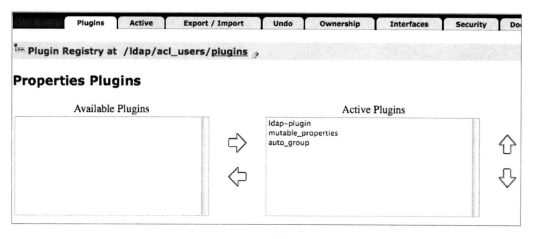

This means that when searching for user properties, PAS will first try the `ldap` plugin, and then fall back on the `mutable_properties` plugin (the standard properties plugin used by Plone), before giving up. Select a plugin and use the up/down arrows to change the priority order.

For the purposes of the Optilux application, we may want to let staff members come from the LDAP repository, but have external users that sign up to the site themselves be created in Plone only. In this case, we need to change the priority for the `User_Adder` interface. Click on **User_adder Plugins** under **Plugins** in **acl_users** and then move the **source_users** plugin to the top, above the **ldap-plugin**:

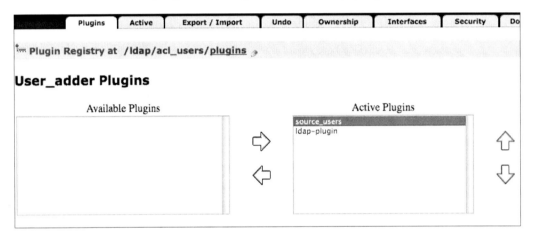

Now, the **ldap-plugin** will only be used if the **source_users** plugin fails. If you wish to disable LDAP user creation entirely, move the **ldap-plugin** to the **Available plugins** list by selecting it and clicking the left arrow.

To learn more about the various PAS interfaces and plugins, you should consult the PAS reference guide at `http://plone.org/documentation/manual/developer-manual/users-and-security/pluggable-authentication-service`.

Summary

In this chapter, we have covered:

- A brief introduction to LDAP and its terminology
- Setting up a minimal LDAP repository for testing
- The Plone add-on products which enable LDAP connectivity
- Configuring LDAP for authentication and mapping LDAP attributes to Plone member properties
- Configuring the PAS interfaces exposed by the LDAP plugins in detail manually

In the next chapter, we will look at how to manage future upgrades and releases.

19
Looking to the Future

We are nearly at an end. Over the past eighteen chapters, we have learned how to build and deploy robust Plone applications. We have seen key principles and professional development practices illustrated through a realistic case study. Hopefully, you now feel equipped to apply these principles and practices to your own Plone development projects.

In this chapter, we will:

- Look briefly at how to manage future releases and migrations
- Review our achievements to date
- Point out where to get more help and information

Making future releases

As any seasoned developer will know, it is much easier (or at least more fun) to build an application from scratch than to extend and maintain an existing one. Plone-based systems are no exception, but there are a few tips that can make life a little easier when the time comes to update or patch an application that is already live.

- In *Chapter 4, Basics of Customization*, we discussed the dangers of relying on settings changed manually through-the-web. It becomes very difficult to manage multiple versions of a code base, if you cannot reliably and automatically set up a blank instance of the site in a test environment. Use a 'policy product' and a GenericSetup base or extension profile to formalize your application configuration as we have done throughout this book. Resist the temptation to make configuration changes on a live server without making sure that this change is represented in developers' sandboxes.

- In *Chapter 16, Zope on the Server*, we described the flow of code from a development environment to a live server. Code travels 'forwards', and should only be changed in a development sandbox. When it has been properly tested, it can be moved to staging and live environments. Data travels 'backwards'. The ZODB and blob storage on the live server can be copied to a staging or development environment for testing and analysis, but should never be overwritten by data from another environment. You will be in trouble if you start to make code changes on a production server or overwrite 'live' data with older data from another server.

- Test. Test again. Then test some more. There is absolutely no excuse for not having automated unit and integration tests for your code. The author would never pay money for code that was not covered by automated tests. (The extensive use of unit and integration tests for the code in this book was not only done to demonstrate good practices it was the only way the author could have any confidence in the code, given the many versions of the code that had to be maintained in parallel.) At the same time, you must perform manual testing and sanity checks on the final functionality. This is doubly true when managing multiple versions of code across multiple environments and dealing with migration code.

- When a new code release is ready, set up a test server with a snapshot of the database from the live environment. If you have written migration scripts, run them and make sure that they work as expected. If things go awry, return to the development environment and attempt to reproduce the problem in a unit test. Then fix the problem and try again.

- Use version control. Even if you are the only developer on a project, not having source code version control is reckless. It is essential to be able to roll back to previous versions of the code and tag a 'known good' collection of packages for a release.

- Keep good backups. This goes without saying, but bears constant repetition.

In other words: prevention is the best medicine when it comes to managing multiple versions of code.

Managing migrations and upgrades

If you have deployed an application and subsequently make a change to its code, you may need a migration script if any of the following are true:

- Have you changed the GenericSetup profile or installation script for your product? Does the new code depend on settings made with the new installation routine? Often, it will be sufficient for users to reinstall the product, but this can sometimes undo configuration settings that may have been changed during operation of the system.

- Have you changed variables and data structures that are stored as part of content objects of the ZODB? If so, you may need to migrate the existing objects.

- Have you fixed a bug that caused existing data to be persisted in an incorrect state? You may need to migrate to the old data that is still affected by the defect.

In all cases, the process is the same: write and run a script or function, which configures the portal and updates persistent objects appropriately.

If you used an extension profile to install a product, you can use GenericSetup's upgrade step support to manage migration scripts and make them available in the `portal_setup` tool.

When using this, it is important to keep track of which version is current. GenericSetup reads this from the `metadata.xml` file that is part of your product's installation profile. For example, we could have the following in `profiles/default/metadata.xml` in a fictitious `guitar.shop` product:

```xml
<?xml version="1.0"?>
<metadata>
  <description>Guitar Shop</description>
  <version>1</version>
</metadata>
```

When making a new release that requires migration, make sure that you bump the version number appropriately.

 The **profile version** listed in `metadata.xml` is usually an incrementing number. It is not the same as the **distribution version** of the package that contains the profile, which is maintained in `setup.py`.

Upgrade steps are written as Python functions, and are registered with ZCML. For example:

```
<configure
    xmlns="http://namespaces.zope.org/zope"
    xmlns:genericsetup="http://namespaces.zope.org/genericsetup"
    i18n_domain="guitar.shop">

    <!-- Installation profile -->
    <genericsetup:registerProfile
        name="default"
        title="Guitar Shop"
        directory="profiles/default"
        description="Extension profile for the Guitar Shop product."
        provides="Products.GenericSetup.interfaces.EXTENSION"
        for="Products.CMFPlone.interfaces.IPloneSiteRoot"
        />

    <!-- Upgrade step for the migration -->
    <genericsetup:upgradeStep
        sortkey="1"
        source="1"
        destination="2"
        title="Upgrade from profile version 1 to version 2"
        description="Fixes the front page title"
        profile="default"
        handler=".upgrades.v1_to_v2"
        />


    <!-- Here is another upgrade, from 2 to 3.
         This one has two steps -->
    <genericsetup:upgradeSteps
        sortkey="2"
        source="2"
        destination="3"
        profile="default"
        >
        <genericsetup:upgradeStep
            title="Upgrade titles"
            description="Fix all other titles"
            handler=".upgrades.v2_to_v3_a"
            />
        <genericsetup:upgradeStep
            title="Upgrade site title"
            description="Fixes a typo with the portal title"
            handler=".upgrades.v2_to_v3_b"
```

```
        />
    </genericsetup:upgradeSteps>

    ...

</configure>
```

Here, we define two upgrade paths: upgrading from version 1 to 2 will call the function `v1_to_v2` in `upgrades.py`. The upgrade from version 2 to 3 is split into two parts, calling `v2_to_v3_a()` and then `v2_to_v3_b()`.

Notice how the upgrade step directive specifies the source and destination version for the upgrade step, as well as a sort key. Sort keys ensure that steps are run in the correct order when upgrading across multiple versions. Also note how the upgrade step explicitly references the extension profile that is being upgraded.

All upgrade step handler functions are passed through the `portal_setup` tool as an argument. As this is stored inside the Plone site root, it can be used as a base from which to acquire other tools or obtain the site root. Here are a few (frivolous) examples of the types of things an upgrade step may do:

```python
from Products.CMFCore.utils import getToolByName

def v1_to_v2(portal_setup):
    """This is a migration step, referenced from configure.zcml

    Here, we "fix" the portal front page.
    """

    portal_url = getToolByName(portal_setup, 'portal_url')
    portal = portal_url.getPortalObject()
    front_page = portal['front-page']
    front_page.setTitle('Welcome to the Guitar Shop')

def v2_to_v3_a(portal_setup):
    """Here is another upgrade step, this one part of a
    two-step upgrade
    """

    portal_catalog = getToolByName(portal_setup, 'portal_catalog')
    for brain in portal_catalog(portal_type = 'Document'):
        brain.getObject().setTitle('All your base are belong to us!')

def v2_to_v3_b(portal_setup):
    """This is the second step
    """

    portal_url = getToolByName(portal_setup, 'portal_url')
    portal = portal_url.getPortalObject()

    # typo in properties.xml - we should fix that one too!
    portal.manage_changeProperties(title="Guitar Shop")
```

Upgrade steps can be invoked from the **Upgrades** tab of `portal_setup`. To run one or more upgrade steps, simply ensure that the relevant boxes are ticked and click **Upgrade**. If you need to rerun upgrade steps that have already been run, you can find them by clicking the **Show** button.

Of course, writing the actual migration code is the hard part. Migration code can often be tricky, because it can be difficult to predict what state the live site may be in. Be defensive, and make few assumptions.

Migration profiles

If you need to manage a large number of migrations, you may want to consider making a special extension profile for each version upgrade and invoking that migration profile as part of a migration step. Plone does this for many of its version migrations.

Since Plone 4, this is explicitly supported with the following syntax:

```
<genericsetup:registerProfile
    name="v2-to-v3"
    title="Migration profile for Guitar Shop v2 to v3"
    description=""
    directory="profiles/migrations/v2_to_v3"
    for="Products.CMFPlone.interfaces.IMigratingPloneSiteRoot"
    provides="Products.GenericSetup.interfaces.EXTENSION"
    />
<genericsetup:upgradeDepends
    sortkey="3"
    source="2"
    destination="3"
    title="Upgrade from v2 to v3"
    description="Runs a migration profile"
    profile="default"
    import_profile="v2-to-v3"
    handler=".upgrades.v1_2_to_v1_3"
    />
```

First, we register an extension profile that will be used to change the site configuration during migration. Then we register an upgrade step that will invoke this profile. Notice how the extension profile is registered for the interface `IMigratingPloneSiteRoot`. This ensures that this profile does not show up during site creation or in Plone's **Add-ons** control panel.

If you want to reuse an existing profile, but only execute some import steps, you can use the attribute `import_steps="step1 step2 ..."` on the `<genericsetup:upgradeDepends />` directive combined with `run_deps="True"` or `"False"` to control whether dependent steps are run.

We can now add XML files to the directory `profiles/migrations/v1_to_v3/` just as we would for a regular extension profile. For example, we could have the following in `properties.xml`:

```xml
<?xml version="1.0"?>
<site>
 <property name="title">The All New Guitar Shop</property>
</site>
```

What we have achieved

Finally, let us quickly summarize our achievements to date.

- In *Chapter 1, Plone in Context*, we discussed Plone's history and community. The Plone community should always be the first place you turn to, if you are stuck or want to get in touch with other developers.

- In *Chapter 2, Introduction to the Case Study*, we introduced the Optilux Cinemas case study, setting the scene for the rest of the book.

- In *Chapter 3, The Development Environment*, we learned how to set up a development environment, using Buildout to orchestrate various dependencies such as the Zope application server and Plone itself.

- In *Chapter 4, Basics of Customization*, we took a look at the various ways in which Plone can be customized and issued a few warnings about the perils of relying too much on persistent through-the-web settings that are difficult to reproduce across environments.

- In *Chapter 5, Developing a Site Strategy*, we created a 'policy package' to manage site policy decisions and configuration settings related to the case study application. We expanded this with new policies in nearly every subsequent chapter. We also emphasized the importance of automated unit and integration tests.

- In *Chapter 6, Security and Workflow*, we explored Plone's security model, and made the case for using workflow as the primary tool for implementing a security policy by showing how to install a custom workflow using GenericSetup.

- In *Chapter 7, Using Add-ons*, we demonstrated how to safely test, install, and customize Plone add-on products.

- In *Chapter 8, Creating a Custom Theme*, we re-branded our growing application with a custom theme using the Diazo engine without modifying the source code of Plone itself.

- In *Chapter 9, Nine Core Concepts of Zope Programming*, we took a break from the example application to look deeper at nine core concepts underpinning Zope and Plone development. If you found that the chapter is a little fast-paced at first, you may want to go back to it, now that you have had more time to see these techniques in practice.

- In *Chapter 10, Custom Content Types*, we dove into the most important skill Plone developers need—building custom content types, which we did using the new Dexterity framework. We also created a custom portlet.

- In *Chapter 11, Standalone Views and Forms*, we looked in more detail at forms and other types of browser views. We used `z3c.form` to generate forms with minimal configuration in Python. We also created viewlets—snippets that can be 'plugged in' to the standard user interface at various points.

- In *Chapter 12, Relational Databases*, we connected our application to an external relational database, using the `SQLAlchemy` library and a little bit of Zope glue. We also used some advanced features of the `z3c.form` library to create a ticket reservations form.

- In *Chapter 13, Users and their Permissions*, we looked at how to manage personalized information, building a form and a portlet to track a user's preferred cinema. We also showed how to create a custom plugin for the Pluggable Authentication Service, integrating Plone with Facebook authentication.

- In *Chapter 14, Dynamic User Interfaces with jQuery*, we improved the user experience of a few of the application's features by using jQuery.

- In *Chapter 15, Summary and Potential Enhancements*, we considered ways in which the example application could be taken further, and briefly looked at issues of internationalization.

- In *Chapter 16, Zope on the Server*, we showed how to move the example application from a development environment to a production server using ZEO (Zope Enterprise Objects) or RelStorage for improved scalability and resilience.

- In *Chapter 17, Setting up a Production Server*, we showed various ways to configure web servers, caching reverse proxies and load balancers in front of Zope, in order to improve performance, stability, and fault-tolerance.

- In *Chapter 18, Authenticating with LDAP or Active Directory*, we connected Plone to an LDAP repository providing authentication services and user properties.

- Finally, in this chapter, we provided some tips on managing releases of a live application and performing migrations.

Where to go next

Undoubtedly, you will have more questions after reading this book. Here are a few places to turn for answers:

- The Plone mailing lists and support forum, as well as the `#plone` IRC chat room on `irc.freenode.net` are the natural places to ask questions and get in touch with the Plone community. See `http://plone.org/support`.

- The Plone website also contains a wealth of other information, such as the documentation at `http://plone.org/documentation`.

- Before attempting to solve a problem yourself by writing a new product, why not find out if others have already done the hard work for you? Make a habit of browsing `http://plone.org/products` or the Python Packaging Index on `http://pypi.python.org/`. Even if you cannot find something that fits the bill perfectly, you will often find solutions to build on or learn from, or other developers with whom you can collaborate.

- Finally, should you need professional help, go to `http://plone.org/support/network` and look for a Plone consultant, developer or trainer.

Summary

In this chapter, we have:

- Offered some tips about managing multiple versions of an application
- Demonstrated how to use the new GenericSetup upgrade-step functionality to invoke migration scripts
- Recapped on the key lessons from this book
- Provided a few pointers to additional resources

And that, as they say, is it.

I hope you have enjoyed this book, and that it has helped you become a better Plone developer. I have certainly enjoyed writing it.

Most of all, however, I hope to see you on a Plone mailing list, in the Plone chat room or, better yet, at a Plone sprint or conference.

Index

B

C

doActionFor() method 131
doctest syntax 176
document 288
Document Object Model. *See* DOM
document_view() method 78
document_view template 288
DOM
  about 389
  manipulating 390-394
DOM manipulation 390-394
draft state 118
DRBD
  URL 441

E

easy_install 32
editable border 292
edit form 241
egg 31
eggs option 57
enabled option 385
Enfold Proxy 432-434
entry points 47
Etag 447
event log 427
exception type
  defining, for reservation errors 327
Expires response header 445
explicit acquisition 181
expression option 385
extends option 413
extension profile
  about 70
  creating 95, 96

F

Facebook authentication API
  about 363
  URL, for info 365
Facebook authentication plugin
  about 363
  features 365
  installing 377-380
  package configuration 366-369
Facebook Graph API 21
Facebook OAuth authentication 369-373

factory 240
Factory Type Information (FTI) 69, 177, 240, 262
features, Plone 4 11
fields 243
film
  screenings, modelling for 324, 325
filmsAtCinema() function 335
Film view
  updating 341
filter option 388
Firebug plugin 451
folderish objects 179
foo property 234
form action
  processing 301
form controller tool 311
form input convertors
  about 303
  boolean 303
  date 303
  default 304
  float 303
  ignore_empty 304
  int 303
  lines 304
  list 304
  long 303
  record 304
  records 304
  required 304
  string 303
  text 304
  tokens 304
  tuple 304
formlib 305
forms
  actions, processing 301
  generating, automatically 305-310
  redirect, performing 303
  submit buttons, verifying for 301, 302
formselector option 388
form.write_permission() directive 258
Four Digits
  URL 150
functional test 165

functional testing 318-320
Funkload 451

G

GenericSetup
  about 69
  imperative configuration 128
  using, for configuration 70-73
GenericSetup-aware tool 69
GenericSetup configuration 71-73
GenericSetup export
  creating 123
GenericSetup extension profile 87
genericsetup namespace 96
GenericSetup profiles
  about 70
  base 70
  extension 70
generic views 290
getAuthenticatedUser() method 75
getFields() method 275
getFoo() method 234
getId() method 179
get() method 276, 277
getObject() method 188, 443
getPath() function 188
getPhysicalPath() method 178, 181
getProperty() method 358, 359
getSite() method 206, 335
gettext system 403
getToolByName() function 206
getURL() method 188, 430
getUtility() method 204, 206
Global Interpreter Lock (GIL) 408, 439
global roles 103
global site manager 204
global template variables
  checkPermission 316
  context_state 316
  portal_state 316
  portal_url 316
global utilities 199, 200
GNU General Public License (GPL) 14
Google Analytics 401
GRANT statement 410

Grok
  URL 198
grokker 198
grokking 198
groups 104, 354

H

handler attribute 129
HAProxy
  about 433, 438
  configuring 437
have_portlets() method 168
haveScore() method 315
high-level class diagram 22
href attribute 145
HTTP Caching Support 447

I

i18ndude 404
i18n:translate attribute 403
IAnonymousUserFactoryPlugin interface 362
IAuthenticationPlugin interface
  about 361, 364
  implementing 374
IBrowserDefault interface 177
IChallengePlugin interface 361
ICredentialsResetPlugin interface 362, 364
ICredentialsUpdatePlugin interface 362
IExtractionPlugin interface
  about 361, 364
  implementing 373
If-Modified-Since request header 446
If-None-Match request header 447
IGroupEnumerationPlugin interface 362
IGroupsPlugin interface 362
ILocalRolesPlugin interface 363
IMigratingPloneSiteRoot interface 470
imperative configuration 128
implementedBy() method 193
implementsOnly() method 193
implicit acquisition 180
IMutablePropertiesPlugin interface 363
IMyType interface 79

RelationChoice field 245
Relative DN 455
RelStorage
  about 329, 409, 410
  configuring 415
  deployment buildout 411-417
  using 410
remove command 424
remove option 385
render() method 223, 315, 391
request container object 181
request review permission 107
REQUEST variable 181
reservations
  modeling 324-326
reservation services 326
reservations form
  implementing 346-350
Resource Registries
  automatic resource merging 444
Restricted Python 132, 133
restrictedTraverse() method 131, 183
retract transition 120
review portal content permission 107
rewrite rule 430
rich text fields 249, 250
roles
  about 108
  manipulating, programmatically 110, 111
Root DN 455
rule files
  adding, to Diazo theme 154-156
rules 144
rules.xml file 145

S

SAN 440
savepoint
  about 183
  setting 183
schema
  about 240-244, 454
  form hints 244, 245
  rich text fields 249, 250
  validation 246, 247
  vocabulary 248, 249

schema extender
  adding 272
  creating 274
  tests, adding 277
  using 271
schema permissions 257
screening
  about 324
  modeling, for film 324, 325
screening view
  implementing 343-345
search form
  creating 296
searchResults() method 131, 188
security assertions 131, 132
security policy
  adjusting 269
security primitives
  about 103
  groups 104
  permissions 104-108
  roles 108-110
  users 104
selected attribute 297
selectedContent() method 300
sendMail() method 309
separate server
  theme, reading from 166
separation of concerns principle 207
server components, Plone
  about 429, 430
  caching reverse proxy 432, 433
  load balancers 433, 434
  virtual hosting 430, 431
  web server 431, 432
server deployment
  elements 418
server deployment, elements
  code dependencies 418
  configuration 418
  custom code 418
  data 418
setFoo() method 234
set() method 277
setProperties() method 358
setTitle() method 83

Thank you for buying
Professional Plone 4 Development

About Packt Publishing

Packt, pronounced 'packed', published its first book "*Mastering phpMyAdmin for Effective MySQL Management*" in April 2004 and subsequently continued to specialize in publishing highly focused books on specific technologies and solutions.

Our books and publications share the experiences of your fellow IT professionals in adapting and customizing today's systems, applications, and frameworks. Our solution based books give you the knowledge and power to customize the software and technologies you're using to get the job done. Packt books are more specific and less general than the IT books you have seen in the past. Our unique business model allows us to bring you more focused information, giving you more of what you need to know, and less of what you don't.

Packt is a modern, yet unique publishing company, which focuses on producing quality, cutting-edge books for communities of developers, administrators, and newbies alike. For more information, please visit our website: www.packtpub.com.

About Packt Open Source

In 2010, Packt launched two new brands, Packt Open Source and Packt Enterprise, in order to continue its focus on specialization. This book is part of the Packt Open Source brand, home to books published on software built around Open Source licences, and offering information to anybody from advanced developers to budding web designers. The Open Source brand also runs Packt's Open Source Royalty Scheme, by which Packt gives a royalty to each Open Source project about whose software a book is sold.

Writing for Packt

We welcome all inquiries from people who are interested in authoring. Book proposals should be sent to author@packtpub.com. If your book idea is still at an early stage and you would like to discuss it first before writing a formal book proposal, contact us; one of our commissioning editors will get in touch with you.

We're not just looking for published authors; if you have strong technical skills but no writing experience, our experienced editors can help you develop a writing career, or simply get some additional reward for your expertise.

Practical Plone 3: A Beginner's Guide to Building Powerful Websites

ISBN: 978-1-847191-78-6   Paperback: 592 pages

A beginner's practical guide to building Plone websites through graphical interface

1. Get a Plone-based website up and running quickly without dealing with code

2. Beginner's guide with easy-to-follow instructions and screenshots

3. Learn how to make the best use of Plone's out-of-the-box features

Plone 3 Theming

ISBN: 978-1-847193-87-2   Paperback: 324 pages

Create flexible, powerful, and professional themes for your web site with Plone and basic CSS

1. Best practices for creating a flexible and powerful Plone themes

2. Build new templates and refactor existing ones by using Plone's templating system, Zope Page Templates (ZPT) system, Template Attribute Language (TAL) tricks and tips for skinning your Plone site

3. Create a fully functional theme to ensure proper understanding of all the concepts

Please check **www.PacktPub.com** for information on our titles

Plone 3 Multimedia

ISBN: 978-1-847197-66-5   Paperback: 372 pages

Embed, display, and manage multimedia content in your Plone website

1. Build a modern full-featured multimedia CMS with Plone and add-on products

2. Use and extend specialized multimedia content-types for images, audio, video, and Flash

3. Set up a custom multimedia CMS by collaborating with external resources such as YouTube, Google videos, and so on

Plone 3 Intranets

ISBN: 978-1-847199-08-9   Paperback: 312 pages

Design, build, and deploy a reliable, full-featured, and secure Plone-based enterprise intranet easily from scratch

1. Install, set up, and use a corporate Plone intranet with ease

2. Secure your intranet using Plone's out-of-the-box features

3. Explore the most useful add-ons for your intranet and learn how to use them

Please check **www.PacktPub.com** for information on our titles

CPSIA information can be obtained at www.ICGtesting.com
Printed in the USA
LVOW130338121011

250053LV00015BA/180/P